East Grinstead

Hartfield

Withyham

Frant

Wadhurst

Rotherfield

Ticehurst

Maresfield

Buxted

Mayfield

Etchingham

Bodiam

Northiam

Iden

Fletching

Burwash

Salehurst

Ewhurst

Beckley

Playden

Peasmarsh

Uckfield

Heathfield

Brightling

Mountfield

Whatlington

Brede

East Guldeford

Newick

Framfield

Waldron

Dallington

Sedlescombe

Udimore

Rye

Isfield

Little Horsted

East Hoathly

Warbleton

Penhurst

Battle

Westfield

Icklesham

Winchelsea

Broomhill

Barcombe

Chiddingly

Ashburnham

Guestling

St Thomas the Apostle Winchelsea

Hamsey

Ringmer

Laughton

Hellingly

Herstmonceux

Catsfield

Crowhurst

Ore

Pett

St.John so Castro

Ninfield

Hollington

Fairlight

Lewes

South Mailing

Ripe

Chalvington

Wartling

Hoee

Bexhill

Hastings

St Leonards

Southover Without

Glynde

Arlington

Hailsham

Iford

West Firle

Selmeston

Pevensey

Beddingham

Alciston

Berwick

Willingdon

Westham

Telscombe

Southease

Tarring Neville

Heighton

Willingdon

Folkington

Rodmell

Piddinghoe

Denton

Alfriston

Lullington

Jevington

Bishopstone

Litlington

Newhaven

East Blatchington

Seaford

Westdean

Friston

Eastbourne

Eastdean

0   kms   20

0   miles   10

AN HISTORICAL ATLAS OF
SUSSEX

SVSSEX

DIEV ET MON DROIT

Surrey

Parte of

Parte of
Hamshire

AN HISTORICAL ATLAS OF
SUSSEX

edited by
Kim Leslie and Brian Short

with maps by
Susan Rowland

An Atlas of the History of the
Counties of East and West Sussex

Phillimore

1999

Published by
PHILLIMORE & CO. LTD.
Shopwyke Manor Barn, Chichester, West Sussex

ISBN 1 86077 112 2

Printed and bound in Great Britain by
BUTLER AND TANNER LTD.
London and Frome

INTRODUCTION

This Atlas traces the development of Sussex from its geological and prehistoric ancestry to the present day. It is published as a contribution towards marking the year 2000, a significant opportunity to survey the many strands that have made Sussex what it is today at the close of the second millennium. There have been many books on the history of Sussex, but this is the first time that its past has been described in the form of an atlas. In this sense it is a landmark publication in Sussex bibliography.

The presentation of county history in atlas form represents a relatively new approach in the publication of local history, even though it actually uses the format of an older generation of scholars – that is to say it is based on the county as a unit rather than any smaller more localised unit such as the parish, and rather than the region, a more fashionable scholarly spatial unit in the 1990s.[1] As noted by Jeremy Black, atlases are among the most conservative of historical forms, although history and historical geography have certainly become 'more varied and adventurous in their interests'.[2] In many cases we have incorporated either topographical or parish boundary information to give context and perhaps provoke questions about geographical relationships, with a spatial index to the 19th-century parish boundaries printed in the endpapers to the volume. Thus, as a county history it is far removed from the antiquarian studies of an earlier generation, written, as Hoskins noted, 'by gentlemen for gentlemen'.[3] For this volume we have assembled 70 completely original maps with accompanying texts, prepared by 62 different authors. Some are archaeologists, some archivists, geographers, historians and planners, representing some of the leading researchers in their fields.

The subject matter is sometimes traditional and sometimes innovatory, although all contributors survey current thinking on their subjects. The maps are likewise a mixture of established techniques and new ideas, moving some way towards Brian Harley's notion of 'a greater pluralism of cartographic expression'.[4] Some material lends itself better to mapping than other: thus it is more conceptually difficult, and indeed perhaps premature, in many ways, to include a map of timber-framed housing, since so much work remains to be done throughout Sussex that the map in this case is better thought of as a statement of work in progress. Other contributions are based largely on primary source material, whether from relatively well-known sources such as the surveys of Bishops Compton (1676) and Bowers (1724), or on the careful assemblage of sources from a wide variety of archives to yield, for example, the spatial patterns of education in Sussex. They are also based on re-interpretations of well-known sources, such as Domesday Book; on up-to-date excavation knowledge, as with the prehistoric distribution maps, or on specialist professional experience, as with the maps dealing with 20th-century planning issues. As ever in such a venture, there were more potential maps and contributors than could be incorporated, but we hope that a sufficiently wide coverage of the county's history is presented to show its essential changes through space and time.

As an atlas, this is a volume which is map-driven. Contributors were asked always to bear this in mind and to convey as much information as possible cartographically, rather than to rely on the text and to use the maps as illustrative material. Each contributor was asked to limit the accompanying text to approximately 1,000 words, which has entailed considerable compression and selection of information, but amplification is provided by the references and bibliographies at the end of the volume. The maps which have emerged represent two broad approaches: some are based on statistical analysis, others are more qualitative in nature, tending towards the narrative. Thus whilst we can deal with demographic data in a quantitative fashion, thanks mainly to the existence of the census from 1801, no attempt has been made, for example, to quantify the agricultural or natural regions of Sussex. We have also included maps of towns within each of the main time periods covered in the atlas: Roman Chichester, medieval Winchelsea, early-modern Lewes, 19th-century Brighton, and 20th-century Crawley.

Maps are unforgiving in demanding exactitude, or seemingly so. They impose their own strict disciplines. Whereas in a written text one can conveniently omit frustratingly elusive detail, on a map such detail is often necessary. We have attempted as much precision as possible, for example, with the boundaries of the spatial units used here, whether they be parishes or rapes or even the county itself. In the latter context, we might therefore note that although there were degrees of imprecision in reality over the boundaries of the county throughout much of its history, and the county itself did not feature as a distinct political entity until the later Saxon period (parts of Kentish Lamberhurst and Horsmonden were in Sussex, for example) we have been as careful as possible to reconstruct the known boundaries. The long and narrow strip, 8 miles north-south and ½ mile wide or less, incorporating North and South Ambersham, only became part of the county of Sussex from 1844 when the Ambershams were transferred from Hampshire as a detached part of the parish of Steep. But the complexity of the situation is further revealed when it is realised that they were to be considered part of Sussex for election purposes from 1832, for all civil purposes by 1844, but until 1890, when the two areas were transferred from the diocese of Winchester to that of Chichester, the inhabitants were expected to baptise, marry, and bury at their parish church in Steep, Hampshire. For ecclesiastical purposes North Ambersham subsequently became united to the parish of Fernhurst, and South Ambersham to Selham. For civil purposes, however, each of the Ambershams remained separate parishes until 1972, when they were dismembered and absorbed in the five adjacent parishes of Easebourne, Fernhurst, Graffham, Heyshott, and Lodsworth. Spatial units are thus highly mutable, depending on the purposes for which they are fashioned.[5]

It must also be remembered that Sussex in the year 2000 is made up of several smaller administrative units, the chief of which are the counties of East and West Sussex, the split between them in the 19th century formalising an historic division between east and west within the curiously elongated historic county. And more recently, in 1997, Brighton and Hove has been carved from East Sussex as an independent unitary authority.

However, despite these internal administrative divisions, the overall boundary of Sussex – with minor adjustments – survives today much as it has been for over 1,000 years. Whilst some counties have been radically altered, dismembered and even re-named, Sussex lives on into the third millennium. This is cause indeed for celebration, and may this atlas be a small but fitting tribute to its survival.

KIM LESLIE
West Sussex Record Office

BRIAN SHORT
University of Sussex

CONTENTS

LIST OF CONTRIBUTORS

Caroline Adams, MA, DAA   Senior Archivist, West Sussex Record Office

Brian Austen, BSc(Econ), MA, M Phil, PhD   Formerly Senior Lecturer in History, Shoreditch College, Egham

John Beard, BSc(Econ), DipTP, FRTPI   Formerly Assistant County Planning Officer, West Sussex County Council

Sue Berry, MSc, PhD   Principal Lecturer in Tourism Management, University of Brighton

Molly Beswick, MA   Formerly teacher and lecturer

John Bleach   Senior Custodian, Lewes Castle and Museums, Sussex Archaeological Society

Sarah Boughton, BSc, MSc, DipTP, MRTPI   Principal Planner (Demography and Housing), East Sussex County Council

Peter Brandon, BA, PhD, FSA   Formerly Head of Department of Geography, University of North London

Steve Brown, MRTPI   Land Use and Transport Planner, West Sussex County Council

John Caffyn, MA   Formerly Chairman, market research company

Andrew Charlesworth, MA   Reader in Human Geography, Cheltenham and Gloucester College of Higher Education

Richard Childs, BA, DAA   County Archivist, West Sussex Record Office

Richard Coates, MA, PhD, FSA   Professor of Linguistics, School of Cognitive and Computing Sciences, University of Sussex

Don Cox   Secretary, Sussex Mills Group

David Crossley, BA, FSA   Hon Reader in Archaeology, University of Sheffield

Roger Davey, BA   County Archivist, East Sussex Record Office

Peter Drewett, BSc, PhD, FSA, MIFA   Reader in Prehistoric Archaeology, Institute of Archaeology, University College London

Tony Duc, BA, DipTP, MRTPI   Planning Consultant, formerly Chief Strategic & Development Planner, East Sussex County Council

Robert Elleray, ALA, FRSA, FLS   Formerly Local History Librarian, Worthing Library

Allen Eyles, BA   Film historian

John Farrant, MA   Formerly Deputy Registrar, University of Sussex

Anthony Freeman, BA, MA, PhD, Dip Ed, FRSA, FRNS   Historical researcher, formerly member of the School Examinations and Assessment Council History Committee

Mark Gardiner, BA, PhD, FSA, MIFA   Lecturer in Archaeology, Department of Archaeological Science, The Queen's University of Belfast

John Godfrey, MA, D Phil   Assistant County Secretary, West Sussex County Council

Fred Gray, BA, PhD   Director, Centre for Continuing Education, University of Sussex

Christopher Greatorex, BA, MIFA   Senior Field Officer, Field Archaeology Unit, Institute of Archaeology, University College London

Keith Grieves, BEd, PhD   Reader in History, University of Kingston

Sue Hamilton, BA, PhD   Lecturer in Later European Prehistory, Institute of Archaeology, University College London

Keith Hardman, BA, MSc, DipTP, MRTPI   Planner, West Sussex County Council

Peter Holtham   Formerly Senior Officer, Brighton Excise

Maurice Howard, BA, MA, PhD, FSA   Reader in the History of Art, School of Cultural and Community Studies, University of Sussex

Annabelle Hughes, BA, MA, D Phil   Historical Buildings Research Consultant

Richard Jones, BA, D Phil   Research Officer, Sussex Archaeological Society

Charles Kay, BA, ALA   Information Librarian, Crawley Library

Kim Leslie, BA, FRSA   Education Officer, West Sussex Record Office

John Lowerson, The Revd, MA, FR Hist S, FRSA   Reader in History, Centre for Continuing Education, University of Sussex

Martin Mace, BSc   Military historian and publisher

Alison McCann, BA, DAA   Assistant County Archivist, West Sussex Record Office

Timothy McCann, BA   Assistant County Archivist, West Sussex Record Office

John Magilton, BA, M Phil, FSA, MIFA   Formerly Director, Southern Archaeology (Chichester) Ltd

John Manley, BA, MA, MA(Econ), MIFA   Chief Executive, Sussex Archaeological Society

David Martin, FSA, IHBC, MIFA   Senior Historic Buildings Officer, Archaeology South-East, University College London

Ron Martin, ARICS   Formerly Chartered Quantity Surveyor

Janet Pennington, MA, Dip English Local History   Archivist, Lancing College

Pamela Platt   History undergraduate, Open University

Mark Roberts, BA   Principal Research Fellow and Director, Boxgrove Projects, Institute of Archaeology, University College London

David Robinson, BSc, PhD   Senior Lecturer in Physical Geography, School of African and Asian Studies, University of Sussex

David Rudkin, BA, AMA, FSA   Director, Fishbourne Roman Palace

David Rudling, MA, BSc, FSA, MIFA   Director, Archaeology South-East, University College London

Neil Rushton, BA, MA   PhD Research Student, Trinity College, Cambridge

June Sheppard, MA, PhD   Formerly Reader in Geography, Queen Mary College, University of London

Brian Short, BA, PhD, FRGS   Reader in Human Geography and Dean of Cultural and Community Studies, University of Sussex

Mark Taylor, BA, MA, MIFA   Senior Archaeologist, West Sussex County Council

John Vickers, BA, BD, PhD   Formerly Principal Lecturer, West Sussex Institute of Higher Education

Wendy Walker, BA   Brighton and Hove Archivist, East Sussex Record Office

Heather Warne, BA, DAA   Archivist, Arundel Castle and Lambeth Borough Archives

Roger Wells, BA, D Phil, FR Hist S   Professor of History, Department of History, Christ Church University College, Canterbury

Sally White, BA, Dip Arch Sci, AMA, PhD   Principal Curator, Worthing Museum and Art Gallery

Peter Wilkinson, MA   Deputy County Archivist, West Sussex Record Office

Rendel Williams, BA, MA, PhD   Reader in Physical Geography, School of Chemistry, Physics and Environmental Science, University of Sussex

Bill Woodburn, MA, FRGS   Brigadier (retired), formerly Royal Engineers

Andrew Woodcock, BSc, MSc, MA, M Phil, PhD, FSA, AMA, MIFA   County Archaeologist, East Sussex County Council

ACKNOWLEDGEMENTS

A considerable amount of teamwork lies behind the production of this atlas and we are most grateful to all those who have given so much help throughout its preparation.

To Susan Rowland, cartographer at the University of Sussex, we owe an enormous debt of gratitude for all her dedicated professionalism in the interpretation of contributors' work with such clarity and skill. Keeping editors and contributors happy, often over the most minute points of detail, has meant a very considerable intrusion into her own free time. To Susan must go the major credit for the presentation and appearance of this atlas.

The original suggestion for a Sussex atlas came from a former West Sussex county councillor, Tommy Gee of Hassocks. As a result, a joint enterprise was set up between the University of Sussex, the Sussex Archaeological Society and both East and West Sussex County Councils. As editors we received support and guidance from an Editorial Board comprising Richard Childs and Roger Davey, the County Archivists for West and East Sussex respectively; John Manley, Chief Executive of the Sussex Archaeological Society, and Susan Rowland. Behind this body has been a Steering Committee made up of members of the Editorial Board plus Jackie Frisby representing Brighton and Hove Council, Caroline Adams, John Godfrey, Jeff Lord and Mark Taylor representing West Sussex County Council and Alan Hibbs representing East Sussex County Council, together with Noel Osborne, Managing Director of Phillimore & Co Ltd.

Thanks are also due to contributors who joined the editors as section co-ordinators, liaising with individual contributors within each of the seven sections into which the atlas is divided: John Bleach, John Manley and David Rudling. Support was also received from staff at the University of Sussex: Hazel Lintott, Martin Wingfield and Anne Woodbridge. Our thanks also go to Sharon Hall for compiling the index. We are also most grateful to Noel Osborne for undertaking on behalf of Phillimore to publish this work and to Nicola Willmot, Production Manager of Phillimore, who has been responsible for the overall design and the final stages of production.

For permission to reproduce illustrations we are very grateful to Ruth O'Shea on behalf of her late husband, Ted (page 106); Susan Rowland (page 112); Cambridge University Collection of Air Photographs (page 16); Sussex Archaeological Society (pages 13, 14, 44, 48, 62); West Sussex County Planning Department (page 30); West Sussex Record Office (pages 38, 68) and Worthing Museum (page 28). Other illustrations used are in the ownership of the respective authors.

Finally we must thank all the contributors who have made this atlas possible. They all readily responded to our invitation to contribute and have shown great patience and forebearance with our questions, suggestions and deadlines over the past two years.

The Editors

THE MAPS

Sussex is a county of major geological interest, with a wealth of rock exposures that provide important insights into Earth history.[1] Although there are no igneous or metamorphic rocks, Sussex is fortunate in possessing a great variety of sedimentary rocks: clays and shales in abundance, ironstones, uncemented silts and sands, and harder siltstones and sandstones, as well as a great thickness of chalk and limited amounts of harder limestone. Many of the rocks are renowned for their well-preserved fossil plants and animals.

All the sediments were originally deposited by rivers or by the sea in horizontal or very gently dipping beds, one on top of another. Subsequent earth movements have folded the beds and created faults. Most of Sussex is situated on the southern flank of a giant upfold, known as the Wealden Anticline, whose central axis crosses the northern part of the county in an east-west direction. A series of minor folds corrugate both flanks of the anticline and trend in the same general direction. Because of the geological structure, the dip of the beds shown on the accompanying geological map is generally to the south. Erosion has stripped away much of the crest of the anticline and its subsidiary folds, exposing the various beds as a series of east-west trending outcrops, which become progressively younger in a north to south direction, as can be seen in the cross-section.

None of the rocks of Sussex is particularly old when viewed against the immensity of geological time. The oldest rocks, belonging to the Purbeck Group, were laid down in shallow water lagoons at the end of the Jurassic Period, around 140 million years ago. They are exposed at the surface only in a core area of the Wealden Anticline, around Brightling and Mountfield. Shales and limestones predominate, but there are also gypsum beds, which are mined and used in the production of plaster and cement.

Overlying the Purbeck Group are rocks laid down after the Jurassic, in the succeeding Cretaceous Period. At the base is the Ashdown Formation and, at the top of the sequence, the Tunbridge Wells Sand Formation, which both consist of silty sands and sandstones, with lesser amounts of shale and clay. These two formations are separated by the Wadhurst Clay Formation, locally rich in ironstone, which provided much of the ore for the wealden iron industry (map 31).

The Ashdown, Wadhurst Clay and Tunbridge Wells Sand Formations, collectively known as the Hastings Group, outcrop in the north and east of the Weald. They appear to be dominantly flood-plain deposits, laid down by rivers, and are not, as was once believed, the infill of a fresh-water lake.[2]

Next in the sedimentary sequence are the shales and clays of the Weald Clay Group, forming a broad belt of lowland around the outcrop of the Hastings Group rocks. Within the Weald Clay Group are layers of flaggy sandstone, known as Horsham Stone, much used in the past for roofing houses and churches. Also present are beds of Paludina Limestone or Sussex Marble, crowded with the fossil shells of fresh water snails, once cut and polished as an ornamental stone. Like the Hastings Group, the Weald Clay Group seems to have been deposited mainly by rivers inundating a vast low-lying flood-plain.

In the middle of the Cretaceous Period, about 110 million years ago, the land slowly subsided and the sea advanced, laying down a series of beds, known as the Lower Greensand Group. The name is unfortunate, since only some of the beds are sandy, and the sand that occurs is seldom green.

At the base of the Lower Greensand is the Atherfield Clay Formation, which closely resembles the underlying Weald Clay in physical appearance. Next in the sequence is the Hythe Formation, which in Sussex consists mostly of sands and sandstones, often interbedded with layers of chert. Best known of the sandstones is the Pulborough Sandrock, still sometimes used for building. The overlying Sandgate Formation is locally very clayey, but more commonly consists of sands and sandstone. At the top of the sequence are the free-draining sands of the Folkestone Formation, much quarried for building sand around Washington and Storrington.

Continued deepening of the sea led to the deposition of marine clays known as the Gault Clay Group, which are arguably the stickiest and least tractable of all the Sussex clays. Sandier sediments were then deposited, known as the Upper Greensand Group. There is much more Upper Greensand in West Sussex than in East Sussex, where deposition of the Gault Clay continued for longer. In West Sussex, the Upper Greensand was once again much used as a building stone.

Starting around 100 million years ago, a calcareous ooze began to accumulate on the sea floor, which later became consolidated into the familiar, soft, white Chalk. The ooze consisted mostly of tiny calcite crystals secreted by planktonic algae that lived in the surface waters of the sea. Scattered particles of silica that also accumulated on the sea floor dissolved, only to re-form as layers and nodules of flint. Sussex preserves one of the most complete and accessible sequences of Chalk strata anywhere in Europe.[3]

The youngest Chalk beds in Sussex are 70-75 million years old. Uplift of the Wealden Anticline now began, and continued after the end of the Cretaceous Period and into the early Tertiary. No rocks dating from this period of uplift are found in Sussex. This is a pity because the end of the Cretaceous was a cataclysmic moment when an asteroid crashed into Mexico and gouged out a crater the size of Belgium, shrouding the planet in a huge dust cloud, creating fires on many continents. This was the time when the dinosaurs became extinct, and mammals began to become more numerous.

The sedimentary record in Sussex resumes in the early Tertiary (Eocene) with a further invasion by the sea and deposition of the sands and clays of the Woolwich and Reading Group. These outcrop on the Coastal Plain, and in places on the Downs as far eastwards as Newhaven and Seaford. They are overlain in many places by clays belonging to the London Clay Group, which in the Selsey Peninsula are overlain by Bracklesham Group clays. The middle Tertiary (Oligocene and Miocene) saw renewed uplift of the Wealden Anticline. Few rocks were laid down in Sussex and there was massive erosion, which continued into the late Tertiary (Pliocene).

Sussex escaped glaciation during the Quaternary, but the climate was sometimes so severe that permafrost developed. Sea-level fell at these times, enabling the rivers to carve their lower valleys far below present sea-level.[4] During the last 10,000 years sea-level has risen considerably as the climate has warmed, and the lower valleys have become infilled with sediments, such as peats and alluvium.

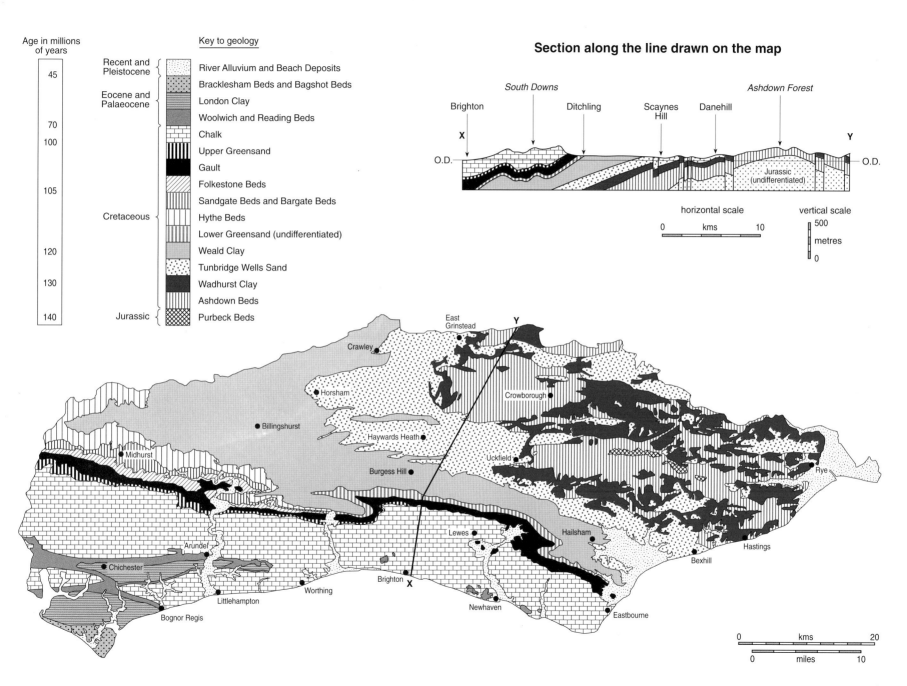

Age in millions
of years

		Key to geology
45	Recent and Pleistocene {	River Alluvium and Beach Deposits
	Eocene and Palaeocene	Bracklesham Beds and Bagshot Beds
70		London Clay
100		Woolwich and Reading Beds
		Chalk
105		Upper Greensand
		Gault
		Folkestone Beds
	Cretaceous	Sandgate Beds and Bargate Beds
		Hythe Beds
120		Lower Greensand (undifferentiated)
		Weald Clay
130		Tunbridge Wells Sand
		Wadhurst Clay
140		Ashdown Beds
	Jurassic {	Purbeck Beds

Section along the line drawn on the map

South Downs   *Ashdown Forest*

Brighton   Ditchling   Scaynes   Danehill
                          Hill

X   Y

O.D.   O.D.

Jurassic
(undifferentiated)

horizontal scale   vertical scale

0   kms   10   500

                            metres

                            0

East
Grinstead   Y

Crawley

Horsham   Crowborough

Billingshurst

Haywards Heath

Midhurst

Burgess Hill   Uckfield   Rye

Arundel   Lewes   Hailsham

Chichester   Hastings

Worthing   Bexhill

Brighton X

Littlehampton   Newhaven

Bognor Regis   Eastbourne

0   kms   20

0   miles   10

3

David Robinson

Soils of significantly different character occur in belts across Sussex from west to east mirroring the outcrops of different geological parent materials, with variations in slope, drainage and past and present land-use, producing more complex mosaics of interrelated soils.

The most extensive and homogenous group are the heavy, poorly-drained soils developed over the impermeable Gault and Weald Clays of the Low Weald. Known as stagnogleys, they are waterlogged throughout most of the winter and early spring when excess rainfall cannot rapidly evaporate nor quickly percolate down through the dense clay subsoil.[1] The upper soil varies in colour from yellow to grey-brown, but below it is predominantly grey due to anaerobic conditions. Water frequently lies on the surface of the land during wet winter weather, but in hot summers the soils dry out, become hard, and crack extensively. The soils are difficult to cultivate and large areas were traditionally under grass, although recent underdraining has greatly extended the use of these soils for arable cultivation.

Stagnogleys are also common on the clay substrates within the Hastings Beds of the High Weald, such as the Wadhurst Clay.[2] Often developed on steep slopes in deeply-dissected countryside, these soils tend to be less intensely waterlogged than those of the Low Weald and are characterised by sub-surface mottles of grey and ochre. These are formed by iron, which is reduced to the grey ferrous state and mobilised by anaerobic winter conditions and then partially re-oxidised to the more stable ferric state during drier summer months.

On the more free-draining parent materials of the High Weald such as the silts of the Ashdown Beds, gleying is less common and brown earths develop. Always brown in colour, those under deciduous woodland tend to be markedly darker than those under cultivation due to enrichment with humus from the decay of annual leaf litter. The upper soil is relatively free-draining with an open structure of well-aggregated soil crumbs. At depth, the soils tend to be less free-draining due to the presence of an argillic horizon formed by the redeposition of clay carried down from the upper soil by drainage water. In some locations, there is sufficient clay to cause impeded drainage and gleying. The freer draining soils are argillic brown earths,

and the gleyed varieties are stagnogleyic argillic brown earths.

Argillic brown earths are the dominant soils of the Coastal Plain where they are developed on a variety of parent materials, including extensive spreads of re-worked wind-blown silt known as brickearth or loess, deposited during cold periods of the Pleistocene; large fans of frost-shattered flint and chalk derived from the Downs, and areas of loamy and pebbly marine deposits.[3] Texture and drainage properties vary with parent material, but all are inherently fertile and produce high quality agricultural land.[4] On low-lying areas of the Coastal Plain, ground water frequently rises into the soil in winter, causing waterlogging and gleying of the lower parts of the profile and the development of argillic gleys. Modern tile drains help to reduce saturation of the surface soil, but in wet winters tillage is difficult because the lower soil can remain waterlogged until late spring.

Argillic brown earths are also characteristic of those areas of the Chalk overlain by Clay-with-Flints. This deposit of more or less homogenous dark brown or reddish tenacious clay, which includes whole or only partially broken flints, is believed to be the remnant of a former cover of Reading Beds, modified by the combined action of periglacial and soil-forming processes, accompanied by solution of the underlying Chalk.[5] Soils developed on Clay-with-Flints are moisture-retentive and difficult to work. The clay-accumulation zone is reddish in colour, which suggests that the clay was washed down during a climatic period warmer than the present, and the soils are therefore classified as paleo-argillic brown earths.[6]

Typical brown earths, without a clay-enriched argillic horizon, develop on outcrops of the Lower Greensand and the Hastings Beds, rich in silt and fine sand. However, on the coarser, sandier members, more acidic brown sands have developed with a lower base status and lower inherent fertility. Over hard sandstones, such as the Hythe Beds, the soils are frequently thin, dry and stony. Although relatively infertile, the soils respond well to fertilizers and in some areas are valued for agriculture, particularly for fruit growing.[7] However, the soils have little structural stability and are susceptible to erosion.

Sand grains within these soils are frequently bleached white due to the mobilisation and removal of

iron oxides. This marks the onset of podzolization, a process of degradation and depletion reaching its full expression beneath the West Sussex heathlands, where deep, free-draining humo-ferric podzols have developed on the coarse sands of the Folkestone Beds. Up to a metre or more in depth, the surface of these podzols is hidden by a matted layer of partially-decomposed plant litter. Beneath lies a black humus-rich layer, followed by a grey ash-coloured layer, 500-750mm deep, from which all iron has been removed. This layer is terminated sharply by a second dark humose layer, beneath which a thin, rust-brown iron-pan is frequently present, together with bands of further iron enrichment for a depth of a metre or more. The soils are acidic and seriously deficient in nutrients. The extreme acidity excludes earthworms and restricts other soil fauna, which partly explains the sharp boundaries between the different soil layers. Where heathland has developed on less free-draining, finer sands and silts, or where compact subsoils exist, such as on Ashdown Forest, shallower stagnogley podzols develop with strongly mottled or whitish-grey subsoil horizons.[8]

Soils developed directly over the Chalk are known as rendzinas. Typically, they rarely exceed 300mm in depth, contain abundant fragments of chalk and flint and are highly calcareous. Under woodland or grassland the soils are humose and dark brown or black, but when cultivated they lose humus and become paler. Their thinness and lack of soil moisture during dry summers restricts their agricultural value, but nearly all are now ploughed for cereals. In valley bottoms, rendzinas thicken and grade into brown calcareous earths which are deeper, more moisture-retentive and less calcareous. Brown calcareous earths are also found along the foot of the Downs, developed on hillwash overlying the Lower Chalk and Upper Greensand. Although sometimes stony, with micro-nutrient deficiencies that discourage the growth of some crops, they give good cereal yields and are of high agricultural value.

All the downland soils of Sussex contain a component of brickearth, which in some locations forms a covering a metre or more in thickness over the Chalk. The surface layers of soils developed in some of these deposits, notably on Lullington Heath, are decalcified, allowing calcifuge plants, such as the heathers *Calluna vulgaris* and *Erica cinerea* to grow in a rare chalk heath community.[9]

In their lower courses, the rivers flow over low-lying tracts of poorly drained, silt-rich alluvium. Ground water lies at, or close to, the ground surface for much of the year, and water stands on the surface in winter producing waterlogged alluvial gleys. Uniformly fine-grained in texture, they are greyish brown, becoming grey with abundant ochreous mottles below the surface. In the past, natural drainage was so poor that peat formed in some areas, but today active peat growth has mostly ceased because of ditching and artificial drainage. Flooding and poor drainage restrict agriculture to pasture, except where artificial drainage allows the cultivation of some arable crops. When drained the soils are fertile, and potentially of high value if the threat of periodic flooding can be removed.

The pattern of soils today is undoubtedly more complex and diverse than that which existed prior to the initial clearance of deciduous woodland for agriculture. The dominant natural soils would be varieties of brown earths, but agricultural activity has led to changes in drainage properties and rates of erosion, and caused nutrient degradation of some soils, but the enrichment and improvement of others. The result has been to accentuate the differences between soils developed on different parent materials and subject to different forms of exploitation and husbandry.[10] Soils are dynamic features of the environment and their management today will determine the character and properties of soils inherited by future generations.

- Stagnogleys
- Argillic gleys
- Argillic brown earths, including paleo-argillic brown earths over chalk
- Typical brown earths and brown sands
- Rendzinas and brown calcareous earths
- Podzols
- Alluvial gleys
- Urban areas

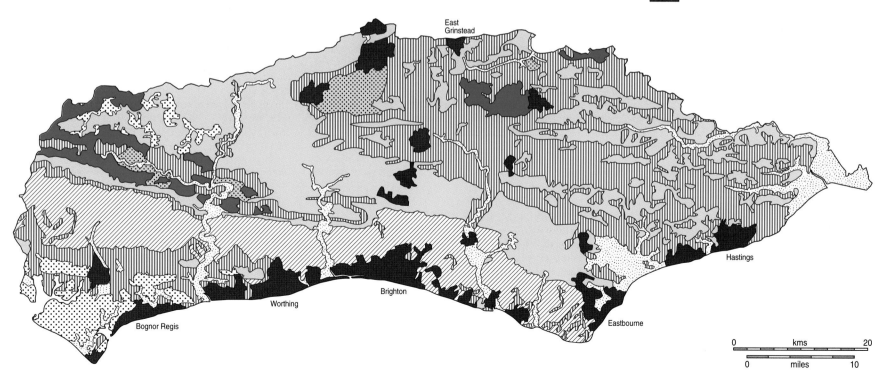

5

The sedimentary rocks of Sussex help to define its topographic and landscape character. The more resistant rocks form the higher ground, while the weaker rocks have undergone greater weathering and erosion and form lowlands. Because the beds tend to run east-west, so do many of the topographic features, giving Sussex a distinct east-west grain. Also, because the beds dip generally southwards, north-facing escarpments have developed along the northern edges of the outcrops of the more resistant rocks.

For many purposes, it is convenient to divide Sussex into five natural regions, each with its own unity and charm.[1] The north and east of the county is mostly quite hilly, with deep, steep-sided valleys ('ghylls') separated by often flat-topped ridges. Known as the High Weald, this region coincides with the outcrop of the Purbeck and Hastings Group rocks, and extends across the Sussex border into Surrey and Kent.[2] The tougher and more massive sandstone beds within the Ashdown and Tunbridge Wells Sand Formations form picturesque cliffs and crags, for example at West Hoathly and at Balcombe.[3] Valley sides cut in the Wadhurst Clay are often steep and tend to suffer from landslipping. Much of this region is 100m or more above sea level, and the highest point is Crowborough Beacon at 240m. Towards the coast, however, the lower valleys of the Brede and eastern Rother, together with Romney Marsh, form a significant area of lowland, best classified as a separate region or sub-region.[4]

Bordering the High Weald to the south and west is the almost flat Low Weald, formed in the relatively weak Atherfield and Weald Clays, nearly all below 50m. Outside Sussex, the Low Weald continues in an arc through Surrey and Kent, completely enclosing the High Weald. Rivers in the Low Weald tend to have wide flood plains and meandering channels, though in many areas they have been artificially straightened and penned in by the construction of high retaining banks. Pevensey Levels, forming an important sub-region of the Low Weald – in medieval times a tidal bay with mudflats and saltmarsh – is now reclaimed pasture.[5]

In West Sussex, the Low Weald is flanked on the south and west by hilly country developed on rocks of the Lower Greensand, Gault, and Upper Greensand.[6] This Wealden Greensand Region is scenically reminiscent of the High Weald. The Hythe Formation is particularly resistant to weathering and erosion, and forms much high ground, as well as a discontinuous escarpment rimming the Low Weald. Blackdown Hill, south of Haslemere, is the highest point in Sussex at 280m. The generally weaker Sandgate Formation forms lower ground, more particularly in the valley of the western Rother. The Folkestone Formation gives rise to further hilly country, the Gault Clay beyond is represented by a narrow vale, while the beds of the Upper Greensand Group form a distinct bench at the foot of the Downs.

The Lower and Upper Greensands thin eastwards and their outcrops become correspondingly narrower. East of the Adur, they cease to affect the landscape, and the Low Weald extends southwards, merging with the Gault Clay Vale

The chalk Downs, covering nearly one third of Sussex, form the most distinctive of the county's five natural regions.[7] It may seem surprising that a rock as soft to touch and easily dissolved as this should form such high ground and such a bold escarpment overlooking the Weald. The explanation is that Chalk is porous, full of small fissures, enabling it to absorb nearly all the rain that falls. Although there are numerous valleys, there are very few streams, and thus under natural conditions relatively little surface erosion. The Chalk is slowly dissolving away, but there is almost no surface flow of water to shape the gently rounded downland summits and distinctive dry valleys.

Four rivers that rise in the Weald, and are thus reasonably well supplied with water, have managed to cut through the Downs. The smallest is the most easterly, the Cuckmere. Its bigger neighbour to the west, the Ouse, has excavated a much wider valley for itself, except at Lewes, where it is closely hemmed in by downland, and has carved river cliffs that it has abandoned. The Adur and Arun have broad, open valleys, similar to that of the Ouse below Lewes. The Arun valley is much the most impressive scenically, with fine abandoned river cliffs.

The fifth of the natural regions is the low-lying Coastal Plain, which extends from the Hampshire border eastwards to Brighton, and reaches its maximum width of about 15km in the Chichester and Selsey areas. It is cut mainly into Tertiary beds, but also in places into the Chalk, and is covered by surface sands, gravels and brickearths of Quaternary age (map 1).

The geology has helped to determine not only topography but also the flora and fauna. Each of the five regions has a distinctive ecological character.[8]

The High Weald is rich in ancient woods and coppice, which harbour wild service tree and other scarce plant species. The region has lost many of the open heaths that it once possessed, although fine heathland remains on Ashdown Forest. The wooded ghylls and sandstone cliffs of the High Weald are home to a remarkable assemblage of liverworts, mosses, ferns (most famously the Tunbridge filmy-fern) and minute snails that require shaded and very damp conditions.[9] Many of the species flourished during the wetter Atlantic Period, 5,000 years ago, and have died out elsewhere in south-eastern England as the climate has become warmer and drier. They are now found mainly in the north and west of Britain. The coastal glens east of Hastings have a similar relict flora. Also of major botanical interest are the shingle ridges that have formed at Rye Harbour, which support sea pea and other rare maritime plants.

The once densely-forested Low Weald has been much cleared for agriculture, but many former coppice woods and wood pastures survive, particularly in the west of the county, for example at Ebernoe Common and The Mens. These support such rarities as the wild service tree and small-leaved lime. As in the High Weald, narrow strips of woodland (shaws) have been left separating some of the fields. Old, unimproved pastures are often rich in orchids, adders-tongue fern and other species that have disappeared from pastures that have received fertilizer and pesticides. Major tracts of grazing marsh have survived along some of the rivers and also on Pevensey Levels. The shingle foreland of The Crumbles (Langney Point) was once famous for its rare plants, but its interest is now sadly diminished owing to the development of the marina and associated housing.

The Wealden Greensand region repeats some of the features of the High Weald. There are very important areas of lowland heath, particularly on the Hythe and Folkestone Formations, and also many ancient woods and remnants of former wood pasture.

The eastern Downs are for the most part remarkably open and treeless. There are some small semi-natural woods and plantations, mainly on the escarpment, but the only extensive wooded area is Friston Forest, which was planted between the wars. The Downs west of the Arun are notably more wooded, and 18th- and 19th-century plantings predominate, but more ancient woods also occur, particularly on the escarpment. Here the occasional veteran large-leaved lime is found, prompting suggestions that this species was an important component of the original downland forests, along with wych elm and other species. Impressive yew woods occur in places, notably at Kingley Vale, north of Chichester.[10]

Clearance of the downland forests by Neolithic and later farmers helped to create extensive tracts of chalk grassland, whose surviving remnants are famous for their wealth of plant and insect species. The plants are adapted to growing on thin, infertile, calcium-rich soil and benefit from frequent grazing by sheep and rabbits. Because of undergrazing, large areas of old chalk grassland have been invaded by hawthorn scrub and by ash and sycamore woodland. Many other areas of grassland have been enriched with fertilizers, ploughed up or planted with trees, again causing serious loss of biodiversity. Most surviving areas of ancient chalk grassland are on steep and unploughable slopes, particularly on the escarpment.

The river valleys that cut through the Downs once supported extensive grazing marshes. Fertilizing and ill-planned drainage schemes have caused major losses of species, but areas of high ecological interest remain, for instance at Amberley Wild Brooks.

The Coastal Plain has suffered greatly from agricultural 'improvement' and from housing development. The few scraps of woodland and semi-natural habitat that survive have a special value, if only because of their rarity. The coastline is unfortunately one of the most developed in Britain, but there are still stretches of unspoilt salt marsh, sand dunes and shingle beach that are of major ecological interest, notably at East Head (West Wittering), Pagham and Climping.[11]

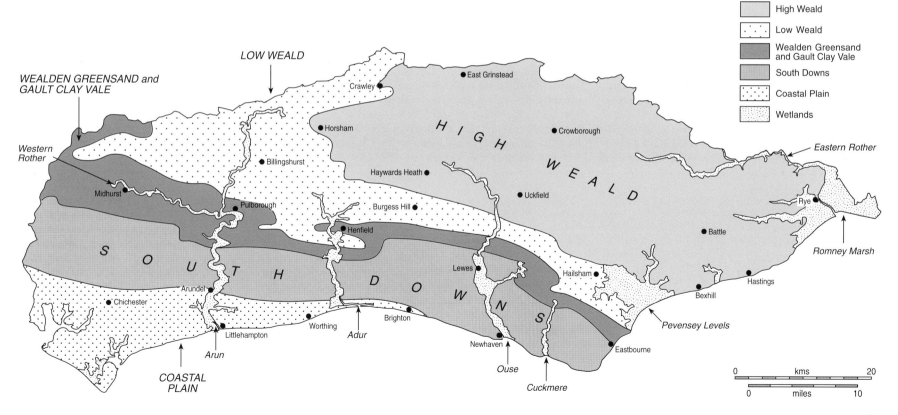

The coastline of Sussex has changed significantly in historic time, in part as a result of the natural processes of erosion and accretion by the sea, but also as a deliberate or accidental consequence of human activity.

The coastline of Roman Sussex was far more indented than it is today. The rivers reached the sea in tidal estuaries which penetrated several miles inland. This was because during the Quaternary ice ages the accumulation of ice caused sea level to fall. At the maximum of the last glacial period, about 15,000 years ago, sea level stood 130-40m below its present level.[1] The rivers flowed south and west across the dry floor of the Channel to a coastline that lay 450-500km distant, excavating deep valleys which were gradually flooded by rising sea level as the climate warmed and the ice melted. The sea appears to have reached close to parts of the present coastline around 5,000 years ago and reached approximately its present height around 3,000 years ago.[2]

The rising sea levels caused the rivers to become increasingly sluggish and infill their valleys with a complex sequence of sediments, a process accentuated by the growth of shingle spits across the mouths of the estuaries, which further impeded the free flow of water to and from the sea.[3] Infilling caused the sea to retreat from these estuaries and today, as the rivers of Sussex approach the present coast, they flow on 30m or more of sediments.[4] Only in Chichester and Pagham Harbours is the process of infill and straightening of the coastline still incomplete (map c).

Under the influence of the prevailing south-west winds, drifting shingle caused the spits to divert the river mouths eastwards. Spits and shingle bars also grew across the mouths of major coastal embayments at Pevensey and Rye Bay, where vast accumulations of shingle formed the cuspate forelands of the Crumbles and Dungeness. There is some uncertainty as to the origin of the shingle and the date of spit formation. There appears to have been a delay of 1,000-3,000 years between sea level reaching its present height and noticeable growth of the spits, possibly because there had to be considerable coastal erosion before a sufficient volume of flint shingle accumulated for eastward drift to cause problems. However, it now seems more likely that the shingle originated offshore, when sea-level was lower, and was driven upwards and shorewards by the rising sea level, initially forming an offshore bar which was then driven onshore.[5]

In Roman Sussex any spits appear to have been insignificant, but by medieval times they were rapidly enlarging and causing major problems for many of the ports. Roman river ports such as Lewes and Bramber lost trade to ports located further downstream such as Seaford and Old Shoreham. In later medieval times these in turn suffered from problems of access and silting, and new passageways had to be cut to the sea through the spits. This led to the creation of new ports such as Newhaven, but the newly-opened mouths were again subject to closure by drifting shingle and many were not stabilised until large breakwaters were built in the late 19th century (maps a and d).[6]

Whilst the sheltered river estuaries and deep embayments were infilled behind spits that grew across their mouths, the open coast suffered erosion and retreat. This was most dramatic in West Sussex where the coast is low lying and backed by soft, easily-eroded materials. Erosion seems to have been particularly severe around Selsey where the sites of the original Saxon cathedral and the former deer park of the bishops of Chichester have been lost to the sea. From the mid-19th to mid-20th centuries, the coast here was retreating from 2.0 to over 4.5m per year and may have retreated by as much as 5 to 7km over the past 2,000 years.[7] Further east, between Pagham and Littlehampton, erosion was also severe and several villages such as Charlton and Ilsham have been lost to the sea.[8]

In East Sussex the coast comprises bold cliffs of chalk and sandstone separated by alluvial lowlands. Today the cliffs are retreating at average rates of 0.3 to 0.5m per year but some stretches are retreating at more than 1.0m per year.[9] Whether such rapid rates of retreat have existed throughout the historic period is uncertain. When sea level reached its present height, some sections of cliff may have been partially obscured and protected from wave action by extensive deposits of rock debris produced by freeze-thaw activity under the periglacial climate of the last Ice Age. It is likely also that, prior to extensive groyning of Sussex beaches and the construction of breakwaters and piers to protect harbour mouths, there was far more shingle protecting the base of the cliffs than there is today. Rising sea levels and slow subsidence of land means that wave height is increasing by between 3 and 6mm per year, and protection offered by the shore platforms at the base of the cliffs is lessening.[10]

The volume of shingle along the Sussex coast has varied significantly over time. For example, between 800 and 300BP vast quantities of shingle accumulated east of Eastbourne to form The Crumbles foreland.[11] Since then around 50% of the shingle has been lost and the seaward margin has retreated more than 1.5km.[12] Between Pett and Rye, the successive accumulation of shingle ridges has extended the shore up to 3km seaward (map e). Camber Castle, built on the edge of the shore in 1539, now lies some 1.75km inland, and the Martello Tower, built at the entrance to Rye Harbour in 1804, now stands 1km inland.[13]

Since the 18th century much of the Sussex coast has been protected by engineering structures such as groynes which capture drifting shingle and by vertical sea walls which repel the waves. Walls continue to be built, most notably at the foot of the chalk cliffs to the east of Brighton where some 2.5km of undercliff wall has been built since the early 1970s. Sea walls are expensive to construct and maintain, and scouring by the reflected energy of the waves causes foreshore erosion and beach loss. As a consequence, in recent decades, cheaper measures designed to absorb rather than reflect the energy of the waves have become increasingly popular. These include the re-charging of beaches at Seaford, Rottingdean and Saltdean; the construction of offshore breakwater islands at Elmer in West Sussex and the installation of riprap and stone revetments to protect the base of some East Sussex cliffs, most notably at Fairlight. Here, in the 1980s, houses collapsed into the sea. Those few areas of coast that remain unprotected continue to retreat, as evidenced by the 1999 Beachy Head collapse. The west coast of Selsey Bill remains particularly vulnerable where breaching of the shingle beach threatens to make Selsey an island once again.

Coastal defence is a never-ending challenge and, with an increasing proportion of the population of Sussex choosing to live near the coast, the threat of erosion and flooding increases each year.[14]

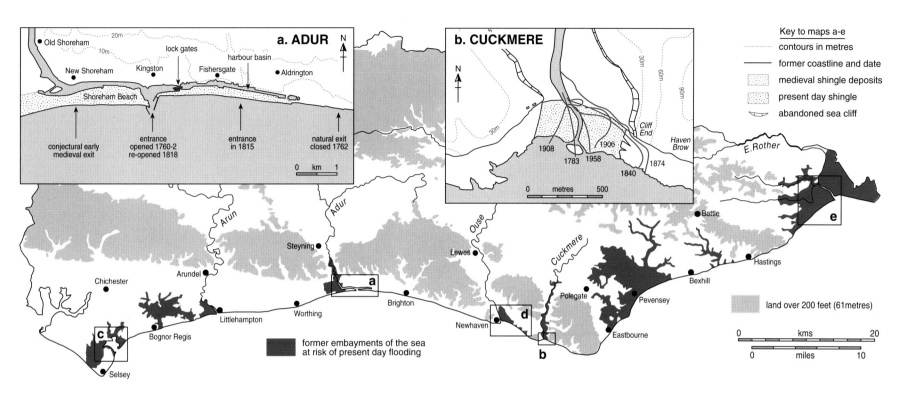

a. ADUR

N

20m
10m

Old Shoreham
New Shoreham
Kingston
lock gates
harbour basin
Fishersgate
Aldrington

Shoreham Beach

conjectural early
medieval exit

entrance
opened 1760-2
re-opened 1818

entrance
in 1815

natural exit
closed 1762

0   km   1

b. CUCKMERE

N

30m

60m

90m

30m

Cliff
End

Haven
Brow

1908
1783 1958 1906
1840 1874

0   metres   500

Key to maps a-e

.... contours in metres

──── former coastline and date

medieval shingle deposits

present day shingle

abandoned sea cliff

E. Rother

Battle

Hastings

Bexhill

e

land over 200 feet (61 metres)

Chichester
Arundel
Steyning
Lewes
Ouse
Cuckmere

Arun
Adur

a

Brighton
Worthing
Littlehampton
Bognor Regis
Selsey

c

former embayments of the sea
at risk of present day flooding

Newhaven
d
Polegate
Pevensey
Eastbourne

b

0   kms   20

0   miles   10

c. PAGHAM

N

2m

Pagham

remnant of 1874
former exit

Saltmarsh

1874
1843
1823
1774
1672

7m

stages in growth
of spit

medieval
estuarine
deposits

0   km   1

d. OUSE

0   km   1

remnant of
medieval channel

30m

N

Newhaven

Bishopstone

30m

30m

breakwater
completed
1890

remnant of
late 17th c.
channel

exit 1698

approximate position
of Roman mouth,
artificially re-opened
c.1539 and again
re-opened 1731-3

approximate
position of
medieval spit

Seaford

Hawks
Brow

medieval exit

**e. RYE
HARBOUR**

Rye

1682   1598

1682

Camber Castle
1539

1594 1755 1765
1803

1695 1845
1927

1899
1950

Winchelsea

Winchelsea Beach

Pett
Level

N

Cliff End

0   km   2

9

The earliest inhabitants of Sussex belong to the Lower and Middle Palaeolithic (or Old Stone Age) periods which, in this country, encompass some half a million years of human history. These people, some of whom may have belonged to a species different from our own, would have led a nomadic lifestyle, not only gathering fruits, berries and other vegetable matter and scavenging the prey of other animals but also hunting and butchering large animals themselves. Since they built no substantial structures, their presence is only normally detected through finds of stone (mainly flint) tools, principally handaxes and the waste associated with their manufacture.

Inevitably, during such a long period, there have been vast changes in the climate and in the geology and morphology of the landscape. Some of the most dramatic changes would have resulted from a series of alternating cold glacial and warmer interglacial periods, which can be reconstructed from changes in oxygen isotope levels in seabed deposits. Although the ice itself never reached Sussex, the intense cold of the periglacial conditions would have produced thick sheets of 'soliflucted' gravels, formed by the mass-movement of semi-frozen rock and underlying deposits moving down the slopes of the Downs onto the present Coastal Plain and into the river valleys.

Fluctuating climatic conditions would also have produced great changes in sea level, at times reaching up to 40m above the present day, at others falling to over 100m below. The evidence for these high sea levels survives in the form of fossil cliffs and raised beaches, now left some distance inland.

Because of these changes, Palaeolithic tools are most commonly found incorporated in later deposits and would have been abandoned in environments very different from the Sussex of today. They are only occasionally found *in situ*, and such sites are particularly rare and important.

Sussex is fortunate in that a number of comprehensive surveys and assessments of Palaeolithic material have already been undertaken.[1] These studies include detailed assessments of individual sites, rather than the more general consideration of distribution patterns discussed here.

With the notable exception of some sites on the West Sussex Coastal Plain, Sussex is not generally a rich area for Palaeolithic discoveries. This is, in part, due to the absence of large-scale gravel extraction, and the consequent disturbance of those deposits in which Palaeolithic tools might be expected to survive. Many sites owe their discovery to former collectors, at a time when collecting Palaeolithic stone tools was fashionable and purchases made from quarry workers. For this reason, the material that survives is biased towards the finished tools, principally handaxes, with relatively little of the associated worked material surviving.

The distribution map therefore represents sites where finds of Palaeolithic tools have been recorded, and not necessarily where they were originally abandoned. Overall the distribution is a product of archaeological prospection and geomorphological processes, and probably not a true reflection of the extent of Palaeolithic activity. Inevitably therefore the distribution pattern reflects the three principal contexts from which Palaeolithic material has been recovered: raised beaches, river gravel deposits, and surface sites. These contexts will now be considered in turn.

Raised Beaches

Preserved on the Coastal Plain, at the foot of the chalk downland, are a series of raised beaches and buried cliff lines.

Although the sequence and date of the various stages of these beaches has yet to be worked out in detail, they can be divided into two main series; a higher, delimited by the Goodwood-Slindon raised beach and cliffline, and a lower, delimited by the Brighton-Norton raised beach and cliffline.[2] The deposits here mark periods when sea level was respectively some 40m and 8m higher than that of the present day.

It is the higher of these raised beaches, and the deposits associated with it (principally the Slindon formation), that is not only the most ancient but the most significant, exemplified by the internationally-important site at Boxgrove (map 6). Only here do we find the associated skeletal remains of large animals (including human remains, *Homo* cf. *heidelbergensis*), micro-animals, other fauna, molluscs and pollen. The Boxgrove site predates the Anglian glaciation and probably dates back around 500,000 years.

The tools from Boxgrove, and nearby contemporary sites such as Slindon, mainly comprise ovate handaxes which are remarkably sophisticated. They clearly demonstrate that the complexity of tools and the quality of workmanship is not necessarily an indication of their age.

The lower raised beach is much more recent in date and is likely to be pre-Ipswichian, probably about 200,000 years old. The most famous exposure of this beach is at Black Rock, near Brighton Marina. Whilst there are some palaeoliths recorded from the raised beach gravels themselves, all could have derived from earlier deposits.

The Brighton raised beach can be equated with deposits at Selsey, on the basis of height, faunal remains and pollen analysis. Lying beneath this beach is an estuarine channel, cut into earlier marine deposits.

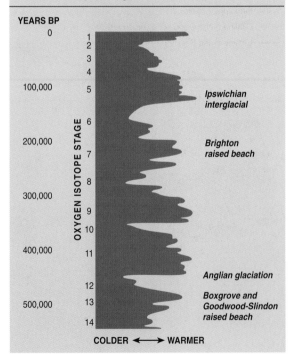

Past temperature changes established from oxygen isotope changes in sea bed deposits

YEARS BP

Ipswichian interglacial

Brighton raised beach

Anglian glaciation

Boxgrove and Goodwood-Slindon raised beach

COLDER ◄──► WARMER

Palaeolithic material (including 'Levallois' flakes) has been found on the foreshore very close to this channel, and probably derives from it.

River Gravels

Prior to the Anglian glaciation the eastern part of Sussex was joined to the continent by a substantial land-bridge, which was eventually breached by water overflowing from an ice-dammed lake in the southern North Sea. The rivers that cut through the Sussex downland today represent remnants of much larger river systems that originally flowed into an embayment south-west of the land-bridge and later into a postulated river flowing south of the present Sussex coastline.

The gravel deposits in the river valleys, within which finds of Palaeolithic tools might be expected to occur, are fragmentary and thin and nowhere are there well-preserved flights of gravel terraces. Moreover, whilst a number of finds have been claimed from the Sussex river gravels, there is not a single authenticated provenance. This situation undoubtedly reflects the lack of commercial exploitation of these deposits, and hence opportunities to search for the archaeological material that must surely survive within them.

Surface Sites

There are abundant finds from the Sussex Downs, particularly between Brighton and Eastbourne, to demonstrate human activity here in the Palaeolithic. Recent evidence from Kent suggests that some of this material may have survived more or less *in situ* and have remained close to the spot where it was originally abandoned.[3] Elsewhere, away from the Downs, there is a scattering of surface finds. These include technologies known to archaeologists as 'Levallois' or 'Mousterian of Acheulian Tradition', material dating from the Middle Palaeolithic of which some may be associated with the presence of Neanderthal Man.

It is unlikely that there will be significant changes to the present distribution map in future years. Certainly new sites will be discovered, particularly on the West Sussex Coastal Plain, where more sites of spectacular importance undoubtedly await discovery and where the commercial exploitation of gravel deposits is presently concentrated. Although further finds will inevitably be made elsewhere, they are likely to reinforce the present distribution pattern of finds, rather than significantly change it.

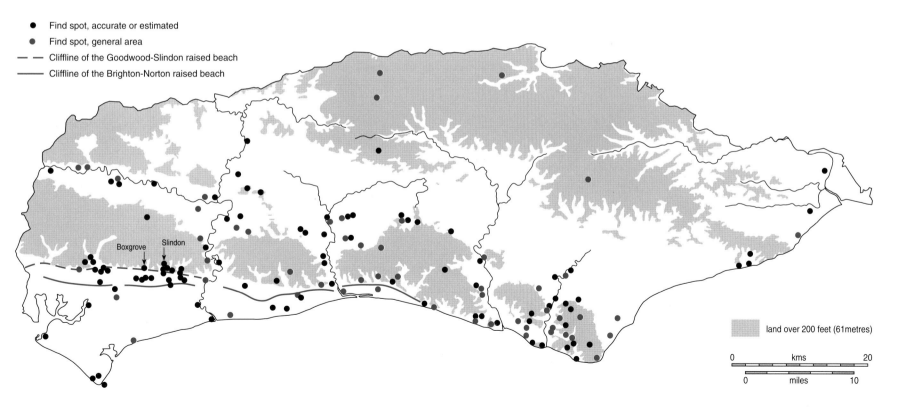

- ● Find spot, accurate or estimated
- ● Find spot, general area
- – – Cliffline of the Goodwood-Slindon raised beach
- —— Cliffline of the Brighton-Norton raised beach

Boxgrove   Slindon

land over 200 feet (61metres)

0   kms   20

0   miles   10

Around half a million years ago hominids first walked into the landmass now known as the British Isles, at that time physically connected to the rest of Europe by a substantial land-bridge, primarily composed of chalk. Thus, the English Channel was only open to the Atlantic Ocean, in the west.[1]

The earliest record of hominid occupation in Middle Pleistocene Britain comes from the South Downs dipslope and the upper Coastal Plain of West Sussex. In this area the palaeogeography was substantially different half a million years ago. A coastal embayment, backed by chalk cliffs, extended over 30km from Portsdown in Hampshire to Arundel in West Sussex. Within the embayment the site of Boxgrove preserves evidence of the activities of the early hominid colonisers and the changing environments within which they operated. In addition, the site has produced the earliest hominid fossil in Britain, a lower limb bone or tibia.

The oldest Middle Pleistocene sediments and preserved land-surfaces of the West Sussex Coastal Plain have been exposed by quarrying along the southern margin of the dipslope of the South Downs, between the River Lavant (SU 857 088) and the River Arun (TQ 020 070). The most extensive exposures, and the only place where the complete conformable sequences may be seen, are in the A.R.C. Eartham Quarry (SU 918 087-SU 924 085) shown on the map. These workings, which cover an area of some 250ha, are located 12km from the present-day coastline and 7km east of Chichester. The quarry complex straddles the parish boundaries of Boxgrove to the west and Eartham to the east but the conformable geological sequences, within which the Palaeolithic archaeology is preserved, are found only in the parish of Boxgrove, after which the site is named.

The Pleistocene sediments at the site are cut into, and unconformably overlie, Upper Cretaceous Chalk of the Campanian Stage. The marine deposits have been formally named the Slindon Formation and comprise three members: the Slindon Gravel, the Slindon Sands and the Slindon Silts.[2] The terrestrial deposits (Eartham Formation), comprise lower and upper gravel members. A transition between interglacial and cold stage sediments is located just above the interface between these two members.

The sediments sit upon, and are contained within, a marine platform and chalk cliff. These features were formed during a Middle Pleistocene high sea level event that entailed a marine transgression moving northwards over the lower Coastal Plain and cutting into the chalk of the dipslope of the Downs. The marine beach complex associated with this high sea level attains a maximum elevation of 43m OD at the junction of the cliff and the wave cut platform; this high altitude being the result of subsequent tectonic activity in the area.[3] Associated with the high sea level are the marine sand member, the Slindon Sands, which grade up into a lagoon/regression unit, the Slindon Silts. The Slindon Silts were laid down when the direct path of the sea into a large embayment, formed by the Downs, was blocked, creating a large salt water, tidally-fed lagoon. At the end of the lagoon phase, following marine regression, a soil developed on the surface of the silts. This represents the most extensive Pleistocene land surface at the site, which has produced most of the archaeological material.

All the sedimentary units at Boxgrove contain cultural material in the form of flintwork, mostly handaxes and debris from their manufacture, and in some units there are also butchered faunal remains, but they are most abundant and least disturbed in the Slindon Silt member and the soil horizon that developed at the surface of the Slindon Silts (plates 1 and 2).[4] Linking the archaeology to the geological and palaeo-environmental evidence demonstrates that the area was occupied over a period of tens of thousands of years.

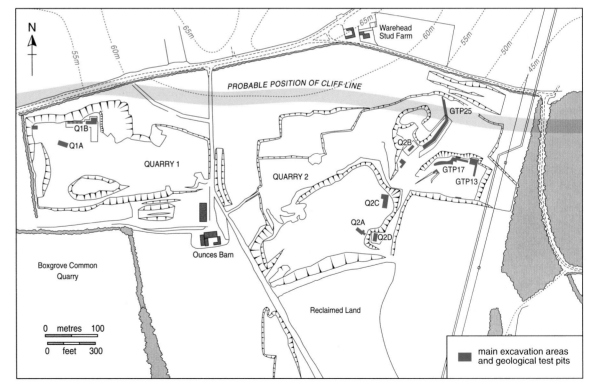

Data from sites throughout the Continent suggest that man first arrived in sizeable numbers from Africa in the interglacial or warm period that began around 520,000 years ago, as attested by the evidence at Boxgrove, and spread rapidly throughout Western Europe. With regard to the tibia from Boxgrove there is only one other piece of fossil hominid that is comparable in age terms, and that is a jaw bone found in a sand pit at Mauer, near Heidelberg in Germany in 1907. The jaw bone was found in isolation from any other archaeological material but in the same sedimentary horizon was a mammalian fauna virtually identical to that at Boxgrove. Thus the Boxgrove hominid has been tentatively classified as *Homo* cf. *heidelbergensis.*

The activities of the hominids at Boxgrove on the mudflats and grasslands in front of the cliff indicate that this area was used for the procurement of carcasses and their subsequent processing. Evidence for the collection of plant material, if such an activity was undertaken in this locale, has not survived. However, it is clear from the distribution and condition of fish bones and marine molluscs recovered during excavation, that these potential food sources were not utilised. It is therefore important to consider how the carcasses were procured, what species of animals were butchered, and how this process was undertaken. Answering these questions will have

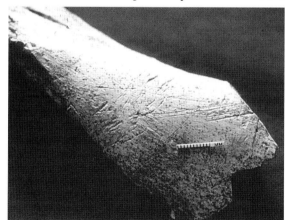

Plate 1. Cut marks made by flint tools on a horse bone (scale in mm divisions).

significant implications for our understanding of the technological capabilities and behavioural repertoire of Middle Pleistocene hominids.

Analysis of the butchered faunal remains from Boxgrove indicate that hominids had access to complete carcasses in very fresh condition. The carcasses are predominantly large mammals such as rhinoceroses, horses and giant deer; and other butchered remains include species such as bear, red deer and bison. The following points attest to carcass condition prior to butchery:

• Body part representation. Evidence from excavation areas Q1B and GTP17 indicates that at the time of butchery all anatomical elements were present.
• The nature of the butchery activities, which follow a logical progression from skinning, through disarticulation to filleting and bone smashing.
• There is no evidence, from the hundreds of butchered bones, of primary access to the carcass by predators, such as lions, or carcass processors such as hyaenas or wolves. Where carnivore puncture marks or gnawing marks are found on butchered bone they always overlie hominid cut marks.

Where isolated butchered body parts have been found, for example in geological test pits or at the edges of main areas, these too exhibit features that point to the carcass being fresh. These features include butchery marks to remove tongues, cut marks in the eye sockets and skinning of the head. The butchered animals are either juveniles or prime of life adults, that show no signs of pathology in their hard tissues.

There are only two viable methods of meat procurement that would result in the combination of features outlined above: confrontational scavenging, and hunting. Confrontational scavenging relies upon other carnivores to kill the prey, the predator is then driven off and the carcass secured. In the area of Q1B the concentration of at least four butchered rhinos, which were unlikely to have had natural predators as mid-life adults, points to a procurement strategy other than confrontational scavenging.

In addition to the strong but still circumstantial evidence for hunting, more direct evidence comes from the horse shoulder blade that was discovered in the

Slindon Silts in Quarry 2 at GTP17. The bone exhibited a curious fracture, towards the middle of the blade: the break was semi-circular and approximately 50mm in diameter. Preliminary analysis indicates that the puncture was consistent with penetration by a projectile.

To evince the hunting hypothesis is crucial to understanding the hominid behavioural repertoire at this period of the Pleistocene. The ability to hunt game removes dependence on other predators and therefore a large element of risk from a subsistence strategy. The nutritional quality and variety of body parts would also be far greater. Access to intestinal fat, lights, offal and stomach contents increases the overall nutritional yield, especially of essential vitamins. Hunting would therefore be the passport to colonisation and exploitation of other ecological niches. Europe, far from being a daunting prospect to early colonisers, would have been quickly opened up.[5] Hunting would also have had implications for the survival of hominids on an annual seasonal basis and also on a broader time-scale between interglacials and glacials. Analysis of the tibia from Boxgrove suggests that the individual was extremely active in life, with immense lower limb strength. Such an individual would have been anatomically well-adapted to hunt and to butcher large fauna.

Plate 2. A typical flint handaxe from Boxgrove.

13

The earliest Mesolithic sites in Sussex (*c.*8000–6000BC) are part of the continental Maglemosian tradition. They include sites at Hassocks, Heath Common at Storrington and Iping Common, all on the Lower Greensand.[1] The site at Iping was excavated in 1960–61 and consisted of a roughly circular area of stained sand about 8m in diameter. Most of the flint assemblage was of cores and waste material (91%). The tools included scrapers, gravers, punches, a pick, a fabricator and 108 microliths together with axe sharpening flakes. It is likely that Iping represents a temporary camp site of a small hunting group.[2] A similar site was excavated at Rackham, where, by plotting the exact position of each struck flake, two or possibly three episodes of flint knapping were identified beside a scatter of fire-cracked flints perhaps representing a small camp fire.[3] The density of Early Mesolithic sites in Sussex remains quite low with most restricted to the Lower Greensand. Many sites on the Downs may, however, have been lost with the erosion of loess particularly in the Early Neolithic. Currently there appears to be little evidence for much Early Mesolithic activity in the Weald.

Between 7000BC–6000BC there was a great expansion in the number of sites in the western Weald. These sites are characterised by numbers of obliquely blunted and basally retouched points often referred to as 'Horsham' points.[4]

Most Mesolithic sites in Sussex belong to the Later Mesolithic, a period from about 6000BC to the arrival of Neolithic ideas around 4300BC. Although many sites were still located on the Greensand they are also found on the Downs, the Coastal Plain and high up into the Weald. Big sites like those excavated at Selmeston and Hassocks, with a wide range of tool types, together with pits, may represent home-bases from which hunting and foraging parties left daily for local resources or seasonally for long range resources like hunting in the High Weald.

Hunting parties camped under the rock-shelters in the Weald. Excavations at Hermitage Rocks, High Hurstwood, revealed a hearth constructed of sandstone blocks associated with 4,329 pieces of worked flint together with large numbers of microliths indicating the importance of hunting. Three carbon-14 dates from Hermitage Rocks of 4850±100bc (Q-1311), 4970±110bc (Q-1312) and 5155±70bc (Q-1562) suggest the site may have been periodically occupied over a number of years.[5] Use of the wealden rock-shelters carried on to the end of the Mesolithic and into the Early Neolithic. High Rocks, Tunbridge Wells, for example, has carbon-14 dates of 3780±150bc (BM-91) and 3710±150bc (BM-40) associated with microliths but with Neolithic round-based pottery under the same shelters.[6]

The wealden rock-shelters may well have been utilised from the home-base camps on the Lower Greensand. Hunting and foraging parties also utilised the Lower Greensand woodland. At West Heath, towards the Sussex-Hampshire border, small scatters of flint tools and waste were associated with temporary camp sites represented by cooking hollows. One of these produced a carbon-14 date of 6150±70bc (Har-645) while another produced two dates of 6820±80bc (Har-7036) and 7090±90bc (Har-

Hermitage Rocks, High Hurstwood

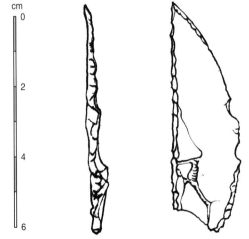

'Horsham point' from rock shelter at Hermitage Rocks

7037). The West Heath activity suggests small hunting and foraging parties using the area during the overlap period between the Early and Later Mesolithic.[7] Further east along the Lower Greensand at Minsted, excavations in 1973 revealed the first evidence for possible manipulation of animals by Mesolithic peoples in Sussex. Pollen analysis of a Mesolithic soil buried under a Bronze Age round barrow showed very high concentrations of ivy (*Hedera*). This suggests forest clearance perhaps to attract game.[8] The ivy may have been deliberately brought to the clearing for winter fodder or may have been growing on dead trees in the clearing.

Evidence for Later Mesolithic activity on the Downs is extensive but largely restricted to flint tools and waste material in the disturbed contexts of modern plough soils. These lithics are often associated with patches of clay-with-flints which may have provided a ready source of flint. Detailed survey of one block of Downland at Bullock Down behind Beachy Head suggests extensive use of woodland resources. Forty-five tranchet axes and twenty other axes together with picks, transverse arrowheads and waste material have been found on Bullock Down.[9] Evidence for Mesolithic activity on the Coastal Plain remains scanty but is on the increase with discoveries on road schemes around Chichester and at Fishbourne Roman Palace. The dozen or so known sites mainly appear to be fairly late in the Mesolithic and probably represent hunter-fishers camping around the many streams and marine inlets formed on the Coastal Plain following post-glacial rises in sea level.[10]

Direct evidence for Mesolithic subsistence strategies in Sussex is very slight due to the absence of much in the way of floral or faunal remains. Hunting is assumed on the basis of the lithic assemblages and information elsewhere in temperate Europe. The oak forests of Sussex would have been home to herds of deer, wild cattle and pig, together with birds and rodents. Rivers, streams and the coastline, we may assume, provided fish and shellfish. The main source of food was, however, likely to have been a wide range of edible plants. Acorns, tubers and roots probably provided staples while nuts and berries would have been available seasonally.[11]

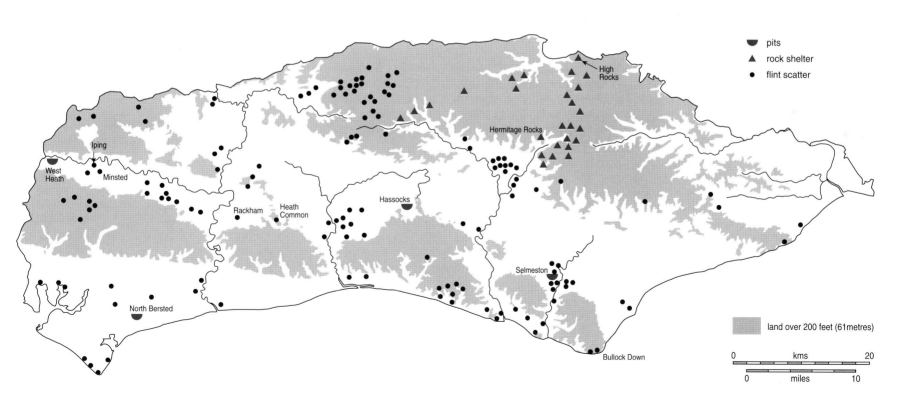

The arrival of 'Neolithic' ideas, manifested in the physical form of communal monuments, the first pottery and polished stone tools, took place in Sussex in the late fifth millennium BC, perhaps by 4300BC. The area that was to become Sussex was already well populated by Later Mesolithic hunters and gatherers and it is almost certain that it was these people who adopted 'Neolithic' ideas by acculturation. There is no evidence for colonisation by farmers from the European mainland. The earliest dates for the Neolithic in Sussex come from the causewayed enclosures in the west at Court Hill (3470±180bc, I-12,893) and The Trundle (3290±140bc, I-11615) together with the flint mines at Harrow Hill (3400±150bc, BM-2098R) and Church Hill, Findon (3390±150bc, BM-181).[1] The earliest well-dated carbonised seed, however, has a date of 2510±70bc (Har-1662). This is the emmer wheat (*Triticum dicoccum*) and six-row barley (*Hordeum vulgare*) from Bishopstone.[2] It therefore remains an open question as to whether agriculture was adopted with other 'Neolithic' ideas at the start of the Neolithic in Sussex. The evidence at present suggests that the domestication of animals, particularly cattle and pigs, took place alongside an essentially hunting, gathering and fishing economy of Later Mesolithic type with agriculture perhaps not being adopted until slightly later.

Clearance of the mixed oak 'wildwood' began in this area in the Late Mesolithic, but intensified in the Early Neolithic.[3] This resulted in soil deterioration and the choking of rivers by erosion products contributing to floodplain development downstream.[4] Molluscan sequences from the South Downs show a mosaic of downland clearance from the Neolithic onwards.[5]

Three types of communal monument were constructed in the Early Neolithic and survive today in the Sussex landscape. They were all constructed on the South Downs but often overlook river valleys, the Coastal Plain in West Sussex, or the Weald. There is evidence for Neolithic activity in the form of flint and stone tools in all these environments. Eight Causewayed Enclosures are known from Sussex although three – Bury Hill, Court Hill and Halnaker Hill – have pit-dug ditches linked below the ground surface making them look superficially like continuously ditched enclosures.[6] The other five enclosures show clear 'causeways' across the circuits of pit-dug ditches characteristic of this type of monument. The three enclosures already mentioned, together with Barkhale, have one circuit of ditches each, while Offham and Combe Hill have two roughly concentric circles. The Trundle and Whitehawk show multiple replacement of ditches probably over many centuries.[7] All the Causewayed Enclosures in Sussex have been sampled by excavation, but only the small one at Offham has been extensively excavated. Although this revealed little trace of activity in the interior, there were deliberately placed deposits within the ditches. These included a pit containing a smashed round-based bowl, a leaf-shaped arrowhead and a careful selection of animal remains, especially teeth of both domestic and wild species.[8] A second deposit consisted of the crouched remains of a young man in his early 20s. The exact function of Causewayed Enclosures remains uncertain, but they clearly involved considerable communal effort, and groups coming together both for their construction and other activities, including those of a ritual nature.

The second type of communal monument constructed in the Early Neolithic are the Long Barrows and the slightly smaller version referred to as Oval Barrows. These barrows consist of mounds of chalk dug from flanking ditches. They are nearly all constructed just below the tops of hills (false-crested) with the Long Barrows having extensive views, often over river valleys and into the Weald. The Oval Barrows have a more downland orientation. Three have carbon-14 dates but it may be assumed that the others are of more or less the same date. The dated examples are North Marden, 2760±110bc (Har-5544), Bevis's Thumb, 2595±95bc (I-11,843) and Alfriston, 2360±110bc (Har-940).[9] Neolithic barrows are generally, but not always, associated with human remains. These are rarely found in sufficient quantities to suggest the use of these monuments for general communal burial.

The bones probably represent those of ancestors of the community living and working within the area from which the monuments are visible. They may therefore represent a physical manifestation of 'place' for specific kin groups, a demonstration of belonging to a particular block of landscape and its resources.

Thirdly, we find flint mines located mainly in West Sussex. Clearly their primary function was to extract flint from the underlying chalk but the process of extraction would have required a range of ritual, evidence for which is provided by specific artifactual deposits. Carbon-14

Offham Hill Causewayed Enclosure near Lewes

dates suggest the use of the mines throughout the earlier part of the Early Neolithic with a date range of 3400±150bc (BM-2098R) from Harrow Hill to 2700±150bc (BM-184) at Cissbury. Flint working areas have been located around a number of the mines as, for example, at Long Down, Church Hill, and Harrow Hill.[10]

Several groups of pits have been located in Sussex both on the Downs, as at North Marden, New Barn Down and Bishopstone, as well as on the Coastal Plain at Copse Farm, Oving. These pits are often thought of as representing domestic sites but the deposits within them and their method of filling suggest a similarity to deposits within Causewayed Enclosure and Long Barrow ditches.[11] Pit deposits may therefore have more of a symbolic than economic role: a way of 'fixing' domesticity in a landscape being tamed.[12] Settlement sites on the Downs are probably represented by scatters of flint tools. Sites with more than five different types of tools have been considered elsewhere as possibly representing settlements, while those with less are probably task-specific areas like surface flint-working sites or hunting camps. Several rock shelters in the Weald, for example, have small groups of flints and may therefore represent hunting camps, while lithic groups around marshy areas perhaps represent camps utilising strand and salt marsh resources.[13] The location of Long Barrows overlooking river valleys, like Long Burgh and Windover overlooking the Cuckmere, suggests that river valleys with rich watermeadows may have been key areas for settlement. This may well have been on a shifting basis without readily recognisable house structures, which remain absent from the archaeological record in Sussex.

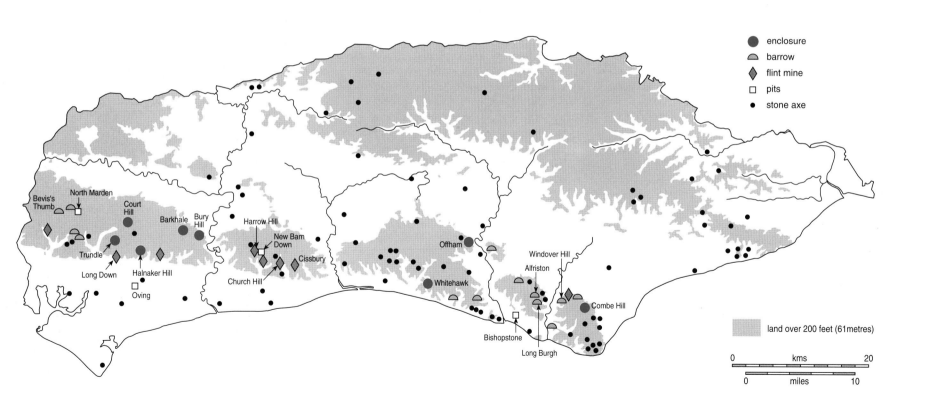

17

The introduction of metals was a fundamental stage in the development of prehistoric technology. However, many cultural traits evidenced in the Early Bronze Age had origins in the Late Neolithic. Certainly the rarity of Early Bronze Age metal supports the contention that conversion from stone to bronze occurred over many centuries. Indeed, the first metal artefacts found in Britain were actually made of gold and copper and date to *c.*2700-2100BC. Bronze only appears in the archaeological record from *c.*2200-1950BC.

Unfortunately, the flat bronze axes which comprise the earliest metal artefacts in Sussex are nearly all casual finds from undated contexts. However, the introduction of metalwork is generally associated with the emergence of Beaker pottery and Round Barrows. A transitional period from *c.*2700-2000BC still retains many 4th-millennium characteristics and is probably best described as a 'metal-using Neolithic'. By *c.*2000BC Beaker vessels are found across the whole region.

The remains of two overlapping enclosures at Belle Tout represent the only adequately excavated Beaker occupation site in the county.[1] Three possible house structures dating to 2000-1800BC were recorded during the investigation of this mixed farming settlement. Carbonised wheat and barley were also recovered, while the enclosure ditches were probably used to control stock. Two other areas of Early Bronze Age activity have been found near Belle Tout. Although lacking structural features, the Kiln Combe and Bullock Down sites both produced Beaker pottery.[2] Pits at Whitehawk and Itford Hill have provided evidence of settlement dating to *c.*2400-1800BC, while a contemporaneous occupation site was recorded at North Bersted.[3] Later Beaker pottery has also been located at Findon.[4] Signs of Early Bronze Age/ Beaker settlement have recently come from Hurstpierpoint, Plumpton and Southerham Grey Pit, Ranscombe Hill.[5] The presence of Beaker artefacts below considerable colluvial deposits at Ranscombe Hill and Kiln Combe suggests that similar sites lie buried in dry valleys.

Exploitation of forest resources is demonstrated by the distribution of bronze flat axes. Indeed, transitory camps have been discovered at Chanctonbury Ring and Pannel Bridge. Another woodland camp at Rackham comprised a flint assemblage, windbreaks or processing racks and two hearths. A carbon-14 date suggests occupation around 2,500BC.[6]

Early Bronze Age archaeology in Sussex is dominated by Round Barrows. Over 1,100 mounds, located mainly on the Downs and Lower Greensand, have been assigned to *c.*2500-1500BC. They display a range of structural forms and are often found in clusters or linear formations. Although some barrows were utilised for purposes other than interment, investigated examples have revealed cremations, inhumations and grave goods.

One such barrow comprising a flint mound with a diameter of 14m was excavated at Crowlink in 1998.[7] This cairn incorporated thousands of worked flints and covered eight cremations and one disarticulated skeleton. No metal or imported artefacts were recovered. In fact 'the richest group of burials under mounds in the South-East came from the Hove area'.[8] The most famous of these monuments is the Hove Barrow which yielded an amber cup, a stone axe and a bronze dagger. A barrow at Oxteddle Bottom contained faience, amber and a bronze ring. Faience has also been retrieved from a burial at

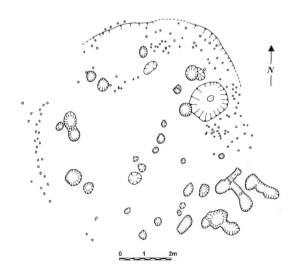

Middle Bronze Age round-house excavated at Patcham Fawcett (Roundhouse IV).[18]

Upper Beeding, while rich mounds were excavated at Newtimber and Washington. A Pyecombe barrow has recently produced a copper dagger and a wristguard (map 1).[9]

The construction of Neolithic ceremonial monuments may have legitimised and displayed the rôle of a powerful minority. This would imply that the establishment of ritual centres advanced the emergence of ranked societies and identifiable élites. Certainly, the presence of rich Round Barrows in Sussex 'suggests the existence of high ranking individuals'.[10] The energy expended on monument construction and the type of grave goods almost certainly reflect the status of the dead. 'Communal monuments hide the individual hand, single burials reveal it.'[11] Drewett has even proposed the formation of a class of specialists with ceremonial responsibilities.[12]

From *c.*1700BC pressure on the best land in Sussex led to a gradual shift from ritual landscapes dominated by barrows to an evolved and efficient agricultural system. Large areas of cleared Downland were brought under the management of organised farmsteads. These small family units utilised round-houses often set on hillslope terraces, grew crops, kept animals and practised a variety of crafts. Many downland settlements were located within extensive enclosures, field systems, trackways and boundaries. They exhibit a high level of social cohesion and were linked by trade/exchange networks. Certainly, a range of habitats would have been exploited.

Much has been written about the many excavated downland settlements of Sussex (map 2). This information will not be reviewed here. However, a recently discovered site at Patcham has provided new material for consideration.[13] The remains included storage/rubbish pits, fence-lines, four-post structures, three large 'scoops' of a type often interpreted as ponds and five round-houses. The settlement lay within a permanent agricultural environment on the edge of a field system. Certainly, cereals and cropweeds were recovered, suggesting that grain was stored and processed on site, while cattle and ovicaprid bones dominate the faunal assemblage. However, neither hunting nor the extensive gathering of wild food was demonstrated. Some small four-post features were perhaps racks for curing hides, drying cereals and leaves, or were skinning frames. The social organisation of the site was not ascertained. Even so, ritual evidence was recorded in the form of animal interments. This corroborates a large body of data suggesting that, after the Early Bronze Age, ritual gravitated from 'monuments in the wider landscape and focused on settlement'.[14] The importance of the site lies in its association with other contemporaneous settlements located near Brighton. Recent discoveries of occupation at Downsview and Varley Halls certainly suggest an intensity of land use not previously suspected for the Downs.[15] However, the possibility of community relocation should not be discounted.

Despite the recovery of stray Middle Bronze Age finds from low-lying areas, settlements have proved elusive. Sites in valleys may be buried under alluvial and colluvial deposits, while much of the Coastal Plain has been exposed to agriculture. However, probable pits were noted at the lowland site of Kingston Buci.[16] Activity beyond the South Downs at Patching has also been confirmed by the presence of a 'burnt flint mound'.[17]

Functions ranging from cooking sites to saunas have been suggested for this monument class.

The Middle Bronze Age in Sussex developed from a period characterised by burial mounds into one dominated by settlements, fields, trackways and boundaries. The evidence suggests that hierarchies and individual status were no longer reinforced through ceremonial monuments located in the landscape. Food production was now the most archaeologically visible priority of Bronze Age society.

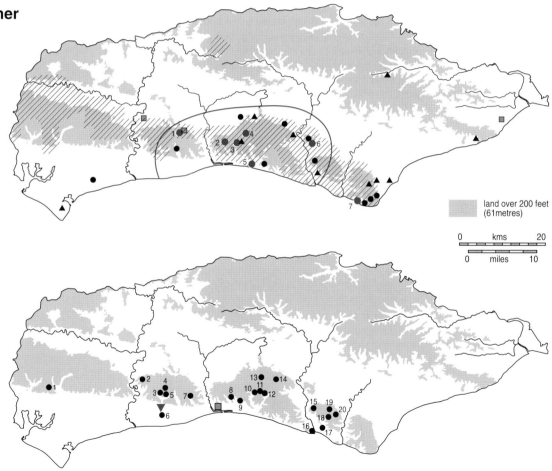

1. Bronze Age Round Barrows and other early activity sites

▲ Bronze flat axe

● Settlement site

▩ Transitory camp

//// distribution of Bronze Age Round Barrows

— extent of rich burials

● Bronze Age Round Barrows
1 Washington
2 Upper Beeding
3 Newtimber
4 Pyecombe
5 Hove
6 Oxteddle Bottom
7 Crowlink

land over 200 feet (61metres)

0   kms   20
0   miles   10

2. Middle Bronze Age settlements

● Downland settlement

▩ Lowland settlement

▼ Burnt mound

1 Kingley Vale	11 Downsview
2 Amberley Mount	12 Varley Halls
3 New Barn Down	13 Ditchling Beacon
4 Cock Hill	14 Plumpton Plain
5 Blackpatch	15 Itford Hill
6 Highdown	16 Castle Hill
7 Park Brow	17 Bishopstone
8 Mile Oak	18 Denton Hill
9 West Blatchington	19 Charleston Brow
10 Patcham Fawcett	20 Black Patch

This period (Late Bronze Age, Early Iron Age and Middle Iron Age) commences with a gradual reorganisation of settlement and ritual traditions, culminating in a complete transformation of the archaeological record.[1] Elements of this reorganisation are: (1) the demise of the Round Barrow burial tradition most prevalent in the Sussex Downs ; (2) the disappearance of the Middle Bronze Age (MBA) settlement pattern of clusters of round-houses in enclosures associated with field systems; (3) the reconfiguration of the landscape with the construction of artificial boundaries (cross-ridge dykes); and (4) the appearance of large, hilltop enclosures, known conventionally as hillforts. There are considerable changes in the ceramic record, with the manufacture of a wider range of vessel types and size, connected with new ways of serving food and drink. These changes culminate in a strong regionalisation in the Middle Iron Age (MIA), evidenced by the emergence of very marked regional patterns in ceramics, fewer but larger landmark hillforts and correspondingly fewer settlements.

Hillforts and Cross-Ridge Dykes

During the Late Bronze Age (LBA) the Sussex Downs were divided into landscape blocks and lesser units by the construction of complexes of linear earthen dykes. At least 60 cross-ridge dykes are known from Sussex.[2] About half of these dykes lie across ridges on the top of the scarp slope of the Downs. The dykes themselves are formed by single, double or multiple banks. These dykes are often near to hillforts (eg Harting Beacon) and settlements and may have co-functioned to redefine access, use and ownership on the Downs; some, however, are distant from known contemporary settlements. Excavated examples have produced LBA and Early Iron Age (EIA) pottery in their primary ditch fills.

The large number of LBA/EIA hillforts (*c.*1000-400BC) in Sussex is striking. Some of these are present by *c.*900BC. Characteristic of some of these sites is their liminal settings, occupying positions on the southern and northern scarps of the Downs (eg Thundersbarrow and Wolstonbury). Some developed from earlier, smaller enclosures established in the LBA (eg Thundersbarrow and Hollingbury). The hillforts vary considerably in size, from the 12ha of Harting Beacon to the 1ha of Highdown

Hill. The majority possess insubstantial enclosing banks and lack evidence for intensive activity in the interior. Harting Beacon is the only hillfort in Sussex (including those dated to later periods) that has produced evidence of four-poster structures, conventionally interpreted as raised store buildings. This lack of internal activity suggests that these sites were peripheral to the main areas of settlement and might be seen more as places from which to access diverse environments, rather than centres of activity in their own right. In the EIA two of these sites (Hollingbury and Highdown Hill) do have more evidence for domestic activity including round-houses.

In the MIA (*c.*400-100BC) there is a dramatic reduction in the number of hillforts. The ones that can be securely dated to this period are Torberry, the Trundle, Caburn and Cissbury.[3] In contrast to the earlier hillforts these occupy more central positions in the Downs, often on obvious landmark hills (eg Caburn). With the exception of the Caburn, little excavation has taken place on these sites, but there is overall evidence for increased activity and a wider range of artefact types (eg billhooks, knives, latch-lifters, slingstones). Pits occur on three of the four sites mentioned (the exception being Torberry). Some of these pits seem to have been receptacles for structured depositions, which included human remains. Pottery finds suggest that there may have been additionally some low-level activity on the six wealden hillforts (eg High Rocks) at this time.

Settlement

LBA pottery find-spots, together with a limited number of pit-features (eg Knapp Farm and Yapton) suggest increased settlement on the West Sussex Coastal Plain at the beginning of the first millennium BC. In East Sussex this is mirrored by the dramatic finds from Shinewater in the Willingdon Levels. Shinewater is a unique site comprising an artificial wooden platform constructed in a watery environment, associated with wooden trackways. A large quantity of LBA pottery and other artefacts indicative of occupation in the 9th century BC was recovered, along with raised hearths. On the Downs the presence of LBA pottery associated with MBA settlements (eg Mile Oak and Downsview) argues for some continuity of use. At Varley Halls there is one LBA house platform,

adjacent to the MBA settlement, and the MBA site of Plumpton Plain A is succeeded by a LBA settlement (Plumpton Plain B). At Heathy Brow, round and rectangular hut-structures and working hollows have been identified, while at Park Brow rectangular structures have been recovered and at Bishopstone four- and six-post buildings have been located.[4]

In contrast to the enclosed hillforts the settlements of the LBA/EIA are largely unenclosed (Bishopstone being the exception).[5] Several of the MIA sites are enclosed (eg Oving and North Bersted).[6] In West Sussex there is some evidence for banjo-enclosures (Carne's Seat, Denge Bottom and Selhurst Park). It is noticeable that the number of MIA settlements and find-spots is reduced, perhaps suggesting a decrease in population during the *c.*5th to 2nd centuries BC.

Production and Exchange

Numerous metalworkers' hoards, particularly concentrated on the West Sussex Coastal Plain, indicate an increase in bronze production and trade during the LBA. Additionally some continental imports are present at the beginning of the first millennium BC (eg pins from Portslade and Brighton, and the Armorican axes from Hollingbury) but are rare by the MIA.

Ritual

There is no evidence for a formal burial tradition. Overt evidence for ritual is difficult to locate, but occasional finds of human bone on settlement sites (eg Oving and North Bersted) and hillforts (eg the Caburn) together with patterned depositions of artefact and animal bones in pits are suggestive of ritual traditions governing disposal practices.

Regionalisation

The MIA evidenced an increased regionalisation of pottery styles within Sussex (see map 2). The more central positions of a few dominant hillforts further emphasise this regionalisation.

1. Late Bronze Age/Early Iron Age

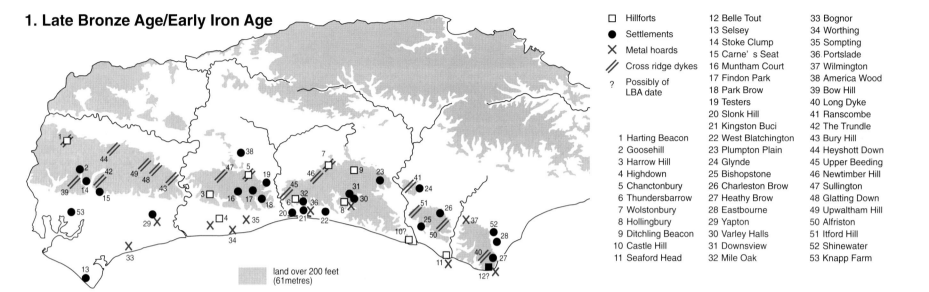

☐	Hillforts
●	Settlements
✕	Metal hoards
⫽	Cross ridge dykes
?	Possibly of LBA date

land over 200 feet (61metres)

1 Harting Beacon
2 Goosehill
3 Harrow Hill
4 Highdown
5 Chanctonbury
6 Thundersbarrow
7 Wolstonbury
8 Hollingbury
9 Ditchling Beacon
10 Castle Hill
11 Seaford Head
12 Belle Tout
13 Selsey
14 Stoke Clump
15 Carne's Seat
16 Muntham Court
17 Findon Park
18 Park Brow
19 Testers
20 Slonk Hill
21 Kingston Buci
22 West Blatchington
23 Plumpton Plain
24 Glynde
25 Bishopstone
26 Charleston Brow
27 Heathy Brow
28 Eastbourne
29 Yapton
30 Varley Halls
31 Downsview
32 Mile Oak
33 Bognor
34 Worthing
35 Sompting
36 Portslade
37 Wilmington
38 America Wood
39 Bow Hill
40 Long Dyke
41 Ranscombe
42 The Trundle
43 Bury Hill
44 Heyshott Down
45 Upper Beeding
46 Newtimber Hill
47 Sullington
48 Glatting Down
49 Upwaltham Hill
50 Alfriston
51 Itford Hill
52 Shinewater
53 Knapp Farm

2. Middle Iron Age sites and pottery

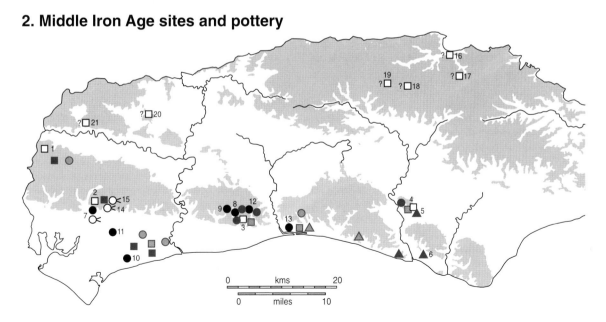

☐	Hillforts
●	Settlements
⊃⊂	Banjo enclosures
?	Possibly of MIA date

1 Torberry
2 The Trundle
3 Cissbury
4 Caburn
5 Glynde
6 Bishopstone
7 Carne's Seat
8 Findon
9 Muntham Court
10 North Bersted
11 Oving
12 Park Brow
13 Slonk Hill
14 Denge Bottom
15 Selhurst Park
16 High Rocks
17 Saxonbury
18 Garden Hil
19 Philpots
20 Piper's Copse
21 Hammer Wood

0   kms   20

0   miles   10

Major decorative motifs occurring on Sussex Middle Iron Age saucepan pottery

● dot impressed horizontal lines

● dot impressed pendant swags

■ tooled wavy lines

■ tooled wavy lines

▲ tooled scrolls

▲ tooled eliptical arcs

THE END OF PREHISTORY *c.*100BC–AD43

Sue Hamilton and John Manley

At some point in the early 1st century BC (Late Iron Age – LIA) there is a conspicuous reconfiguration of the settlement and economic pattern of Sussex. This is particularly evidenced in three ways. One of these is the disappearance of hillforts from the South Downs, with the exception of Devil's Dyke, together with the development of settlements on the West Sussex Coastal Plain such as Oving and North Bersted. The second is the appearance of ritual centres such as the cemetery at Westhampnett and the shrine at Lancing Down. The third major change is fundamentally economic, with the establishment of iron working sites such as Crowhurst Park and Sedlescombe (Footlands), and the more centralised production of pottery, including the production of wheel-thrown cordoned wares in West Sussex and hand-made grog-tempered wares in East Sussex. In addition, local coin production commences, for example at Ounces Barn, Boxgrove. Broadly contemporary with this we find a gradual increase in imported Roman goods, particularly linked to the growing proximity of Roman influence, consequent on Caesar's conquest of Gaul.

Hillforts

It is not until the LIA that hillforts become fully established in the Weald. These sites include promontory enclosures such as Philpots and High Rocks.[1] There is a general consensus that these sites relate to more intensive exploitation of the iron sources of the Weald. Thus there is evidence of smelting and forging of iron in Garden Hill where a number of iron-working hearths were associated with two round timber structures. The presence of a poorly-built bath building in the Roman period at Garden Hill may indicate both continuity of indigenous community and activity, and a desire to indulge in a more Romanised way of life.

Settlements

There is a marked increase in the number of settlements and find-spots in the LIA. The most co-ordinated changes are in West Sussex where a series of enclosed farmsteads, such as Oving, reach their most developed form.[2] The exploitation of this fertile environment is only possible through extensive drainage networks which may have been collectively organised from a number of dispersed settlements.

Production

During this period the first evidence for centralised ceramic production occurs. This production probably took place at specialist pottery production sites such as Chelwood Gate and Horsted Keynes in the High Weald, ideally located to exploit the excellent potting clays of the region.[3] In West Sussex the first wheel-turned vessels appear using quartz-sand temper from the Lower Greensand.[4] The origins of the Roman iron industry of the Weald can probably be traced to this period at sites such as Goffs Park, Broadfield and Crowhurst Park.[5]

Ritual Centres

Formal cemeteries and ritual centres appear in LIA Britain and are represented in Sussex by the extensive cremation cemetery at Westhampnett and the shrine at Lancing Down.[6] The former probably acted as a communal burial ground for several different communities on the coastal plain, the individual cremations being set out around a symbolic central space that resembled a round timber structure. At Lancing Down the Romano-British masonry temple was preceded by a small wooden rectangular structure associated with LIA coins and pottery.[7]

Coinage and Trade

Physical evidence of coin production in Sussex is restricted to the moulds from Ounces Barn, Boxgrove, which may date from the very end of the Iron Age.[8] The appearance of coins signifies not solely a growing emphasis on trade and exchange, but also a desire on the part of ruling aristocracies to emphasise their identities. Commius, Tincommius and Verica were successive leaders of the Atrebates, who controlled the Chichester area. Names of such leaders appear on both gold and potin (derived from tin) coinage. The overall distribution of coins is skewed very much in favour of western Sussex (map 2). Indeed, a concentration of imported and British coins from the Chichester region, mostly dating from the middle third of the 1st century BC, may suggest settlement of a group of people from across the Channel.[9]

Chichester Dykes

These large linear bank-and-ditch earthworks have attracted the attention of antiquaries since at least the 17th century. The current consensus would date the earthworks to somewhere between the 1st century BC and the first few decades AD. The ditches form three distinctive blocks: those west of the Lavant that have been traditionally identified as defending a territorial *oppidum* – an extensive area containing diverse foci of settlement and production; those east of the Lavant; and those in the vicinity of the Arun – 'War Dyke'. An alternative or additional interpretation of the dykes is to see them, in association with the minor rivers and streams, as forming the boundaries to several land-blocks each possibly controlled by a separate but powerful ruler.[10]

Romanisation and Change

Some of the changes apparent in LIA Sussex have been attributed to contact with the Roman world and are indicated by the presence of imported Roman goods such as Dressel 1B amphora (wine containers) and fine tableware including Arretine and Samian ware from Italy and *terra nigra* and *terra rubra* from Roman Gaul. These at the very minimum suggest a change in eating and drinking habits and it may be that the trade in these goods was rigorously controlled by high status communities and individuals. These changes culminate in the very close allegiance between Verica, chief of the Atrebates, and the Roman imperial household. Verica must have been completely familiar with Roman lifestyles and was presumably also familiar with the written word. The flight of Verica to the Emperor Claudius in AD40 signals the end of prehistory and his plea for Roman intervention signifies not a desire for foreign imposition but a request for the maintenance of an already Romanised way of life in his part of southern England.

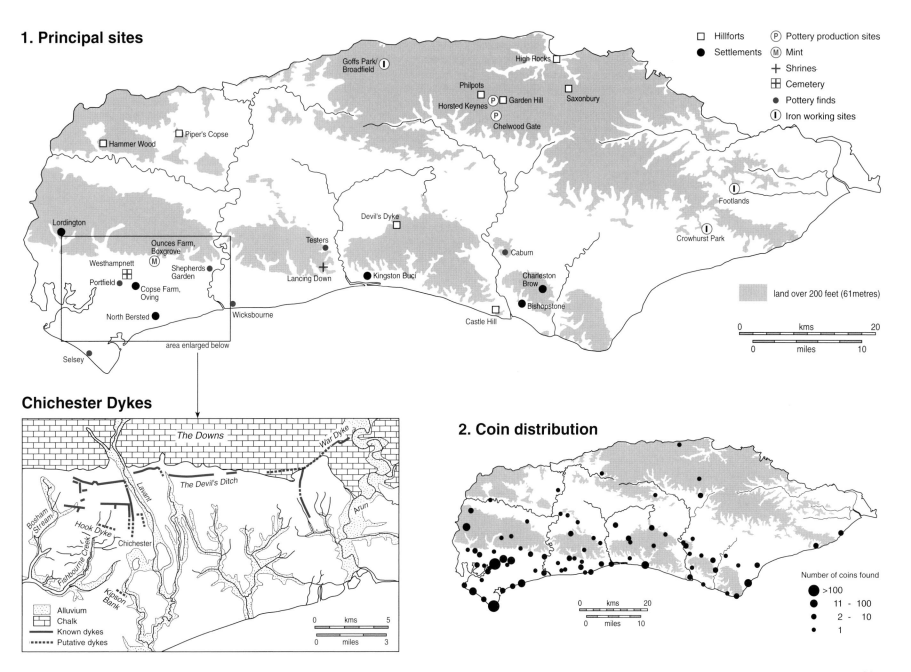

1. Principal sites

Hillforts
Settlements
Pottery production sites
Mint
Shrines
Cemetery
Pottery finds
Iron working sites

Goffs Park/Broadfield
High Rocks
Philpots
Horsted Keynes
Garden Hill
Saxonbury
Chelwood Gate
Piper's Copse
Hammer Wood
Footlands
Devil's Dyke
Crowhurst Park
Lordington
Testers
Ounces Farm, Boxgrove
Caburn
Westhampnett
Shepherds Garden
Charleston Brow
Portfield
Copse Farm, Oving
Lancing Down
Kingston Buci
Bishopstone
North Bersted
Wicksbourne
Castle Hill
Selsey

land over 200 feet (61 metres)

0 kms 20
0 miles 10

Chichester Dykes

The Downs
War Dyke
Lavant
The Devil's Ditch
Arun
Bosham Stream
Hook Dyke
Chichester
Fishbourne Creek
Kipson Bank

Alluvium
Chalk
Known dykes
Putative dykes

0 kms 5
0 miles 3

area enlarged below

2. Coin distribution

Number of coins found
>100
11 - 100
2 - 10
1

0 kms 20
0 miles 10

23

The Conquest

The flight to the protection of Rome of the pro-Roman king Verica provided the Emperor Claudius with a reason for invading Britain – the restoration of Verica to his kingdom located in parts of Sussex, Hampshire, Berkshire and Surrey. Until recently, however, the general view was that in AD43 the Roman forces landed at Richborough (Kent). In 1989 an alternative theory was put forward: that the invasion forces landed along the south coast. Here were safe harbours and the Romans could expect political support from among the local inhabitants.[1] Various excavations at Fishbourne have revealed evidence which supports the idea that this area played a major part in the Claudian invasion.[2]

Client Kingdom

After the invasion, part of Sussex, and probably also areas to the north and west, became a client kingdom ruled by Tiberius Claudius Togidubnus.[3] Togidubnus was successful in introducing elements of Roman culture into his kingdom, as evidenced by finds from Chichester and by some of the large early villas which are a distinctive feature of Sussex during the 1st century.[4] The wide distribution of the large early villas may be very significant, with each located on a distinct block of land which may 'represent the territory over which the land-owning aristocracy held control'.[5] Could this pattern be a clue to one distribution of the tribal sub-units, the *pagi*, about which so little is known?[6] At Fishbourne, both the Proto -Palace and the Flavian Palace have been suggested as houses that may have belonged to Togidubnus, although definite proof (eg inscriptions) is lacking.[7] Following the death or retirement of Togidubnus his extensive kingdom was integrated into the Roman province of *Britannia* and probably divided into three regional tribal units, with much of Sussex, especially the area to the south of the Weald, and part of south-eastern Hampshire, forming the civitas of the *Regni*, with its capital at Chichester.[8]

Communications

Perhaps the main traces of early military activity in Sussex are the major roads, some of which (eg Stane Street) have associated posting stations.[9] Roads linked Chichester to London via a crossing of the Arun at Pulborough; to Winchester and Silchester (ie other *civitas* capitals); to Selsey; and, via an extension of Stane Street, to a postulated harbour on Fishbourne Creek.[10] Other major roads include the Greensand Way, which lies to the north of the Downs and links Pulborough with two important roads: London-Hassocks and London-Lewes. The two north-south roads probably provided transportation routes to/from the western group of iron-working sites. Another north-south road connected the eastern group of iron-works to Rochester. The many other minor Roman roads are likely to have served a wide variety of rural farms and industries. Other important communications would have been by boat, by sea and river. Though little evidence is available about maritime routes, the association of the Roman fleet, the *Classis Britannica*, with the eastern iron-works is attested by the discovery at some sites of tiles stamped *CL BR*.[11] The main outlet for iron from this area was presumably by sea from the estuaries of the rivers Brede and Rother. Elsewhere the importance of river transport is probably indicated by the locations of settlements close to the Arun, Ouse and Cuckmere. The Arun is one of the few rivers in Britain for which we know its Roman name: *Trisantona*.[12]

Rural Settlement

The only town in the territory of the *Regni* was Chichester.[13] Other much smaller nucleated settlements occur in association with posting stations, as at Alfoldean, or at other road junctions, as at Hassocks.[14] At the Hardham-Pulborough-Wiggonholt triangle there was apparently a concentration of settlement and industry.[15]

Throughout much of southern Sussex (ie the fertile Coastal Plain, the chalk Downs and on or near the Upper Greensand), the majority of Roman sites were associated with farming. The settlement pattern is characterised by two aspects: 'a strong element of continuity, many sites originating well back into the preceding Iron Age or even earlier, and a very marked discrepancy in wealth'.[16] In addition, the distribution of rich and poor settlement is not random, the poorer farms being fairly evenly dispersed over the Downs and the Coastal Plain, whilst the richer establishments tend to be located where the soil is more productive: the Coastal Plain, the southern margins of the Downs, and the Upper Greensand, and/or where there were good communications and access to markets. These more wealthy establishments, with buildings which significantly reflect the Roman style of life, are known as villas. The initial phase of villa building in Sussex, the large early villas (see above), appear to have been imposed on the Iron Age settlement pattern. The owners were probably rich tribal notables. During the 2nd and 3rd centuries there was a big expansion of villa-ownership by 'middle-rank' farmers. Many of these villas developed gradually from more humble origins, as at Beddingham where the domestic building with masonry foundations was located adjacent to a Late Iron Age or early post-Conquest timber round 'house'.[17] During the later 3rd and 4th centuries villas began to decline in certain areas of Sussex, especially the Coastal Plain. This decline may be linked to such factors as pirate raids and the establishment of a military presence at Pevensey. In other (inland) areas villas continued to develop, and at Bignor the relatively humble 3rd-century villa grew into a large and luxurious courtyard villa.[18] It is probable that during the 4th century there was a reversion to a much smaller number of villa-owners, some of whom were very rich with large households. Little information is available about the final phases of villa life in Sussex, but at Beddingham parts of the site may have been occupied by Saxons during either the late 4th or early 5th century. In contrast, some of the downland farmsteads, including even those located near to the coast, as at Bishopstone, show signs of continued occupation through the 4th century, and perhaps into the 5th century.[19]

Much of the Weald appears to be devoid of Roman farms. This situation may be due to the lack of archaeological fieldwork, but may be determined by poor soils, woodland, and perhaps the existence of an Imperial Estate designed to control the valuable iron-works (see below).

Religious sites constitute another aspect of the rural landscape. Thus whilst no shrines have been identified in East Sussex, several rural temples, including Chanctonbury Ring and Lancing Down, are known for West Sussex. The important temple on Hayling Island (just in Hampshire) may have been used by people living in the Fishbourne/Chichester area.[20] Several temples (eg

Lancing and Hayling Island) have revealed evidence for continuity from the Iron Age. In addition to the Romano-Celtic temples, there is some evidence for the ritual re-use of Bronze Age Round Barrows.[21]

Industry

The most important industry in Roman Sussex was iron-making, and during the 2nd century there was a major expansion of this wealden industry.[22] There were two main groups of iron-works, a western 'private' zone and an eastern area linked to the *Classis Britannica* (see above). These links, and other factors, have led to the suggestion that the Weald may have formed an 'Imperial Estate'. By

the mid-3rd century the iron industry was in decline, and the eastern group of sites was abandoned.

Other rural industries included farming, the manufacture of pottery, tiles and salt; the quarrying of stone and forestry. Surface evidence of Roman field systems still remains on the Downs. This area was primarily concerned with the growing of cereals and the keeping of sheep. Cattle rearing was concentrated on the lower lands with greater access to water. Sites for the manufacture of pottery and tiles were often located near roads and markets, and products from the Hartfield tilery were transported by road as far north as Beddington (historic Surrey) and as far south as Beddingham.[23]

The End of Roman Sussex

During the 3rd and 4th centuries various factors had a dramatic impact on Roman Sussex, including Saxon raiding; the construction in *c.* AD293 of a fort at Pevensey (*Anderitum*) and the adding of defences to Chichester.[24] Villa life in some areas, especially near the coast, began to decline, whilst further inland some villas, as at Bignor, continued to thrive and expand. By the late 4th century there are signs of a decline in standards at Chichester, but here, as on many villa sites, there is little evidence about the nature and dating of the final phases of occupation. At Pevensey, sub-Roman occupation continued until the late 5th century.[25]

town
mansio/vicus
large early villa
villa
probable villa
temple
road
pottery kiln
tile kiln
major iron works
fort
other Roman sites/finds
(selection only)

W. Rother
Pulborough
Bignor
Stane Street
Chanctonbury
Fishbourne
Arun
Lancing
Chichester
Hayling Island
Adur
Hassocks
Greensand Way
Ouse
Beddingham
Cuckmere
E. Rother
Pevensey

land over 200 feet (61 metres)

kms 0 — 20
miles 0 — 10

25

Chichester was the only large Roman town in Sussex. Its Roman name *Noviomagus*, a compound of two Celtic words meaning 'Newmarket', reflects the importance of the Chichester area before the Conquest as a redistribution centre of pottery and, presumably, other continental imports.[1]

Chichester was sited near the south-western end of the Roman road known as Stane Street which ran from Chichester Harbour to a river-crossing at Pulborough below the confluence of the Rother and Arun and ultimately to London. At a point which later became the East Gate, the road was cut through one of the Late Iron Age Chichester dykes, which became the eastern boundary of the town. The other major route ran west from Chichester towards Havant (Hampshire) and, when a street grid was established, this became its axis. Lesser roads led from the South Gate to the Manhood Peninsula, and from the North Gate towards Silchester.[2]

The Chichester area was not immediately absorbed in *Britannia* after the Conquest but retained some independence as a client kingdom under Togidubnus, assumed to be a successor of Verica, the local ruler whose flight to Rome gave Claudius his excuse to invade.[3] Its status as a town (perhaps the only town) in Togidubnus' kingdom ensured that Chichester made rapid early progress towards urbanisation. The inscription now in the Assembly Rooms façade, North Street, usually dated to Nero's reign, records the erection of a temple to Neptune and Minerva by a guild (perhaps of shipwrights, given the dedication). A lost inscription from East Street seems to be from a contemporary equestrian statue.[4]

One of the major public buildings was the baths, the earliest phase of which was Flavian.[5] Marble wall veneer and flooring sections were used, some imported from Greece and Italy, and worked on site. These provide a link with Fishbourne Palace; the craftsmen employed there may later have found jobs in the nearby town. East of the baths was the forum (market place), the gravelled surface of which has often been found in excavations, although the basilica (town hall) which should have adjoined it is unlocated.

Private houses were usually sited away from the main streets. The earliest were small, numerous and timber-framed, but were replaced by larger houses with stone foundations which by the later 3rd century were being embellished with mosaics and hypocausts.

Chichester's walls, erected in the later 3rd century, perhaps in response to Saxon raiders in the Channel, consisted of an earthen rampart fronted by a flint wall with two V-shaped ditches beyond.[6] On the west, and perhaps elsewhere, houses had to be demolished before the defences could be built. In the 4th century, projecting artillery towers were added and a wide, flat-bottomed ditch replaced the earlier ditches.

Cemeteries lined Chichester's approach roads. Beyond East Gate, north of Stane Street, was a (largely) cremation cemetery of *c.*AD70 to the early 3rd century. A 4th-century inhumation cemetery lay outside the West Gate, and both types of burial occur outside the North Gate.[7] The only major extramural public building (although perhaps abandoned before the walls were built) was an amphitheatre, one of only a few in the country still visible today.[8]

Chichester's decline is plain from archaeological evidence.[9] Its once well-equipped houses were sub-divided, with hearths built on tessellated floors, and the drains flanking the pot-holed streets were no longer cleaned. The baths were repaired after *c.*AD370 but, commercially, Chichester may have been declining long before the late 4th century, a period for which there are few coins in the archaeological record. Not until the 10th century was it again an urban centre.

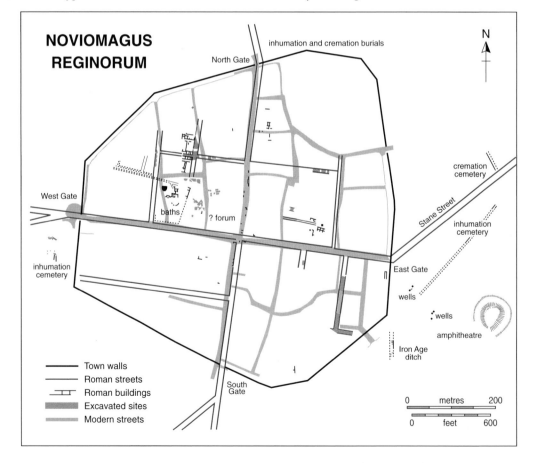

Fishbourne Palace, 2km west of Chichester at the head of Fishbourne Channel, was discovered by chance in 1960 and excavated over the next nine years. Barry Cunliffe, the director, identified several phases of activity.[10] The first, represented by the ground plans of two large timber granaries or store buildings, contemporary road surfaces and associated military artefacts, was interpreted as part of a supply base for Vespasian's campaign in the South West soon after the Claudian invasion. In the following phase the granaries were replaced by civilian timber-framed houses which were succeeded in *c.*65/70 by two substantial masonry buildings. One – with a large bath complex and clearly of high status – was interpreted as a proto-palace and tentatively linked with the local client king, Togidubnus.[11]

The most impressive phase was represented by the substantial remains of a four-winged structure surrounding a formal garden, of which bedding trenches, plant pits, post-holes and a water supply system survived. The building, covering 2.1ha, was constructed in *c.*75/80 and is interpreted as a palace because of its size, its high quality decoration and assumed connection with Togidubnus. The west wing, on higher ground overlooking the garden, had a central room with an apsidal end, and probable pedimented façade approached by a flight of steps. This is interpreted as an audience chamber and the focal point of the complex. The north wing, built around two courtyards or gardens, appears to have comprised separate suites of rooms. Many original mosaics survive, mainly black geometric designs on a white background, and replacement polychrome mosaics of the following phase, including the famous Cupid on a Dolphin. This wing is open to the public and the most significant excavated finds are displayed in an adjacent museum.[12]

A fire, possibly accidental, destroyed the north and possibly the west wing in 270/80, after which the remainder was dismantled.[13] By the late 4th or 5th century, bodies were buried in the rubble and eventually all evidence for the buildings disappeared from view.

Excavations in 1983, 1985-6, 1992 and 1995 revealed extensive activity running east from the Palace for at least 300m.[14] The excavations of the 1980s uncovered traces of both masonry and timber buildings, whilst pits, post-holes and bedding trenches were interpreted as semi-formal gardens. All excavations encountered an aqueduct, supplied from feeders from the north, probably leading to a bath-house in the east wing. From the base of one of the feeder ditches a 1st-century gold signet ring was recovered.[15] Inscribed in reverse TI CLAUDI CATUARI, it was the property of Catuarus, perhaps a British nobleman given Roman citizenship by Claudius or Nero, and possibly a kinsman of Togidubnus.

Since 1995 excavations immediately east of the Palace have uncovered the foundations of a large masonry building tentatively identified, largely on the basis of its plan, as a *principia* (military headquarters).[16] Apparently constructed between AD50 and 60, it survived alongside the Palace until the 3rd century. Its presence may support the belief that a significant part of the Claudian invasion occurred in the Chichester region.

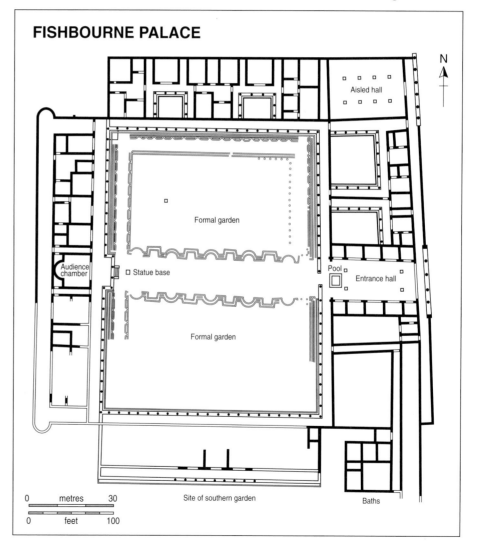

FISHBOURNE PALACE

There are very few historical sources which shed any light on early Saxon Sussex. The earliest is Gildas' *De Excidio Britanniae* which was written in the mid-6th century. Later writers such as Bede in the 7th century and the Anglo-Saxon Chronicle, begun in the 9th century, drew extensively on Gildas and fleshed out his historical framework with names and dates. For early Saxon Sussex the Chronicle has only three references: to the arrival of Aelle and his sons in 477, a battle near the banks of a river in 485 and Aelle's attack on *Anderitum* (Pevensey) in 491. Given the time gap between the events described and the writing of any of the books, it is likely that the framework is fairly accurate but the dates far less so. There are no lists of kings for the South Saxons as there are for some other kingdoms.

Archaeological information to help fill out this picture is very limited. Since the early Saxons built in wood, rather than stone, there are no upstanding building remains as there are for the Romano-British period. Very few settlement sites have yet been identified. Most archaeological information for this period comes from finds such as jewellery, pottery, glass and weapons which were buried as grave-goods in pagan Saxon cemeteries such as those at Alfriston and Eastbourne. These cemeteries contain few objects of Roman origin and there is virtually no evidence to show what happened to the Romano-British population which occupied this area before the Saxons arrived. This paucity of evidence means that the speed of the transition to Anglo-Saxon from Romano-British culture, and the mechanisms of change, are unclear. However, neither the end of Roman Britain nor the start of Saxon Sussex were sudden events. The Roman administration and economy were in decline well before the 'official' end of Roman Britain in *c.*410. Historical sources describe the use of mercenaries from the area between the rivers Elbe and Weser in northern Germany to help maintain peace in southern Britain. Their numbers grew and they revolted against their former employers in the late 5th century. In time the Saxon culture became dominant but this must have been preceded by many years during which the two cultures co-existed to a greater or lesser extent.

Highdown Hill, just to the north-west of Worthing, has been identified as the possible site of one of these early mercenary settlements. It has been suggested by Welch that there are up to ten 4th-century Romano-British graves in the cemetery, which lies within the ramparts of a prehistoric enclosure, and that they represent a small Romano-British community which initially supervised the Saxons.[1] In the 5th century the objects used as grave-goods show that Saxon culture became dominant. The cemetery was in use up to the early 7th century but the site of the associated Saxon settlement has never been found. In 1997 a hoard of 23 gold *solidi*, 25 silver coins, 2 gold rings and a quantity of scrap silver was found at Patching, only 2km from Highdown. It forms the latest Roman hoard found in Britain and was buried in or around 465. The gold coins were minted over a period of 80 years, from 381-461, and the earliest silver coins date from 333. The scrap silver includes both late 4th-century fragments and a 5th-century chape fitting of continental manufacture. Since the sites are so close, and inter-visible, and because Highdown cemetery is thought to have been in use by the time the hoard was buried, it is very tempting to suggest that there was some connection between the two sites.[2]

Highdown is the only 5th-century cemetery which has been found outside the area between the Ouse and Cuckmere.[3] This area is also one where there was apparently little Romanisation and it may be that land here was offered as part of a treaty arrangement with groups of Saxons. The capture of the Saxon Shore Fort at Pevensey by Aelle towards the end of the 5th century enabled the Saxons to break free of Romano-British control. Aelle went on to become the first King of the South Saxons. Judging by the distribution of cemeteries, Saxon settlement spread west as far as the Downs north-west of Chichester, and east as far as the area around modern Eastbourne, during the 6th century. However, in spite of the excavation of the two cemeteries at Apple Down and five graves at Westhampnett, both near Chichester, the area west of the Arun has still produced relatively little evidence of a strong Saxon presence.[4] The areas to the north of the Downs and to the east of Eastbourne are apparently devoid of cemeteries or settlements.

Gold solidi from the Patching Hoard
(enlarged to twice actual size)

The Emperor Gratian (AD367-83)   *The Emperor Severus III (AD461-5)*

In the late 6th and early 7th centuries various forms of burial structure became more common and grave-goods were included less often. There are a number of barrows in Sussex from this period, found either singly or in groups along the Downs. Post-holes, thought to be from several forms of raised burial structure, were found in the later cemetery at Apple Down. These structures may be an alternative to grave goods as a way of indicating the status of the deceased.

Only three settlement sites have been partly excavated: Bishopstone is on a hilltop close to a 5th-century cemetery which overlooks the Ouse estuary, Beddingham is also close to the Ouse, and Botolphs is in the valley bottom close to the Arun.[5] The settlement at Bishopstone partly overlay fields linked to the Romano-British occupation of the site. Only part of the settlement has been excavated, but traces of 22 buildings were found in this area. They were not all occupied at the same time. Three were sunken featured buildings, a type of small hut often associated with craft work. The majority of the other structures were rectangular post-built halls. The settlement seems to have gone out of use by the early 7th century.

The excavations at Beddingham Roman villa have produced evidence of occupation by Saxon 'squatters', or at least people using Saxon pottery, during the late 4th or early 5th centuries.

The early Saxon settlement at Botolphs is much smaller than that at Bishopstone and had a shorter lifespan, although the site was re-occupied in the later Saxon period. The early settlement was occupied from the mid-5th to mid-6th centuries and the presence of two antler pottery dies shows that pots were made on the site. The only structures found were three sunken featured buildings and one post-hole, but there may well have been more buildings scattered over an area larger than that excavated.

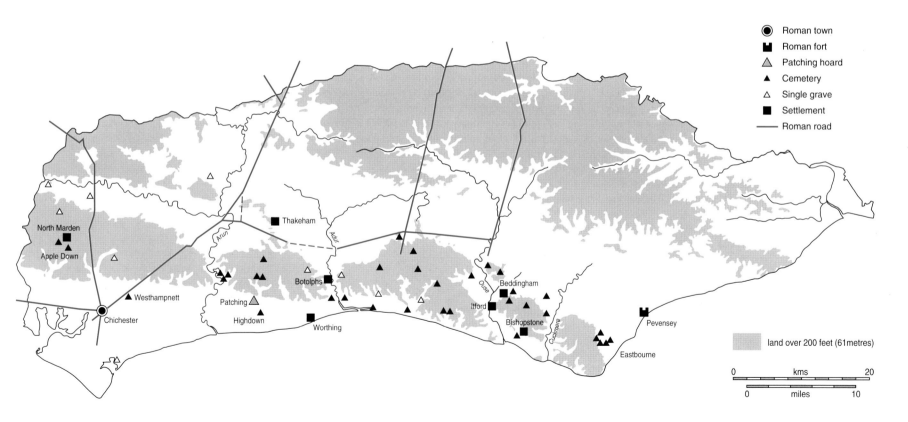

The 400 years covered by this map was a period of immense change. In the 7th century there were no recognisable towns, if we discount the ruins of the Roman period, and there were very few central places of any sort. Indeed, there were perhaps no settlements within the county larger than a hamlet. By the mid-11th century a network of towns and other centres performing administrative, commercial and Christian religious functions had developed. The emergence of a hierarchy of settlements both acting as central places and performing specialist roles was a reflection of the developing commercial and administrative complexity of English society. We can trace the development of the central places by considering how functions were concentrated at key places.[1]

The land of Saxon Sussex was divided into a series of large estates or holdings.[2] By the 10th century many of these estates were being split into very much smaller areas and it is only possible to identify hints of the earlier pattern where, for various reasons, this process had not advanced very far. The estate of South Malling stretched from near Lewes as far as Lamberhurst near the county boundary, and that of Bosham occupied a large tract to the west of Chichester. Estate centres at which rent was given were clearly important places. It is not possible to identify all the estate centres, and indeed the pattern was continuously changing as estates were partitioned and new centres were established. The will of King Alfred provides a list of the estates which he held as his private property in the 880s and therefore gives a view at one moment in time of the centres of a major landholder.[3] The main administrative unit of Late Saxon Sussex was probably the district known as the rape. We know very little about how these worked, or even their boundaries, since the pattern was extensively modified by the Normans (see map 20). The Saxon rapes were subdivided into hundreds, which served as taxation and administrative districts. In England generally these contained a nominal 100 hides (a measure of taxable value linked to land area) but in Sussex they were generally much smaller. The meeting of the hundred court to administer justice was generally held at a central spot, sometimes a notable landmark, a central settlement or an area of no-man's land between a number of estates. The courts were attended by all freemen within the district, and that large gathering also provided an opportunity for goods to be bought and sold. Markets commonly developed at hundred meeting places, particularly where the sites of the hundred were near an estate centre rather than a remote location.[4]

Religious centres were no less important than the secular foci. The county was served by a series of minster churches. The minsters covered a much larger district than the later medieval parish churches and were each staffed by a number of priests. Some of the districts attached to the minster churches, known by historians as *parochiae*, can be plotted from later evidence and the minimum area of three of these has been shown. The *parochia* of Peasmarsh, for example, covered an area between the county boundary and the River Tillingham. Many of the minster churches were situated at estate centres. In the north of Sussex there were apparently very few minster churches, reflecting the under-developed character of the Weald (and see also map 18).[5]

The impact of Viking raids on Sussex is poorly documented. Only with the battle at Ellingsdean near West Dean (West Sussex) in 1001 is it possible to reconstruct enough of the detail to get some impression of the Viking threat and the response by the defenders.[6] The main fortifications were a series of strongpoints known as *burhs* which could be held against the Vikings. Many were situated on rivers and were intended to halt the Viking advance into the interior of the county, but all the larger *burhs* had a secondary role, to provide commercial and perhaps administrative centres. The success of this policy can be seen from the map. Burpham was evidently superseded by Arundel and only *Eorpeburnan*, probably to be identified with Castle Toll near Newenden on the county border, failed to develop into a borough.[7]

As commercial activity grew in Sussex from the early 10th century onwards a number of mints were established to issue coin, and from 973 to undertake the periodic reminting of coins. Most of the mints were established at the main commercial centres. However, at Cissbury near Worthing, if it has been correctly identified, an emergency mint was established within the circuit of the Iron Age hillfort for a brief period in the early 11th century. The foundation of the mint at Steyning at about the same time reflects the need for a permanent mint in central Sussex, reflecting the wealth and population of the area.

The burh *at Burpham*

The final category of sites on the map is that of the pre-Norman ports. The evidence is almost certainly incomplete, for it is necessary to rely upon miscellaneous references and inference. Arundel, for example, had a port in 1086 and a church dedicated to St Nicholas, the patron saint of sailors, which may suggest that it had a landing place earlier, in the Late Saxon period. The port at Arundel, like those at Lewes and Steyning, was not situated on the coast, but some way inland on the river. By contrast, the ports at Hastings and Winchelsea were on inlets on the coast. Eastbourne has been added tentatively, as there is a reference to an 'old hythe' at East Hale in a charter of 963.[8] Places for which the sole evidence is fishing have been omitted.

The evidence plotted on the map is both miscellaneous and incomplete, and yet some interesting patterns do emerge. It is possible to pick out a series of places with a cluster of functions. All these had emerged as towns by the end of the 11th century, with the exception of Eastbourne. The failure of Eastbourne, which was never in the first rank of centres, is probably as much to do with its proximity to Pevensey and the promotion of that place by its Norman lord, Robert of Mortain. A second point apparent from the map is the clear concentration of central places in the south of the county, particularly in western and central Sussex. The settlement hierarchy of eastern Sussex developed much more slowly, and even in the mid-13th century there were relatively few commercial centres.[9]

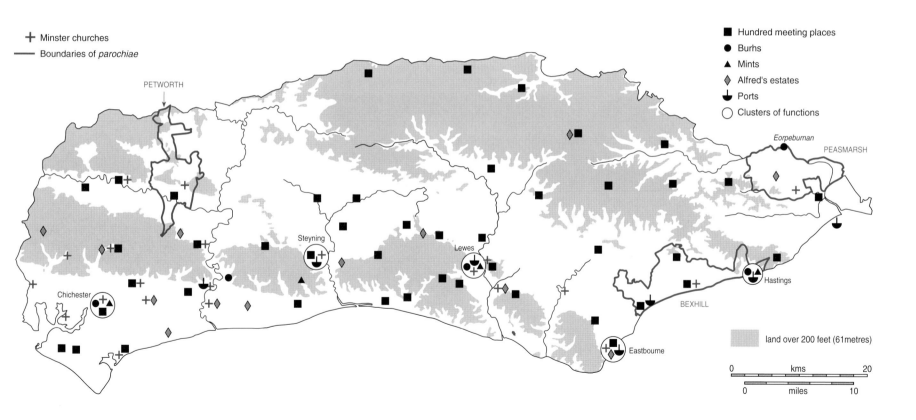

Minster churches
Boundaries of *parochiae*

Hundred meeting places
Burhs
Mints
Alfred's estates
Ports
Clusters of functions

land over 200 feet (61 metres)

PETWORTH

PEASMARSH

Eorpeburnan

Chichester

Steyning

Lewes

Hastings

BEXHILL

Eastbourne

kms   20

miles   10

Sussex is distinctive in having virtually no surviving Brittonic Celtic place-names. Even the ancient names of Chichester and Pevensey have vanished. The South Saxons used several different words and formative elements to construct place-names which meant or implied a community in some sense. Names in Old English *-ingas* (eg Hastings, Poynings, Ashling) are literally words for groups of people associated with a person (rarely some other entity) whose name appears as the preceding element. The genitive case of such 'community' names may appear with other final elements (eg Rottingdean, Chiddingly). It is no longer believed that names in *-ingas* represent the earliest phase of settlement, nor that they originally denoted bands of colonists under a leader whose name usually appears in first place; so Climping is no longer seen as the colonial territory of one Climp(a), with a name for his followers used as a place-name.[1] The *-ingas* names may belong to a slightly later (though still perhaps 6th/7th-century) phase of consolidation.

The prototypical community, for our purposes, is the farm designated by several different words in a fluctuating pattern which is still only partly understood. *Ham* was used early, and appears to have meant a substantial enterprise; places so named often developed importantly in the Middle Ages (probably Patcham and Pagham). The word was used in *wic-ham*, a compound word (developing into a name) applied to significant, possibly still functioning, Romano-British inhabited places of which there were several in Sussex.[2] *Ham* is difficult to distinguish from *hamm*, a topographical term for 'partially-isolated land', later 'watermeadow' or even just 'enclosure'; *ham* should not be assumed lightly since *hamm* survived in local dialect and in the names of many later small holdings. Names in *ham* 'estate', meaning manor and *-ingaham* seem to be a possible early stage; *ham* went out of use in place-name construction quite soon, though it survives as the ordinary word *home*. But it may not be possible, as formerly thought, to establish a reliable fine-grained chronology of the use of these early name-types.

Many farms which developed in Saxon times have names in *tun*, originally meaning 'enclosure' in some physical sense like 'hedge', 'fence'. It appears as an Anglo-Saxon name-element relatively late, and its increasing visibility in the record after the 8th century may accompany the reorganisation of land exploitation whose archaeological traces are called the Middle Saxon Shift.[3] It became, as elsewhere in England, the dominant element for naming farming communities. No fewer than 66 historic parishes and two extinct ones bear a name in *tun*. There were also 38 others known to the editors of *The Place-Names of Sussex* which did not achieve parish status.[4] That is, well over half were important enough to fulfil other social and administrative functions. They cluster markedly on or adjacent to the downland east of the Ouse, are quite frequent in the western rapes, especially in the western downland and close to the boundary of Arundel and Bramber rapes; but are sparse in the rape of Hastings. Quite a few such places on the Coastal Plain never became parishes (eg Drayton; Almodington) or have been extinguished.

They can be categorised according to the first elements with which they are constructed: 1. Those with ordinary lexical words, usually descriptive of the site or relating it to another (Clayton, Compton, Sutton, Westmeston), this type being dominant in the Weald where, however, *tun* is in any case unusual. 2. Those with personal names (Bepton, Alciston); the relation between the person named and the place (free or bond tenant, lord) is not known for certain, but one Ælfric was a free tenant of Alfriston before 1066.[5] 3. Those with words for categories of person (Preston, Kingston), of which at least the Kingston type may testify to a more general policy towards the assembling of food-renders. 4. Those which, with their first element, probably formed a lexical word of fixed meaning (Laughton, 'vegetable garden', (Little)hampton, sense unclear, a major agricultural unit of some kind); these should probably be seen as applications of *leac-tun* and *ham-tun* rather than of *tun* as such.

A major additional sub-type is that formed with *-ing-tun*. The first element of these names is almost always a personal name (Barlavington, Wilmington), and what this implies as distinct from category (2) is not known for certain; the concentration of these on and near the Downs east of the lower Cuckmere is remarkable. Sometimes, but rarely, the *-ing* may descend from the genitive of *-ingas* (Ashington, Yeverington). It is not always easy to decide from early sources whether a particular name enshrines *-ing-tun*, or *tun* following the genitive of a name in *-a*, viz. *-an* (Durrington); sometimes *-ing-* appears to be optional (Walderton). Occasionally the *-ing* may belong with the first element to form a lexical word of some kind; this may be so for Sullington and Norlington.

It has recently been suggested that the *tun*-names indicate an economy based on stock-rearing.[6] Since this is likely to be a live issue, and since such names are still not fully understood, *tun*-names have been chosen as the subject of map 2, which illustrates their distribution and linguistic categorisation. *Tun* persisted as a word for 'farm', '(nucleated) village', in medieval times and is found in such names as Town Littleworth, but it rarely becomes permanent in a place-name at this late date.

Other words in use for inhabited places include *wyrth*, 'toft, curtilage; house-plot and attached land', found even in early documents such as a late 8th-century land-grant to Selsey cathedral by Aldwulf, *dux* of the South Saxons. Relatively few major places are so named, and it is normally accepted that they represent small holdings, perhaps sub-parts or in some cases grants away from larger enterprises. In Sussex they are overwhelmingly formed with a personal name, and this pattern contrasts markedly with the differentiated pattern of *tun*. Extraordinarily few became medieval parishes, all of these being in the western Weald (Worth, Lodsworth, Petworth, Fittleworth; the last three nearly contiguous) as shown on map 1.

Other terms indicating habitation are *cot(e)* and *wic*. *Cot(e)* is found in three instances of Walcot, 'slaves' or Britons' cottage(s)' and nine others, including the parish Woodmancote. Some of these were clearly specialist, and quite humble, establishments and not primarily farms (Saltcote, Woodmancote); some may be post-Saxon. *Wic* (ultimately from Latin *vicus*) is hard to evaluate as its application may have continued to be current in the Middle Ages, by which time it has come to mean 'dairy-farm' or some other sort of specialised enterprise, but it is found in some very early names, notably the instances of *wic-ham* referred to above.[7] *Wic* is rare with a personal name, and *cot(e)* never occurs with one.

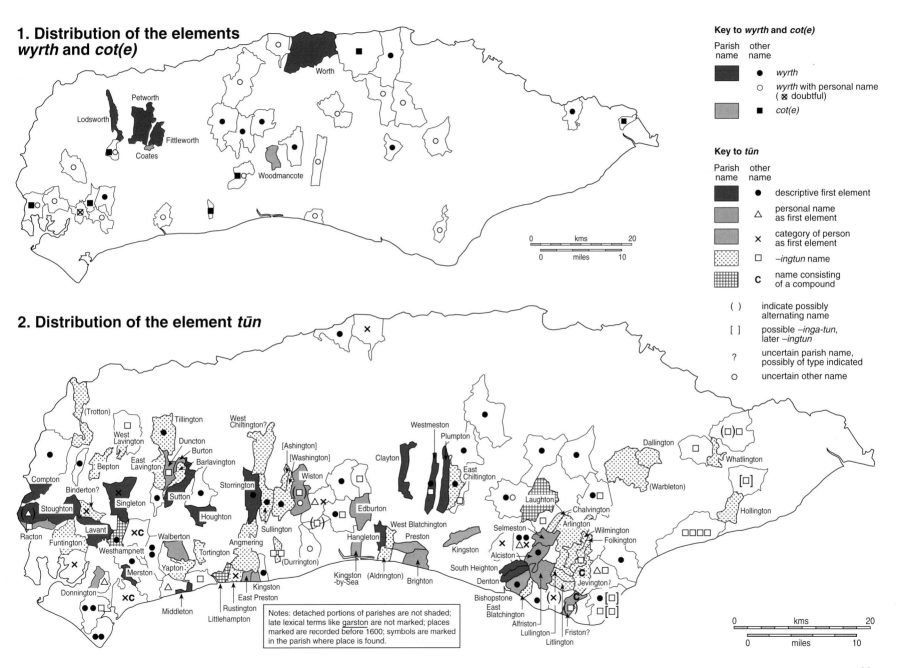

1. Distribution of the elements *wyrth* and *cot(e)*

Key to *wyrth* and *cot(e)*

Parish name / other name

- ■ (dark shading) / ● *wyrth*
- / ○ *wyrth* with personal name (⊗ doubtful)
- ▨ (light shading) / ■ *cot(e)*

Worth

Petworth

Lodsworth

Fittleworth

Coates

Woodmancote

Key to *tūn*

Parish name / other name

- (dark shading) / ● descriptive first element
- (medium shading) / △ personal name as first element
- (grey shading) / × category of person as first element
- (dotted shading) / □ –ingtun name
- (grid shading) / C name consisting of a compound

- ( ) indicate possibly alternating name
- [ ] possible –inga-tun, later –ingtun
- ? uncertain parish name, possibly of type indicated
- ○ uncertain other name

0 kms 20
0 miles 10

2. Distribution of the element *tūn*

(Trotton)

West Lavington

Tillington

Bepton

East Lavington

Duncton

Burton

Barlavington

West Chiltington?

[Ashington]

[Washington]

Westmeston

Plumpton

Dallington

(□)□

Whatlington

Compton

Binderton?

Stoughton

Singleton

Sutton

Storrington

Wiston

Clayton

East Chiltington

[□]

(Warbleton)

Racton

Lavant

Houghton

Sullington

Edburton

Hollington

Funtington

Walberton

Tortington

Angmering

Hangleton

West Blatchington

Preston

Kingston

Laughton

Chalvington

Arlington

Selmeston

Wilmington

Folkington

Alciston

Donnington

Westhampnett

Merston

Yapton

(Durrington)

Kingston -by-Sea

(Aldrington)

Brighton

South Heighton

Denton

Jevington

Middleton

Rustington

Littlehampton

Kingston East Preston

Bishopstone
East Blatchington

Alfriston

Lullington

Friston?

Litlington

C

Notes: detached portions of parishes are not shaded; late lexical terms like garston are not marked; places marked are recorded before 1600; symbols are marked in the parish where place is found.

0 kms 20
0 miles 10

33

Interpreting Domesday Book

In 1086, when the Domesday Survey was made, Sussex had recently been divided into five new baronies, locally called rapes, each with at least one town and a castle. The inquiry ordered by King William sought to find out what land each person held. The results of the investigation were entered into a book (or correctly two books) which became known as Domesday Book (DB).

Before we can begin to interpret DB, it is necessary to understand the purpose for which it was made. It was both a record of the feudal owners of estates or 'feodary', and a record of the taxable value of lands or 'geld list'. DB does not record individual settlements, but lists the manors. Some were small, consisting of little more than a farm or two. Others were enormous, stretching many miles northward as far as the borders of Surrey and Kent. The larger manors might comprise either a continuous block of land, or a core of land in the south of the county and separate areas in the woodlands of the Weald to the north. The likely extent of these large manors may sometimes be inferred from later records. A few examples may be given. It is probable that the 145 tenants with 34 ploughs taxed at Washington (value £53) included people living around Horsham. Some of the tenants of the bishop of Chichester's manor of Bishopstone (£20; 39 tenants, 30 ploughs) may have lived at Heathfield, and those of the archbishop's manor of South Malling (£70; 254 tenants, 73 ploughs) at Mayfield and Wadhurst.

Many previous maps of Domesday Sussex have given a misleading impression of the location of settlement and distribution of wealth. They have failed to indicate the extent of the lands in the north of the county.[1] The general pattern of association between manors in the coastal areas and their lands in the Weald is shown diagrammatically in map 1. DB does, however, provide a more detailed account of the farms in the Weald due to territorial changes in the areas around Battle, East Grinstead and a broad tract around Burwash and Ticehurst. Typically, the settlements in these areas occupied the lands in the river valleys, while the upland waste and woodland remained as common land and for hunting.

Rural Settlement

In the Downland, where many of the named Domesday settlements lay, recent research reveals an endemic pastoral economy.[2] At Stanmer later evidence indicates that the archbishop's demesne and permanent sheep down left only 600 acres (243ha) for the villagers' ploughs. It seems likely that half the Domesday population (59 families, 26 ploughs) were at Lindfield and elsewhere in the Weald.[3] At Clayton, a spring-line parish, there was no villagers' ploughland at all. The 14 ploughs of the 31 families in the manor were all elsewhere, to the north and south.[4]

In the Weald, at Wivelsfield, part of Stanmer in 1086, a few families shared about 750 acres (304ha) across various soils, providing them with arable, meadow and wood.[5] Worth, whose Saxon church later controlled a large parish on the Surrey border, then contained scattered farms and hamlets contributing to Earl Warenne's income under Ditchling and Patcham.[6] Individual farms in Worth would have been of similar value (5s to £1 each) to those enumerated around the new abbey of Battle and in other areas affected by the formation of the new rapes of the counts of Mortain and Eu. In one of those areas, East Grinstead, 11 farms are mentioned, ten of which were slightly down on their Saxon values. At another, near Burwash, 22 out of 25 independently assessed farms had maintained their Saxon values.

While the economic character of life may have remained broadly stable in the remote wealden farms, their overlords did not. Over the county as a whole 400 English lords were replaced by Normans as heads of manors. Around Petworth, for example, sheriff Robert's new estate had displaced around 40 English lords (map 2). By controlling manorial revenues, franchises and the profits of mills and mines, the ruling group of Normans had appropriated the greater part of the county's wealth.[7]

Tenure and Economy

The pattern of landholding in 1086 cannot be simply summarised. The boundaries of the Domesday estates can rarely be mapped precisely and instead the parish boundaries have been used, which, although not the same,

1. Manorial types, and relationship between manorial centres and their outlying lands

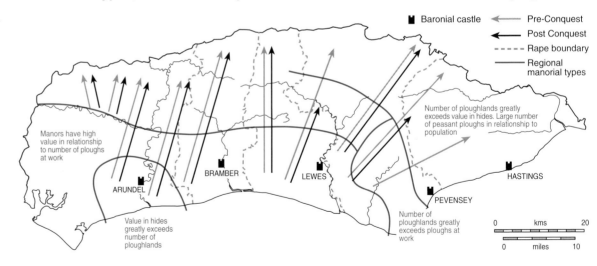

provide a useful guide. Map 2 seeks to show the general pattern of landholding by individuals but also indicates those parishes where a significant multiple lordship can be identified. The general picture is clear. King William had very little land in Sussex: he possessed only the manor of Bosham, and the manor of Rotherfield which had come into his hands on the forfeiture of the lands of Bishop Odo. The lords of the rapes, as one might expect, were major landholders with lands not only adjoining their castles, but also some distance away. This is particularly clear at the western end of Sussex, where Earl Roger had lands remote from his castle at Arundel. The map also shows the relatively small area held by the count of Eu in the rape of Hastings.

Most of the estates of the bishop of Chichester lay around the cathedral city. The archbishop of Canterbury also had land in that area, at Pagham, Lavant and Aldingbourne. The bishop of Exeter, Hyde Abbey (in Winchester) and Battle Abbey were the other main English ecclesiastical landholders. The French abbeys of Fécamp, Almenesches, Séez and others had been granted lands in the county by Norman lords. The lands of the abbey of Fécamp, which may have been given before the Conquest, were close to the ports of Hastings, Steyning and Winchelsea.

The regional character of Sussex in 1086 may be further explored by examining the data in DB (map 1). A number of measures of taxable value are given, including the hide, which had been used before the Conquest, and the ploughland, which seems to have been intended as a new measure of taxation. It also lists the numbers of lords' and peasants' ploughteams at work on the land, and figures for these and for the population and the value of the manor, probably its rentable value, may all be compared.

The analysis picks out a group of manors around Arundel which had been highly valued in terms of hides before the Conquest, but were assessed more moderately in ploughlands. The reasons for this disparity can only be guessed at – had they been taxed excessively, perhaps? The reverse is true for the area of eastern and north-eastern Sussex where the assessment of ploughlands greatly exceeded the hidage. The explanation is clearer here – it was an area of expanding agriculture and the revised taxation estimates reflect its increasing wealth.

The valuation in ploughlands of many vills in Sussex was similar or identical to the sum of the ploughteams at work on the lords' and peasants' land. In a few places there is a considerable disparity. A number of vills at the edge of the chalk downland and extending out on to the Weald Clay had many fewer ploughteams at work than one might have expected from their valuation. It is not clear if these manors were under-resourced or their taxable wealth was derived from other sources apart from arable cultivation. One of the most informative statistics is a measure of the value of each manor divided by the number of plough teams at work. The highest values come from those manors which have most productive arable, demonstrating very clearly the wealth of southern and western Sussex in contrast to the less productive north and east of the county.

2. Landholding in 1086

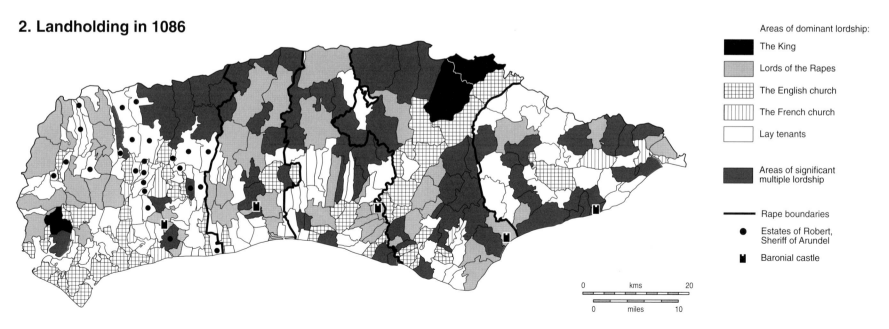

Areas of dominant lordship:

- The King
- Lords of the Rapes
- The English church
- The French church
- Lay tenants

Areas of significant multiple lordship

— Rape boundaries

● Estates of Robert, Sheriff of Arundel

▮ Baronial castle

0   kms   20

0   miles   10

Mapping the 11th-Century Church

Domesday Book (DB) provides the fundamental documentary source for tracing the distribution of churches in 11th-century England.[1] The survey notices the existence of a church in a manor or a town with the phrase *ibi ecclesia*. But, it has long been realised that DB is a temperamental guide to the actual existence of churches in 1086 – best demonstrated in Kent where the text of the almost contemporary *Domesday Monachorum* increases the number of churches recorded in DB in that county by over 100%.[2] In Sussex, DB records the existence of 106 local churches whilst implicitly suggesting the existence of a further 18, usually by reference to a priest or cleric. Unfortunately, Chichester Cathedral did not emulate Canterbury in the production of a comprehensive list of 11th-century churches in its diocese, but, if the DB evidence is augmented with architectural and archaeological evidence as well as with other documentary sources, a viable distribution of churches in existence by 1100 can be mapped.[3] Architectural evidence is obviously reliant upon there being standing features of the original stone church in existence today, whilst archaeological evidence is dependent upon the limited coverage of field work in the county. Despite these restrictions, architectural/archaeological evidence accounts for a further 37 definite 11th-century churches in Sussex.[4] These can be supplemented by churches named in the surviving pre-Conquest charters and in the early post-Conquest cartularies of Chichester, Lewes and Sele, which add a further 49 churches.[5]

When mapped, the distribution of known 11th-century churches suggests that the parochial system of the later Middle Ages was not in place county-wide by 1100. Large numbers of the southern parishes of the three most westerly rapes were endowed with a parish church by 1100, but elsewhere, especially in wealden areas, the later parishes cannot be shown to have had a church within their boundaries. This suggests that, at this time, the less populated areas of Sussex were still being served by mother churches, the minsters of Anglo-Saxon *parochiae*, although questions about the number of early wooden churches and the debate about the chronology of wealden settlement still hamper any definitive

conclusions.[6] A closer study of the development and erosion of the minster system may help elucidate the general picture.

The Development and Erosion of the Minster System

The parochial system of the pre-Viking Church seems to have been based on a network of minster churches whose religious communities performed pastoral duties over areas that could form several later parishes.[7] Page postulated that these *parochiae* often coincided with the shire hundreds, whilst the minster church itself often stood in the hundredal town. This correlation cannot be taken too far for Sussex – it is perhaps more useful to see minster *parochiae* as developing as an integral part of an earlier system of land division that can be traced in charter evidence. The *monasterium* of Stanmer, for instance, was commissioned by one Hunlaf, *comes*, as the parochial centre of the large estate, which stretched almost to the Surrey border, granted to him by King Eadwulf at some time between 760 and 771.[8] But, by the time of DB, Stanmer's minster status had already been downgraded and its importance subsumed by St Michael's at South Malling. Also, by this time, the parochialisation of the Stanmer *parochia* was complete. Components of the original *parochia* – Westmeston, Ditchling and Wivelsfield – had developed into autonomous parish churches with their own boundaries which part-imitated the topographical alignments of the old *parochia*.[9]

In contrast, Selsey seems to have retained its minster status over a large part of Manhood hundred until as late as the 12th century. Its size, prestige and income allowed it to survive the potential jurisdictional encroachments from the type of proprietary churches which were carving up the *parochia* of the poorer minster of Stanmer.

The identification of a church as having minster status can sometimes be derived from the DB entry – if the church is recorded as holding more than one hide of land, as at Bosham where the church held 112 hides, then it can be insinuated that it supported a number of ministering clergy who would have served the *parochia*. Sometimes, the DB entry explicitly states that there are a number of clerics – at Aldingbourne they are even named.[10]

Map 1 shows all churches which would have had minster status at some time in the 11th century; the extent to which their parochial rights had been infringed by 1100 can be seen by the completeness of parish church coverage around them (map 2). The inset map shows the likely area of the *parochia* of Petworth minster within and without Rotherbridge hundred. Petworth's DB entry gives no clue to its minster status, but from later charters of confirmation made to Lewes priory it is disclosed that Lurgashall and Duncton churches as well as the chapels of River and Tillington were daughters to the church at Petworth. They were also still paying pensions to the mother church at the end of the 12th century. In 1145 a new church at *Bleteham* (Egdean) was dedicated with the proviso that it paid its income of *romscot* (a church tax) to Petworth – a late example of what had probably already happened at the other churches: the founding of a proprietary church followed by the growth of an autonomous parish and the erosion of the minster's jurisdictional rights which became fossilised in later pension rights over its former dependencies.[11]

The *Taxatio* of 1291

Map 2 adds to the churches in existence by 1100 a further 66 Sussex churches recorded in the taxation of Pope Nicholas IV in 1291.[12] The *Taxatio* is not comprehensive in its coverage of 13th-century churches, and it would be legitimate to say that most 19th-century parishes were constituted with their own parish church by the end of the 13th century – but it is the first systematic documentary source after DB which provides a comparison with the 11th-century situation. Allowing for the unquantified amount of rebuilding of pre-1100 wooden churches, the distribution of 1100-1291 churches suggests that parochialisation in the wealden areas of Sussex was in general later than 1100. However, examples of late parochialisation in areas such as Selsey suggest that the growth of the parish in 11th- and 12th-century Sussex was less to do with the chronology of settlement, and more to do with the ability of minster churches to retain their former jurisdictional rights.

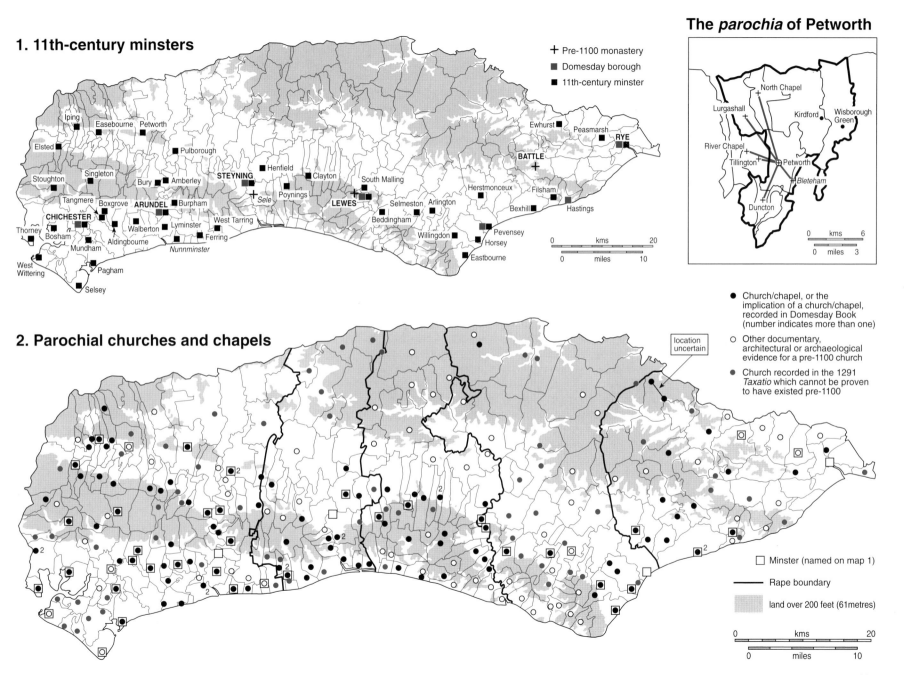

1. 11th-century minsters

✚ Pre-1100 monastery
■ Domesday borough
■ 11th-century minster

Iping
Easebourne
Petworth
Ewhurst
Peasmarsh
RYE
Elsted
Pulborough
BATTLE
Stoughton
Singleton
Bury
Amberley
Henfield
Clayton
South Malling
Herstmonceux
Filsham
Tangmere
STEYNING
Poynings
Selmeston
Arlington
Bexhill
Hastings
Boxgrove
ARUNDEL
Burpham
Sele
LEWES
CHICHESTER
Lyminster
West Tarring
Beddingham
Walberton
Willingdon
Thorney
Ferring
Pevensey
Bosham
Aldingbourne
Nunnminster
Horsey
Mundham
Eastbourne
West Wittering
Pagham
Selsey

The *parochia* of Petworth

Lurgashall
North Chapel
Kirdford
Wisborough Green
River Chapel
Tillington
Petworth
Bleteham
Duncton

2. Parochial churches and chapels

● Church/chapel, or the implication of a church/chapel, recorded in Domesday Book (number indicates more than one)

○ Other documentary, architectural or archaeological evidence for a pre-1100 church

● Church recorded in the 1291 *Taxatio* which cannot be proven to have existed pre-1100

location uncertain

□ Minster (named on map 1)

— Rape boundary

land over 200 feet (61 metres)

37

In the medieval period, as in later times, there were obvious benefits in adopting specialist agricultural regimes which allowed the crops best suited to the local soils to be grown. The market was sufficiently well developed from at least the mid-13th century to allow the exchange of produce between regions, so that the oat-producing area of the Weald might purchase wheat grown on the better soils in the south of the county, and the coastal regions could produce wool for export.

It is not possible to map the agricultural regimes of the whole county with equal confidence. The survival of documentary sources and the work undertaken by scholars have allowed only small areas to be studied in detail, although general statements may be made about much of the remainder. Where detailed account rolls have survived, it is possible to identify the crops sown and the stock kept on the lords' land. We know very much less about the agricultural regime of their tenants. The map is based mainly on records of the mid-14th century, a period for which there is a relative abundance of evidence.

The most wealthy area of Sussex included much of the Coastal Plain, the downland and the scarp foot of the Downs (Region I). Large acreages of wheat and barley were grown and fertility was maintained by growing legumes which obviated the need for fallowing. Large flocks of sheep were kept, particularly on the Downs in eastern Sussex, but also on the coastal marshes near Broadwater and Pagham. The soils of the Coastal Plain were not uniformly fertile and a sub-region (Ia) of poorer soils is distinguished on the map. The sub-region included Cakeham and the stony soils on the southern edge of the chalk where larger areas of oats were grown. At Poling in 1365 oats covered 24% of the sown acreage, and the figure for West Stoke earlier in the century was similar.[1]

The western Rother valley and the Low Weald claylands formed a region of moderate fertility (II). The manors here grew wheat and oats and kept flocks of sheep, though in smaller numbers than those of the preceding region, and some cattle. Large flocks of sheep were kept on the Pevensey and Winchelsea Marshes (III). Manors

in this region grew oats, but a greater proportion of wheat and barley than the manors in the High Weald (IV) which had the poorest soils in the county. Oats were sown on more than half the arable fields and this was the only region in which rye was grown in any quantity. Only a very limited acreage of legumes was planted. The main livestock kept was cattle; sheep were only present where there was access to pasture in the river valleys or marsh.

The regional basis of agriculture is also reflected in the distribution of open fields. These large unfenced arable fields, subject to communal regulation, were never as widespread in Sussex as in some of the Midland counties. The map published by Gray in 1915 differentiated an area of open fields in the southern half of Sussex from the area of holdings in severalty or individual occupation in the north of the county.[2] However, more recent work has shown that this is too simplistic. The manors on the fertile Coastal Plain often had two, three or four large fields or groups of fields which were cropped on a fixed, cyclic basis. North of the Downs the system was more flexible. There were either many smaller fields or more than one crop might be sown in the same field.[3] Not all land was held in open fields, even on the coastal fringe, and further

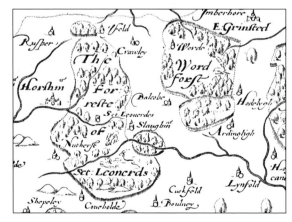

The Forests of St Leonards and Worth depicted by Christopher Saxton, 1575

north an increasingly large portion was held in severalty. In the northern half of the county open fields have not been convincingly demonstrated, although in some places areas of meadowland were regulated communally.[4]

The distribution of deer parks provides further evidence of the character of the medieval landscape. Parks varied considerably in size, but there is often insufficient evidence to allow the area of each to be indicated on the map. Nevertheless, the general pattern is clear. Parks were established on the poorer soils, the clays of the Weald or the clay-with-flints of the Downs. There were few parks on the Coastal Plain and in the eastern half of the South Downs. The Downs in western Sussex, which are more heavily wooded, had a greater number of parks. Some were established shortly after the settlement of the Normans, as at Bramber and the Great Park at Arundel.[5] Others were made in succeeding centuries to preserve tracts for hunting as the cultivated area increased. Parks were often situated near to the lord's house, such as Knepp Castle (Shipley) and the excavated moat at Hawksden (Mayfield).[6] Rabbit warrens were another type of park but are not shown on the map. These are generally less easily identified than deer parks, but they could be equally large in area. However, the warren at Petworth, which lay near to the deer park, is particularly well documented.[7]

Some of the gaps in the distribution of parks are filled by forests. The term 'forest' is strictly applied only to areas under royal jurisdiction and need not imply a wooded landscape, but it was often used more widely for land, often woodland, subject to special rules of the lord of the rape. An exception to this definition seems to be the Forest of Waterdown (Frant) which, as a possession of the Count of Gloucester, was presumably treated as an outlying part of Tonbridge lowy (an administrative district) in Kent. Sussex forests were administered through special wodemote or woodplea courts at which fines were paid by offenders or those using the wood. The largest of all Sussex forests was that of Arundel, which covered the whole of the Downs from the Arun westwards as far as Compton and extended almost as far south as Chichester.[8]

1 Middle Park
2 Up Park
3 Down Park
4 Stansted Great Park
5 Stansted Little Park
6 Westbourne
7 Cakeham
8 Trotton
9 Dumpford
10 Stoughton
11 Bosham
12 Treyford
13 Cocking
14 North Park
15 Cowdray
16 Downley
17 Selsey

18 East Dean
19 Halnaker
20 Tangmere
21 Aldingbourne
22 Shripney
23 Barlavington
24 Woolavington
25 Sutton
26 Upwaltham
27 Selhurst
28 Slindon
29 Shillinglee
30 Great Park
31 River (Treve)
32 Petworth Little Park
   and Coney Park
33 Ifold

34 Downhurst
35 Medhone
36 Flexham
37 Egdean
38 Fittleworth
39 Coates
40 Coldwaltham
41 Arundel Great Park
42 Arundel Little Park
43 Ford
44 Atherington
45 Pallingham
46 Pulborough
47 Wiggenholt
48 Batsworth
49 West Chiltington
50 Warminghurst

51 Goring
52 Findon
53 Heene
54 Stock
55 Solewick
56 Strood (Wiston)
57 Bramber
58 Dedisham
59 Broadbridge
60 Chesworth
61 Sedgewick
62 Knepp
63 Hawksbourne
64 Roffey
65 Shelley
66 Bewbush
67 Slaugham

68 Ewhurst
69 Shermanbury
70 Twineham
71 Albourne
72 Stretham
73 Woodmancote
74 Poynings
75 Hurstpierpoint
76 Cuckfield
77 Worth
78 Crabbet
79 Wakehurst
80 Ditchling
81 Westmeston
82 Chailey
83 Warningore
84 Lavertye

85 Standen
86 Horsted Keynes
87 Sheffield
88 Blackham
89 Buckhurst
90 Newham
91 Maresfield
92 Buxted
93 Plotsbridge
94 Isfield
95 Little Horsted
96 Plashett
97 Broyle
98 Moorland
99 Laughton
100 Glynde
101 Firle

102 Hamsell
103 Rotherfield
104 Frant
105 Frankham
106 Mayfield
107 Bentley
108 Saperton
109 Chiddingly
110 Michelham
111 Hawksden
112 Bivelham
113 Warlington
114 Lime
115 Wartling
116 Herstmonceux
117 Old Court
118 Eastbourne

119 Pashley
120 Burwash
121 Dudwell
122 Bexhurst
123 Mountfield
124 Park Farm
125 Bodiam
126 Whatlington
127 Battle Great Park
128 Battle Little Park
129 Broomham
130 Buckholt
131 Crowhurst
132 Brede
133 Udimore
134 Hastings
135 Iden

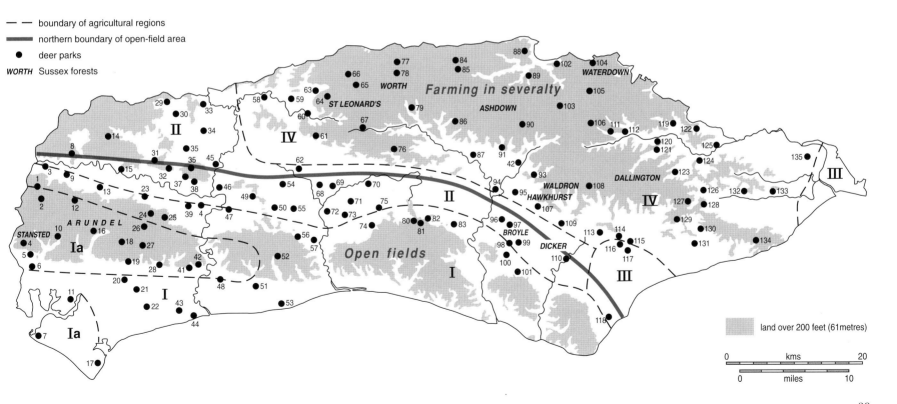

- — boundary of agricultural regions

━━ northern boundary of open-field area

● deer parks

WORTH Sussex forests

land over 200 feet (61 metres)

0 kms 20

0 miles 10

39

Civil and ecclesiastical administration in medieval Sussex was managed respectively through the geographical and jurisdictional units of the shire, rape, hundred and manor, and the diocese, archdeaconry, deanery and parish. All these units were in existence or, in the case of parishes, in the course of formation by about 1100, and remained the major units of administration through the Middle Ages.

The county of Sussex and the diocese of Chichester have been approximately coterminous for over 1000 years, and both have been 'time out of mind' divided in two. And yet the boundaries of division are not coincident. The pre-1974 division between the two counties is the same as the border between the rapes of Bramber in West Sussex and Lewes in East Sussex, but throughout its length

it is generally one hundred removed eastward from the border between the archdeaconries of Chichester in the west and Lewes in the east. Possibly the boundary between the rapes of Bramber and Lewes originally corresponded with that between the deaneries of Storrington and Lewes, but was realigned before 1086. This would give the deanery boundaries a date before 1086, possibly 1075, as argued by Hudson.[1]

There is coincidence and divergence between the boundaries of the major deaneries and rapes. Working from east to west, the deaneries of Hastings and Dallington correspond to the area covered by the rape of Hastings. The deanery of Pevensey corresponds to the rape of its namesake apart from the large area

covered by the deanery of South Malling, which came under the separate jurisdiction of the archbishop of Canterbury. However, parts of Mayfield and Wadhurst were in the rape of Hastings and may have been outside the deanery of South Malling.[2] Lewes deanery again corresponds to the rape of the same name on its eastern border, apart from the parish of East Grinstead, which was not included until the 16th century. Along the length of its western side, the deanery boundary overlapped into the rape of Bramber, and a narrow strip of land had divided loyalties. The deanery kept the hundreds of Fisheresgate and Wyndham complete whereas the rape boundary broke them up; the eastern half-hundred of Wyndham (Bolney and Twineham parishes) was

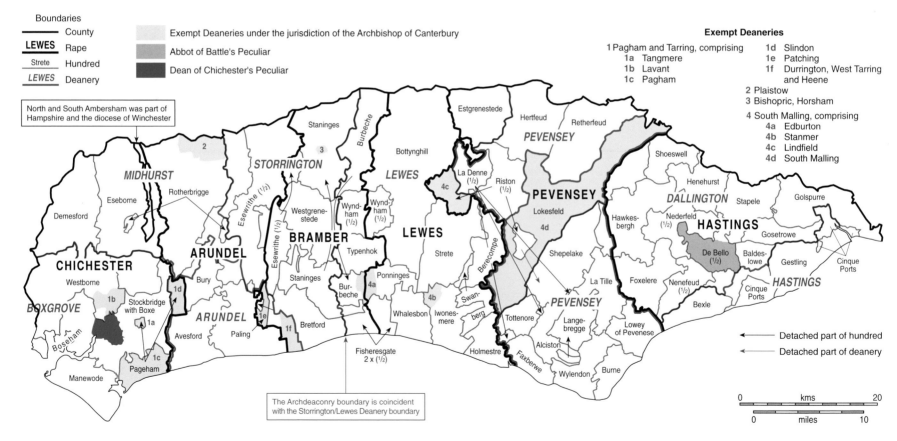

identified as a separate entity for assessment in 1296 within the rape of Lewes.[3]

On the west of Bramber rape, the border may have diverged substantially away from that of the deanery of Storrington in order to compensate for the loss of land on the east side of the rape. The large hundred of Esewrithe was kept intact inside the Storrington deanery, but the rape border divided it. The western deanery boundaries reflect the fact that the rapes of Chichester and Arundel were not separated until the 13th century, and it is possible that an original boundary between the rape of Bramber and the far western fifth rape corresponded with the western border of the deanery of Storrington.

The rape boundaries not only divided hundreds, but in some cases also manors. By the end of the 13th century, further fragmentation of hundreds had occurred, with name-changes perhaps reflecting the meeting places of the hundred courts.[4] For the most part the hundreds within rapes are self-contained, but some are split, such as Burbeche, which is separated by Typenhok and Wyndham. This reflects the custom in Sussex of landholdings – manors, parishes and hundreds – having outliers to take advantage of the different soil conditions to be found from the north to the south of the county. The tendency of parishes and hundreds to run northwards from the Downs may have contributed to the shape of the rapes.

The rapes were essentially units of Norman lordship and taxation, although they may have held some status before the Conquest. The origin of the word 'rape' does not appear to be Norman, but might derive from the Saxon territorial division *hrepp*, or the Saxon word *rap*, meaning a measuring rope. These corridors of power provided a network of communication between the coast and London. William the Conqueror originally farmed out the rapes to those closest to him, giving each to a tenant-in-chief. West of Lewes Rape, Sussex may have been given originally to Earl Roger of Montgomery. By 1073 an additional rape was formed for William de Braose, with its centre at Bramber. As late as 1248 there was no sixth rape, when the Pleas of the Crown still treated the hundreds for Arundel and Chichester together, but in 1262 they recorded a group of hundreds under the 'Bailiwick' of Chichester. By 1275 the Hundred Rolls recorded the new rape's name. Arundel and Chichester rapes had only twelve hundreds between them, whereas the other rapes had more than ten each.

Hudson suggests that William the Conqueror had set up the deaneries in order to remove disputes over jurisdiction from the hundred courts, which were in private hands.[5] There were eight diocesan deaneries in Sussex, and the deans of Chichester and Battle and the archbishop of Canterbury administered separate jurisdictions from those of the bishop and his archdeacons.

The map shows the situation around 1278, when Edward I issued commissions and articles of enquiry, whose returns are now known as the Hundred Rolls.[6] The enquiry looked into the usurpation of royal rights and privileges by ecclesiastical magnates, nobles and manorial lords, and the result gives a brief survey of local administration. Those surviving for Sussex are mainly the 'Extract Rolls' containing only the salient facts. The hundred names recorded there are used on the map.[7]

MEDIEVAL CHICHESTER
Alison McCann

A charter granted by King Stephen to the Bishop and reeves of Chichester in 1135 confirmed to them the rights of borough and gild merchant as they had enjoyed them since the reign of William I. In 1226 the citizens were granted the custody of the city at farm and, by 1239, the city had a mayor.[1]

The bishop's seat had been moved to Chichester following the decree of the Council of London in 1075. In 1147, William D'Aubigny confirmed to the church of the Holy Trinity whatever it held by right in the south-west quarter of the city. By the late 12th century, the Bishop had a separate court for the palace, and the Dean had his own court. In the mid-14th century, agreements were made between the Bishop, the Dean, and the citizens to resolve disputes about jurisdiction.[2]

Chichester contained nine ecclesiastical parishes. The largest of these was St Peter the Great, which used part of the Cathedral as its parish church. The parish also included considerable land outside the city walls. The Dean of Chichester's jurisdiction covered this area too, together with the parishes of St Pancras outside Eastgate, St Bartholomew's outside Westgate, and Fishbourne to the west, and Rumboldswhyke to the south-east of the city.

Within the city there were other areas as well as the Bishop's Palace outside the Dean's jurisdiction. The parish of All Saints was a peculiar of the Archbishop of Canterbury, and as such had its separate court. The Franciscans came to Chichester before 1245, and moved to the site of the former castle in 1269. Their popularity among the townspeople would have contributed to the decline of the parish of St Peter sub Castro, whose church stood near the castle gates. It was already impoverished by the mid-13th century. The church was finally demolished in 1574, when it had been long disused.[3]

The Dominicans were established in Chichester sometime after 1253, and in 1289 they obtained permission to close two lanes which ran through their property. Their site took over a very large portion of the parish of St Andrew in the Pallant, which disappears after this date. The other lost parishes are those of St Mary in Foro, and St Peter in Foro. A licence having been granted for the destruction of the latter church in 1229, its two parishioners were probably taken over by 1551 by St Mary's. The parish of St Mary in Foro was itself unserved because of its poverty.[4]

1 St Peter the Great parish
2 St Peter North Street parish
3 St Peter sub Castro parish *(conjectural)*; later part of St Peter North Street
4 St Peter sub Castro parish *(conjectural)*; later part of St Peter North Street
5 St Martin's parish
6 St Olave's parish
7 St Andrew Oxmarket parish
8 St Mary in Foro parish *(conjectural)*; formerly St Peter in Foro, later part of St Peter the Great parish
9 St Andrew in the Pallant parish *(conjectural)*; later part of St Peter the Great parish
10 Blackfriars, extra parochial; formerly part of St Andrew in the Pallant parish
11 St Pancras parish; formerly part of St Andrew in the Pallant *(conjectural)*
12 All Saints parish, Archbishop of Canterbury's peculiar jurisdiction
13 The Cathedral Close
14 The Bishop's Palace

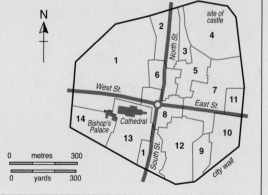

MEDIEVAL MARKETS AND PORTS

John Bleach and Mark Gardiner

The maps portray two major and integral parts of the trading network of the Middle Ages, markets and ports.[1] Identification is based on documentary evidence but detailed categorisation of their relative importance and, in the case of ports, of their chronology is not possible. Market locations appear in three categories – boroughs, where a market is presumed; non-boroughs named in a market charter; and non-boroughs with no such charter but where the right to hold a market was claimed or for which there is other evidence that a market existed. Market days are identified, where known, and the earliest date of borough or market status is given. Medieval boroughs in Kent, Surrey and Hampshire within about five miles of the county boundary are identified.[2]

The long coastline, the proximity of continental Europe and the abundance of fish, particularly herring in the inshore waters, encouraged the development of medieval ports in the county. The most important of these lay at the east end of Sussex near the shortest crossing to the Continent. Hastings was one of the Head Ports of the Cinque Ports, and Pevensey, Winchelsea and Rye, as members of the confederacy, had a privileged status in return for contributing towards providing ships for the king. Other members, such as Hydneye (in Willingdon) and Northeye (in Bexhill), were much smaller places which even by 1300 had dwindled into insignificance.

Changes in coastal and riverine morphology led to the decline of numerous other ports during the medieval period. New Shoreham replaced Steyning and Bramber as the main ports on the Adur, just as Seaford superseded Lewes on the Ouse. Many of the smallest ports relied, however, not on the protection of the rivers, but were established on gently sloping shingle beaches. Fishing boats sailed in pursuit of herring as far as Great Yarmouth from the beaches of Brighton and Hove. Goods were traded from many of the coastal landing sites and inlets. The creeks around Chichester provided numerous landing places for cargo ships, but the most important of these was Dell Quay (in Apuldram), whence goods could be taken overland to Chichester. Quays on the eastern Rother were used for loading wood which was shipped to the Low Countries and London. Unlike the major ports,

many of these landing sites, such as Lancing, Aldrington, and Rottingdean, did not themselves become markets.

Doubtless market activity of an informal nature took place throughout the Middle Ages wherever people were gathered together, but it is in the nature of such activity to be unrecorded. The more formal weekly market activity is based either on the grant by the Crown to a named individual for a particular place or, as in the case of most of the boroughs, on customary usage. It is this formal activity which is discussed below.

In the earlier Middle Ages market activity was concentrated on and near the coast. The Domesday boroughs of Chichester, Arundel, Steyning, Lewes, Pevensey, and probably also Rye and Hastings were local, if not regional, market centres. Before 1100 they had been joined by Battle, Bramber and Winchelsea, and from the mid-12th century by Seaford. From about 1200 the increasing population and a consequent growing commercialisation of the economy, coupled with the growth of a royal monopoly of the licensing of markets, heralded 150 years of intense, recorded activity in the granting of market rights throughout the county (see table).

Evidence for market penetration of the Weald dates from 1202-3 when Michael de Poynings received a licence from the king to hold a market every Friday at his manor of Crawley. This nascent economic activity was consolidated with the development of Uckfield from about 1220 and the emergence of boroughs at Horsham and East Grinstead by 1235. These wealden locations were far more dependent on roads for their trade routes than was the case with the Domesday and other early boroughs, all of which, with the possible exception of Battle, had navigable water nearby.

The early 1250s witnessed a significant expansion of the formal economy in both the eastern Weald and Rother valley with market grants for Wadhurst, Burwash, Salehurst, Robertsbridge and Hailsham, and for Cuckfield in the central Weald. The apparent success of some of these market centres which performed, in part, the functions of towns in the coastal parts of the county, is in marked contrast with the five intended markets for which grants are known from the previous 25 years. Thus, no evidence is known of any weekly market activity at Preston (near Brighton), Rockland (in Wartling), Wisborough Green, Newbridge (across the Arun from Wisborough Green), or Henfield.

A further intensive burst of activity in the first quarter of the 14th century may have had as much to do with political expediency on the part of the Crown as with the demands of the local economy or economic self-interest on the part of manorial lords. After 1325 the granting of market rights slowed to a trickle but the emergence in the 15th century of Alfriston, Storrington and West Tarring as local market centres should be noted. Contemporary with the establishment of new market centres, the borough markets at Pevensey, and on the Adur at Bramber, Shoreham and Steyning, continued their long decline from a peak of prosperity earlier in the Middle Ages. Many markets survived into the early-modern period, however, and provided a weekly arena, as they had done for centuries past, in which local inhabitants could buy and sell the necessaries of life.[3]

Number of recorded grants of market rights in Sussex, 1201-1350						
1201-25	1226-50	1251-75	1276-1300	1301-25	1326-50	Total
4	5	11	5	21	4	50

The granting of market rights was no guarantee that a market would take place. Undoubtedly many did function, and the evidence for this survives in contemporary references to income received from a market, such as at Broadwater, Eastbourne, Findon, Horsham, Wadhurst and Westbourne. The record of a market place at Hurstpierpoint and Ticehurst, and the partial survival of a ?late-medieval market cross at Alfriston, indicate potential functioning markets. For over 30 of the non-borough market locations shown on the map, however, such as Ringmer, West Grinstead, Tangmere and Wepham, there is no evidence of the rights, whether granted or claimed, being used. It should be noted that this lack of evidence could be due as much (and probably more) to gaps in research or paucity of relevant documentation rather than to the non-utilisation of market rights.

1. Ports and landing places

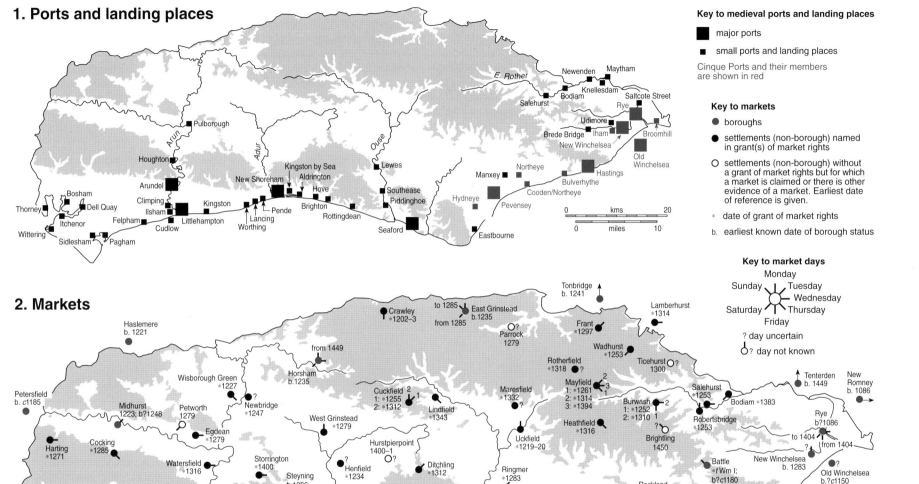

Key to medieval ports and landing places

■ major ports

■ small ports and landing places

Cinque Ports and their members are shown in red

Key to markets

● boroughs

● settlements (non-borough) named in grant(s) of market rights

○ settlements (non-borough) without a grant of market rights but for which a market is claimed or there is other evidence of a market. Earliest date of reference is given.

∗ date of grant of market rights

b. earliest known date of borough status

Key to market days

Monday
Sunday — Tuesday
Saturday — Wednesday
— Thursday
Friday

? day uncertain
○? day not known

Map 1 labels

E. Rother
Newenden · Maytham
Knellesdam
Bodiam
Salehurst
Saltcote Street
Rye
Udimore
Brede Bridge · Iham
New Winchelsea
Broomhill
Old Winchelsea
Pulborough
Northeye
Manxey
Hastings
Bulverhythe
Cooden/Northeye
Hydneye
Houghton
Lewes
Arundel
New Shoreham · Kingston by Sea · Aldrington
Hove
Southease · Piddinghoe
Bosham
Climping
Kingston
Thorney · Dell Quay
Ilsham · Pende
Brighton
Pevensey
Itchenor
Felpham · Lancing
Rottingdean
Eastbourne
Wittering
Cudlow · Worthing
Littlehampton
Seaford
Sidlesham · Pagham

0 kms 20
0 miles 10

2. Markets

Map 2 labels

Tonbridge b. 1241
Haslemere b. 1221
Crawley ∗1202–3
to 1285 East Grinstead b.1235 from 1285
Parrock 1279
Frant ∗1297
Lamberhurst ∗1314
from 1449
Horsham b.1235
Wadhurst ∗1253
Tenterden b. 1449
New Romney b. 1086
Petersfield b. c1185
Wisborough Green ∗1227
Rotherfield ∗1318
Ticehurst 1300
Cuckfield 1: ∗1255 2: ∗1312
Lindfield ∗1343
Maresfield ∗1332
Mayfield 1: ∗1261 2: ∗1314 3: ∗1394
Burwash 1: ∗1252 2: ∗1310
Salehurst ∗1253
Bodiam ∗1383
Midhurst 1223; b?1248
Petworth 1279
Newbridge ∗1247
West Grinstead ∗1279
Uckfield 1219–20
Heathfield ∗1316
Robertsbridge ∗1253
Rye b?1086
to 1404 from 1404
Harting ∗1271
Cocking ∗1285
Egdean ∗1279
Hurstpierpoint 1400–1
Brightling 1450
New Winchelsea b. 1283
Old Winchelsea b.?c1150
Watersfield ∗1316
Storrington ∗1400
Henfield ∗1234
Ditchling ∗1312
Ringmer ∗1283
Battle ∗t Wm I; b?c1180
Westbourne 1231–2
Slindon ∗1314
Steyning b.1066
Wepham ∗1303
Preston 1. ∗1228 2. ∗1307
Lewes b.1066
Cliffe 1. ∗1331 2. ∗1345 3. 1409
Hailsham ∗1252
Rockland 1226; 1251; 1325
Bulverhithe ∗1310
Hastings b.?1066
Tangmere ∗1314
Findon b.∗1086
Bramber 1. c1087 2. ∗1316 b. 1294
Brighton ∗1312
Wartling ∗1337
Bosham ∗1218
Arundel b.1086
East Angmering ∗1384
New Shoreham b.1208–9
Alfriston ∗1406
Willingdon ∗1301
Pevensey b.1066
Chichester b.1066
Goring ∗1301
Pagham 1. ∗1204 2. ∗1316
West Tarring 1. 1348 2. ∗1444
Broadwater 1. ∗1245 2. ∗1312
2:1312–75; 1383–?<1440
2:1375–83; ?<1440–<1493
Seaford c1140; b.1235
Eastbourne ∗1315
Birling ∗1267

land over 200 feet (61 metres)

0 kms 20
0 miles 10

43

In 1252 a great storm broke through the sea walls at Winchelsea, to the south of Rye, and caused havoc. By 1271 part of the church of St. Thomas had been washed away. Because of its importance to the commerce and defence of the realm, Edward I took the initiative to move the town to a new location overlooking the River Brede in 1280. Having acquired the manor of Iham on a hill to the west, in 1283 Edward instructed commissioners to lay out the new town.

The rent roll was drawn up in 1292. Of the 150 acres (61ha) available, Edward reserved 12 acres (5ha) for himself and 802 plots were allocated on the remainder – 723 on the hill and 79 by the harbour. Surprisingly, the commissioners placed the administrative and commercial centre without direct access to the gates and harbour. The central plots commanded the highest rents – rents were cheapest in the southern and western suburbs. In addition to Iham's existing church, New Winchelsea was planned with two churches, those of St Thomas (the principal) and St Giles, together with a house of Grey Friars and three hospitals. The hospitals were located within the southern suburbs, but the other ecclesiastical sites were more central.[1] In 1318 the Black Friars were given permission to set up a house within the suburbs, although they later moved to a more central location.[2]

Already by 1321, at the King's command, the Mayor and Barons were strengthening the town's defences.[3] Of the gates, the Strand Gate and the (later rebuilt) Pipewell Gate survive, as does the New Gate (so called by 1330) at the extreme southern end of the town. Fragments of the turreted town wall can be seen to the south of the Strand Gate. The initial defences had too long a circuit, a factor which favoured the French during their raids on the town.

The first 30 or 40 years on its new site represent the period of Winchelsea's greatest prosperity (map 1).[4] Recognition of its seaborne strength is found in 1303 when Gervase Alard, a leading citizen and merchant of Winchelsea, was made Captain and Admiral of the fleet. The town was regarded as the chief port of Sussex and was able to maintain its trade at or above its previous level.

Its principal import was wine, the significance of which is well illustrated by the large number of vaulted undercrofts: 32 are still accessible. During the year 1306/7,

15 Winchelsea ships of between 83 and 190 tons were involved in the wine trade with Bordeaux. Over an eight-month period within this year alone 14,400 hogsheads (ie 737,000 gallons) were imported from south-west France. Fishing was also significant. The import trade was otherwise varied and included the necessities for a large town and its rural hinterland: cloth, corn, wax, earthenware, mirrors, cups, leather, fruits, and spices were amongst them. The principal exports were wood, dairy produce and salt.[5]

The outbreak of the Hundred Years' War brought interruption to Winchelsea's trade. There is evidence to suggest that the town was sacked and burnt by the French in February 1326, but the town escaped the raids of 1339, despite neighbouring Rye and Hastings being burnt. Even so, in 1342 (six years before the Black Death) 94 tenements were uninhabited and, by 1358, 25% of its properties lay abandoned. By far the most devastating French attack was in 1360, when large numbers of men landed, took the town and killed the inhabitants. This attack should, however, be kept in perspective – Winchelsea ships had been in the forefront of attacks on French towns. Six years after the raid no fewer than 385 tenements (almost half the total) were 'waste, burnt and uninhabited'. A further French raid in 1377 was successfully repelled, but the town's decline had become such that in 1378 Chichester supplanted Winchelsea as the chief Sussex port. Just two years later the French surprised the town and again sacked it.[6]

Although the remainder of the century saw a gradual improvement in its fortunes, Winchelsea now consolidated itself within the north-eastern corner of its site, the suburbs being largely abandoned (map 2). Before 1414 the old administrative centre near the Grey Friars had been abandoned in favour of a more convenient location near the church of St Thomas. That the town officials accepted the reduced size as permanent is indicated by their petitioning the King in 1414 to reduce the defended area. An inquiry allows the precise line to be ascertained. The new defences would enclose 21 of the original 39 quarters, placing the parish church of St Giles near the south-western corner. The precinct of the Grey Friars would occupy the south-eastern corner and the Black Friars the north-western corner. St Thomas's

church and the new administrative centre stood centrally within the contracted site. The proposed wall would destroy just five dwellings, a clear indication of the abandoned state of the suburbs. That Winchelsea was still of some importance is suggested by the King's grant of 600 marks towards the costs. Payment was made out of the exchequer in 1417, but following a peace treaty with France payments stopped and the work was abandoned.[7]

During the 15th century another threat to the town became apparent – the harbour was silting. The port was still able to receive vessels of 200 tons in 1433, but towards the close of the century the silting worsened. In 1524 the town provided four ships manned by 15 mariners, but by 1544 it could provide but six hoys; by 1561 there were no 'ships, boats or crayers' based at Winchelsea. Having relied primarily upon its seaborne trade, the town's fate was inevitable. During the first 30 years of the 16th century houses within the commercial centre itself were abandoned, and the attrition rate was accelerating. By 1565 there were only 109 inhabited houses remaining – the number had fallen to 60 by 1575.[8] Even so, in 1573 the burgesses were able to entertain the Queen, who referred to Winchelsea – one feels rather tongue-in-cheek – as a 'Little London'.[9] Being located further down the estuary and not yet affected by the silting, Rye now prospered at Winchelsea's expense.

Medieval seal of Winchelsea

1. Winchelsea in the early 14th century

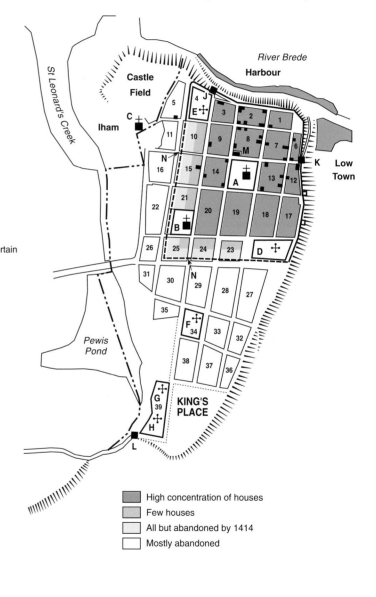

St Leonard's Creek

River Brede
Harbour

Castle Field

Iham

C ✝

J

5 4 3 2 1

11 10 9 8 7 6

Town Quay

16 15 14 **A** ✝ 13 12

K

21

22 20 19 18 17 **B** ✝

BUTCHERIES

26 25 24 23 **D** ✝

MONDAY MARKET

HUNDRED PLACE

31 30 29 28 27

35

F ✝ 34 33 32

Pewis Pond

38 37 36

G ✝ 39 ✝ **H**

L

A Parish church of St Thomas
B Parish church of St Giles
C Parish church of St Leonard, Iham
D Grey Friars
E Blackfriars (founded 1318 - site uncertain moved 1339, and again in 1358)
F Hospital of St John
G Hospital of Holy Cross
H Hospital of St Bartholomew
J Pipewell Gate
K Strand Gate
L New Gate (so called by 1330)
M Town Hall (moved site)
N Proposed new gates on line of new town wall (not built)

– · – Line of proposed new town wall as planned in 1414

■ Accessible vaulted undercroft

Note: The numbers shown on the plan are the numbers of the blocks as given in the 1292 founding rental. They were still in use in documents of the 17th century.

	60d per acre (49 prime plots)
	48d per acre (79 harbour plots)
	40d per acre (584 plots)
	36d per acre (90 plots)

2. Winchelsea in the early 15th century

St Leonard's Creek

River Brede
Harbour

Castle Field

Iham

C ✝

5 4 **J**
E ✝ 3 2 1

11 10 9 8 7 6

N

16 15 14 **A** ✝ **M** 13 12

K
Low Town

21

22 20 19 18 17 **B** ✝

26 25 24 23 **D** ✝

31 30 **N** 28 27
29

35

F ✝ 34 33 32

Pewis Pond

38 37 36

G ✝ 39 ✝ **H**
KING'S PLACE

L

	High concentration of houses
	Few houses
	All but abandoned by 1414
	Mostly abandoned

0 metres 500

0 feet 1000

45

The conversion of Sussex, the last English Kingdom to acquire the seat of a bishopric, began in 681 almost a century after St Augustine's mission to Canterbury. According to Bede the credit belongs to Wilfrid, his fellow Northumbrian, but there was already a Christian presence when he arrived. A small community of Irish monks was based at Bosham. Whether any influence from late Roman Christian tradition had lingered is a matter for speculation. Wilfrid was granted land at Selsey and founded the cathedral at Church Norton.[1] From the outset, the boundary of the diocese approximated to that of Sussex.

Monastic life in England in the four and a half centuries between St Augustine and the Norman Conquest has left only a hazy impression. There were Celtic monastic communities already present in England when St Augustine arrived in Kent and introduced the monastic way of life based on the Rule of St Benedict. Both Benedictine and Celtic traditions could be found in 7th-century England, but in time Benedictine observance was pre-eminent. In the early years the religious communities, whether monks or clerics, carried out a missionary function. The major churches in the diocese, the *minsters* (of which the cathedral was the chief minster) were staffed by communities of clerics that led a common life resembling that of monks. The name *minster*, in effect the vernacular form of *monasterium*, suggests (according to Blair) that in the 7th and 8th centuries 'it is difficult to draw a hard line between "minsters" which had parochial duties and "monasteries" which did not'.[2] However, monastic communities later develop which appear to follow more closely the Benedictine ideal of withdrawal from the everyday world. The Rule stipulates the importance of self-sufficiency and lays down precise requirements for life within the monastery. It implies that at the outset a community required a range of buildings, besides the church, to fulfil their needs. These early monasteries comprised an informal group of buildings. The 'conventual' plan based around the church and cloister which originated on the Continent may have made its appearance in the 10th century during the period of monastic revival.[3]

There was a small religious community at South Malling probably founded before Wilfrid's departure. Aldulf, ruler of the South Saxons, is recorded as granting land *c.*765 to a monastery. In the 8th century there are hints of Saxon colleges of canons at Ferring, and King Offa granted land for the service of God at Bexhill and Beddingham, which may have been colleges. At Steyning there is some evidence for a possible minster of secular canons before 858, when Ethelwulf, father of King Alfred, was buried here. In Edward the Confessor's reign Steyning was granted to Fécamp Abbey. At Chichester, the Benedictine nunnery of St Peter was displaced to accommodate the canons from Selsey when the Cathedral was moved in 1075. A monastery certainly seems to be implied by a charter in 956 of King Edwy to the brethren of Chichester and William of Malmesbury suggests a pre-Conquest minster of St Peter, perhaps a double monastery.[4]

After the Norman Conquest, reform and reconstruction continued at a brisk pace. Every major church was rebuilt in England in the decades following 1066.[5] Where appropriate, cathedrals were moved from rural areas to urban centres, and thus Selsey was abandoned and the cathedral rebuilt in Chichester *c.*1070-75.[6] In 1066 there were about 50 Benedictine monasteries in England. By the end of the 11th century the number had more than doubled. All were Benedictine with the exception of five Cluniac houses.

The first-generation Norman barons, preoccupied with consolidating their hold on their newly acquired land and wealth, tended to enrich existing French monasteries or endow small daughter houses. Boxgrove illustrates a small scale monastery modelled upon the layout of greater abbeys.[7] The upsurge in new foundations did not take place until the 12th century, but two major houses were established in Sussex soon after 1066. Battle Abbey was founded on the spot where Harold fell, notwithstanding objections from the monks of Marmoutier to the impracticality of such a hilly site.[8] At Lewes, William de Warenne, Duke William's seneschal, persuaded the abbot of Cluny to send monks to begin a

monastery which became the chief house of the English Cluniac Order. The great priory church of St Pancras, at Lewes, with its high steeple and vault 28m over the high altar (half as high again as the nave of Chichester Cathedral) would have been the largest and most spectacular church in the diocese had it survived the Dissolution.

In the 12th century other Orders developed from the Benedictine mainstream, re-establishing the early values of a simple, austere life of work and prayer. Of these, the Cistercians came to have the most far-reaching influence in English monastic life. Robertsbridge is the only Sussex example. The Premonstratensian canons, like the Cistercians, pursued an austere life in remote places away from everyday life. Bayham Abbey, on the Kent border, was directly dependent upon the mother house of Prémonstré – a privilege only allowed to one other English foundation. Durford, on the Hampshire border, was a smaller and less successful house. For some decades before 1066, there existed in parallel with communities of Benedictine monks a body of regular clergy known as the Canons of St Augustine. Minsters had been served by clerks or canons, separate from monks, who lived under stricter religious vows. Augustinian canons lived a communal, quasi-monastic life but were often married. Reform had begun in the late 10th century, but after 1066, the Normans, influenced by continental practice, enforced strict vows. The Augustinians were popular. Their houses, modest in size and more readily endowed by the lesser nobility, are therefore numerically well represented at Tortington, Shulbrede, Easebourne, Michelham, Hardham, Pynham near Arundel, and Hastings.

The Friars arrived in the 13th century. Preaching and teaching, they served the poor and needy, living in poverty themselves and relying on gifts of food. They are found in urban sites at Chichester, Lewes, Rye, Shoreham and Winchelsea, often on marginal land close to rivers or the sea.

Medieval hospitals under a chaplain, assisted by brethren or sisters, followed a strict rule which was effectively monastic. Although some institutions cared for the sick, others helped the poor and aged or lodged travellers. They were usually based in the midst of the community they served or close to key routes or crossing points for travellers and pilgrims. By contrast leper hospitals, naturally, were at a distance from the town – Maudlin and St James (both outside Chichester); Bidlington by Bramber; St. Leonards, Seaford (destroyed by the sea in 1368).

The military orders were present at Poling where the Knights Hospitaller were granted land, at Shipley where the Knights Templar were granted the manor and church, and at Saddlescombe where they were granted a manor, the property passing to the Hospitallers when the Templars were suppressed.[9]

Monasteries did not simply exist for the sake of monks within the cloister, they performed an important function in society, undertaking on behalf of their founders and benefactors onerous penances which they would otherwise be unable to perform. Masses held for the souls of the departed reassured the living against the uncertainties of the hereafter. They often provided an honourable career for the younger sons and daughters of the nobility who could not expect to inherit.[10] Reform may have been overdue when they were suppressed in the 16th century but the wholescale destruction of the monasteries was an unparalleled act of vandalism.

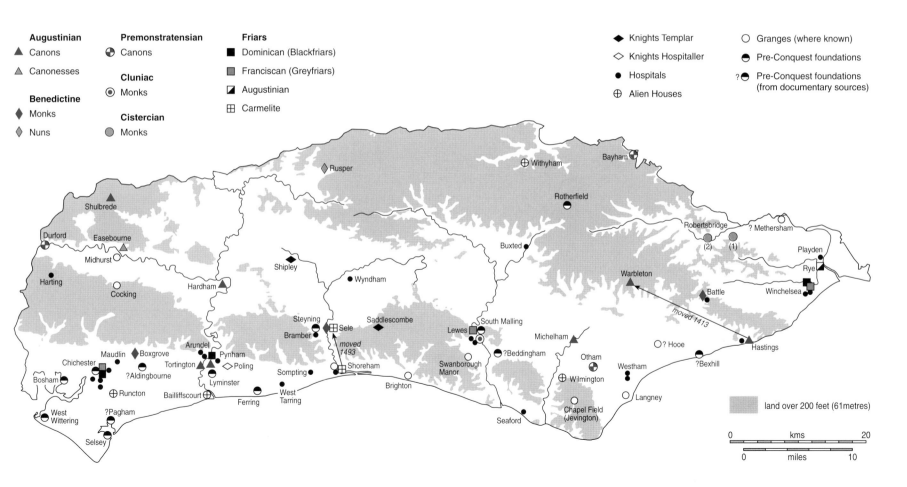

47

This map shows 109 deserted settlements in Sussex, including some lost to the sea. The figure is, however, an underestimate of the true total for the county; in this century work by Burleigh, Gardiner, Holden, Hurst, Tebbutt and others has added numerous sites to the research begun in Sussex by the Revd Hussey in 1848. The sites noted on the map and their names are derived from the Sites and Monuments Records of East and West Sussex County Councils, the Medieval Settlement Research Group and the Royal Commission on the Historical Monuments of England.[1]

In 1954 Beresford's pioneering work *The Lost Villages of England* defined these as follows:

> ...those villages where we have clear evidence of their existence as communities in the Middle Ages; but where we now have no more than (at most) a manor house and a farm and a church. In many villages...we shall have only one of these...and in quite a number of cases, not even these.[2]

However, within the last 20 years it has been considered that the phenomenon of deserted settlements is only one episode in a continuous shifting of sites throughout time. Current opinion suggests that deserted settlements, such as Kingston-by-Ferring (28), are those that are much reduced from their former size, whilst other settlements have actually shifted in location, but the demonstration of such shifts is notoriously difficult to trace. As more research is undertaken on so-called deserted sites all over the country as well as in Sussex, the growing feeling is that the nucleated settlement was a transitory feature in the total history of settlement.[3]

Deserted settlements vary in physical appearance and may be seen as crop marks or as a pattern of raised platforms and hollow ways which indicate their layout. There may also be associated pottery, and field names and aerial photography can provide evidence for these lost settlements.

The desertions are concentrated in downland and coastal regions, with few represented in the Weald. This possibly reflects difficult settlement conditions combined with the poor drainage of the Weald Clay. On the other hand absence of fieldwork in this area might contribute to the lack of evidence. The most productive land was the most densely settled: the scarp foot zone, the spring line, the river valleys of the South Downs and, to a lesser extent, the Coastal Plain.

It is impossible to give precise reasons for desertion of many sites, though tentative conclusions can be drawn for some. For example the Black Death was severe in Sussex in 1348-9, and after the plague there may have been a retreat from the downland to coastal areas. Holden concluded that at Hangleton (55) – the first deserted medieval settlement in the county to be excavated in a scientific manner in the 1950s – the Black Death was the final blow to an already impoverished village.[4]

Environmental changes connected with the climate and the rise in sea level during the 13th century were extremely significant. Storms ravaged the Sussex coastline during the late 13th century: Old Winchelsea (108) was deserted and Cudlow (24) and other coastal settlements were eroded by the sea. Northeye's (89 & 90) desertions reveal a combination of factors: drainage of the surrounding marshland, storms and economic hardship.

Economic reasons in particular contributed to the pattern of desertion. The early and middle 13th century was a period of land colonisation when many villages were expanding and utilising more marginal land. Burleigh feels that, with an increasing population, perhaps land became scarcer and more expensive, and that expansion did not reflect increased wealth. Lands possibly also became unproductive and infertile. Another cause of depopulation was the emparking of land and the displacement of villages such as probably occurred at Binderton (16) and Wiston (42). The *Nonarum Inquisitiones* of 1341 (enquiries relating to agricultural production during 1340) indicate shrinkage in the area of arable land during the 14th century. It reveals that land was lying uncultivated because of the poverty of parishioners and their inability to find seed; land had been destroyed by the sea, and bad weather caused harvest failures and the death of livestock.[5]

The Act of Parliament 1489 forbidding conversion of ploughland to pasture reflected the increasing problem of enclosure and sheep grazing, with resulting depopulation. However, this does not seem to have been much of a problem in Sussex compared with some other counties, as the depopulation of the Downs occurred earlier and is more likely to have been caused by a movement away from more marginal land, rather than enclosure by landlords, as in the Midlands and the east of England.[6]

A coastal county such as Sussex has always been vulnerable to attack; war as a depopulating agent must be considered. In Exceat (84) only two houses remained in 1460, when the church was in ruins. Local tradition, supported partly by the *Nonarum Inquisitiones*, favours devastation by the marauding French.[7]

Some sites are no longer visible, such as Hangleton (55) and Worthing (38), now covered by housing developments, whilst others remain easily accessible by public footpath and bridleway. It is even possible to walk along the deserted streets of Charlton (44) and Monkton (8) whilst noting the former house platforms of the long-forgotten occupants.

The excavation of Hangleton medieval village, 1953. Eric Holden is using a measuring rod to indicate the width of an oven.

1 Downley	20 Glatting	39 Pende	58 West Blatchington	77 Tilton	96 Faulkners Farm
2 Broadwash Bridge	21 Binsted	40 Shermanbury	59 Pyecombe	78 Alciston	97 Lye Green
3 Racton	22 Yapton	41 Buncton	60 Pangdean	79 Winton	98 Coleham
4 Lordington	23 Ilsham	42 Wiston	61 Stanmer	80 Arlington	99 Daleham
5 Walderton	24 Cudlow	43 Charlton Court	62 Balmer	81 Sutton	100 Church Field
6 Up Marden	25 Atherington	44 Charlton	63 Balsdean	82 Chinting	101 Buckham
7 North Marden	26 Ford	45 Wyckham	64 Telscombe	83 Poynings Town	102 Isfield
8 Monkton	27 Poling	46 Botolphs	65 Southeram	84 Exceat	103 Buxted
9 Linch	28 Kingston-by-Ferring	47 Coombes	66 Iford	85 Birling	104 Salehurst
10 East Itchenor	29 Coldwaltham	48 Old Erringham	67 Rodmell	86 Hydneye	105 Bodiam
11 Bracklesham	30 Greatham	49 Kingston Buci	68 Southease	87 Manxey	106 Saltcote Street
12 Almodington	31 Lee Farm leper settlement	50 Woodmancote	69 Piddinghoe	88 Hooe	107 Iham
13 Wardur	32 Chantry Bottom	51 Albourne	70 Beddingham 1	89 Northeye 1	108 Old Winchelsea
14 Wytheringe	33 Lower Barpham	52 Edburton	71 Beddingham 2	90 Northeye 2	109 Broomhill
15 Merston	34 Cobden	53 Newtimber	72 Tarring Neville	91 Bulverhythe	
16 Binderton	35 Muntham	54 Perching	73 Heighton	92 Priory Valley	
17 East Dean	36 Myrtle Grove	55 Hangleton	74 Norton	93 Shelley Church	
18 Burton	37 Upper Barpham	56 Aldrington	75 Bishopstone	94 Tinsley Green	
19 Duncton	38 Worthing	57 Hove	76 Heighton St Clere	95 Shantytown	

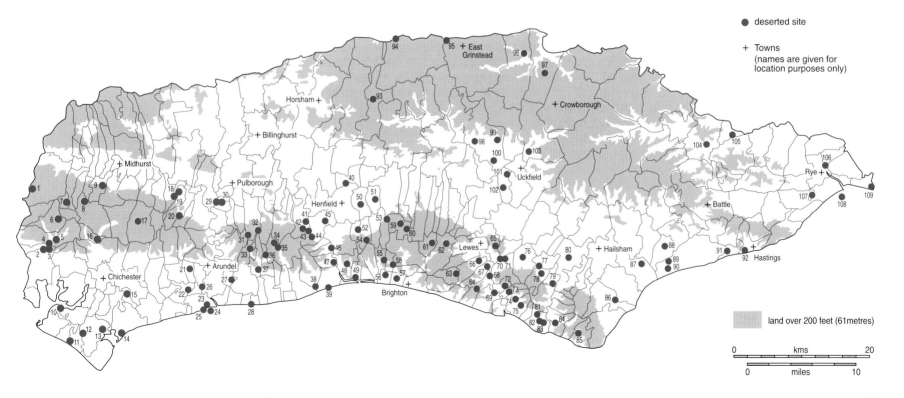

● deserted site

+ Towns
(names are given for
location purposes only)

land over 200 feet (61metres)

49

Sussex was not without fortifications before 1066. Masonry walls surrounded the Roman sites of Chichester and Pevensey. The fortifications at Chichester were re-used by Alfred and his son, Edward the Elder, in the late 9th and 10th centuries, and further earthwork defences were built at Burpham, Lewes, Hastings and *Eorpeburnan*, forming burghal centres from which to defend the kingdom of Wessex against Viking raids.[1] It was only after the Norman Conquest, however, that the county saw an explosion of private defences or castles which stood in marked contrast to the communal defences of previous periods, Sussex possessing the first documented post-Conquest castle at Hastings as depicted on the Bayeux Tapestry.

Stemming from its geographic position, the military role of Sussex was unique. Between 1066 and 1204, Sussex was not only a frontier zone, sharing common military roles with the Northern and Welsh marches, but was also the crucial link between Norman and Angevin powerbases either side of the channel. The rapal division of Sussex into north-south corridors has been interpreted not simply as a means of administering the county, but also the means by which the king could guarantee his progress from London to Normandy and beyond. Each rape had its major castle (Hastings, Pevensey, Lewes, Bramber, Arundel, and later, Chichester) all located close to the coast, granted to major magnates with close affinities with the royal family. Possession relied on loyalty to the Crown. Disloyalty led to siege, twice laid to Pevensey in 1088 and 1147, and to Arundel in 1101, or dispossession in the cases of Bramber and Knepp on the forfeiture of William of Braose. From the major centres secondary castles were subsequently established inland, as was the case for Knepp and Bramber, the former used by King John as a hunting lodge. These eventually formed a complex, and as yet poorly understood, network of defensive sites which looked to their mother establishments.[2] In addition to their defensive function, the rapal castles fulfilled offensive roles as garrison centres dominating large hinterlands, and acting as centres for administration, places *from which* the county was governed and *at which* fealty was paid.

Lesser lords, pre-occupied with defending their individual interests, and wishing to reinforce their elevated social status, constructed castles across the county. For the most part, the right to fortify was carefully supervised, but in times of political vacuum, for example during the anarchy of Stephen, adulterine castle building took place across the country. No castles in Sussex, however, can be shown categorically to have their origins in this lawlessness, although the semi-fortified site of Clay Hill, Ringmer, may have been constructed at this date. Lack of archaeological investigation and historical documentation means that few Sussex castles can be closely dated but motte-and-bailey and ringwork forms suggest that private castle building began early – probable examples being Church Norton, Chennells Brook near Horsham, and Pulborough – reaching its zenith in the 12th and 13th centuries in parallel with the national trend. Typological grounds for dating remain dangerous since, unable to support the costs of new masonry castles, lesser lords may have copied outdated fortification types. Variations of design and dates have been identified in the early Norman ringwork at Old Erringham, Shoreham, the square keep at the bishop of Chichester's castle at Aldingbourne constructed in the 1160s, the mid-12th-century shell-keep at Midhurst, and concentric ditches and walls of Sedgewick near Horsham, licensed for crenellation in 1258.

The loss of Normandy in 1204 appears to have had no immediate impact on Sussex, although 13th-century pottery recovered from Selham motte and Hartfield might suggest that these two fortifications were constructed to defend against a foreign threat. The first discernible effects of growing tension between England and France were the measures taken to defend coastal towns. Murage grants were given to Chichester (1261), Lewes (1264), Winchelsea (1283), Arundel (1295) and Rye (1329), with further grants being given throughout the Hundred Years' War. Obvious targets, such as Battle Abbey, where the gatehouse was built and the abbatial enclosure strengthened in 1338, and Lewes Castle, where a barbican was added in the 1340s, also took precautionary action. By the late 1370s and into the 1380s not only the war but also social unrest encouraged further defensive work. The bishop of Chichester received licence to crenellate Amberley, both Michelham and Wilmington priories were partially fortified, and Edward Dallingridge constructed his fortified manor at Bodiam.[3] Surveys have shown that, while Bodiam is intrinsically weak, considerable efforts were made to secure the site from within. The lord's range including hall, chambers and kitchen, for example, could operate independently from the rest of the castle.[4]

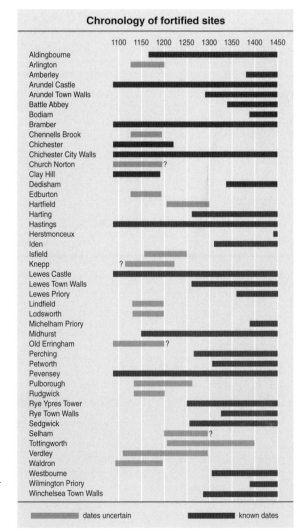

Chronology of fortified sites

	1100	1150	1200	1250	1300	1350	1400	1450
Aldingbourne								
Arlington								
Amberley								
Arundel Castle								
Arundel Town Walls								
Battle Abbey								
Bodiam								
Bramber								
Chennells Brook								
Chichester								
Chichester City Walls								
Church Norton								
Clay Hill								
Dedisham								
Edburton								
Hartfield								
Harting								
Hastings								
Herstmonceux								
Iden								
Isfield								
Knepp								
Lewes Castle								
Lewes Town Walls								
Lewes Priory								
Lindfield								
Lodsworth								
Michelham Priory								
Midhurst								
Old Erringham								
Perching								
Petworth								
Pevensey								
Pulborough								
Rudgwick								
Rye Ypres Tower								
Rye Town Walls								
Sedgwick								
Selham								
Tottingworth								
Verdley								
Waldron								
Westbourne								
Wilmington Priory								
Winchelsea Town Walls								

▬▬▬ dates uncertain   ▬▬▬ known dates

The established network of major strongholds was further supplemented by smaller sites with defensive potential, in particular moated sites. These include both sites which can be considered truly *defensive* and those which were simply *defensible*. Over 235 moated sites are known in Sussex, although no definitive survey has been undertaken.[5] This figure is comparatively high, but undoubtedly relates to geology – in particular the Wealden clay – rather than to social, economic or military needs specific to Sussex. Studies elsewhere demonstrate that most were constructed between 1150 and 1500 with a period of rapid expansion between 1200 and 1325. It is probable that Sussex examples followed this chronology. The reasons for their construction appear diverse. While defence may have been a consideration it need not have been the prime motivation for moat construction. Even a site such as Bodiam could not have withstood the determined assailant for long. Rather it seems that moated sites soon attained a social and symbolic cachet, being associated with aristocratic, ecclesiastic or other manorial dwellings, which led to their later adoption by those in the lower echelons of society. As such they have much in common with sites such as Isfield, Waldron and Tottingworth (Heathfield), built to resemble their more noble cousins.

The full development of the castle, from the earliest earth and timber designs through to the late medieval sham, can be traced in Sussex, together with all other medieval defensive measures. The variety of solutions found to solve defensive requirements attests to the continuous importance not only of defending individual and local interests, but the nation as a whole, throughout the period 1066-1450.

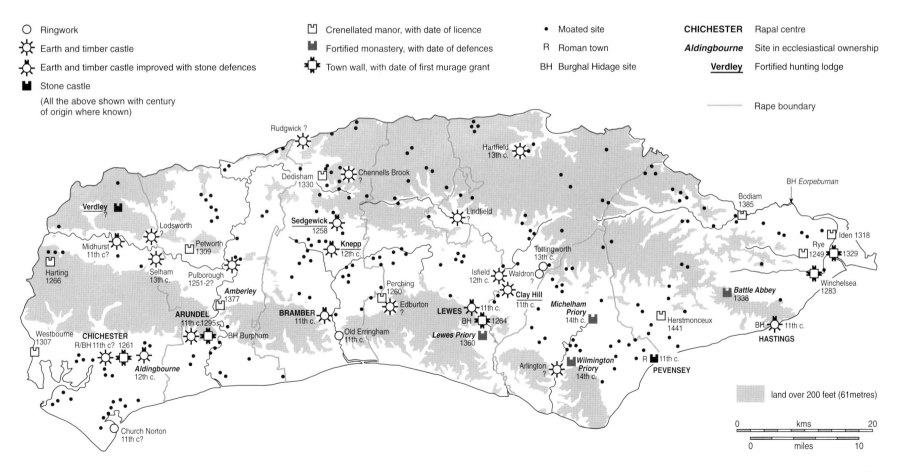

Key:

- ◯ Ringwork
- ☼ Earth and timber castle
- ☼ Earth and timber castle improved with stone defences
- ◼ Stone castle

(All the above shown with century of origin where known)

- ⌂ Crenellated manor, with date of licence
- ◼ Fortified monastery, with date of defences
- ✦ Town wall, with date of first murage grant

- • Moated site
- R Roman town
- BH Burghal Hidage site

CHICHESTER Rapal centre
Aldingbourne Site in ecclesiastical ownership
<u>Verdley</u> Fortified hunting lodge

—— Rape boundary

land over 200 feet (61 metres)

Map labels:
Rudgwick ?
Hartfield 13th c.
Dedisham 1330
Chennells Brook ?
BH *Eorpeburnan*
Bodiam 1385
Verdley ?
Lindfield
Bodiam 1385
Iden 1318
Lodsworth
Sedgewick 1258
Midhurst 11th c?
Petworth 1309
Knepp 12th c.
Tottingworth 13th c.
Rye 1249 1329
Harting 1266
Selham 13th c.
Pulborough 1251-2?
Amberley 1377
Isfield 12th c.
Waldron
Perching 1260
Clay Hill 11th c.
Michelham Priory 14th c.
Winchelsea 1283
Westbourne 1307
CHICHESTER R/BH 11th c? 1261
ARUNDEL 11th c.1295
BH Burpham
BRAMBER 11th c.
Edburton ?
LEWES 11th c.
BH 1264
Herstmonceux 1441
BH 11th c.
Aldingbourne 12th c.
Old Erringham 11th c.
Lewes Priory 1360
Wilmington Priory 14th c.
R 11th c.
PEVENSEY
HASTINGS
Church Norton 11th c?
Arlington ?
Battle Abbey 1338

0 kms 20
0 miles 10

When Henry VIII died in 1547, he left behind an English national Church which could roughly be described as Catholic but secular. Catholic, because its beliefs and liturgy were largely traditional, and secular because it had divested itself of obligations to Rome and connections with religious orders. In the succeeding six years of Edward's short reign, the pendulum swung steadily towards Protestantism.

It was the next decade, the five years of the reign of the Catholic Mary, and the first six years of her Protestant sister Elizabeth, that brought the grass-roots changes in Sussex and throughout the English counties.

The map charts the progress of the new Protestant religion in the crucial mid-century decade. It shows the acceptance at local level of the new forms of worship and theology. Its complicated pattern reflects also the diverse ways in which the changes arrived.

In the most notorious phase of the Marian reaction, the laity of the county paid a heavy price. Out of a likely national figure of 288 Protestants burnt at the stake, 41 victims came from Sussex. Thirty-six of them can be identified with specific parishes and the place of execution of 27 is known.[1] Surprisingly, the impetus for the persecution may have come as much from the conservative local magistracy as from central government.[2] There are two reasons why the county – and specifically its eastern half – should have been perceived as dangerously radical. Most obviously, its geography made it open to the influences of continental Protestantism. There seem also to have been links with the Lollards, who had been active in west Kent and eastern Sussex long before Henry's Reformation.[3] So while the burnings were witnessed in towns across the whole of the county, the victims were drawn from just 18 parishes in the east – with the majority coming from the High Weald and most of the remainder from the eastern seaboard.

But the principal participants in the events of the decade were the clergy – and their changing fortunes reflect the ebb and flow of the national tide. The weapon used against them by Mary's (and later Elizabeth's) governments was deprivation: the removal of a priest from his parish living or cathedral office; and it is important to note that the deprivations were imposed by national, rather than diocesan, authority.

The principal crime which Mary's deprivations punished was clerical marriage. A royal proclamation forbidding married clergy to minister was issued in December 1553. Action followed rapidly. By May 1554 clergy had been removed from 18 livings, and by the end of the year the figure had risen to 52 clergy. Twelve followed during the years 1555-6, and there was one further deprivation before the end of the reign. The distribution shows the divergence between the conservative west and the radical east: the former suffered 37 deprivations and the latter 28.[4] The cathedral clergy seem to have had a slightly easier time. The Protestant bishop, Scory, was replaced, within days of Mary's accession, by his predecessor, Day; but only four prebendaries lost their places.[5] The final total for the county was 70 out of 320 parish livings and 38 cathedral appointments.

It is difficult to trace the subsequent careers of the parochial clergy. But we can establish that deprivation was not necessarily the end. Around 16 received Marian appointments to other livings, and there were perhaps five appointments to curacies. Presumably this meant that they had disposed of their wives. Of those who refused to do so few, perhaps seven, were reinstated to their living in Elizabeth's reign on the deprivation of the men who had ousted them. Around eight reappeared from oblivion to receive different Elizabethan livings. Almost half cannot be traced.

In November 1558 Mary died and her Protestant sister succeeded her. But the immediate target of Elizabeth's religious settlement continued to be the clergy. Whereas the Marian priests were judged on celibacy, the Elizabethan were now asked to demonstrate loyalty and conformity. After the 1559 Acts of Supremacy and Uniformity re-established the break with Rome and re-introduced the Book of Common Prayer, royal officials administered statutory oaths to the clergy. Those who failed to comply were deprived.

This time it was the senior clergy who suffered the most severely. The government perceived that the security of the newly re-established Church of England would depend on loyal men of godly learning who could persuade their congregations. As the spearhead of such a body, the cathedral clergy must be sound. Seven posts were purged by the end of 1560 and a further nine in the next four years. The parochial clergy were not left unscathed. Thirty-nine incumbents were deprived – in an unexpectedly similar ratio to the previous reign: 23 in the east and 16 in the west. Thus in this second wave a total of 55 of the county's benefices lost their clergy.[6]

The later careers of these men are even more tangled than those of their Marian counterparts. Those deprived for refusing the oath held no further appointments in Elizabeth's church; and at least eight are known to have pursued Catholic ministries abroad or in the households of Catholic magnates. Surprisingly at least eight more deprivees did hold Elizabethan benefices – but it appears that their deprivation was not the result of their conscience but either of pluralism (holding more than one living) or the return of their deprived predecessor.

During the period 1558-64 other events were affecting the religious stability of the county. Forty-three incumbents resigned their livings – 18 in the east and 25 in the west – and additionally four members of the cathedral chapter.[7] The figure is relatively high, and as well as reflecting normal moves to new appointments must also include a number of retirements. Clerical retirement was something of a rarity, as there was normally no provision for a pension; and so the figure suggests that a number of older men could not in conscience continue under the new regime.

But the most powerful instrument of change was not under the control of any politician or ecclesiastic. The years 1558 and 1559 saw an influenza epidemic as virulent as most of the plague outbreaks. The English clergy seem (perhaps through a combination of age and stress) to have been particularly vulnerable. Certainly death cut a deeper swathe than Mary or Elizabeth. In the five years up to 1564, the clergy of 83 benefices died (evenly divided in death with 41 in the east and 42 in the west). Seven of the chapter also succumbed.[8]

In the end the bare statistics point to the turmoil the county had experienced in the past 12 years. In only 30 parishes can we find evidence of an incumbent remaining at his post throughout. In the years 1559-64, a quarter of the incumbents of the county's 320 parishes had died. Over the whole period 225 had been removed by deprivation, death or voluntary resignation.

When, in 1564, Bishop Barlow wrote a report on his diocese to the Privy Council, he could look back over 11 years of turbulence and forward to a future still fraught with dangers. Though Sussex had embraced the Elizabethan Settlement, it cannot be said that Sussex had embraced Protestantism. Though the machinery of the newly-established church was in place, it was precarious. If the later years of the 1560s presented a relatively peaceful appearance, it stemmed more from truce than victory. In the west, Catholic sympathies and Catholic magnates would pose major problems for a century to come. In the east, radicalism and later Puritanism would prove equally intractable. The Church of England's *via media* was still generations away.

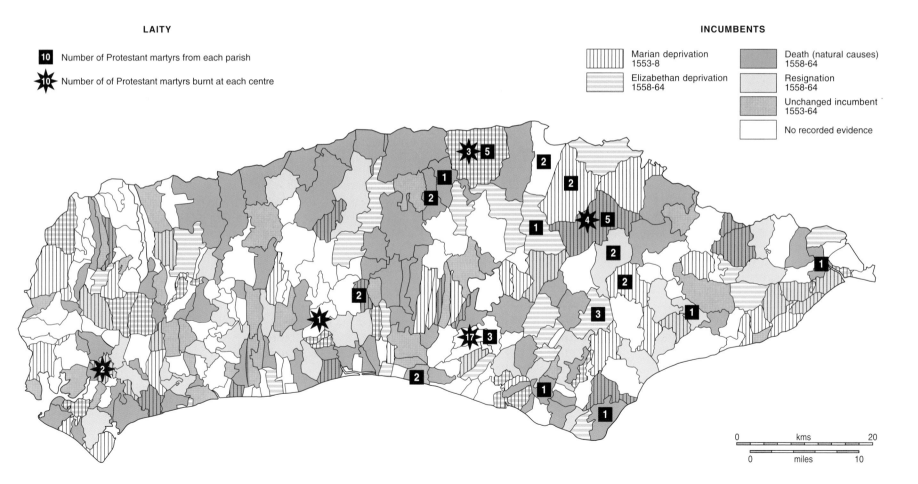

LAITY

10 Number of Protestant martyrs from each parish

10 Number of of Protestant martyrs burnt at each centre

INCUMBENTS

Marian deprivation 1553-8

Elizabethan deprivation 1558-64

Unchanged incumbent 1553-64

Death (natural causes) 1558-64

Resignation 1558-64

No recorded evidence

0   kms   20

0   miles   10

The term 'great house' can be defined as a large, undefended domestic structure, most typically found surrounded by parkland or large gardens, built at the behest of aristocrats, members of the upper gentry or high-ranking clergymen. By the late 17th century such houses were often described as 'country seats', implying residence for only part of the year. The great house can also, however, be used to describe grand, free-standing houses built on the outskirts of towns or villages, more often for patrons wealthy from commercial success, whether locally or in London. The national picture of the building of large houses, both in country and town, suggests an enormous upturn from the early 16th century until about 1630, then between four and five decades of relatively modest construction, followed by another upswing at the end of the 17th century, lasting well into the next.[1] Sussex roughly follows this pattern although, despite one or two spectacular examples of great houses of the period 1680-1700, the county never matched the intensity of building witnessed elsewhere during those latter years. New building was at every period often a question of re-encasing and modernising the old. Very few great houses of the early 16th century were built on totally new sites and even well-established structures that externally did not change their appearance may have had radically new interiors. Even the castles of earlier times, like the late 14th-century Bodiam and the 15th-century Herstmonceux, would have been substantially altered, and more than once for changing household needs within the outer castle walls.[2] In the later 16th century, for reasons of fashion, changes in the arrangement of large estates which moved the centre of power, and new ideas about the siting of houses for the benefit of health, a greater number of houses were built on new, more elevated sites, such as the Goring's house at Danny.[3] Houses often signify new wealth and social climbing, but they were not always built at the optimum time of financial solvency or security of tenure in political or social position. They marked the point of arrival and were often a statement of the family's potential longevity as great landholders.

The most significant factor in releasing land and building materials for great new houses was the upheavals in the Church during the Reformation. Sussex had only a small presence of late medieval great ecclesiastics who built large domestic structures for themselves only to find their properties subject to re-distribution or exchange at the behest of the Crown in the later years of Henry VIII.[4] The Bishop of Chichester was busy at Cakeham in the 1520s and the Archbishop of Canterbury's great house at Mayfield was later owned by a succession of court or London figures, including Sir Thomas Gresham, founder of the Royal Exchange. The Dissolution of the monasteries meant that their buildings passed into a variety of hands, especially gentry families, as at Michelham and Wilmington, and in one case a man of the highest influence at court, Sir Anthony Browne, at Battle. The systematic destruction of Lewes Priory, an unusual procedure in the south-east of England, meant the release of stone, particularly valuable Caen stone from northern France, into the locality and the building or transformation of several great houses, including Southover Grange and Hangleton Manor.

The aristocracy are generally thought to have benefited just as much as 'new men' from the Dissolution. It enabled aristocrats to consolidate their estates and sometimes build further houses. Among the established aristocracy, the Fitzalan family, Earls of Arundel, at Stansted and Arundel, and the West family, Lords de la Warr, at Halnaker, can be said perhaps to have been mainly resident in the county. The Howards, Dukes of Norfolk, at Chesworth, in Horsham, still counted their East Anglian estates as their true power base and the Percy family at Petworth were strong in Northumberland and Middlesex. One branch of the powerful Sackvilles controlled the vast estate of Buckhurst in the north-east of the county. Of the new aristocracy, raised by service to the Tudor monarchs, the Brownes, Viscounts Montague, were the most prominent at both Battle and Cowdray; the latter was inherited by Sir Anthony Browne in 1542 from his half-brother, Sir William Fitzwilliam, holder of great offices at Henry VIII's court. The Brownes remained

Catholic yet outwardly loyal; Elizabeth I enjoyed one of the most famous 'entertainments' of her many royal progresses at Cowdray in 1591.[5]

Other major courtier figures from the early 16th century whose 'great house' was in Sussex were Sir John Gage at Firle, Sir William Pelham at Laughton and John Shurley at Isfield. At the end of the next century, Lord Grey of Warke, Lord Privy Seal to William III, rebuilt his family house at Uppark between 1685 and 1690. Wealthy Londoners were responsible for a small number of significant houses, at Albourne, Parham, Barnham and the lost house of Woolavington, for which a builder's contract of 1586 survives.[6]

Cowdray House, Midhurst. Built between 1520 and 1550, left in ruins after the fire of 1793.

There is no especially significant pattern in the placing of great houses except the noticeable void in the eastern and western extremities of the Weald, where the presence of industries meant small and profitable estates rather than large landholdings. The handful of houses built at the behest of wealthy ironmasters, such as Rowfant and Batemans, were predictably close to the centre of their owners' industrial wealth. The availability of building materials certainly determined or limited the owners' choice, with a marked use of local flint on the Downs. Yet the widespread presence of brick, usually locally-made, meant that a good many houses where new wings were added, or the exterior modernised, happily mix brick with stone, flint or half-timbering. There was clearly a preference for brick among fashion-conscious courtier figures in the early 16th century and many houses ostensibly of stone were in fact stone revetments over a brick core, as at Cowdray, or consisted of a brick surface, lightly-rendered. Generally, the great Sussex house is said to be stylistically conservative, yet the county has several startlingly novel houses across the two centuries, with either distinctive surface enrichment or ingenuity of plan or elevation. Among these are the use of terracotta ornament at Laughton in the 1530s, the only example of this decorative addition to brick houses outside East Anglia and the Thames valley; the lost centrally-planned house of Michelgrove with its raised central tower prefiguring later Elizabethan houses; the extraordinary Barnham Court c.1640, so close in design to the house later known as Kew Palace in Surrey; and the great park front of Petworth of the 1680s.[7] Some houses are also outstanding examples of particular features of style or planning typical of this period, such as the E-shaped entrance fronts of Danny and Wiston, and therefore are of national significance among the great houses of the Elizabethan age.

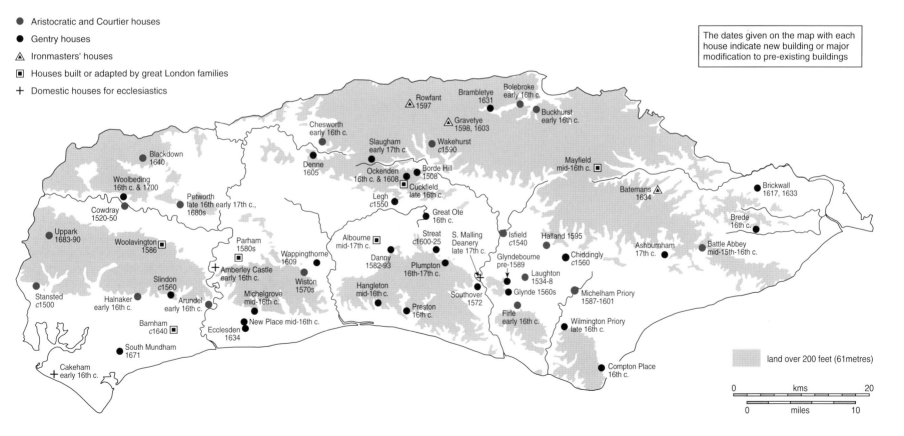

● Aristocratic and Courtier houses

● Gentry houses

△ Ironmasters' houses

▣ Houses built or adapted by great London families

+ Domestic houses for ecclesiastics

The dates given on the map with each house indicate new building or major modification to pre-existing buildings

Rowfant 1597
Brambletye 1631
Bolebroke early 16th c.
Buckhurst early 16th c.
Chesworth early 16th c.
Gravetye 1598, 1603
Blackdown 1640
Slaugham early 17th c.
Wakehurst c1590
Mayfield mid-16th c.
Woolbeding 16th c. & 1700
Denne 1605
Ockenden 16th c. & 1608
Borde Hill 1508
Cuckfield late 16th c.
Batemans 1634
Brickwall 1617, 1633
Petworth late 16th early 17th c., 1680s
Cowdray 1520-50
Legh c1550
Brede 16th c.
Uppark 1683-90
Great Ote 16th c.
Woolavington 1586
Parham 1580s
Albourne mid-17th c.
Streat c1600-25
S. Malling Deanery late 17th c.
Isfield c1540
Halland 1595
Ashburnham 17th c.
Battle Abbey mid-15th-16th c.
Wappingthorne 1609
Danny 1582-93
Glyndebourne pre-1589
Chiddingly c1560
Slindon c1560
Amberley Castle early 16th c.
Wiston 1570s
Plumpton 16th-17th c.
Laughton 1534-8
Stansted c1500
Halnaker early 16th c.
Arundel early 16th c.
Michelgrove mid-16th c.
Hangleton mid-16th c.
Southover 1572
Glynde 1560s
Michelham Priory 1587-1601
Barnham c1640
Ecclesden 1634
New Place mid-16th c.
Preston 16th c.
Firle early 16th c.
Wilmington Priory late 16th c.
South Mundham 1671
Cakeham early 16th c.
Compton Place 16th c.

land over 200 feet (61metres)

0 kms 20

0 miles 10

Religious observance in the sense of church attendance was legally compulsory during the 17th century, but the apparent regularity of attendance revealed by presentments of absences at visitation or quarter sessions probably means no more than that the bare requirements of the law were satisfied. Those who attended their parish church, and those who refused to attend divine service for religious reasons, whether as Catholic recusants or nonconformists, are shown on the maps, which are based on the figures provided by the Compton Census of 1676.[1]

Post-Reformation Catholicism in England has been described as essentially a seigneurial religion, with its survival depending on the numerous gentry households which provided shelter for their co-religionists and access to the sacramental life. Sussex Catholicism was centred on the estates of families such as the Brownes, Viscounts Montague, at Cowdray in Easebourne; the Shelleys at Michelgrove in Clapham; the Carylls at Ladyholt in Harting; the Kempes at Slindon; the Gages at Firle and the Thatchers at Priesthawes in Westham. These Catholic households later developed into the 18th-century missions of Cowdray, Arundel, Burton, Slindon, Ladyholt and West Grinstead. Catholics were singled out for harsher penalties than the fine of 12d. imposed by the Act of Uniformity 1559 for non-attendance at church. Statutes of 1581 and 1585 against recusants raised the penalty for non-attendance to £20 a month (calculated on a 13-month year), with confiscation of their goods and two-thirds of their property for non-payment. Erratic conformity and the persistence of occasional conformity, together with the unreliability of official returns, make it difficult to assess the incidence of recusancy in Sussex in the 17th century. The 1603 Returns of Communicants covered only 250 parishes out of some 315 in Sussex and the total number of adult recusants was put at 262 – 109 men and 153 women.[2] The detailed lists for 81 parishes in the Archdeaconry of Lewes record only 53 recusants, less than 0.5% of the communicant population, whereas an analysis of presentments for the Archdeaconry of Chichester and its associated peculiars to five assizes

between 1624 and 1628 reveals that 552 individuals were reported as recusants, though the highest total for a single return was 300.[3] Of these recusants, almost a half lived in the parishes of Midhurst (211) and Easebourne (56) under the patronage of Viscount Montague. A list of recusants presented to the April 1625 Quarter Sessions at Chichester lists 237 people, of whom 123 came from Midhurst.[4] The 1641 Protestation Returns, which include recusants, are now thought to be significantly unreliable as a guide to the incidence of Catholicism.[5] In Midhurst, for example, 210 adult males signed the Protestation on 18 February 1642, and 54, classed as 'Recusant Papists', refused. Two days later, 35 of the 54 capitulated and took the oath, though they were still classified as 'Recusant Papists'. The Churchwardens' Presentments for Midhurst in 1641 record the names of 129 Catholics, of whom 75 were women and only 54 were men and, of these, only 38 appear in the Protestation Returns.[6] In the same year 168 people were presented as recusants in the eastern division of the county and 139 of them lived in one of the centres of rural Catholicism.[7] In 1657, as a result of the Act of 26 June 1657, 222 recusants were brought to account in Sussex.[8] The Compton Census, recording 385 recusants scattered in 47 parishes, but with three-quarters of their number concentrated in only ten parishes, suggests a Catholic population of less than 1%, but it is unlikely to have fallen so low. A significant fact revealed by these statistics is that two-thirds of the parishes in which Catholics were listed and three-quarters of the individual Catholics were in western Sussex. The secular clergy were well organised, with nine priests working in the county in 1631, and a number of chaplaincies funded by the laity, while after 1600 Jesuit and Benedictine missioners were to be found in many Catholic houses.[9]

Dissent from the teaching of the established Church led to the formation of nonconformist sects such as Anabaptists, Independents and Presbyterians as well as Quakers. Protestant nonconformity was more widely spread than recusancy, especially in the eastern half of the county. Although the term recusancy was originally

used to describe Protestant dissenters as well as Catholics, neither group was mentioned in the 1603 Returns, and it is unlikely that there were more than a few Protestants who would have refused to attend their parish church. Household religion was the essence of Puritanism and, until permanent meeting places were provided, worship took place in private rooms, which might exist for only a short period, so that locations of Protestant nonconformity changed relatively frequently. Many Puritan clergy undoubtedly conformed in the first decades of the 17th century, though ten were deprived in the aftermath of the Hampton Court Conference and, until the rise of Arminianism, the Puritan gentry were not fundamentally opposed to the Established Church.[10] The Arminian reforms of Bishops Montague and Duppa led to the emergence of a Puritan party among the gentry.[11] During the Civil War and Commonwealth the hierarchy of the Church of England was abolished, attempts were made by Presbyterians to become the established church and nonconformist congregations flourished. Following the Act of Uniformity 1662 large numbers of clergy were ejected from their livings for refusing to comply with the Revised Book of Common Prayer, 65 Puritan ministers were ejected from their livings in Sussex, and dissenters were subject to persecution.[12] In the 1669 Return 50 Protestant Conventicles were recorded in Sussex, and Lyon Turner, assuming an estimate of between 50 or 90 hearers, suggested a total of 3,000-4,000 nonconformists. Caplan argued that even the lower estimate of hearers was probably too high, since the Compton Census gave a figure of 2,452, or about 5% of the total population.[13] Yet the 1669 Return did not record Conventicles at Chichester or Horsham. The Toleration Act 1689 permitted freedom of worship for all Protestant dissenters, and purpose-built meeting houses began to be erected. The Common Fund Surveys made in 1690-91 show that there were then 23 dissenting ministers working in the county.[14]

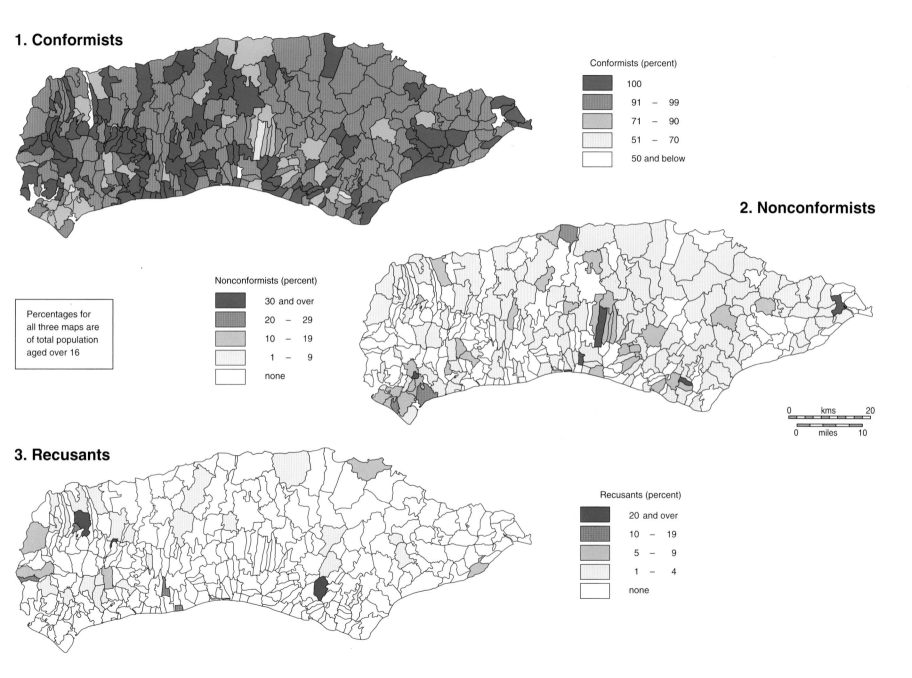

1. Conformists

Conformists (percent)
- 100
- 91 – 99
- 71 – 90
- 51 – 70
- 50 and below

2. Nonconformists

Nonconformists (percent)
- 30 and over
- 20 – 29
- 10 – 19
- 1 – 9
- none

Percentages for
all three maps are
of total population
aged over 16

3. Recusants

Recusants (percent)
- 20 and over
- 10 – 19
- 5 – 9
- 1 – 4
- none

0   kms   20

0   miles   10

Whilst Sussex was not the site of great battles of national significance, the pattern of events during the Civil War reveals one county's experience of the complex social, political and economic factors that determined support for either Crown or Parliament. The key resource of the Sussex iron industry, its nearness to London and its position as a possible source of royalist arms and money from France – as well as the King's potential escape route – meant that it was a region that Parliament needed to keep under firm control.[1] In the broadest sense, it is usually argued that there was a divide between a staunchly Parliamentarian eastern half or even two-thirds of the county, and a more instinctively royalist west which therefore was fought over, but from which the King's supporters were never able to penetrate east.[2] Yet this rough geographical divide conceals differences of loyalty within certain urban areas, particularly the city of Chichester where merchant classes supported Parliament but resident clergy and gentry from surrounding estates supported the King.[3] There were more pockets of royalist allegiance in downland areas than along the Coastal Plain. It is noteworthy that, despite the potential benefits that towns on a relatively long coastline might gain from the imposition of Ship Money, only Hastings held out for the King.[4] As the 1640s progressed, grievances, especially about religious practice, and resulting disturbance emerged less from underlying loyalty to the monarchy than from discontent with a Parliament now accepted as the effective government.

Activity in late 1642 centred on the control of Chichester, where supporters of both sides trained near each other, until mid-November when royalist forces led by Sir Edward Ford of Uppark took control. Ford then attempted to march towards Lewes but was stopped at Haywards Heath. Early in December, Sir William Waller, fresh from his capture of Farnham Castle and the city of Winchester for Parliament, prepared his attack on Chichester by first taking Arundel Castle, garrisoned by 100 royalist troops. Chichester surrendered to Waller on 28 December after a siege of eight days. Much of 1643 proved quiet, though Colonel Herbert Morley described the county as 'full of neuters and malignants'. The year

was to end, however, in the most dramatic events involving the greatest numbers of the entire war in Sussex and certainly the costliest in terms of lives and structural damage. In late November, the royalist Lord Hopton moved into the county from Hampshire, took Petersfield and the lightly-garrisoned houses of Stansted and Cowdray and moved on to Arundel where, after the surrender of 9 December, he established a garrison of 1,000 men. The Parliamentary response was swift, Waller raising 10,000 troops, re-taking Cowdray and laying siege to Arundel on 13 December. It finally fell on 6 January 1644 after considerable starvation and lack of water and 6,000 troops were subsequently garrisoned here. This victory secured Waller the title of major-general, a title he held over the four associated counties of Hampshire, Surrey, Sussex and Kent.

The fall of Arundel effectively ended the first Civil War in Sussex and there was thereafter no serious threat to Parliamentary supremacy. In fact, during 1645 troops were removed from Chichester and Arundel to the Parliamentary siege of Basing House in Hampshire, causing some alarm whenever small bands of royalist forces mustered on the western borders. Discontent manifested itself at this time in the rise of the Clubmen, associations of men devoted to seeking disarmament. The 600 who met at Duncton Down and the 1,000 at Rooks Hill on 17-18 September precipitated the summoning of troops who then attacked the Clubmen's headquarters at Walberton four days later. In October it was noted that disquiet made the raising of money for Sir Thomas Fairfax's army extremely difficult. There remained a running sore of royalist activity, particularly during 1648 when insurgents at Horsham, having refused to pay taxes the year before, had to be dispersed and fined, a plot to seize Chichester was unmasked and an attempt was made on the magazine at Rye. These events reveal more, however, about nervous anticipation of French and Dutch raids on the coast than any serious threat to Parliament's control. By 1651, it was against the background of relatively assured supremacy and quiet vigilance that the drama of the last leg of Charles II's escape after defeat at Worcester took place; the Sussex militia had been ordered

to Oxford earlier that year and only two bodies of troops remained in the county. More than a month after the battle, the King moved in disguise between safe houses in Sussex before departing the country from Shoreham on 15 October.[5]

Destruction of property within the county was quite widespread but, in common with the south-east of England generally and unlike areas such as the Midlands or the Welsh borders, there was little deliberate razing of buildings.[6] Some larger towns and the city of Chichester suffered more than smaller market towns; Chichester in particular was subject to some wholesale demolition for needs of defence, especially in the suburbs. A few churches were badly damaged, notably that at Arundel, whose tower was used by Waller to attack the castle at the end of 1643. Great houses that had been fortified were sometimes

Sir William Waller

damaged by powder explosions. Moves by the Sussex Committee in November 1644 to pull down a number of houses that had proved sites of contention, such as Cowdray, were thwarted, the houses being garrisoned or left empty, their outer walls and doors removed instead.[7] By 1648, claims for damage were officially heard; 38 claimants at Arundel had property losses amounting to £3,772.[8]

Arguably the greatest impact of the Civil War was the shift of the old polarisation in religious adherence. Certain Catholic strongholds, usually centred on great houses, remained. As Parliament forced Puritan incumbents on many parishes after 1648, the result was that after the post-Restoration Act of Uniformity of 1662 one quarter of the clergy were ejected or resigned their posts.[9] Significantly, many of the poorest classes turned away from the old Puritan-High Anglican divide to become Quakers and Baptists. George Fox founded the Society of Friends at Horsham in 1655 and thenceforward many communities of dissenters flourished, so that by 1669, for example, 200 Quakers were established at the small town of Steyning.[10]

The accompanying map, greatly indebted to Armstrong's example, shows only the major troop movements of the winters of 1642 and 1643, some major skirmishes of those campaigns and the re-taking of Horsham and Rye for Parliament after the risings of 1648.[11] The significance of Chichester and Arundel for both sides, and a small concentration of royalist great houses commanding the approaches to these places, account for military activity being largely concentrated in the western extremes of the county.

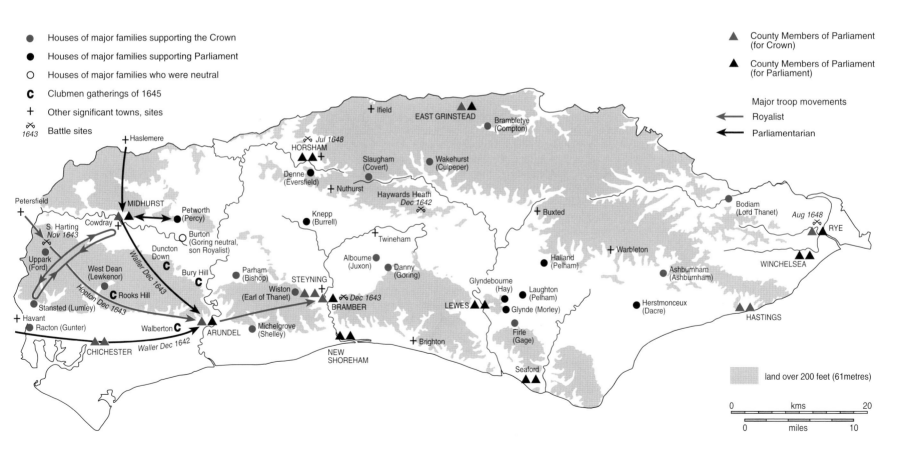

59

The study of vernacular timber-framed buildings in Sussex was pioneered by R.T. Mason, a surveyor, during the late 1940s, at much the same time that the first listings were being carried out.[1] At first, he worked almost alone but, in the 1960s, a group of those who had been inspired by the work of both Mason and J.R. Armstrong formed the Wealden Buildings Study Group, producing detailed studies of Charlwood (Surrey), Steyning, Horsham and Rudgwick.[2] Subsequent years saw the birth of the Weald and Downland Open Air Museum at Singleton, the Surrey Domestic Buildings Research Group and the Rape of Hastings Architectural Survey.[3]

The combined researches of these groups and individuals are now facilitating a more informed approach to the recording and evaluation of the construction and historical development of timber-framed buildings in Sussex.

It is accepted that most vernacular houses in Sussex from the late 13th century to the mid-16th century were built with box-frames and common rafter roofs. In plan these consisted of a large room without a first floor, known as an open hall, flanked by floored bays at each end. These are called solar and service, which are terms borrowed from supra-vernacular houses, and relate to the functions of the rooms. These houses were heated with a single hearth towards the middle of the open hall. The roof construction was, in the main, of the type known as 'crown-post with collar purlin', with each pair of rafters collared. For the student of framed buildings this is the period classified as 'medieval'.

The most widely misused description of a medieval timber-framed house is 'wealden', which tends to be applied to any such house in the Weald. This term has been ascribed to Mason, and was used to define a very particular type of building; one with a single span roof over an open hall and floored ends, but where the upper floors of the ends were jettied forward, giving the hall the appearance of being recessed. He observed a number in his area with these features in common, but we now know that this style can be found country-wide, in most areas where there is timber-framing. The best known example is Bayleaf at the Weald and Downland Open Air Museum,

and now we know even that to be atypical, as it was not built at one time.

A combination of socio-economic change and building innovation fuelled the most significant transition. The open hall 'medieval' building was changed to the 'post-medieval' fully-floored house with built-in smoke control, be it a plastered timber hood, bay, or masonry chimney. Timber-framed buildings constructed without an open hall are classified as 'post-medieval', although this is an over-simplification. In parallel with the development of new constructions went the adaptation and extension of older buildings, and the use of other materials such as brick, stone and flint in combination with timber-framing.

From these classifications have emerged a number of sub-divisions, many of them warranting separate treatment. More detailed study has identified a number of early buildings, dating from *c.*1250 to *c.*1350, with features which reflect a period of transition from more primitive constructions and plan forms. Roofs of collared rafters without purlins or crown-posts, with parallel bracing and corner ties, aisles, base crucks and evidence of variations from the 'normal' plan, have all challenged our understanding of building and development.

Increased recording has also begun to demonstrate a pattern of changing ratios from east to west between open halls with crown-posts and those with side-purlins (more predominant in Hampshire). It is highlighting differences between parishes, illustrating in a positive way the variations in socio-economic conditions, and it has revealed examples of 'foreign' constructions, sometimes explicable through documentary sources.

The distribution maps of recorded buildings are based almost entirely upon a simplistic division between medieval and post-medieval construction. Apparent anomalies and lacunæ may be accounted for both by the lack of current information on many parishes, and by variations in economic and social factors. The west of the region suffers from a lack of investigators, though not from a lack of surviving buildings. The coastal area has suffered from modern development, which has swept away most earlier buildings.[4]

It must be stressed that the buildings which survive to be recorded generally represent less than 50% of the buildings existing in the 17th century. To get a more rounded view comparisons must be made with contemporary distributions of population and taxation. There are also surviving vernacular buildings constructed from flint, brick and stone, although these tend to be from the post-medieval period, and specific to certain localities. Current data suggests that medieval houses survive best within the wealden towns and large villages, compared with a more general post-medieval spread. But when plotted against household densities in 1724 (map 3), survival appears generally better in the east of Sussex than in the central and western parishes – an unexplained pattern which requires further investigation by the increasing numbers of enthusiasts from different backgrounds, united by a shared fascination with the buildings themselves.

A typical open-hall house at Sayers Common

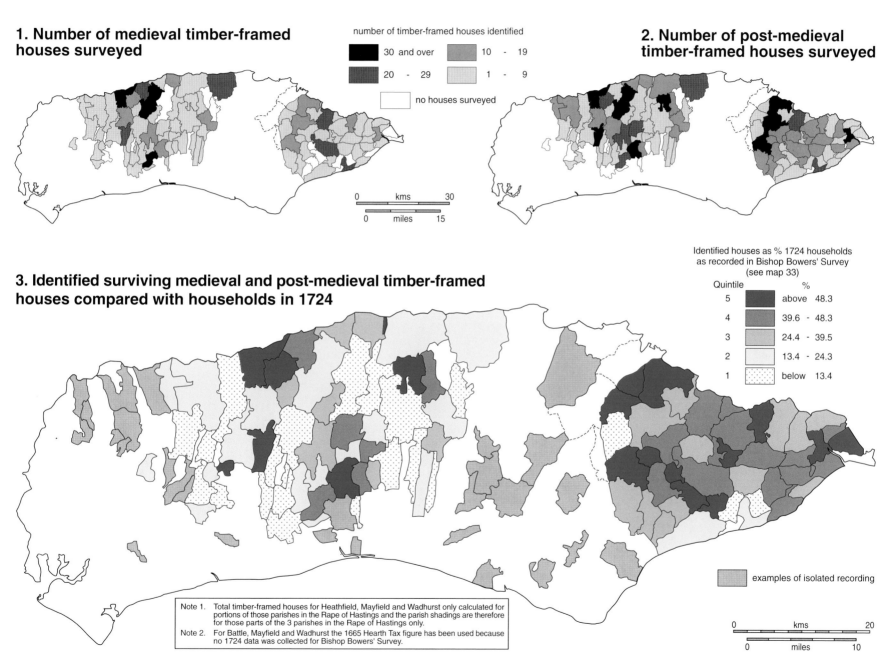

1. Number of medieval timber-framed houses surveyed

number of timber-framed houses identified

- 30 and over
- 20 - 29
- 10 - 19
- 1 - 9
- no houses surveyed

2. Number of post-medieval timber-framed houses surveyed

0 — kms — 30

0 — miles — 15

3. Identified surviving medieval and post-medieval timber-framed houses compared with households in 1724

Identified houses as % 1724 households as recorded in Bishop Bowers' Survey (see map 33)

Quintile		%
5		above 48.3
4		39.6 - 48.3
3		24.4 - 39.5
2		13.4 - 24.3
1		below 13.4

examples of isolated recording

Note 1. Total timber-framed houses for Heathfield, Mayfield and Wadhurst only calculated for portions of those parishes in the Rape of Hastings and the parish shadings are therefore for those parts of the 3 parishes in the Rape of Hastings only.

Note 2. For Battle, Mayfield and Wadhurst the 1665 Hearth Tax figure has been used because no 1724 data was collected for Bishop Bowers' Survey.

0 — kms — 20

0 — miles — 10

61

David Crossley

The map of post-medieval Sussex industries emphasises the reliance of ironmasters on supplies of ore and charcoal, and their need to site furnaces and forges on reliable rivers and streams. For the glass industry the need was largely for fuel; sand and clays were essential in small quantities, so could come from a wider area. The distribution of the iron industry follows the wealden clays, whence ore was dug, and where soil favoured managed woodlands rather than agriculture.

Particularly important was the fuel from coppices, and although archaeological attention has concentrated on the making of iron and glass, the woods provided for a wider trade. To the east, in Kentish as well as Sussex parishes, it was essential in the dyeing of cloth.[1] Wood went to urban industrial and domestic hearths: the northern Weald supplied London, the south-east fed a coastal trade. Structural timber was required for buildings and for shipping, and management allowed for this by leaving standards growing amongst the coppice stools. Competition in the firewood market produced biased accounts of the activities of wealden ironmasters, who were accused of felling woods.[2] This was no doubt for coppicing, to produce poles suited to charcoal production. This affected the interests of town firewood merchants, as those of the Cinque Ports, who were shut out of lands whose owners had either built ironworks or leased mill-sites to ironmasters, in agreements which included dedicated coppice. In the 17th century approximately one quarter of the surface of the ironmaking district of the Weald had to be under coppice to satisfy the iron industry, leaving the rest to agriculture, to commons on poorer lands, and to woods used for other purposes.[3] The development of iron production in the western Weald, in the second half of the 16th century, led to competition with the traditional glass industry, intensified by the arrival of immigrant French glass makers in the decades after 1567.[4] In the early 17th century, attacks on the glass industry's use of wood led to its rapid and total conversion to the use of coal by 1620.

If the woods of the Weald were the essential basis for the siting of iron and glass production, the rapid growth

of these industries stemmed from demographic and political circumstances. The regional market for iron in the 16th century increased in line with the wealth of London and its supply areas. The city's population quadrupled over the century and, as farmers in the home counties prospered as a result, they improved their equipment and their buildings. Although the vernacular architecture of the region (map 30) was based on timber, a typical house also used quantities of iron for fastenings and fittings. Similarly, the thriving coastal and deep-sea shipping fleets used iron on some scale. Added to this long-term growth in the market for iron was the sporadic need for armaments. Armies, navies and coastal fortifications required iron, notably the naval ships built in the dockyards of the Thames and Portsmouth, during the period of the political isolation of Henry VIII and in the Spanish wars of the reign of Elizabeth. In the 17th and 18th centuries fluctuating demand for arms imparted more instability, particularly in the final century of the wealden industry, although it remained a major supplier of ordnance to the Crown.[5] These guns amounted to a dangerously large proportion of regional iron output, at a time when much of the common trade was being supplied from elsewhere in England.

The industry at the end of the Middle Ages, which was the basis for this growth, is not well researched. Such archaeological and archival evidence as exists indicates unpowered bloomeries in the 14th century, sited on wooded ore outcrops and sufficient to supply the Crown with iron products in time of war. We

would expect that in the later Middle Ages there would have been a shift to the valleys as water power was used, as elsewhere in Britain and on the continent of Europe. The evidence is slight, confined to the excavated hammer forge at Chingley, just over the border in Kent. In the 16th century the picture changes. The continental development of the blast furnace, producing molten iron for casting, in contrast with the solid product of the bloomery, is known from the 13th century onwards in Scandinavia and in Germany.[6] The blast furnace appears to have been brought to the central High Weald by French

The Richard Lenard fireback, 1636

ironworkers in the half century after 1496, accompanied by a perfected means of converting high-carbon, brittle, cast, (pig) iron into malleable bar in the finery forge.[7] The archaeology of the post-medieval iron industry has confirmed these changes, and those sites in Sussex and nearby parts of Kent where substantial excavation has taken place are indicated on the map. Blast furnaces have been excavated at Batsford (Herstmonceux), Chingley (Lamberhurst, Kent), North Park (Fernhurst), Maynards Gate (Rotherfield), Panningridge (Dallington) and Pippingford (Hartfield), and Scarlets (Cowden, Kent).[8]

Forges have been examined at Ardingly, Blackwater Green(Worth) and at Chingley.[9] The essential features of the two types of site are now established, and the similarities with those known on the Continent, notably in north-east France, are clear. Furnaces were stone towers, about 5m square, with a height of probably 6m, as established from survivors elsewhere in Britain and Europe, and from continental drawings. Their bellows were driven by water wheels supplied from the ponds where earthwork remains are frequently encountered in wealden valleys. The location of furnaces can also be

established from adjoining deposits of slag. In the case of furnaces producing castings such as guns, rollers, or pipes, a typical feature is the timber or brick-lined pit in which moulds were set. Forges also were water-powered, and there is evidence that some occupied the sites of former water-powered bloomeries. Their buildings were less substantial than those of the blast furnace, giving little archaeological information about covering structures or conversion hearths, but usually containing significant remains of hammers, in the form of ground-level timber frames and pits for the bases of anvils.

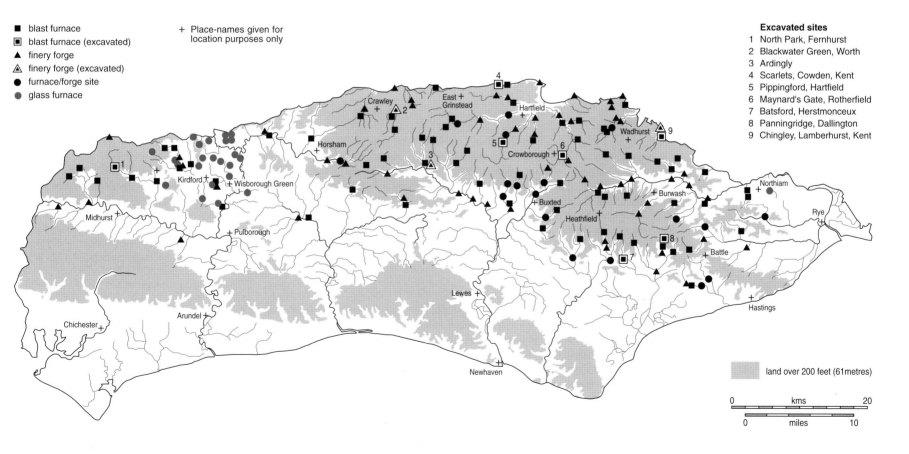

- ■ blast furnace
- ◨ blast furnace (excavated)
- ▲ finery forge
- △ finery forge (excavated)
- ● furnace/forge site
- ● glass furnace

+ Place-names given for location purposes only

Excavated sites
1 North Park, Fernhurst
2 Blackwater Green, Worth
3 Ardingly
4 Scarlets, Cowden, Kent
5 Pippingford, Hartfield
6 Maynard's Gate, Rotherfield
7 Batsford, Herstmonceux
8 Panningridge, Dallington
9 Chingley, Lamberhurst, Kent

land over 200 feet (61 metres)

0   kms   20

0   miles   10

63

Lewes is located on a spur of the Downs which borders the broad, alluvial valley of the Ouse on the north and east and that of the Winterbourne on the south (map 1). With the steep-sided Paddock to the north-west, the land-bridge onto the spur is on the west where 'a defence of earthworks, probably of Saxon date, can still be traced each side of the site of the medieval West Gate' [a - see map 2].[1] This readily defensible site almost certainly was the location of the Anglo-Saxon *burh* recorded at Lewes in the Burghal Hidage of *c.*AD900. [2]

The historically distinct and independent settlements of Cliffe to the east and Southover to the south eventually became part of Lewes at its incorporation as a borough in 1881. For centuries prior to this the town was perceived as an ancient borough, though nominally it was subordinate to the lords of the manor through the manorial courts over which the lords' official presided.

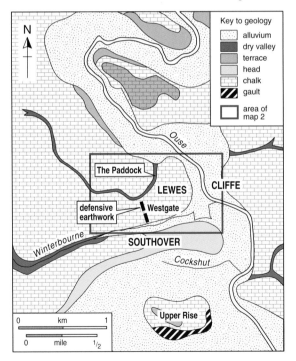

1. The geological setting of Lewes

In practice, however, the jury of the court leet had come to acquire a semi-autonomous existence known as the 'society', 'company' or 'fellowship' of the twelve, from which two members were appointed each year as high constables of the town.[3]

By the early 17th century Lewes had expanded beyond the promontory, though hardly beyond the bounds of the 'borough'. Two contemporary maps describe a linear settlement along the High Street from St Anne's church, 'where the bounderstone of this Burrowe lyeth over against the east end of the Chauncell', to the river bridge, new-built in 1561 and again some 40 to 50 years later.[4] Side streets and twittens at regular intervals, particularly on the south side of the High Street, join the encircling roads at the bottom. Some of them, notably St Mary's Lane (now Station Street), were built up, but, with the exception of the extensive remains of the castle, there are very few buildings shown behind the north side of the High Street towards St John's church. There is evidence to suggest, however, that parts of this area were built on at times during the medieval period; thus, some shrinkage or relocation of the urban area by about 1600 may be deduced.[5] A few metres outside the borough, west of St Anne's church, are shown a post mill [b] and the remains of the medieval hospital of St Nicholas [c], later used as a poorhouse for St Anne's parish. A number of crofts ranging in size from two roods to six acres (0.2 to 2.4ha), the larger ones often developed with barns and outbuildings, occupied much of the open ground on the promontory.[6]

Lewes appears to have been a relatively prosperous town in the later 16th century. Norden, for example, characterises it in 1595 as 'a plentifull market town [which] standeth in a most firtilly place for corne, pasture, woode, fish, fowle, sheepe and health'.[7] In addition to its fertile hinterland (Norden might well have included iron in his list) two other factors contributed to this perceived prosperity – that the town was an administrative centre for the eastern half of the county, and that it controlled river traffic (north/south) and a downland routeway with a river crossing (east/west).

During the 16th century Lewes emerged as the focal point in eastern Sussex from which local government and justice were administered. Country gentry and

lawyers found it convenient to have a base in Lewes, and upwards of 30 gentry and titled families were resident and/or property owners in the town between 1615 and 1620. Indeed, so fashionable did Lewes become that, in the first half of the 17th century, it served as the centre of a marriage market for the gentry community of eastern Sussex.[8]

Lewes was also well located for business, and the Ouse was the conduit along which flowed much of the trade on which local prosperity was based. Southdown grain and wool and wealden iron were sent down the river bound for London and elsewhere, and groceries, wines, spices, textiles and salt, amongst other goods, were imported for local sale and distribution – thus, in the 1620s, Richard Newton imported currants, prunes and spices for sale at his shop on the north-west corner of Watergate Lane [d].[9] Access to the town by road was good and it was the first bridging-point of the river from the sea. The town's provision and produce markets and the livestock fairs were important weekly and annual events in the economy of central Sussex.

Perhaps the most obvious manifestation of the wealth brought into, and created within, Lewes during the latter half of the 16th and early 17th centuries was in the fabric of the town itself. From about 1550 town houses for the gentry and substantial homes for local professionals and merchants appeared along and adjacent to the High Street.

Prominent among these buildings on the south side of the High Street were The Friars [e], built probably by John Kyme, steward to Sir William Petre, secretary of state from 1543 to 1566, on the ruins of the friary at the eastern entrance to the town; the Pelham family's first town-house [f] (now the *White Hart*), refashioned in 1568; courtier George Goring's mansion [g] (now Pelham House) of 1579 in St Andrew's Lane; and brother Henry Goring's town-house of 1583 [h] (now the Westgate Centre) tucked in behind the *Bull Inn* [i] (itself 15th-century with 16th-century additions and, along with the *White Horse* [j], the *Star* [k], and the *White Lion* [l], one of the main taverns in the town in 1620).

On the north side was Barbican House [m], with a surviving fireplace of 1579, which was rebuilt at this time by merchant and sometime high constable, John Holmwood; whilst its neighbour on the opposite corner of Castlegate [n] was extended for William Dodson, the goldsmith, in the 1620s. Outside the West Gate and up the hill towards Ireland's Lane stood the old *Vine Inn* [o] (now the *Shelley's Hotel*) which was rebuilt in 1577 by Thomas Pelland, a Southover brewer, and sold in 1588 as a town-house to Thomas Sackville, Lord Buckhurst, in whose family it remained for 75 years. In addition to these and many other private buildings, the market house outside Castlegate [p] and, about 150 metres east, the Sessions House [q], both in the road, were built in the 1560s, and the House of Correction [r] for the Rapes of Lewes and Pevensey in 1610.[10]

Lewes was, perhaps, the most urbanised settlement in eastern Sussex at this time. Certainly, Camden considered that 'for populousness and extent it may be ranked among the principal towns in the county'; and it is demonstrably the case that a Lewesian was less likely to describe himself, or be described, as either a yeoman or a husbandman, those twin pillars of rural society, than his counterpart elsewhere in eastern Sussex. Of those grooms and sureties whose residence and occupation were recorded in marriage licences within the archdeaconry of Lewes between 1615 and 1620, only 16% of Lewesians were described as yeoman or husbandman. This figure increases to 34% at Hastings, 65% at East Grinstead, 78% at Hailsham, and to 100% at Westmeston.[11]

For all the new building, however, the townscape experienced by this urban population was dominated by the medieval castle, notwithstanding that parts of it were being dismantled and carted away at 4d a load in the 1620s for building work elsewhere. Four hundred years later the surviving remains of the castle continue to overlook the administrative capital for most of eastern Sussex and, furthermore, have themselves become the focal point of a thriving tourist trade.

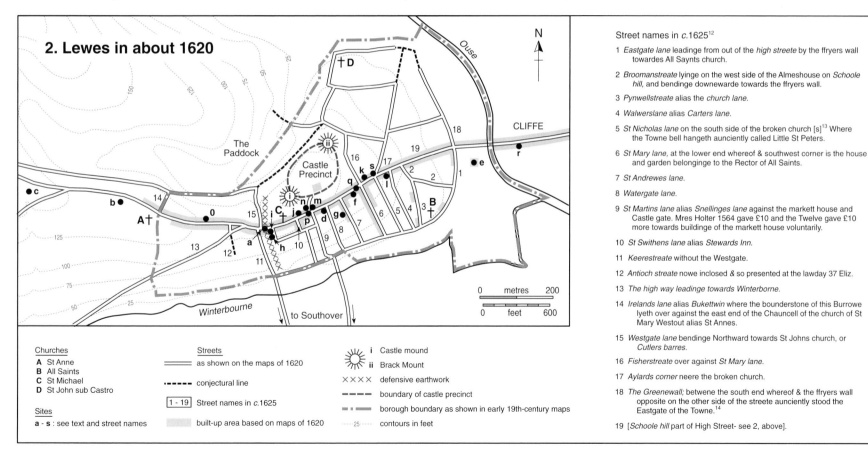

2. Lewes in about 1620

Churches
A St Anne
B All Saints
C St Michael
D St John sub Castro

Sites
a - s : see text and street names

Streets
——— as shown on the maps of 1620
▪▪▪▪ conjectural line
1 - 19 Street names in *c*.1625
built-up area based on maps of 1620

i Castle mound
ii Brack Mount
×××× defensive earthwork
▬ ▬ boundary of castle precinct
▬ ▪ borough boundary as shown in early 19th-century maps
····25···· contours in feet

65

David Martin, Brian Short and Peter Wilkinson

The Compton Census 1676

Henry Compton (1632-1713), Bishop of London from 1675, was entrusted to ascertain the numbers of inhabitants, and Catholic and Protestant nonconformists in the country:

'First, What number of persons or at least families are by common account and estimation inhabiting within each parish subject under them [i.e. the Bishops]. Secondly, what number of Popish recusants, or such as are suspected of recusancy, are there among such inhabitants at present? Thirdly, what number of other Dissenters are resident in such parishes, which either obstinately refuse, or wholly absent themselves from, the Communion of the Church of England at such times as by law they are required?'[1]

The survey was undertaken within each parish by the incumbent, churchwardens and archdeacons. Compton received the returns, drawn up in three columns corresponding to the questions. Their accuracy in revealing the numbers of Catholics and Dissenters is certainly open to question, so too is the use of the aggregate figures for demographic purposes.[2] What, for example, was being counted? It was intended that all males and females over 16 in each of the three categories would be revealed, and this was almost certainly the most common practice. However, some dioceses just returned heads of household, or all males. Some returned the entire population, some may (or may not) have counted servants, and the first column of the returns in the original manuscript sometimes refers to inhabitants and sometimes to conformists. In order to arrive at entire populations for each parish, the use of multipliers is normal, but such a practice gives population figures which can vary quite widely, depending on the multiplier chosen and the assumption as to what actually is counted in the original data. Following the recent work of Crockett and Snell, building upon that of Whiteman, we can be fairly certain that the initial column in the case of Sussex did represent conformists.[3] Adding all three columns together, therefore,

gives totals for adults (16 years and over) which have been plotted here as densities per 100 acres (40ha). No multiplier is used for the reasons given, and because no overall multiplier could be assumed to remain constant for all rural and urban parishes in the different regions of Sussex.[4]

Bishop Bowers' Survey 1724

Whilst the Compton Census was taken on a national scale, the 1724 enquiry was a local device to assist Thomas Bowers, Bishop of Chichester from 1722 to 1724, in managing the diocese efficiently.[5] Each incumbent was now presented with 13 questions on such topics as the state of the church building and parsonage, the frequency of services, parochial charities, and numbers of families, together with Papists and Dissenters.[6] The practice of making such enquiries was becoming fashionable, pioneered by Archbishop Wake for Lincoln in 1706 and Canterbury in 1716.

The seventh question asked for 'the number of families residing in the parish; and if any Papists, how many families? Also if any Protestant dissenters, how many of them and of what sort?' The answers will again present problems to the demographer. Would the incumbent try to enhance his image by understating the numbers of nonconformists, and how would this affect his totals? Probably the Bowers' returns are no more scrupulous in counting nonconformists than other contemporary surveys, which frequently did understate nonconformist numbers. Did he distinguish between a family and a household? And how accurate was his arithmetic? Definitions of 'family' are lacking, and numbers are suspiciously rounded. A further difficulty is that the catchment for the survey excluded the Dean's Peculiar of Chichester and the Archbishop's Peculiars of South Malling and of Pagham and Tarring. In the latter case, however, figures from Archbishop Wake's 1716 survey can be inserted.[7] By so doing, 268 parishes out of 312 have figures, compared with Compton's 284. Despite these reservations, Bowers provides a useful complement to Compton. At the most basic level the survey provides for some parishes where the 1676 survey was defective.

Population Trends

During the 16th and early 17th centuries population continued to grow following its late medieval decline. Natural growth (ie a surplus of christenings over burials) characterised the eastern Weald and, from the early 17th century, growth consistently outstripped that on the Downs and Coastal Plain. But growth everywhere was punctuated by localised epidemics, and more generally by the plague of 1665-6. These, coupled with the uncertainties of the Civil War and migration to London, contributed to a static or even declining population after about 1640.[8] Other localised factors included the loss of employment in the wealden iron industry, marshland malaria, and downland depopulation related to agricultural engrossment and extensification. By 1676 there were high densities in the eastern and western ends of the Weald and in the Coastal Plain, compared with the Downs and Marshland, and the pattern was echoed in 1724.[9] An overall estimate for adults in 1676 in Sussex gives 60,934 and for the entire population 79,824.[10] In 1724 there were an estimated 18,416 families, and multipliers of 4.25 and 4.5 yield total populations of only 78,268 or 82,872. Even allowing for multiplier errors and omissions, population was clearly static. By 1801, however, population had grown to over 159,000, and the processes by which the population standstill of the 17th and early 18th centuries was replaced by one of rapid growth is explored elsewhere in this volume.

Extracts from Q.7 of the Bishop Bowers' Survey 1724
(original spellings retained)

Burwash: There are about 200 families in the parish. There are no papists in it, or no dissenters, except a small meeting of presbyterians to which about 6 or 7 families of this parish resort.

Roegate: Families, 60. No dissenters of any sort, except 2 of the weaker sex.

West Wittering: About 70 families. All goers to church (except 2 families). No Roman Catholick.

Horsted Parva: About 20 families. No protestant dissenters. One family of popish servants, belonging to Sir William Gage.

West Firle: The number of families 34. 8 popish, 4 Anabaptists and 1 Presbyterian families.

1. Compton map, 1676

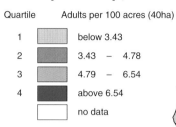

Quartile		Adults per 100 acres (40ha)
1		below 3.43
2		3.43 – 4.78
3		4.79 – 6.54
4		above 6.54
		no data

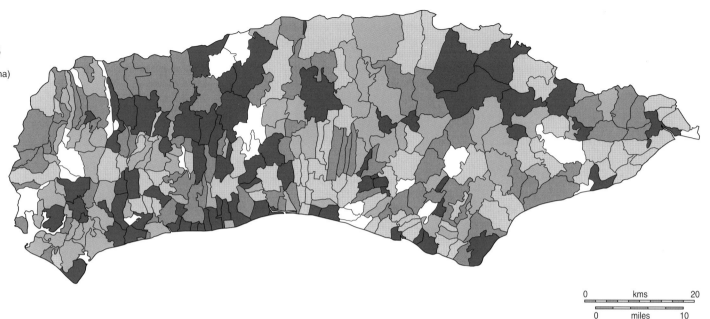

Lewes and Chichester have each been treated as a single parish. As the data of the two towns cannot be easily compared, they have simply been put in the highest quartile without specific figures.

Certain pairs of adjacent parishes for which one survey gives combined data have been combined for both surveys - ie Clayton and Keymer, Edburton and Fulking, Iping and Chithurst, West Dean and Binderton, Hastings St Clement and All Saints, Lyminster and Warningcamp, Tarring Neville and South Heighton.

2. Bowers map, 1724

Quartile		Families per 100 acres (40ha)
1		below 1.06
2		1.06 – 1.49
3		1.50 – 2.10
4		above 2.10
		no data

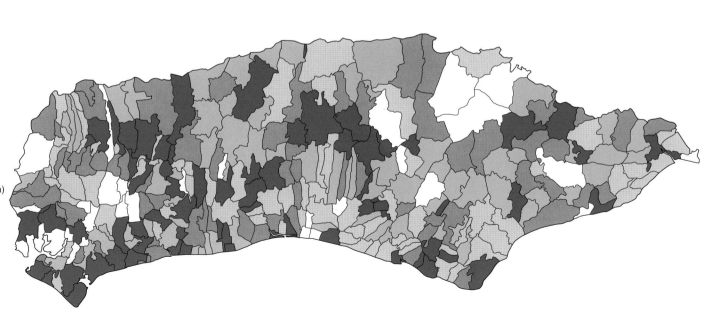

An 'Abstract of a Particular Account of all Inns, Alehouses etc. in England with Their Stable-Room and Bedding in the year 1686' in the Public Record Office presents, by county, in alphabetical order of place, columns headed *guest beds* and *stabling for horses*. No individual inn names are noted. The Sussex list has been transcribed by a clerk with no apparent knowledge of local place-names, which renders several of the locations meaningless. The document lies in a miscellaneous War Office class which suggests the abstract was made for the purpose of billeting, but the particular account cannot be traced.[1]

However, the reasons behind the Return can be deduced from the Journals of the House of Commons.[2] In the year following the failed Popish Plot of 1678, Parliament resolved 'That a Committee of the whole House do take into consideration how to improve the Militia for the Safety of the Kingdom...'. In 1683 the failed Rye House Plot to assassinate Charles II and his brother nevertheless also caused widespread horror, and James II's coronation on 6 February 1685 was followed in June by the Monmouth Rebellion. By the autumn of that year James had an army of *c.*20,000 men and on 12 November 1685 Parliament discussed bringing in a Bill 'to render the Militia more useful'. Six days later a committee was formed to consider the matter and a chairman appointed. Parliament was prorogued by the king on 20 November. Apart from five further prorogations, there are no other entries in the Journals until the Prince of Orange's Declaration of 10 October 1688 from his Court in the Hague.[3] We therefore have a nation-wide billeting return, probably organised by Sir Thomas Meres, chairman of a militia improvement committee. Agents were presumably dispatched to take details of possible billeting places in case of further danger to the king and country. Sussex, an important coastal county, was at the forefront of trouble from overseas.[4]

Innkeepers who were postmasters were meant to be exempt from billeting, though whether this worked in practice is unknown. What is certain is that soldiers were often not paid enough to cover their billeting dues, and inn and alehouse keepers were complaining of much indebtedness by the troops and lack of pay from the government.[5]

Of the 212 Sussex places listed, four are untraceable, and ten are suppositions on reasonable evidence. What is immediately apparent is that Horsham dominates the map with far more stabling facilities (365) than any other town, followed by East Grinstead (247), Lewes (245) and Chichester (221). There is a 50% drop to Petworth (122), Midhurst (118) and Brighton (95). Other port towns and those with good access to the sea, such as Arundel, Steyning, Shoreham, Eastbourne and Hastings, each have similar figures, with 40-50 stablings.

When guest bed numbers are analysed, East Grinstead (103) tops the list, with Lewes (99), Chichester (84) and Horsham (83) not far behind. Midhurst (53), Petworth (45) and Hastings (40) are the next group, then Arundel, Steyning, Shoreham, Brighton and Rye follow, with 25-31 beds each.

The list shows that 31 places have beds but no stables and eight have stables and no beds. These are likely to be alehouses. There are 88 with 1-2 beds on offer, a mixture of alehouses and small inns, while 45 have 3-5 beds, being perhaps small inns. Only 12 towns and villages have more than 20 beds. There is a big increase in stabling, with 21 places having 20-50 stablings each, but only seven towns in the county have more, between 95 and 365 stablings. The larger inns would, of course, be concentrated in the latter group.

It can be seen that Horsham is the pivotal town for travellers crossing the treacherous clay of the Weald, supplying opportunities for the hire and exchange of horses as well as livery. The main route, from London to Shoreham and Brighton, was via Dorking, Horsham and Steyning. East Grinstead, Chichester and Lewes are next in the hierarchy, and the coastal towns of Brighton and Hastings compare favourably with Midhurst and Petworth inland. Arundel, Steyning, Shoreham, Eastbourne and Rye form the next group, following by Westbourne, Battle, Rotherfield and Wadhurst. There are a few disproportionate figures, such as Nutley with 26 stablings but only nine guest beds, Crowborough with ten stablings and three beds and Whatlington with 11 guest beds and a stable for only one horse. Reasons need to be sought for these anomalies, such as that inns situated on or near steep hills would have needed an extra supply of horses.

Geological features are influential in the siting of many inns. Horsham is situated at the western end of the Hastings Beds which project here into a sea of clay, and in close proximity to the headwaters of the rivers Arun, Adur and western Rother. The High Weald is well supplied with middling accommodation, though more small-to-average inns serve the general wealden area. Fewer inns and alehouses exist in the predominantly clay areas. Alehouses are in abundance to the east of Chichester, with a scattering to the north of Hastings. Their fairly even distribution throughout the Weald clay possibly reflects the difficult and isolating nature of the terrain at all times of the year, except during the driest of summers. The easier travelling area of the chalk downland is thinly supplied with accommodation, though again stabling outweighs beds. However, the Low Weald between the Surrey border and the sandy soils of the Pulborough area shows a plentiful north/south supply of horse stablings. Horsham was the favoured and necessary port of call for those journeying from London to Chichester, Shoreham

Inn sign, East Wittering. This inn name dates from the Restoration of Charles II in 1660.

and Brighton. East Grinstead was the equine supplier for travellers going on to Lewes, Eastbourne, Hastings and Rye.

The Coastal Plain south of Chichester presents a barren scene, apart from Sidlesham which has many more guest beds than stablings (13/5) in contrast to other coastal towns which all provide more stabling than beds.[6]

The overall picture is of a county dominated by the need for stabling. More people were travelling by coach in the late 17th century, but the roads were so bad in the county, even in summer, that frequent stops and mount exchanges were required. In Henry VIII's reign 'Souseks full of dyrt and myre' had been well-known for its abominable travelling conditions. Contemporary letters and diaries up to the mid-18th century refer frequently to the dangers of travel on horseback within the county, as well as the difficulties for coaches.[7] Fuller in the mid-17th century describes Sussex as 'A fruitful county, though very dirty for the travellers therein, so that it may be better measured to its advantage by days journeys than by miles. Hence it is, that in the late order for regulating the wages of coachmen at such a price a day and distance from London, Sussex alone is excepted, as wherein shorter way or better pay was allowed.'[8]

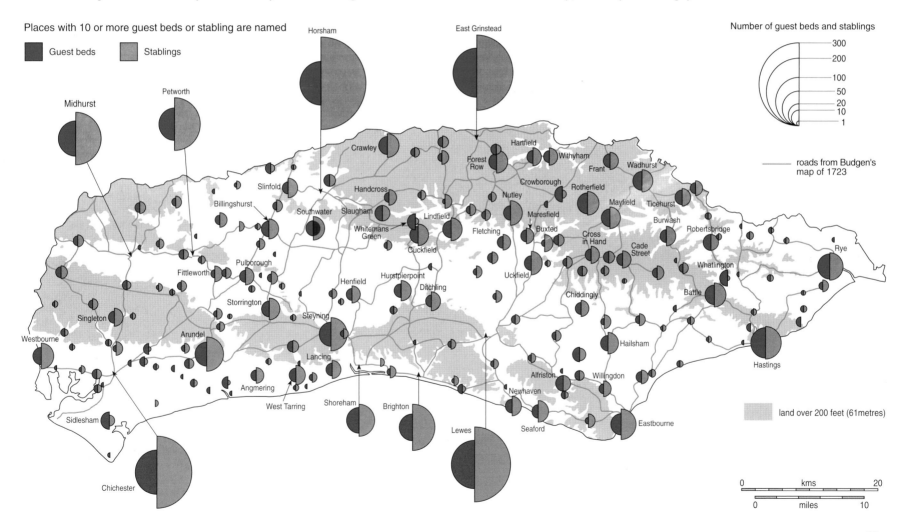

Places with 10 or more guest beds or stabling are named

Guest beds   Stablings

Number of guest beds and stablings

300
200
100
50
20
10
1

roads from Budgen's map of 1723

land over 200 feet (61 metres)

0 kms 20
0 miles 10

69

The Old Poor Law 1700-1835

Many parishes had either poorhouses or workhouses in this period (map 1).[1] Those sharing workhouses – notably through the adoption of Gilbert's Act 1782 – are not individually identified. The Gilbert Unions, and administrations formed under Local Acts, are also shown.

The 1601 Act, forming the statutory basis for poor-law administration until the 1834 Poor Law Amendment Act, contained little on accommodation.[2] Parochial officials were to provide 'convenient houses' for the impotent poor without any work provision. Ambiguities over the meaning of 'impotent' were responsible for synonymous 18th-century usage of 'workhouse' and 'poorhouse'. Some were rented, others purchased and altered; few were purpose-built, though exceptions include those by Local Act authorities at Chichester (1753) and Brighton (1810). Buildings holding over 50 were uncommon, though Eastbourne's purchase of the redundant army barracks (*c.*1816) accommodated 200.

Additionally, parishes owned cottages for letting to families, though rows of tenements could resemble a poorhouse without a master; the Framfield exemplar partly functioned as a village brothel. Parishes only having cottages are excluded from map 1.

Rising poor-relief costs, fears over the growing numbers of paupers and relief paid to able-bodied claimants, strengthened concepts of the 'deserving' and 'undeserving' poor, and generated interest in provision to combine discipline, economies of scale, and profits through the sale of goods made by inmates. Knatchbull's permissory Act 1722 enabled parishes to combine to finance workhouses and impose residency as a condition of relief to the able-bodied, but no Sussex parishes appear to have combined under the Act, though Northiam added a new manufactory to its existing house (1770s). Many parishes, including Rye and Battle, experimented with contractors paid on a per capita basis for their charges; they sought further profit from manufacturing. Cuckfield's 'Manufactory of Woollen and linen Cloths' still functioned in 1835. Accommodation for the non-able bodied, especially the aged, was a key component of Gilbert's Act, permitting combinations of parishes sharing provision and costs under Boards of Guardians, and was widely adopted in western Sussex (map 1).

Sussex had the unenviable distinction of the highest poor-relief costs during the agricultural depression from 1815 to the 1830s. Poverty was aggravated by demobilised servicemen and the not-unrelated acceleration in the birth rate. Unemployment depressed wages; escalating allowances and various parochial work schemes ensued. Poorhouses were packed with orphaned and deserted children, the old, the infirm, the chronically sick and the insane. Costs threatened to bankrupt the worst-hit parishes, but administrators still used institutional provision to discipline difficult claimants, including insubordinate youths.[3]

Workhouses were particularly loathed in Sussex working-class circles. By 1834-5 Assistant Commissioner Hawley, faced with the awesome task of reforming relief provision, was appalled over inmates' rich diets, lax discipline and inter-mixing.

Workhouses under the New Poor Law 1835-1900

Ironically, workhouses became pivotal for radical reforms following the 1834 Poor Law Amendment Act.[4] The critical issue of non-medical relief to the able-bodied invoked the concept of 'less eligibility', activated by the workhouse test. Those unable to maintain their families would be forced to become inmates, with even lower living standards than those outside. Inmates were classified: able-bodied, elderly and infirm, children, and then separated by gender. Families were divided, strict discipline imposed. Able-bodied males' work included bone-crushing and hand-milling corn. Able-bodied females and older women did housework, while schoolteachers provided elemental education for children.[5]

In 1835 widespread violence followed the conversion from cash to payments in kind of the allowances made to the able-bodied. Most of the new Sussex Unions created after 1835 inherited several workhouses, but few were sufficiently substantial. The Commission agreed to use different workhouses within Unions to effect classification. The majority started with at least two existing houses for different inmates. Uckfield began with no less than eight: Horsham's able-bodied went to the biggest building in the town itself, while the children, aged and infirm, went to dilapidated workhouses at Shipley and Warnham. In both Unions, children were housed miles from parents, and wives from husbands, provoking riots and arson against Guardians' property (see map 37).[6]

Multiple workhouses were costly, and Boards were encouraged to build central single establishments (1836-1842) among them Hastings, Horsham, Steyning and Uckfield. Other Unions achieved this by altering the grandest Old Poor Law institutions, including the former Gilbert houses at Easebourne and Westhampnett.

Map 2 reveals considerable differences in the size of Unions. Grandees such as the Earl of Chichester refused to amalgamate 'his' parishes with those of Lewes town, which ended up with just two adjacent rural parishes. His downland empire went into Newhaven; that Board rejected the unruly smuggling centres of Alfriston and Seaford, which were foisted on Eastbourne. Lord Gage likewise kept his sphere of influence separate from Lewes; the resultant Chailey Union half ringed the town, with other parts embraced by the tiny West Firle Union. Rationalisation came only in the 1890s. Even greater problems came from obdurate Gilbert Unions, Sutton, East Preston and Arundel, who refused to dissolve.

Popularly-elected Guardians in Brighton, Chichester and Lewes knew that political survival dictated parsimonious regimes to sustain low rates for numerous small ratepayers. The predominantly rural Unions, particularly Petworth, evaded outdoor relief prohibition orders to the able-bodied. By the 1840s most Unions rarely imposed the workhouse test on the able-bodied. But workhouses were hated and certainly did deter potential claimants. The aged and infirm, orphaned and abandoned children became the principal inmates.[7] Nevertheless, Brighton extended its 1822 house, and in the late 1860s erected a new building, now the General Hospital.

The anti-New Poor Law movement exploited scandals and maladministration, emanating from the hated 'Bastilles', and Cobbett repeatedly attacked the Duke of Richmond's Westhampnett Union. Violence was endemic, and often mutual between governors and delinquents. Some former Sussex workhouse girls entered prostitution; some boys became professional criminals. The enduring fear of 'the house' was thoroughly deserved.

1. Pre-1835 Poorhouses, Workhouses, Gilbert Unions, Incorporations and Local Acts

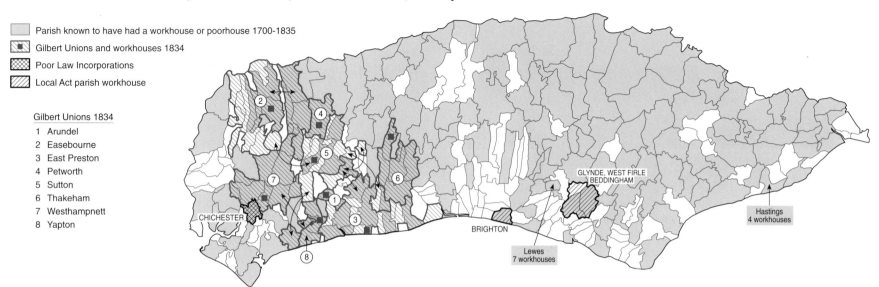

Parish known to have had a workhouse or poorhouse 1700-1835

Gilbert Unions and workhouses 1834

Poor Law Incorporations

Local Act parish workhouse

Gilbert Unions 1834

1 Arundel
2 Easebourne
3 East Preston
4 Petworth
5 Sutton
6 Thakeham
7 Westhampnett
8 Yapton

CHICHESTER

BRIGHTON

Lewes
7 workhouses

GLYNDE, WEST FIRLE
BEDDINGHAM

Hastings
4 workhouses

2. Post-1835 Poor Law Unions, Gilbert Unions, Incorporations and places under Local Acts

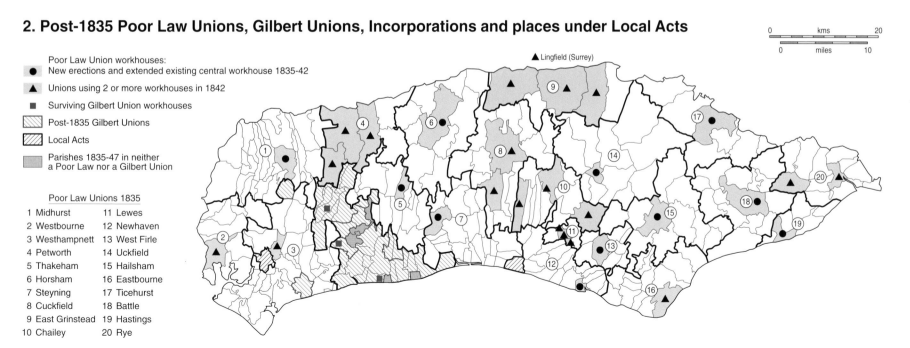

Poor Law Union workhouses:

● New erections and extended existing central workhouse 1835-42

▲ Unions using 2 or more workhouses in 1842

■ Surviving Gilbert Union workhouses

Post-1835 Gilbert Unions

Local Acts

Parishes 1835-47 in neither a Poor Law nor a Gilbert Union

Poor Law Unions 1835

1 Midhurst	11 Lewes
2 Westbourne	12 Newhaven
3 Westhampnett	13 West Firle
4 Petworth	14 Uckfield
5 Thakeham	15 Hailsham
6 Horsham	16 Eastbourne
7 Steyning	17 Ticehurst
8 Cuckfield	18 Battle
9 East Grinstead	19 Hastings
10 Chailey	20 Rye

▲ Lingfield (Surrey)

kms 20

miles 10

Richard Childs

'In 1801 the six English counties of the southern coastline accounted for one third of all England's MPs, though they contained only 15 per cent of its population.'[1]

The structure of parliamentary representation had remained essentially unaltered since the first parliament of 1295. Each county returned two MPs, as did boroughs, designated by royal charter. The system reflected medieval England, not an 18th-century country at the dawn of the Industrial Revolution.

In Sussex, ancient boroughs such as Bramber and Steyning, which had been important places in the Middle Ages, each returned two MPs, while elsewhere large manufacturing towns such as Birmingham and Leeds remained unrepresented.

Not only did the system not reflect population size, but the vast majority of men, and all women, did not have the vote. Based on a 40-shilling property qualification dating from 1430, less than 10% of adult males could vote in county elections. The franchise for borough elections was even more arcane, varying from inherited rights; membership of closed corporations; ownership of certain plots of land; payment of poor rates (scot and lot); resident householders; and freeholders.

Even if a man had the vote, he was not necessarily free to use it as he wished. Before the Ballot Act 1872 votes had to be cast in public, and after the elections poll books were published, revealing exactly how people had voted. Elections took place in a festive, not to say riotous, mood, often marked by bribery and drunkenness.

Elections were also expensive affairs. The qualification to stand as a candidate was ownership of property worth £600 per annum for a county seat and £300 per annum for a borough seat. Candidates would often have to pay the travelling and accommodation expenses of 'their' voters to visit the polling town. Elections were frequently a substantial drain on the candidates' purses, and it naturally followed that candidates came largely from the gentry and upper-middle classes.

Parliamentary elections were often uncontested. Between 1734-1832 no more than 190 of England's 489 seats were contested at any one general election. Local patrons often held constituencies as their personal fiefdoms by appointing their own candidate and controlling the votes of the electorate. In Sussex, for example, boroughs such as Horsham returned the Duke of Norfolk's candidates and, at East Grinstead, the Duchess of Dorset's nominees. Before 1832 more than half the English parliamentary boroughs had fewer than 300 electors and more than 50 boroughs had fewer than 50 voters.

There had been a wide range of proposals for reforming the system since 1770. One scheme came from the Sussex magnate, the radical 3rd Duke of Richmond, who introduced a parliamentary bill for enfranchising all adult males.[2] But all reform was resisted and it was only through a combination of factors in the next century – including an economic slump, agrarian unrest (the Captain Swing riots in the south-eastern counties), divisions in the Tory Party, and the ascendancy of the Whigs – that the first Reform Act was passed in 1832.

Under the Act, 56 of the smallest 'rotten' English boroughs were disenfranchised. Sussex lost Bramber, East Grinstead, Seaford, Steyning and Winchelsea. Other small boroughs had their representation reduced from two seats to one. The larger industrial towns of the North, including Leeds and Manchester, were enfranchised for the first time. In Sussex a new parliamentary borough of Brighton was created. County seats were also redistributed and Sussex was to return four members, two each for the Eastern and Western Divisions.

Though the 40-shilling franchise for the county electorate remained substantially unaltered by the 1832 Act, the various borough franchises were replaced by a £10 householder franchise, ie owners or occupiers of a property worth £10 per annum. The Act also established the production of registers of electors.

The Act went some way towards redressing the unrepresentative distribution of seats, though the rural areas of the South remained over represented. The Act led to more contested elections and a decline in aristocratic influence and patronage in the boroughs, if not in the counties. It benefited the urban middle classes, though not the working class. Corrupt practices remained, as the Act failed to introduce a secret ballot.

Notwithstanding Chartist agitation in the 1840s, further reform had to wait 35 years. The Reform Act 1867 may have owed a lot to Disraeli's political opportunism in attempting to increase the popularity of the Conservative Party with the urban electorate. Its practical effects were to extend the borough franchise to all adult male householders and male lodgers occupying premises with a rent of £10 per annum or more. But the county franchise, though modified slightly, still remained largely the preserve of the 40-shilling freeholder.

Seats were also redistributed under the 1867 Act. Boroughs with fewer than 10,000 residents lost seats to those with more. Chichester, Horsham, Lewes, Midhurst and Rye each lost one seat, while Arundel was disenfranchised.

Nationally, the 1867 Act doubled the size of the electorate. However, it still left the majority of men and all women without the vote. Particularly noticeable was the largely unenfranchised male population in the county seats.

The 1872 Ballot Act introduced the secret ballot to elections. Its effects were far from instantaneous, as many voters remained unconvinced of the absolute secrecy of the vote. It did, however, remove the carnival atmosphere of the hustings, and gradually removed the voting pressure which landlords or employers could exert on their tenants or employees.

The Franchise Act 1884 and Redistribution of Seats Act 1885, collectively known as the Third Reform Act, extended the 1867 borough franchise to the counties and redistributed 160 seats. The old county divisions were divided into single member constituencies. Sussex was divided into six rural divisions while the boroughs of Hastings and Brighton returned one and two members respectively. 'The county constituencies ceased to be historic communities but artificial units based approximately on numbers.'[3]

The 1884-5 reforms made the electoral system far more representative than it had been at the beginning of the century, but universal adult male suffrage would have to wait until 1918, and universal suffrage until 1928.

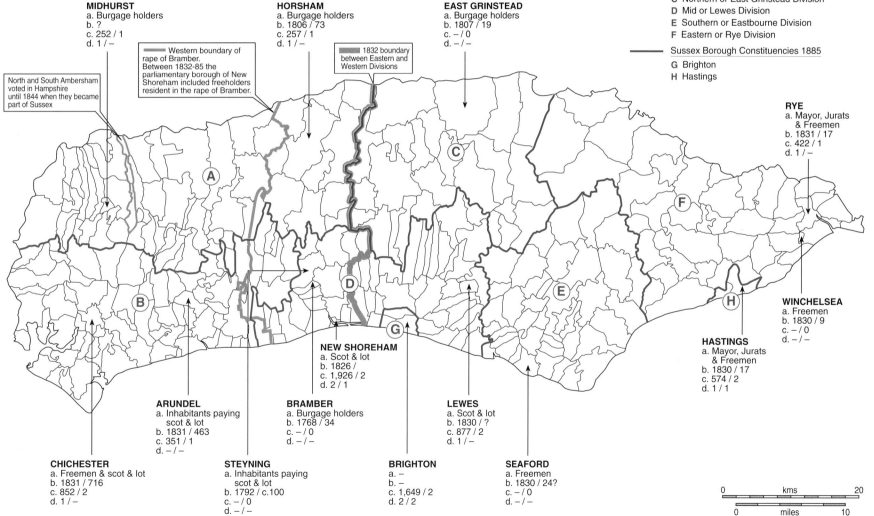

COUNTY ELECTIONS

Population (Census)	Date of election	No of voters/Registered voters	%
233,019 (1821)	1826	3,187	1.4
272,012 (1831)	1832	5,803	2.1
363,735 (1861)	1868	31,847	8.7
490,505 (1881)	1885	74,658	15.2

TOTAL NUMBER OF SEATS IN SUSSEX

Period	County	Borough	Total
pre-1832	2	26	28
1832-67	4	14	18
1868-85	4	11	15
1885	6	3	9

Key to borough representation

a. Nature of franchise
b. Last pre-1832 contested election/no. of voters
c. No. of registered electors/no. of seats 1832
d. No. of seats 1868/1885

───── Sussex County Constituencies 1885

A North-Western or Horsham Division
B South-Western or Chichester Division
C Northern or East Grinstead Division
D Mid or Lewes Division
E Southern or Eastbourne Division
F Eastern or Rye Division

───── Sussex Borough Constituencies 1885

G Brighton
H Hastings

MIDHURST
a. Burgage holders
b. ?
c. 252 / 1
d. 1 / –

HORSHAM
a. Burgage holders
b. 1806 / 73
c. 257 / 1
d. 1 / –

EAST GRINSTEAD
a. Burgage holders
b. 1807 / 19
c. – / 0
d. – / –

───── Western boundary of rape of Bramber. Between 1832-85 the parliamentary borough of New Shoreham included freeholders resident in the rape of Bramber.

───── 1832 boundary between Eastern and Western Divisions

North and South Ambersham voted in Hampshire until 1844 when they became part of Sussex

RYE
a. Mayor, Jurats & Freemen
b. 1831 / 17
c. 422 / 1
d. 1 / –

WINCHELSEA
a. Freemen
b. 1830 / 9
c. – / 0
d. – / –

HASTINGS
a. Mayor, Jurats & Freemen
b. 1830 / 17
c. 574 / 2
d. 1 / 1

NEW SHOREHAM
a. Scot & lot
b. 1826 /
c. 1,926 / 2
d. 2 / 1

ARUNDEL
a. Inhabitants paying scot & lot
b. 1831 / 463
c. 351 / 1
d. – / –

BRAMBER
a. Burgage holders
b. 1768 / 34
c. – / 0
d. – / –

LEWES
a. Scot & lot
b. 1830 / ?
c. 877 / 2
d. 1 / –

CHICHESTER
a. Freemen & scot & lot
b. 1831 / 716
c. 852 / 2
d. 1 / –

STEYNING
a. Inhabitants paying scot & lot
b. 1792 / c.100
c. – / 0
d. – / –

BRIGHTON
a. –
b. –
c. 1,649 / 2
d. 2 / 2

SEAFORD
a. Freemen
b. 1830 / 24?
c. – / 0
d. – / –

0 ──── kms ──── 20
0 ──── miles ──── 10

Sussex, often represented as an idyllic landscape, was far from quiescent. Indeed 'In parts of the south and east two separate worlds faced each other, the one trying to impose its view of the countryside, justice and history on the other.'[1] Only a fraction of protests are shown here, owing to under-reporting; nor do blank areas signify deferential workforces, since other tactics, among them go-slows and the taking of crops and wood, constituted part of the poor's resistance against the wealthy. Class collaboration also occurred, because small farmers differed little in their plight from labourers working on larger farms.

Food Riots

Although the most frequently-staged 18th-century protest comprised food riots, Sussex stood on the edge of its principal theatres – industrialising districts, manufacturing towns and cities. Sussex incidents were scattered and sporadic, though when they occurred they drew in rioters with different occupations from both town and countryside who feared at times for the safety of their food supplies, demanding *local* produce at fair prices (map 1). [2]

Arson and the Swing Riots

By contrast, the Swing protests left little of Sussex untouched, with inhabitants of non-participatory parishes often joining protests in neighbouring villages (map 2). The revolt followed 14 years of agricultural depression, aggravated by the demobilisation of veterans after the French wars and the most rapid demographic growth ever recorded. Under- and unemployment exerted heavy downward pressure on rural wages, as the depression further undermined job security. In the Downs and Coastal Plain farmers deployed threshing machines, depriving labourers of indoor winter work with the flail.

Following a thin harvest in 1830, winter prospects looked bleak. Risings, beginning in East Kent, moved westwards into Sussex by the end of October.[3] Labourers demanded wage advances, fuller stable employment, and restored poor-relief levels. In the eastern Weald, farmers joined workers in transient alliances to demand tithe and rent reductions. Arson, threatening letters signed 'Swing' and often depicting gibbets, public confrontations and

the destruction of threshing machines followed. While the army belatedly contained the situation in eastern Sussex, the west was engulfed, but here swifter action was taken by the Duke of Richmond with yeomanry and special constables.[4] Some semblance of order was restored; prisoners were tried for arson, robbery, riot, machine-breaking, and assault, and were variously executed, transported or imprisoned. Most farmers and vestries agreed to wage and poor-relief increases, whilst many vicars and some landlords respectively reduced their tithe and rent demands.

However, many of the farmers who dominated most rural communities reneged on these agreements, and incendiarism intensified (map 2). Some, however, advocated constitutional reform as the sole prerequisite to an enduring reform of the grievances. Radical posters and newspapers circulated in the countryside, but if this, and the prolonged Reform Bill crisis of 1832, politicised rural workers and small farmers, they were to be disappointed by the mediocrity of political change achieved by the 1832 Reform Act.

Anti-Poor Law Protests

Inadequate Poor Law benefits had constituted a main grievance of the Swing protesters, and the riots were seized upon by utilitarians and Whigs to reconstruct the poor relief system (see map 35). As the new Unions were formed, farmworkers feared losses in incomes, and Sussex again experienced protests from the mid-1830s. Riots attempted to prevent the segregation of inmates between and within workhouses, and Guardians were intimidated as their boards convened. These protests never achieved the intensity of their Swing antecedents, but participants from Willingdon, Ringmer, Horsham, Steyning and elsewhere were fined or imprisoned. Thereafter, rebellions by workhouse inmates became commonplace, while Guardians remained the targets of incendiarism.

Trade Unionism

An agrarian trade union, the United Brothers of Industry, was formed in 1835 with its headquarters at Rye, spreading across the Weald and eastern Downland (map 3).[5] Aiming to enforce wage increases to compensate for the loss of allowances in-aid-of earnings, it was smashed

by a lock-out orchestrated by two members of the Curteis family, both Whig MPs. Arson, poaching, cattle maiming and revolts recurred, but surplus labour supplies limited the efficacy of rural unionism before the 1870s, although there was much union activity amongst the skilled workers in Sussex towns, such as Brighton.

The Kent and Sussex Labourers' Union (KSLU) was centred on Maidstone (Kent) from 1872 until its collapse in the early 1890s. In 1872-3 the KSLU expanded into eastern Sussex, attaining 17,000 members at its peak in the late 1870s, but westward expansion was stopped by the appearance of Joseph Arch's National Agricultural Labourers' Union (NALU).[6] The progress of Arch's Union in Sussex is poorly documented, but map 3 demonstrates that its presence was not negligible. Only in far eastern Sussex did the KSLU reign supreme for 20 years. Its principal tactic was to negotiate wage increases and reduced hours, the strike weapon rarely being used. But employers instituted lock-outs in 1873-4 and 1878-9, and despite high levels of membership the KSLU found itself at best having to negotiate wage reductions and at worse being comprehensively beaten. Nevertheless it did achieve some successes, including 25% wage increases in the early 1870s, and in promoting emigration, perceived as a key weapon in reducing labour surplus. Both unions, like the United Brothers, drew on the services of experienced trades unionists in the towns, including Brighton, Hastings and Maidstone.

The locations of these recorded protests are not always easily explicable. Wealden agrarian poverty can be invoked in an understanding of the Swing protests and trade union branch formation. But food riots were both urban and rural; arson was as widespread in its recorded incidence in southern Sussex as in the Weald; and anti-poor law protests were spread uniformly. It should finally be noted that such old parliamentary constituencies as Chichester, Horsham, Lewes and Rye, as well as the new powerhouse of southern Chartism, Brighton, were also foci for dissent. So too were smaller towns, such as Battle, Billingshurst and Ditchling, and their role should therefore also be superimposed on distributions of 18th- and 19th-century protest.[7]

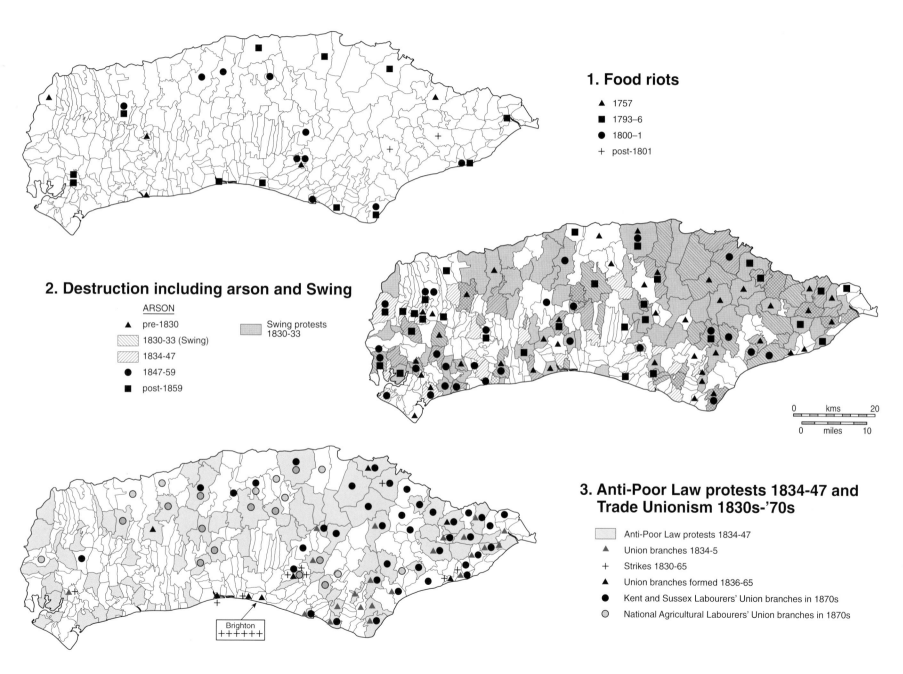

1. Food riots

- ▲ 1757
- ■ 1793–6
- ● 1800–1
- + post-1801

2. Destruction including arson and Swing

ARSON

- ▲ pre-1830
- ▨ 1830-33 (Swing)
- ▧ 1834-47
- ● 1847-59
- ■ post-1859

Swing protests 1830-33

0 kms 20
0 miles 10

3. Anti-Poor Law protests 1834-47 and Trade Unionism 1830s-'70s

Anti-Poor Law protests 1834-47
- ▲ Union branches 1834-5
- + Strikes 1830-65
- ▲ Union branches formed 1836-65
- ● Kent and Sussex Labourers' Union branches in 1870s
- ◉ National Agricultural Labourers' Union branches in 1870s

Brighton
++++++

38 RELIGIOUS WORSHIP 1851

John Vickers

For the first and only time a census of places of worship in England and Wales was organised at the time of the decennial population census in March 1851. Its purpose in the eyes of the authorities was to determine how far the provision of churches and chapels, and of the seating they provided for worshippers, was keeping pace with the rapid growth of the population and its radical redistribution as Britain became industrialised. The main questions asked were about the number of sittings (free and 'appropriated') and the number of worshippers and 'Sunday Scholars' attending in the morning, afternoon and evening on 30 March. Although a response was not legally enforceable, information was received from a high proportion of the known places of worship in Sussex, despite encouragement from the Anglican hierarchy for clergy to boycott the enquiry. But not all returns gave the required information and a number of gaps had to be filled subsequently by the local Registrars from whatever sources they could tap.

The results of the census were published as a Parliamentary Paper in 1854 and refuelled the controversy that had begun before census day as to the propriety and accuracy of its findings. Since the original returns became available at the Public Record Office in 1951, the debate has been renewed, this time in academic circles, concentrating on the (sometimes intractable) problems of interpreting the figures, especially for attendances. The returns for an increasing number of counties, including Sussex, have been published, facilitating a comparative study of the patterns of church attendance in different parts of the country and different types of community (e.g. urban and rural, or 'open' and 'close' parishes).[1] In this context, county divisions are of little significance and, as Coleman has shown in a study of Southern England, the most meaningful unit of comparison is the Registration District.[2] Coleman found clear divisions within the county, both between east and west and between the coastal region and the wealden hinterland, and affinities between some registration districts in Sussex and their neighbours across the county boundaries.

Despite this sharing of some characteristic features with the adjoining counties of Kent, Surrey and Hampshire, Sussex had discernible features of its own. It was one of the few areas still with more Anglican than

Nonconformist places of worship. With seating for 56.5% of the population it was just below the national average of 57% in the provision of accommodation: lower than Hampshire's 58.7%, but well above Kent's 53.1%. The statistics for attendances are more problematical, but a broad picture emerges as the map opposite demonstrates. Total attendances represented 34% of the population, against a national average of 34.2% and compared with 36% in Kent and 40% in Hampshire, where both Nonconformity and Methodism were appreciably stronger.[3] Even more than in the country as a whole, morning services were by far the best attended, reflecting the prevailing Anglicanism and despite the fact that in

many Nonconformist chapels the evening congregation was the largest of the day.

The most obvious feature was the continuing Anglican predominance, with figures noticeably higher than in England as a whole, not least in comparison with the industrial North. The Church of England had 66.7% of total attendances (compared with the national average of 49.5%) – well above the figures for Kent (62.1%) or Hampshire (58%). Again, a distinction can be made between eastern and western Sussex. In the west (i.e. closest to the focal point of the diocese of Chichester) the percentage of the population attending worship was lower than in the east; but at the same time, the Anglican share

RELIGIOUS DENOMINATIONS	Number of Places of Worship and Sittings		Number of Attendants† at Public Worship on Sunday, March 30, 1851			Number of Places *open for Worship* at each Period of the Day, on Sunday, March 30, 1851; and Number of Sittings thus available					
						Places of Worship open			Sittings ‡		
	Places of Worship	Sittings*	Morning	Afternoon	Evening	Morning	Afternoon	Evening	Morning	Afternoon	Evening
TOTAL	617	160,988	88,748	66,794	34,639	440	382	204	135,549	107,362	59,408
PROTESTANT CHURCHES:											
Church of England	350	108,076	62,593	52,745	14,066	273	249	34	93,839	82,589	22,138
Independents	78	17,787	9082	2854	6599	45	23	49	13,779	4415	12,576
Baptists:											
General Baptists	4	795	301	48	72	4	1	2	795	145	450
Particular Baptists	34	7997	4800	3038	3396	23	20	20	6994	4836	5629
Baptists (undefined)	12	2380	1368	1072	280	8	9	4	2000	1930	770
Society of Friends	5	1057	235	160	...	5	4	...	1057	895	...
Unitarians	5	1852	793	148	402	4	1	4	1502	350	1552
Wesleyan Methodists:											
Original Connexion	63	11,018	4293	3639	5587	32	42	50	7439	7246	9625
Primitive Methodists	5	506	297	335	501	3	3	5	411	321	506
Bible Christians	12	1211	227	586	730	5	6	12	557	776	1211
Calvinistic Methodists:											
Lady Huntingdon's Connexion	5	1963	1359	36	1550	3	1	4	1633	80	1883
Isolated Congregations	32	4819	2385	1638	928	26	15	15	4106	2472	2043
OTHER CHRISTIAN CHURCHES:											
Roman Catholics	8	902	785	311	200	6	4	1	862	682	400
Catholic and Apostolic Church	1	300	150	100	200	1	1	1	300	300	300
Latter Day Saints	2	250	40	68	88	1	2	2	200	250	250
Jews	1	75	40	16	40	1	1	1	75	75	75

* The number of *sittings* is not returned for 83 of the above 617 places of worship. Of these, 64 belong to the Church of England; nine to the Independents; three to the Particular Baptists; one to the Unitarians; one to the Bible Christians; four to Isolated Congregations; and one to the Roman Catholics.
† The number of *attendants* is not returned for 52 of the above 617 places of worship. Of these, 34 belong to the Church of England; seven to the Independents; three to the Particular Baptists; one to the Unitarians; five to Isolated Congregations; and two to the Roman Catholics.
‡ Out of the 440 places *open* in the morning, 54 did not return the number of their *sittings*; and a similar omission occurred with respect to 41 out of the 382 open in the afternoon, and 17 out of the 204 open in the evening.

Total Sussex population 1851 - 336,844

Reprinted from *Parliamentary Papers 1852-53: Report on the Census of Religious Worship 1851*, ccxxv.

of attendances was much higher.

The figures for Protestant Dissent were correspondingly low: 32% of total attendances, compared with the national average of 45.9%. The Independents were strongest, with Baptists and Wesleyan Methodists trailing behind. The older Dissenting bodies (Independents and Baptists) tended to be strongest in the rural parishes of the Weald and in the east of the county. In one or two western districts (Thakeham and the adjoining Steyning) the Anglicans enjoyed a virtual monopoly. Faced with the relative Anglican and Nonconformist strength and the predominantly rural nature of the county, Wesleyan Methodism remained weak and unevenly distributed (as

to a large extent it still is outside the urban areas). The other brands of Methodism scarcely existed in the county. Roman Catholic congregations were few and small and, like those of other minority groups, are not individually represented on the map.

Given that in England as a whole attendance levels were invariably higher in rural parishes than in the towns and cities, the relatively low attendance figures for Sussex, which was still a predominantly rural county, raise intriguing questions, but ones to which the answers remain largely conjectural. Did the lack of competition in so many parishes make for Anglican complacency? In the absence of alternatives to the parish church, were many, especially

of the 'poorer classes', expressing their Nonconformity by staying at home? Certainly, where rivalry to the Established Church was at its strongest (notably in Hailsham, Lewes, Ticehurst and East Grinstead districts) the overall attendance was above the county average.

With rural parishes far more compact than the sprawling industrial parishes of northern England, and Nonconformity relatively weak in most districts, the low overall attendance figures raise intriguing questions about both the effectiveness of the Church of England and the failure of Methodism to gain more than a toehold in most of the county.

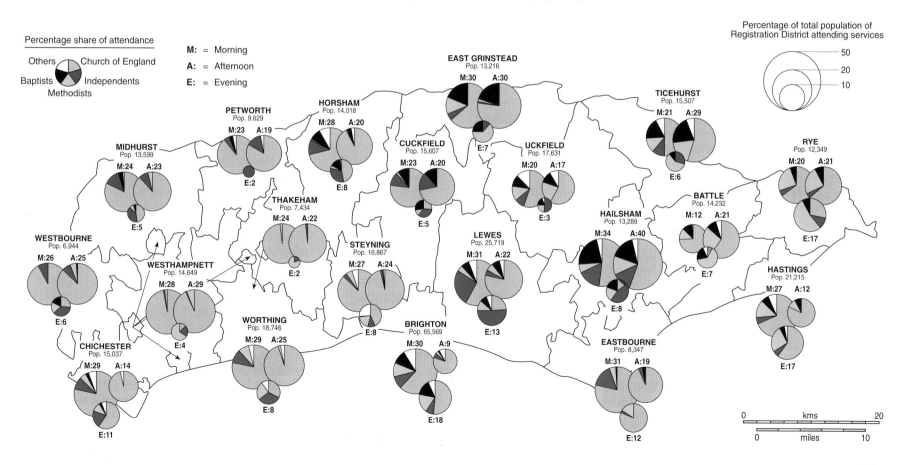

Richard Budgen was the first to map the road network of Sussex, for his survey of the county published in 1723. He picked out 63 routes on the map by dots at one mile intervals, most labelled with the distance from the origin. If Tenterden, just in Kent, is added to the 13 Sussex towns which he identified as having markets, 51 of the routes had a market town as either origin or destination. Three of the others radiated from Tunbridge Wells, a major spa town, and four started from the coastal settlements of Eastbourne, Emsworth (Hants.), Newhaven and Pevensey, where some seaborne goods were handled. That left only four routes, in the eastern Weald, and the 100km ridgeway on the summit of the Downs between South Harting and Eastbourne.[1]

Budgen saw some 1,100km as the primary road network, linking the settlements between which most traffic flowed, and comprising the routes recommended to travellers. That, however, says nothing about their condition - which depended mainly on physical factors and to a lesser degree on the traffic. Maintenance was funded by the parish, whose residents had little interest in keeping up the roads for through travellers, and supervised by its unpaid surveyor. For east-west travel the firm, well-drained surface of the chalk provided good riding at all seasons but was not easily accessible to wagons. These routes probably received little maintenance and for their repair flint was readily available, though they were constrained by the location of the bridges or ferries across the north-south rivers (the main bridges were maintained by the Justices in Quarter Sessions). But large areas of the Low Weald and, to a lesser extent, the High Weald were cloaked with clay that had no hard beds of rock sufficiently near the surface to provide a foundation to the roads which were reduced to quagmires in rainy seasons. Yet here originated the bulkiest and heaviest products, timber and ironwork, for which carriage by water rather than land would have been more efficient.

Budgen marked only the rivers Arun, Adur, Ouse, Brede and eastern Rother as navigable. On only the Arun could barges reach any significant distance into the Weald, and even on the lower reaches they risked grounding on

shoals. Navigation had deteriorated as land on the margin of the rivers was embanked and taken into agriculture, thereby reducing the volume of water entering on the rising tide and scouring the river bed and the outfall as it flowed out. The estuarine harbours had shallow and tortuous entries, due to longshore drift from west to east, and the man-made works of previous generations were in decay. But the creeks of Chichester Harbour and the shingle beaches of the main coast provided some further places where bulk cargoes were handled.[2]

The harbours were the first target of deliberate improvement, with piers completed at both Newhaven and Littlehampton in 1735 and at Shoreham in 1763. None was maintained in the condition then achieved, but lost ground was recovered in the 1790s, 1820s and 1816-19 respectively. Large expenditures at Rye from 1724 achieved no useful result.

Improvement of the roads, through the instrument of turnpike trusts, began in earnest in Sussex in 1749, and by 1764 improvements were authorised to existing roads radiating from London to 11 of the 13 market towns on the map. In the late 1760s schemes for cross-country routes emerged, particularly in the vicinity of Tunbridge Wells and north-east of Lewes. Brighton's emergence as a resort was reflected in several projects of 1770 to speed access from London; by then all 13 market towns were encompassed. In the 1770s a large series of cross-routes of relatively local importance was also begun, but between 1777 and 1801 few new schemes were launched.[3]

During this lull, improvements were made to the waterways with substantial works being undertaken on the Arun (from 1785, culminating in a continuous line of navigation between London and Portsmouth, opened in 1823), the Ouse (1790-1812), the western Rother (1791-4) and the Adur (1808-12, and from 1825). Smaller improvements opened up navigation on the Cuckmere (probably in the 1790s) and on Glynde Reach (1796-1803).

Marketing needs were the dominant consideration in nearly all the earlier transport improvements. Perhaps because the harbours and waterways were better able to handle bulk goods, leisure travel by contrast, was a more conspicuous influence on road building by 1800, first to

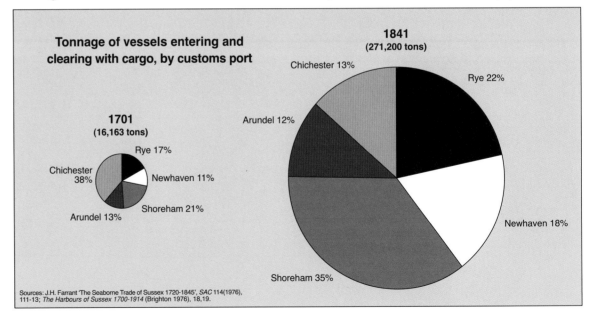

Tonnage of vessels entering and clearing with cargo, by customs port

1701
(16,163 tons)

Rye 17%
Chichester 38%
Newhaven 11%
Arundel 13%
Shoreham 21%

1841
(271,200 tons)

Chichester 13%
Rye 22%
Arundel 12%
Newhaven 18%
Shoreham 35%

Sources: J.H. Farrant 'The Seaborne Trade of Sussex 1720-1845', *SAC* 114(1976), 111-13; *The Harbours of Sussex 1700-1914* (Brighton 1976), 18,19.

Tunbridge Wells and then to the burgeoning seaside resorts. Although the interior filled out with improved roads, these did not include those ancient routes confined to the top of the South Downs escarpment.

From 1801 turnpiking resumed, with schemes for relatively short links in the general network and for new routes between existing destinations. Standards of engineering and maintenance were rising from around 1820 under the influence of J. L. McAdam who advised the trusts east of Lewes in 1817. In 1840 Sussex had 1,091km of turnpiked road, in addition to 3,811km

repaired by the parish surveyors. The last scheme was authorised in 1841 – the year in which the London to Brighton railway opened. Faced with competition from the railways, most trusts could no longer generate enough income from users to maintain the roads, and all the trusts were wound up between 1864 and 1885.

Nearly all these transport improvements were financed by borrowing which was to be repaid from charges on users. Many were never economically viable, in that they did not pay the lenders their interest, let alone return their capital. But that may be less evidence of

unneeded or excess capacity, than of poor engineering, weak management and inflexible toll charges in inflationary times. The volume of traffic increased greatly over the period of the improvements, even if few statistics are available to track it. One indicator is the tonnage of vessels entering and clearing Sussex ports with cargo. This rose from some 16,000 tons in 1701, to 100,000 tons in 1789/90 and 271,000 tons in 1841, at an average annual growth rate of 2% and a 17-fold increase overall.[4]

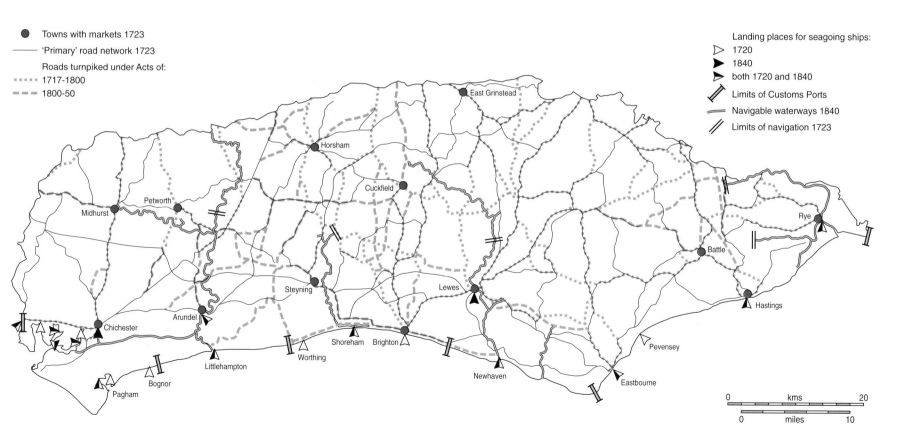

As with turnpiking, railway building came relatively late to Sussex. That the first main line, opened in 1841, was from London to Brighton reflected the changed urban hierarchy compared with a century earlier. The London, Brighton & South Coast Railway (LBSCR) extended its network, east and west from Brighton, to St Leonards (1846) and Havant (1847), with branches to Newhaven (1847), Eastbourne and Hailsham (1849) and, from the London line, to Horsham (1848). In 1851-2, the South Eastern Railway (SER) crossed the Kentish border with lines from Tunbridge Wells and Ashford to Hastings and St Leonards. Lines were built through the gaps of the rivers Arun (1863) and Adur (1861), and short branch-lines served inland towns and coastal resorts. To defend its eastern flank against the SER, the LBSCR added two lines to Tunbridge Wells, one from the main line via East Grinstead (1866), the other from Lewes via Uckfield (1868).[1]

As early as 1861, LBSCR shareholders were concerned that lines were being constructed through rural areas which would provide little revenue. In 1867 it was revealed that many of these lines were indeed making losses and the LBSCR was at some risk of bankruptcy. New construction in Sussex virtually ceased for a decade, and the main additions thereafter were further routes from Tunbridge Wells and East Grinstead towards the coast. At its maximum extent, between 1902 and 1933, the railway network in Sussex was 579km long. History was to show that the lines added later were indeed the least viable. Of the 373km opened up to mid-1864, 17% were to be closed by 1983 - and of the remaining 206km opened subsequently, 77% were closed.[2]

Sussex had no extractive industries or bulky manufactures of more than local significance. Bulk goods were moved by rail only for local consumption. But the marketing of agricultural produce (including imports from France via Newhaven and, briefly, Littlehampton) and of fish was extended by the faster movement of perishable goods to London. Farmers also increasingly bypassed the old market towns or used the livestock markets by the stations at Haywards Heath and Heathfield.

Passenger traffic provided an exceptionally large proportion of the companies' revenue, and the seaside resorts were crucial in this respect, as the early pattern of line building indicates. The railways facilitated the percolation of seaside holiday-making down the social scale and day excursions were introduced, but within the frame of resorts already established before 1840. The only substantively new resort, Bexhill, developed 40 years after the opening of the line hugging the coast between Pevensey and Hastings. Inland, in the Weald, were more instances of new settlements around a railway station, mainly in the form of villas for the middle classes and the supporting services, as at Haywards Heath, Hassocks and Burgess Hill and at Heathfield and Crowborough. Horsham and East Grinstead also became centres for villa development. Inland parishes without good railway access (and indeed non-urban coastal parishes) tended to lose population in the later 19th century.[3]

The railway quickly transformed the transport network of Sussex. The revenue of turnpike roads and waterways dropped sharply when a railway line opened to offer an alternative routing. As the turnpike trusts were wound up, responsibility for maintenance reverted to (and in most cases remained with) the parishes. Road conditions in general declined until after the new county councils from 1889 assumed the full burden of maintaining 'main roads'. A motoring guide of 1906 found most Sussex main roads in good condition. By 1900 metalled roads were graded, and nearly all the first-class roads at that date had been turnpikes in 1850, the few exceptions being important east-west highways such as the Worthing-Arundel-Chichester road. Notable among the former turnpikes not becoming main roads were some of the ancient downland routes.[4]

Broadly for the roads there was continuity of usage, though their administration changed, and in the 20th century the motor car and lorry were to challenge the primacy of the railways. For the waterways it was otherwise. They virtually went out of use as commercial arteries. The canal between Ford and Chichester closed as such in the year after the railway opened, 1847. Commercial traffic ceased during the 1860s or early 1870s on the upper Ouse, the Baybridge Canal (on the Adur) and the Wey & Arun Canal; on the western Rother in 1888; on the canal from Chichester Harbour to the city's canal basin, c.1906; and on the Royal Military Canal in 1909. On the eve of the First World War, waterborne traffic – on a minuscule scale – had regressed to the tidal sections of the rivers as used before the 18th-century improvements, and even that fell victim to the motor lorry in the 1930s.[5]

Selectively the harbours were able both to flourish through an alliance with the railways and, eventually, to

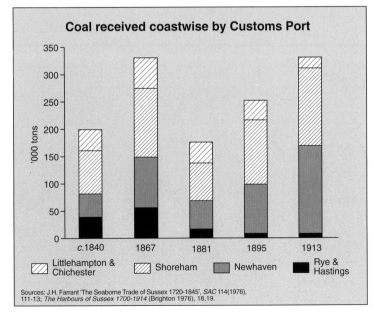

Coal received coastwise by Customs Port

'000 tons

Littlehampton & Chichester   Shoreham   Newhaven   Rye & Hastings

Sources: J.H. Farrant 'The Seaborne Trade of Sussex 1720-1845', SAC 114(1976), 111-13; The Harbours of Sussex 1700-1914 (Brighton 1976), 18,19.

compete with them. The alliance was in cross-Channel traffic, as the LBSCR sought to maximise its share of traffic to the Channel coast. Since the mid-18th century, the beach and then the Chain Pier at Brighton had been the principal Sussex transit for passengers to France, with the ships berthing at Shoreham. From 1849 services to Dieppe were transferred to Newhaven, and from 1863 the LBSCR exercised its new powers to own and operate steamboats. In 1878 it gained effective control over the harbour and began major investments which from 1889 allowed a fixed timetable, not dependent on the tide.

The railway's competition was first felt in the distribution of goods from the harbours. As the network expanded, the railway took traffic away from shipping. The regular sailings to and from London faded away around 1850, and foreign trade concentrated on major ports. From 1849, the LBSCR was distributing coal from its wharf at Deptford and from the mid-1860s it was taking Midlands coal brought by the new link lines across or round London. This practice spelt the end of regular shipping at Hastings and accelerated the decline at Chichester, Littlehampton and Rye. However, the

harbour commission at Shoreham had responded energetically and in 1851-5 turned the eastern arm into a floating dock, beside which were built the largest gasworks in Sussex (from 1874) and an electricity generating station (from 1906). With steam colliers appearing from 1884, the harbours with docking and unloading facilities were able to increase their trade substantially. But by the First World War only two commercial harbours of any significance, Newhaven and Shoreham, remained in Sussex.[6]

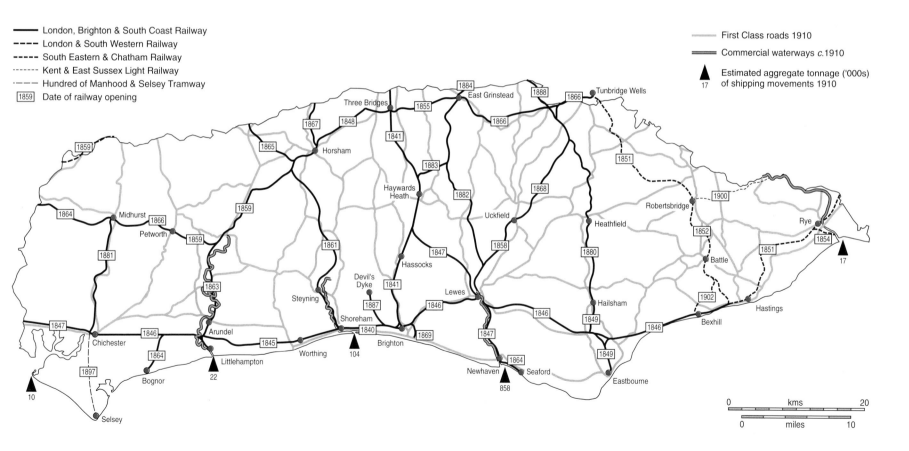

The map features every school known to have operated at some point in the 18th century. It is necessarily incomplete. There are no comprehensive central records of schools in this period, and the details derive from a wide range of diverse sources.[1] The map omits (particularly in East Sussex) a large number of dame and petty schools that did not find a place in any surviving records; it probably omits some small schools for the sons of local gentry kept by clergymen, and one or two workhouse and Sunday schools.

Symbols in red indicate that the school was wholly or partly a charity school, but it should be noted that few charity schools were only charity schools: the schools were small, the master's salary meagre, and it was expedient to allow him to take a number of paying scholars in addition to the charity children.

Under each place name schools are listed in chronological sequence of the earliest date reference we have to them. Schools in existence when the century began are shown in italics. Most private schools were relatively small, their scope and ethos determined by their master or mistress, and when a school changed hands it is shown on the map as a separate school. This does not apply to continuing family schools, or to private schools grafted onto endowed charity or grammar schools.

Most schools were Church of England establishments, but the map shows other religious affiliations of principals where these are known. It will be seen that there was a significant dissenting presence in the county – and this is likely to be understated on the map.

The schools must be set against the small population of the county (see map 33). Towns were small, villages tiny, and the map reveals a substantial educational involvement relative to population size.

The century began with the charity school movement, promoted by the SPCK.[2] In 1701 there were seven elementary charity schools in the county [C], plus one provision for some charity schooling [pC]. In the first quarter of the century, 32 charity schools were set up, plus eight provisions for charity schooling, or 40 new educational facilities in total. Some of these were small, some may not have lasted very long, but the momentum of this initiative continued through the century; the number of charity schools and provisions for charity schooling operating at some point in each quarter-century steadily increased, reaching 85 in the last.

As elsewhere, in Sussex the free grammar schools decayed in the 18th century. A classical education had become increasingly irrelevant to poor parents; trustees were often lax and ineffective. At the beginning of the century, there were nine free grammar schools [GS]. One soon failed, and by the early 19th century three others had become purely elementary. The grammar schools that flourished were private schools that widened their curricula beyond Latin and Greek, and in most cases these appropriated to themselves the buildings and income of charitable trusts intended for the benefit of poor boys.

There are references to workhouse schools in Sussex from the 1730s [W]. With some exceptions, the education given was minimal, but they were significant on two counts: firstly, for acceptance of the idea that it was expedient for schooling to be provided out of the poor rates; secondly, for the fact that the 'scholars' were from the paupers at the very bottom of the social hierarchy. There were also a few parish schools supported by the poor rates [P]; in some parishes the workhouse children were put out to respectable dame schools; and throughout the century many parishes paid for the occasional schooling of individual children. These developments prefigured Forster's Education Act 1870, which promoted (but did not compel) primary education of all children, largely paid for out of local rates.

Sunday schools [SS] were one-day-a-week charity schools, and capable of teaching children to read. At least 18 were set up between 1785 and the end of the century (by 1819 there were 91). Their significance lay in the large number of children that they taught, for comparatively little cost. As Malcolm Dick has noted, the Sunday school was the first major expression of mass schooling.[3]

There was a wide diversity of private schools [eg B, BB, B&GB, G, GB, S]. Numerous dame schools taught small children to read for 2d. a week. There were small village schools, often taught by the parish clerk. Several clergy boarded a few boys and prepared them for public schools or university. Of larger schools, increasingly during the century many schools were promoted as educating boys for 'business', and there was a very marked increase in the number of boarding schools (from five in the first quarter of the century, to 101 in the last).

Behind the symbols in the map were other key changes. There was widespread reaction against harsh discipline (the word 'tenderness' entered the vocabulary of school advertisements around 1770). There was an emphasis on the health of scholars, and all the Sussex boarding schools promoted their healthy location. There was rapid expansion in school curricula: in the last quarter-century at least 43 boarding schools offered French; at least 37 boys' schools offered higher mathematics; 'sciences', such as history, geography, astronomy and natural history, began to be taught at girls' schools; there are occasional mentions of such subjects as chemistry, electricity, shorthand and domestic economy. There was a successful co-educational boarding school, providing a full education for both sexes, even with balls laid on for the scholars and their parents or guardians; the first cadet corps; the introduction of secular libraries and newspapers into schools; prizes, and prize days; the involvement of schoolchildren in charitable and religious activities, in extra-curricular school plays and other public performances.

In short, the educational thrust of the 18th century shaped and anticipated many of the educational developments that were to come.

AA academy of drawing (1 day a week)
AD academy of dancing (in some cases only 1 day a week)
B boys' day school
BB boys' boarding school
BC boys' charity school
BBC boys' boarding charity school
B&GB boys' and girls' boarding school
C charity school (Cs, two or more)
CSg charity schooling (other than for individual children)

D dame school (Ds, two or more)
D charity dame school
Ev evening school
F farm school
FEv French evening school
G girls' day school
GB girls' boarding school
GC girls' charity school
GS boys' free grammar school

J Jewish school
P parish school supported by poor rate or church
pC provision for charity schooling
S school (Ss, two or more)
Sg singing school
SI school of industry (girls)
SS Sunday school (SSs, two or more)
T tutor (at his own house)
W workhouse school

Suffixes
(F) French only language spoken in the school
Affiliation of proprietor/head:
(Bt) General Baptist
(CH) Countess of Huntingdon Connexion
(D) Dissenter
(M) Methodist
(PB) Particular Baptist
(RC) Roman Catholic

■ 1801 population over 2,000

Under each town or village, schools are shown in chronological order of their opening

Italics: school operating before 18th century

Unplaced schools
BB: S: G: G: S:
[French C?]: BB: GB

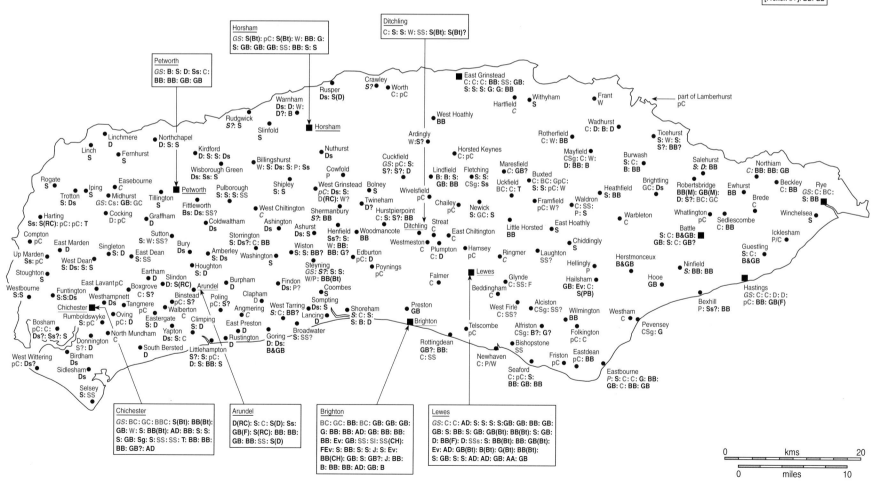

Horsham
GS: S(Bt): pC: S(Bt): W: BB: G: S: GB: GB: GB: SS: BB: S: S

Ditchling
C: S: S: W: SS: S(Bt): S(Bt)?

Petworth
GS: B: S: D: Ss: C: BB: BB: GB: GB

Chichester
GS: BC: GC: BBC: S(Bt): BB(Bt): GB: W: S: BB(Bt): AD: BB: S: S: S: GB: Sg: S: SS: T: BB: BB: BB: GB?: AD

Arundel
D(RC): S: C: S(D): Ss: GB(F): S(RC): BB: BB: GB: BB: SS: S(D)

Brighton
BC: GC: BB: BC: GB: GB: GB: G: BB: BB: AD: GB: BB: BB: BB: Ev: GB: SS: SI: SS(CH): FEv: S: BB: S: S: J: S: Ev: BB(CH): GB: S: GB?: J: BB: B: BB: BB: AD: GB: B

Lewes
GS: C: C: AD: S: S: S: S:GB: BB: GB: GB: S: BB: S: GB: GB(Bt): BB(Bt): S: GB: D: BB(F): D: SSs: S: BB(Bt): BB: GB(Bt): Ev: AD: GB(Bt): B(Bt): G(Bt): BB(Bt): S: GB: S: S: AD: AD: GB: AA: GB

83

The map seeks to illustrate progress during the 19th century towards universal free (or publicly subsidised) education at elementary level, with a brief glance at the very limited provision for secondary schooling.[1] It is divided for local comparison into districts based on the poor law unions of 1835 (as modified by 1900), which were the basis for school attendance districts under the Education Act 1876. For each of these districts, four 'snapshot' surveys of the existence of free or subsidised elementary schools are given in the tables below, the years chosen being 1801 (A), 1841 (B), 1869 (C), and 1901 (D). Sunday schools are not included, though they played a significant rôle early in the century. Comparable population totals for the districts are shown underneath (but the year 1869 is chosen for school totals, rather than the census year 1871, in order to illustrate the picture immediately before the establishment of school boards).[2]

The picture thus provided needs to be viewed with caution. Evidence for the existence and nature of schools is patchy in the first half of the century, and further work may yield more. Definitions can be imprecise and inconsistent. Also, school sizes varied considerably, from small village schools with a dozen or so children, to large urban ones subdivided into boys', girls' and infant departments (subdivided schools are here treated as one school). Evidence of pupil numbers, and therefore of the sufficiency of local provision, is not always readily available. The number of (ancient) parishes in each district is noted on the map, since most schools were parish-based, and the density of buildings on the ground was affected by the parish structure.

1801: Almost all public elementary day schools existing at this date were based on charitable endowments or local philanthropy, and some were of many years' foundation. A handful of endowed schools would survive into the 20th century, but most shortly became (or had their income diverted to) National or church schools. Some 58 are noted here (excluding endowments for children to attend schools in neighbouring parishes, etc).

1841: Two major national movements were established in the early 19th century to help fund the education of the poor: the National Society by Andrew Bell in 1811, and the British Society by Joseph Lancaster in 1812.[3] In addition some church or parochial schools were provided independently. The National Society had a Chichester diocesan branch (co-terminous with the county), which besides funding local schools established training colleges for men and women teachers at Chichester (1840) and Brighton (1842) respectively. The earliest National schools so far noted were at Chichester and Brighton (1811), and at Henfield, Horsham and Steyning (1812), but several places had them by 1820. For the purposes of this map the various charity (endowed), Church of England, National, parochial, and other general 'village' or 'neighbourhood' schools are treated as a single category. Some 144 have been identified by 1841. British or nonconformist schools were far fewer in number: Brighton, Lewes and Chichester had schools by 1812, and there were some 13 in all by 1841. From 1833 government grants were available towards building schools.

1869: Many more voluntary schools had been established by 1869, reflecting not only the powerful movement in support of the education of the poor, but also the steep rise in population (especially in coastal towns) which was to be such a notable feature of Sussex to the end of the century. Altogether 316 schools can be assigned to the National/CE category by 1869, with 21 British, and 9 Roman Catholic schools.

1901: The Education Act 1870 sought to achieve the universal provision of elementary schooling, and compulsory attendance, through a mixture of continuing voluntary establishments as before, with a new form of statutory body, the elected school board, which could be set up voluntarily or compulsorily in areas where school places were lacking (or where provision could not keep pace with population growth, or where the financial base was inadequate). Some 54 boards were set up in Sussex between 1871 and 1900, in both urban and rural areas, and built many new schools. A few National/CE schools transferred to the boards, though new schools were still established, and most British schools did so (notably in

Brighton).[4] School board areas are coloured on the map to illustrate the areas of greatest perceived need in the last quarter of the century. On the eve of the Education Act 1902, when county and county borough councils gained responsibility for education, there were 100 board schools in existence (which would become 'council' schools), and 342 voluntary ones (309 National/CE, 8 British, and 25 Roman Catholic).

Free or subsidised (boys') secondary education was almost non-existent in Sussex for much of the 19th century. Attempts were made by the Charity Commissioners to introduce new schemes for old grammar school endowments, resulting in the new boys' grammar schools at Hastings (1878), Midhurst (1882), Steyning (1883), Rye (1884), and Horsham (1889). Endowments were also re-directed to provide exhibitions for secondary education in suitable private schools at Lewes (1885) and East Grinstead (1888).

'Higher Grade' establishments offering more advanced technical education for older children were introduced by 1900 as church schools at Brighton, Eastbourne, St Leonards, and Worthing, and as a board school at Brighton (1884). Other technical (science and art) education was provided at a number of places in the later 19th century, but public provision of secondary education was only to be tackled systematically by local authorities under powers conferred by the Education Act 1902.

Although it is only possible here to feature free and subsidised 'public' education, private, fee-paying schools were always numerous (if sometimes short-lived). They ranged from elementary dame schools in villages, to major establishments such as Brighton College (1847), Eastbourne College (1867), and the Woodard Schools (Lancing 1848, Hurstpierpoint 1849, and Ardingly 1858). Most secondary schooling was private, and boarding establishments attracted pupils from all over the country. A directory of 1867 lists 402 such establishments in Sussex, of which half (200) were in Brighton and Hove.[5] The ratio of designated girls' to boys' schools at this time was 2:1 (180 to 87 respectively).

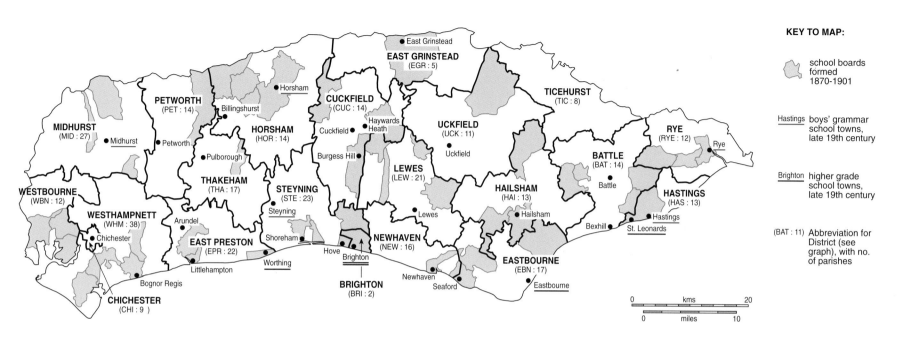

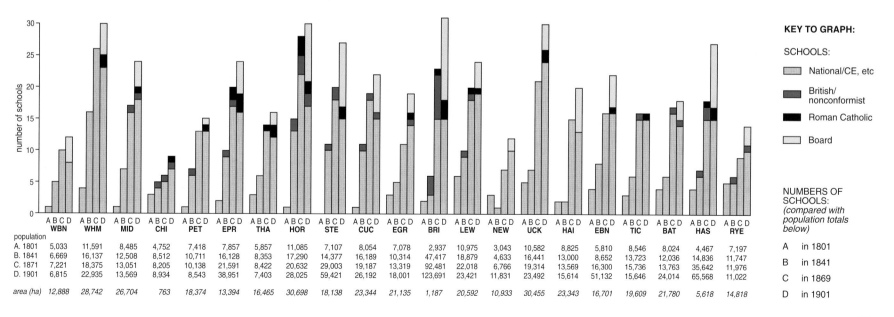

KEY TO MAP:

school boards formed 1870-1901

Hastings boys' grammar school towns, late 19th century

Brighton higher grade school towns, late 19th century

(BAT : 11) Abbreviation for District (see graph), with no. of parishes

KEY TO GRAPH:

SCHOOLS:

National/CE, etc

British/nonconformist

Roman Catholic

Board

NUMBERS OF SCHOOLS: (compared with population totals below)

A in 1801
B in 1841
C in 1869
D in 1901

Map labels:

MIDHURST (MID : 27), Midhurst, Petworth
PETWORTH (PET : 14), Billingshurst, Horsham
HORSHAM (HOR : 14), Pulborough
EAST GRINSTEAD (EGR : 5), East Grinstead
CUCKFIELD (CUC : 14), Cuckfield, Haywards Heath
UCKFIELD (UCK : 11), Uckfield, Burgess Hill
TICEHURST (TIC : 8)
RYE (RYE : 12), Rye
BATTLE (BAT : 14), Battle
HASTINGS (HAS : 13), Hastings, St. Leonards, Bexhill
WESTBOURNE (WBN : 12)
WESTHAMPNETT (WHM : 38), Chichester, Arundel
THAKEHAM (THA : 17)
STEYNING (STE : 23), Steyning, Shoreham
EAST PRESTON (EPR : 22), Littlehampton, Worthing
LEWES (LEW : 21), Lewes
HAILSHAM (HAI : 13), Hailsham
NEWHAVEN (NEW : 16), Newhaven, Seaford
EASTBOURNE (EBN : 17), Eastbourne
BRIGHTON (BRI : 2), Hove, Brighton
CHICHESTER (CHI : 9)
WESTHAMPNETT, Bognor Regis

Scale: 0 — kms — 20 / 0 — miles — 10

number of schools (y-axis: 0 to 30)

	WBN	WHM	MID	CHI	PET	EPR	THA	HOR	STE	CUC	EGR	BRI	LEW	NEW	UCK	HAI	EBN	TIC	BAT	HAS	RYE
population																					
A. 1801	5,033	11,591	8,485	4,752	7,418	7,857	5,857	11,085	7,107	8,054	7,078	2,937	10,975	3,043	10,582	8,825	5,810	8,546	8,024	4,467	7,197
B. 1841	6,669	16,137	12,508	8,512	10,711	16,128	8,353	17,290	14,377	16,189	10,314	47,417	18,879	4,633	16,441	13,000	8,652	13,723	12,036	14,836	11,747
C. 1871	7,221	18,375	13,051	8,205	10,138	21,591	8,422	20,632	29,003	19,187	13,319	92,481	22,018	6,766	19,314	13,569	16,300	15,736	13,763	35,642	11,976
D. 1901	6,815	22,935	13,569	8,934	8,543	38,951	7,403	28,025	59,421	26,192	18,001	123,691	23,421	11,831	23,492	15,614	51,132	15,646	24,014	65,568	11,022
area (ha)	12,888	28,742	26,704	763	18,374	13,394	16,465	30,698	18,138	23,344	21,135	1,187	20,592	10,933	30,455	23,343	16,701	19,609	21,780	5,618	14,818

85

In Sussex, as elsewhere, there was a strong correlation between types of common and the soils available: sheep pastures on chalk Downs, common meadows in flood plains, common pastures on poor sands or difficult clays. Many commons still existed in the 18th and 19th centuries and rights of common were still widely practised on them; but many had already been enclosed before 1700, that is, divided internally into hedged plots in private ownership, all former rights of common extinguished.[1] Between 1750 and 1900 many more were enclosed under Parliamentary legislation. Their distribution is shown on the map in 26 areas across Sussex. These areas are based both on the local terrain, and on administrative or economic ties, all important factors in the loss or survival of commons. For example, area 9 represents the River Adur and its hinterland, in which a paucity of commons reflects its earlier history in baronial control; 18 was the area of economic dependence on the Ashdown Forest (17) at its centre.[2]

The scarcity of commons in the eastern High Weald (area 23) is remarkable and may be due to Pelham family activities *c*.1788-1812.[3] Moreover, the lack of common brooklands in the tidal estuaries around Rye, Bexhill and Pevensey (areas 25-26) contrasts starkly with similar estuaries of the Ouse (area 16) or Arun (area 5) in which extensive commons persisted into the 19th century; and Chichester Harbour (area 1a) where 961ha of tidal marshes are still held in common of the manor of Bosham.[4]

The Forests

Of the hunting 'forests' of Sussex Arundel had been on chalk, occupying the length of area 2.[5] The rest were on the High Weald sands and clays: St. Leonards, Worth and Ashdown occupying areas 10, 14, and 17 respectively; Waterdown and Dallington within areas 19 and 24 respectively. Ashdown was declared a forest after 1066 but was a common at heart and is therefore treated below. The forests had always supported some tillage for their wardens, and all had at least a few common rights such as

pannage for hogs for people living nearby. By the 18th century the latter had generally lapsed (except at Ashdown, where extensive rights of common were practised) while agriculture had advanced. Waterdown was reclaimed from scrub in the 1500s, as part of the Eridge estate, seat of the Earls of Abergavenny. The 'Great Park', Downley, and other 'walks' in Arundel Forest, were farms by 1750. St Leonards and Worth forests, their timber rifled by iron makers, were by then mainly heath and scrub, considered in 1818 as 'incorrigible at any expense'. Iron production lingered on around Dallington Forest, affecting the woodland management there.[6]

Agriculture and forestry progressed during the 19th century. Worth was divided into new estates, over 400ha each; and by 1872 St Leonards Forest supported 17 farmers. The very success of forest reclamation in Sussex is witnessed by the many grand houses of the landowners, 'prettily' located in fashionable sylvan settings.

Common Tillage and Common Meadows

Villages in which the local landholders each had a share in a common-field system, growing their crops in a communal area, governed by common regulations, were once predominant in the Coastal Plain of Sussex (area 1), the chalk Downs (areas 2, 6, 12, 21), the tidal river valleys (areas 5, 9, 16) and the scarp foot and greensand parishes (areas 3, 7, 12, 22). Seasonal hay crops, taken from separate common meadows in the vicinity, were usually part and parcel of the same system.[7] The map shows those localities where arable commons had survived into the 18th century, but which were enclosed by Parliamentary methods after that. It is not possible, however, to plot those places where private agreements caused the enclosure of arable, such as Eastbourne (area 21) because, as yet, insufficient data has been gathered.[8]

Pasture Commons and the Ashdown Forest

The pasture commons of Sussex ranged from the Manhood of Selsey Peninsula (area 1), coastal marshes and greens, sheep pastures on the chalk Downs, oaken,

wood-pastures on clay (areas 4, west part; 8, 15) to the true heaths on the Greensands in West Sussex (in areas 3, 4, 5 north part, and 7) and on the Upper Tunbridge Wells and Ashdown beds (areas 14, 17, 18, 20, 23). Wood-pasture on clay, such as The Mens (area 4), could turn to open gorse and fern if trees were cut down, for example, at The Dicker (area 22).[9] From 1700 to 1900 pasture commons were still being actively used by their commoners; and by many other poorer cottagers who had perhaps encroached with new cottage plots and had often not legally established their rights to out-pasture livestock or to gather materials. 'Stinting' usually limited the number of animals that could be out-pastured: the larger wealden commons, such as Ebernoe (area 4), hosted at least one stock fair a year and they were usually driven in autumn, events that centred round the local inns. Materials cut or gathered, known as 'litter', were invaluable for poorer farmers: gorse and holly mulched as animal feed, bracken for use in stalls and byres, vital in areas where straw was hard to obtain. It was usually possible to dig materials, such as peat, gravel or clay, by licence, a facility that enabled brick and tile-making to grow as a trade among cottagers throughout the clay commons of Sussex (see map 53).

The pressure for enclosure after 1750 often sprang from the commoners themselves, or at least, the wealthier among them. Where commons were exhausted from over-stocking and over-cutting they hoped for a better return from their new, private, allotments. But commercial factors were also strong in Sussex as at Burgess Hill (area 12). Political motives were behind the enclosure of Horsham Common (area 8) in 1813; while developing seaside resorts converted many coastal greens into new, untraditional uses. At Littlehampton (area 5) in 1818 humble locals, accustomed to drying their clothes on bushes or digging stone behind the beach, were told to stop, because it was considered 'dangerous' for persons 'walking, riding and in carriages'.[10] Despite these pressures, a remarkable number of commons did survive, 353 in total. Some downland survivals are substantial, such as Harting (209ha, area 3) or Telscombe (91ha, area 11). Expansive heaths cluster round Midhurst, Black Down and Chailey (areas 3, 4 and 13 respectively). The map totals all surviving commons per area.[11]

The resources of the surviving commons were often stretched to the limit during the 19th century. Ditchling Common (area 12) was run by the parish in the depressed 1830s, to employ the poor.[12] Nowhere was the pressure felt more keenly and nowhere were the arguments for 'saving' a common more cogently put than on the Ashdown Forest. Since early medieval times its commoners had reiterated their rights. In 1693 a settlement was reached allowing 2,600ha as common and 2,800ha as enclosure. Barring some nibbling at the edges, thus it stood in 1876-82 when evidence was prepared for the High Court from a stream of commoners, adamant in the defence of their customary rights. Their stand heralded a calm future for Ashdown Forest under official regulation and a halt to further enclosure.[13] The quiet perseverance of custom in the myriad of smaller commons in West Sussex has ensured that common land is an enjoyable characteristic in the county today.

COMMONS ENCLOSURES 1750–1900, AND SURVIVALS IN HECTARES PER AREA						
Area 1	1a	2	3	4	5	6
■ 1,846	0	606	0	0	2,929	624
▣ 737	0	500	1,388	185	494	266
● 24	961	240	1,384	951	343	0
Area 7	8	9	10	11	12	13
■ 143	0	295	0	279	0	0
▣ 401	515	47	0	329	228	206
● 17	4	40	0	158	73	469
Area 14	15	16	17	18	19	20
■ 0	0	1,327	0	0	0	0
▣ 0	35	0	2,424	79	0	760
● 0	67	0	2,586	215	87	1
Area 21	22	23	24	25	26	
■ 0	0	0	0	0	0	
▣ 256	1,606	0	0	18	0	
● 8	28	4	0	2	0	

☐ Pasture commons enclosed before 1700

■ Commons including arable enclosed 1750–1900

▣ Pasture commons enclosed 1750–1900

● More prominent registered commons open in 1994 (see table)

+ Towns
(names are given for location purposes only)

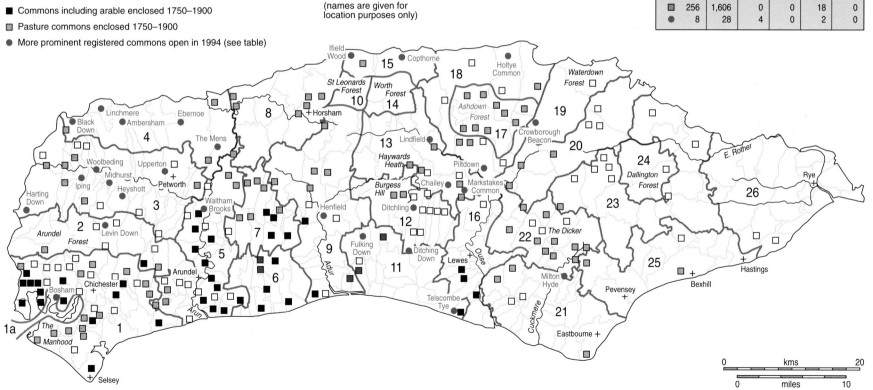

87

For the study of population from 1801 we have the advantage of the decennial census, following the passage on 31 December 1800 of 'An Act for taking an Account of the Population of Great Britain, and of the Increase or Diminution thereof'. This was a time of national population growth that has hardly ever been surpassed before or since, with gross reproduction rates reaching a peak in 1806.[1] Within South-East England as a whole population growth 1801-51 was the norm, and the population growth of Sussex from 159,471 in 1801 to 336,844 in 1851(111%) was greater than that of Kent (98%) although behind that of Surrey (154%). Growth rates in the intercensal years were highest in 1811-21(23% compared with England and Wales 18%) and lowest in 1831-41 (10% compared with England and Wales 13%). By 1831 23.7% of Sussex's population lived in the coastal towns, 2% at the ports, 16.3% at other towns and 58% in rural areas.[2]

From 1841 the census was overseen from the office of the Registrar-General, whose enumerators were appointed on a District basis.[3] The Sussex Registration Districts are shown on map 1. Between 1801 and 1851 all Sussex Registration Districts showed increases of at least 25%, although the changes at the parish level, as in map 45, demonstrate greater variability. The interior Weald increased its population by 72% overall, but there was great variation between the lesser growth of the far eastern High Weald and western Low Weald parishes on the one hand and the more sustained growth of the central wealden communities. At Crawley, Lower Beeding and Slaugham the populations more than doubled.

The greatest growth was in those urban parishes on or near the coast where the rates of increase reached to between 100% and 200% or more (map 2). This was exemplified by Brighton's fourth-ranking place in the density of its urban population by 1831, behind only Southwark, Dover and Woolwich within the South East. The 1801 population of *c.*7,000 rose to 24,000 by 1821 with the intercensal increase 1811-21 being the fastest of any town in England, and reaching a combined population with Hove and its other suburban parishes of over 70,000 by 1851. Other Sussex resorts demonstrated less spectacular growth, although the overall Hastings population of 3,848 in 1811 grew to 6,085 in 1821, and

included a huge 1,200% growth at the new town of St Leonards. The urban dominance of Hastings and Brighton was indeed such that their combined populations accounted for no less than two-thirds of the total urban population of Sussex by 1841. There was a genteel visitor trade at Eastbourne, Bognor, Seaford, Worthing and Littlehampton, although more convincing growth had to await the full impact of the railways after 1850. Along the coast, commercial activities also grew with the county's ports and harbours, bringing population growth to Shoreham and Southwick and Newhaven, although older sea-faring settlements such as Rye and the defunct port of Winchelsea showed somewhat slower growth rates.

Also by contrast, there were lower than average population densities by 1831 in several areas on the eastern South Downs such as at Patcham, Poynings, West Firle, Beddingham or Willingdon. The Downland in fact was an area of low growth rates, thereby continuing a trend established in earlier periods. Such rates characterised the Alfriston area, with some parishes showing overall demographic decline in the 50-year period, and there

were similarly low rates over much of the western Downs from Upper Beeding westwards to the Hampshire border.

Before 1831 population growth had characterised both urban and rural Sussex. But between 1831 and 1851 there was an important demographic turning point: while urban growth continued unabated, rural populations began to decrease, at first only relative to the urban increase, but then also absolutely. Emigration since 1831 was noted in the 1851 Census Abstract for such parishes as Beckley, Northiam and Udimore, and by 1851 at least 15 parishes in the eastern Weald registered population decreases in an arc from the Kent border through Brede to Bexhill.[4] Despite the presence of railway labourers (there were 600 in 1851 in Battle alone) by 1851 the Registration District of Battle which had shown above-average densities in 1831 now had a density below that of the surrounding area, such was the decline. A similarly low density now also prevailed in western Sussex in the Westhampnett and Westbourne Districts. The theme of rural depopulation is taken up in map 45, but its origins as more than a purely localised phenomenon should be

1. Density of population by Registration District 1851

Note 1: densities calculated separately for outliers of Chichester and Worthing Registration Districts and densities re-calculated for Chichester City and the main part of Worthing District.
Note 2: Ticehurst Registration District also included Lamberhurst, mostly in Kent.

Density of population per 100 acres (40ha)

- above - 37.9
- 24.0 - 37.9
- 21.1 - 23.9
- below - 21.1

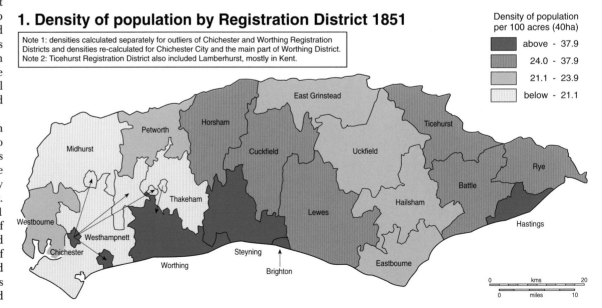

noted prior to 1851. Emigration to Upper Canada was unprecedented in its scale in the 1830s, when as many as 1,800 individuals left Lord Egremont's lands and other parishes in western Sussex.[5] Poverty and under-employment, isolation, the threat of the New Poor Law and the lure of urban jobs and better housing forced many families and individuals to quit rural Sussex at this time. Indeed, the scale of population loss would have been even greater by 1851 were it not for temporary residents working on the railways.

However, many market towns continued to reflect an agricultural prosperity in their hinterlands. At Cuckfield, Battle or East Grinstead most of the tradespeople were tied in with agriculture in some way or another, and shops grew in importance as the older open markets and fairs consequently lost trade. The resulting appearance of solidity was noted by William Cobbett at Horsham and Petworth. Such towns also prospered during the Napoleonic Wars, as corn and cattle transactions flourished and toll income rose steeply as at Chichester, where the Revd Alexander Hay noted a doubling in income from tolls over the previous ten or eleven years before 1804.[6] In eastern Sussex, Lewes c.1830 had breweries, tanyards, brick kilns, chalk pits, a small iron foundry, paper mill, Baxter's the printers, and a small dockyard area. Other than these towns, there was little inland urban population, except perhaps at Frant where Tunbridge Wells spilled over into Sussex, since once again the stimulus awaited the full impact after 1850 of the arrival of the railways.

The period 1801-51 was therefore one of spectacular urban growth at the coast, more selective and more muted growth inland, and low growth or losses of population in many downland parishes. Rural under-employment and the pull of the towns was now beginning to be felt, accelerating in the last decade of the period as the railways came to exert their influence more widely.

2. Population change 1801-51

Note: temporary population increases due to railway construction in 1851 have been included on this map

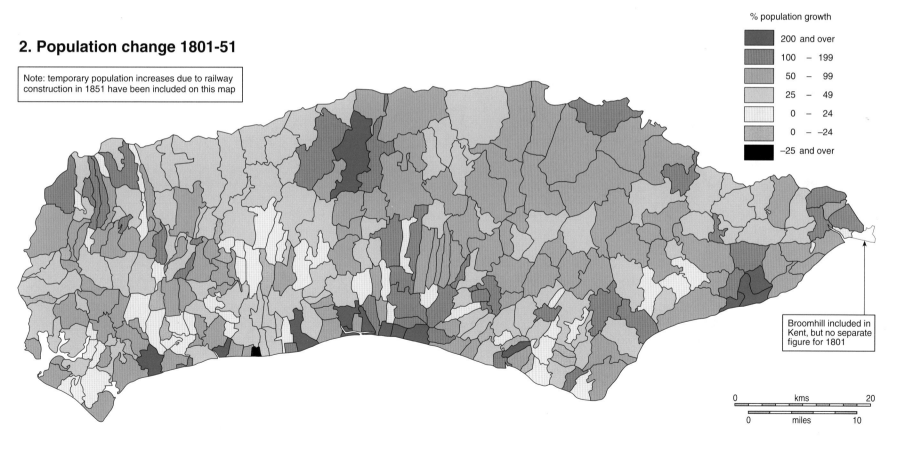

% population growth

	200 and over
	100 – 199
	50 – 99
	25 – 49
	0 – 24
	0 – –24
	–25 and over

Broomhill included in Kent, but no separate figure for 1801

0 kms 20

0 miles 10

The population of Sussex doubled between 1851 and 1911 (336,844 in 1851; 633,378 in 1911), but the changes were far less evenly distributed than during the previous half century. The most rapid growth took place in parishes along the coast and in the central inland district, whilst inland districts towards the east and west of the county experienced population loss.

The first of the two major areas of rapid growth was the coastal strip between Bognor and Hastings. Brighton, with Hove, remained the largest urban centre in Sussex throughout this period (70,588 in 1851; 173,763 in 1911), with local expansion particularly a feature of Hove and the northern suburb of Patcham. Certain other resorts, however, exhibited far greater percentage increases, notably Eastbourne (1,174%), Bexhill (613%) and Worthing (346%). It was the effect of rapid increase in numbers in the resorts, and also in the port towns of Newhaven and Shoreham, that produced the discontinuous but conspicuous zone of the darker red shades along the coast on the map.

The second major area of over 100% growth straddled the principal railway line linking Brighton to London. Some of the existing small towns in this zone had seen a significant increase in population, such as Cuckfield, Crawley and East Grinstead, but the biggest impact had come from the development of the new towns of Burgess Hill and Haywards Heath around railway stations located on former common land. Of all these inland towns, however, only Burgess Hill experienced growth rates that rivalled those in the coastal zone.

A large proportion of the population growth in these two zones had been fuelled by migration. Some migrants moved in from the rural hinterland, but the majority came from London and other urban areas in southern England. The congenial physical and social environment of the resort towns attracted many comparatively wealthy retired and semi-retired residents, with the result that by 1911 several of these towns were distinguished by relatively high percentages of inhabitants aged 65 and over (see graph). Certain inland towns, such as Cuckfield

and Burgess Hill, also had high percentages of over 65s, though others such as Haywards Heath and East Grinstead, better located to attract those of working age and with families, exhibited more normal age structures. To provide services for both the prosperous permanent residents and the numerous holidaymakers who swelled the resort population each season, other less wealthy migrants were drawn into these centres, including large numbers of female domestic servants who found work in private homes and the proliferating hotels and boarding houses. Since there was already a predominance of women among the elderly migrants to the coast, it is not surprising to find that by 1911 many resorts exhibited an exceptionally high ratio of females to males (Hastings, Worthing, Hove and Cluster A on the graph). Most inland towns were included in Cluster B on the graph, with male: female ratios close to the national average for that date (94 males: 100 females). The overall effect of the sexual imbalance in the resorts was to give Sussex one of the most feminised populations among all the counties of England.[1] The graph also highlights the population structure of the port of Newhaven, unique in Sussex with its deficit of both females and the elderly.

High Weald parishes on either side of the main north-south communication links formed the largest area of moderate (50-99%) and low (under 50%) growth, with fingers of pink shading on the map extending south across the Low Weald where railways reached towards the coast. Moderate growth characterised the town of Horsham and the 'urban villages' that had grown up after the Hailsham to London railway was completed in 1880 in places such as Crowborough, Heathfield and Waldron. The parishes with low growth were more rural, and had experienced two contrary migratory streams, an outward movement of young people searching for work, and an inward movement of comfortably-off families from London seeking spacious family homes in the healthy uplands; over the six decades the balance had tipped just in favour of growth. A smaller area of modest to low growth lay on the Greensand hills of the north-west, where there was

easy access from Haslemere station across the county boundary. A third area stretched along the northern fringes of Chichester Harbour, where again reasonable communications were combined with an attractive environment.

The grey shades on the map that indicate population decline occupy two large clusters of parishes towards the eastern and western ends of Sussex, linked by smaller groups of Low Weald parishes across the centre. Some of these parishes had lost population during every one of the six decades between 1851 and 1911, while others had experienced a period of decline followed later by gains too small to outweigh the earlier loss. As in many other English rural areas, the number of people employed in agriculture and local services had fallen, leading to a sizeable proportion of the young people leaving to find work in the towns.[2] Although local birth rates remained high, those who remained were too few to sustain population numbers. Distance from London and limited access to a railway station meant that these areas attracted few migrants from the towns, while locally there were additional discouraging factors such as low-lying and damp terrain in the Low Weald, and the virtual impossibility of obtaining property in certain downland parishes where large estates prevailed.

Many of the features of population change exhibited by Sussex during this period were shared to some extent with other counties in the region. What made Sussex distinctive was its possession of a long coastline studded with high-class resorts that had proved especially attractive to female and elderly residents. With around half of the population living in such resort towns by 1911, their demography had come to dominate that of East and West Sussex and to differentiate them from their neighbours.

Age and sex characteristics of 1911 administrative districts

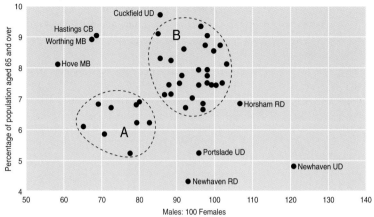

Percentage of population aged 65 and over

Cuckfield UD
Hastings CB
Worthing MB
Hove MB
B
A
Horsham RD
Portslade UD
Newhaven UD
Newhaven RD

Males: 100 Females

Cluster A comprises Bexhill MB, Bognor UD,
Brighton CB, Eastbourne CB, East Grinstead UD,
Haywards Heath UD, Littlehampton UD, Seaford UD,
and Steyning East RD.

Cluster B comprises most inland UDs and all RDs
except Horsham and Newhaven.

Note: alterations to parish boundaries and temporary distortions
of 1851 population numbers due to railway construction have
both been taken into account when calculating change. Parishes
were amalgamated where boundary changes were complex.

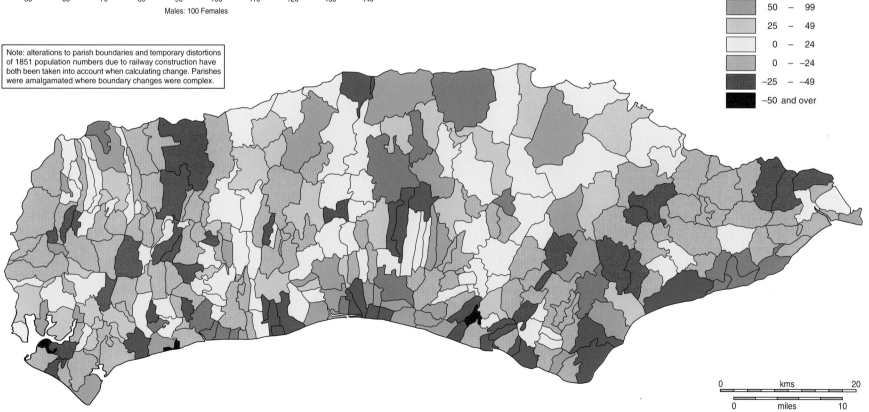

% population growth

	200 and over
	100 − 199
	50 − 99
	25 − 49
	0 − 24
	0 − −24
	−25 − −49
	−50 and over

0   kms   20

0   miles   10

In 1750 Sussex was a rural county within which market towns acted as conduits for agricultural products that went mainly overland to London. In spite of the length of the coastline, there were few coastal ports. Most of the population lived in the inland Weald. By 1914, by contrast, many market towns were backwaters and seaside tourism dominated employment and urban development. Sussex was one of the first coastal regions in the world to be transformed by tourism from an agrarian economy with a rural settlement pattern dominated by small market towns to a service sector economy dependent on seaside tourism. Major seaside resorts had developed along the coast and they commandeered most of the agricultural products that the southern part of the county produced. There was little industrial employment in the county throughout this period other than in the market towns, the ports or the seaside resorts. By 1914, Brighton had a major railway workshop, iron foundries and breweries all of which supported tourism.[1]

In 1750, the market towns of inland Sussex were the main centres of population. Most were on bridging points of rivers (Arundel, Lewes, Steyning) or had other important attributes such as the support of the major landowner (Petworth). Chichester and Lewes were the largest towns with the widest range of services. Both were social centres for the gentry, wealthy farmers and professionals, where the wealthy gentry either owned or rented town houses. In Lewes, the houses of the Pelham and the Gage families, for example, still survive.[2]

The market towns retained their importance to the economy of Sussex until the 1840s. However, London's dominance of Sussex as a market and as a source for goods was already being undermined by the development of the seaside resorts and the emergence of Portsmouth as a major naval centre requiring supplies. As the railway system developed, it helped farmers to by-pass local markets and supply both London and the resorts directly. The emergence of large shops in London, and markets in the resorts, helped the farmers to cut out local middlemen. Some landowners helped farmers by investing in facilities such as dairies that dealt directly with town shops, Lord Hampden's dairy at Glynde being a good example.[3]

Whilst the majority of inland towns ossified in the late 19th century, a few did develop as market centres: Hailsham, Crawley and Haywards Heath are examples. Burgess Hill, Crowborough, and Heathfield were all intended to be residential towns, but they did not develop much until after 1914.[4]

In 1750, only six small towns existed along the county's lengthy coastline: Rye, Hastings, Seaford, Brighton, Shoreham and Littlehampton. Winchelsea had long ceased to function as a port. All of the others were in decline. The four ports that were by river mouths were suffering because all of the rivers required investment in harbour improvements and most were only navigable for short distances inland. When the present mouth of the Ouse was finally stabilised from the later 18th century and the river made navigable to Lewes, Newhaven could develop as a port.[5] But the harbour improvements isolated Seaford, once a port at the mouth of the river when its out-fall was further to the east. The fortunes of Shoreham and Littlehampton improved after the river mouths of the Adur and the Arun were similarly stabilised. Connections to the railway system also benefited these ports.[6]

Although Hastings lacked a river, this port still exported goods from its wealden hinterland. The town's once thriving long-distance fishing industry had by now declined. Brighton had exported some grain from the nearby downland farms, to Portsmouth, London and elsewhere, but had been far more dependent upon the long-distance fishing industry than Hastings. The history of Brighton during this period is summarised in map 47.

By the 1750s, seaside resorts were emerging in the South-East of England. The demand was mostly from visitors who lived within the region: wealthy people who had frequented spas such as Tunbridge Wells and Bath, and Londoners seeking a change from their local spas such as Epsom, were amongst the potential market. Between 1730 and 1750, Brighton, Hastings and Margate (Kent) were amongst the coastal places that were visited for leisure bathing.[7]

At first, the number of visitors was so small that only a few places could profit from seaside tourism. Brighton and Margate were the earliest resorts in the South-East, soon to be joined by Hastings. The coast of Sussex won most of the London market, mainly because it was far more accessible than that of Kent.[8]

Brighton and Hastings were small towns that sought employment; Brighton was in dire straits (see map 47). Both towns had basic facilities such as shops and inns, cheap accommodation to rent, and plenty of people looking for work. By 1780, much of Brighton's town centre had been rebuilt and the cost of living was rising in the town.[9] Hastings grew more slowly and kept more of the earlier buildings in the area that is now called Old Town.[10] It was the success of Brighton that generated imitations

Brighton Chain Pier (John Bruce, History of Brighton, *1835)*

such as Hothampton (Bognor), Worthing, and the scattered developments in the parish of Eastbourne, such as Meads and Seahouses.[11] The number of resorts increased during the Napoleonic Wars when the army acted as a magnet for families and young ladies seeking marriage, but the market was not big enough to support them all, and only Worthing managed to develop into a small resort town.[12] In the 1830s, all the resorts suffered either directly from the economic recession or indirectly because of its impact on London.

The major period of resort development along the coast was between 1850 and 1914. By 1860, most of the resorts were near a railway line and those without a station were lobbying to have one.[13] Landowners also recognised the potential of housing development as a source of income, especially when agricultural rents fell during the later 19th century. But whilst the Stanford family profited handsomely from Hove and Preston in the late 19th century, the Dukes of Devonshire failed to gain from Eastbourne and withdrew from development.[14]

By 1914, the town councils along the coast were substantially composed of townspeople who viewed the surrounding countryside as land on which to build houses, golf courses and as a source of water and other supplies for their towns. Facilities were sought not only for tourists, but also for the growing number of retired residents who were attracted by the leisure facilities and ambience. The visitors and the residents were now using their cars to explore the countryside before 1914, seeking tea gardens (as at Litlington in the Cuckmere valley) and antiquities. Rambling and bicycle societies began to treat the rural hinterlands as free recreation zones too. Already tourism had sowed the seeds for a conflict between town and country within Sussex.[15]

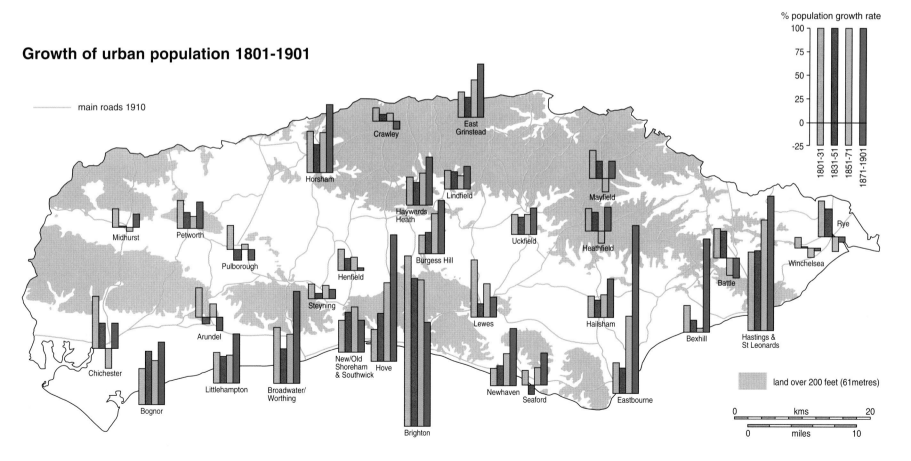

Growth of urban population 1801-1901

93

Brighton has been one of Britain's major resorts since the 1770s and its success directly inspired the development of both Worthing and Hove before 1850.[1] The large coastal dormitory settlements at Rottingdean, Saltdean and Peacehaven that emerged from the late 19th century became very heavily dependent upon Brighton for services and for employment. Today, Brighton and Hove (which were merged into one administrative area in 1997) form the main urban centre in the South-East of England outside London. The town remains important as a resort for day-trippers, the conference industry and for long-term residents.[2]

Beginnings

Little is known about the early history of Brighton before the beginning of the 16th century. The scant surviving evidence suggests that it was a small agricultural and fishing community that was normally called Brighthelmstone.[3] More important than the neighbouring downland villages such as Patcham and Preston, Brighton nevertheless lacked the services and roles assumed historically by the town of Lewes, to the north-east.[4]

Fishing Town

By the 1550s, Brighton was developing a large fishing fleet that worked the North Sea. By 1650, the population had grown from about 1,500 to about 3,000. But during the late 17th century, the loss of the seafront area on which the vessels were berthed combined with the decline in the herring fishing industry to contribute to a fall in the population. Neither the fossilised open field system that surrounded the town, nor the declining coastal carrying trade supported the population that fishing had sustained (map 1). Young people began to emigrate, mainly to London. In the early 1700s, Brighton was seeking financial support from nearby parishes and the town was described as poor and decayed.[5]

Seaside Resort

During the early 18th century sea bathing became a fashionable pastime and coastal towns such as Brighton and Margate were able to develop new roles as holiday and health resorts. At the seaside, they copied the routines and rituals of inland spas, such as Bath, adding such novelties as the newly-invented bathing machine. Brighton's first recorded sea bathers arrived during the 1730s when the town was very much cheaper than inland spas such as Tunbridge Wells. Dr. Richard Russell, a well-known figure in Sussex society, was also a passionate advocate of the curative powers of spa and seawaters and by 1750 he was sending patients to Brighton. There he built a house at the front of the Steine in 1750 (where the *Royal Albion Hotel* now stands). He also published *A Dissertation on the use of Seawater in Diseases of the Glands* (English translation from the original Latin, 1752) which enhanced his reputation. Russell encouraged businessmen from Lewes to invest in Brighton, since capital was unavailable locally.[6]

Accessibility has always been a key to Brighton's success as a seaside resort. The closest south coast town to London, Brighton had a ferry service to Dieppe soon after 1760 and became a popular stop en-route to the Continent. Road transport improved rapidly and in the 1780s coaches could reach London in 5 hours. Proximity to Lewes and to Tunbridge Wells was also very important to Brighton during the early years because many of the town's visitors were drawn from the region.[7]

1. BRIGHTON PARISH c.1740

— — parish boundary
· · · · boundary of Laines
---50--- contours in feet

to Ditchling
to Lewes
PRESTON PARISH
N
to Preston
PRESTON PARISH
Sheep Down
to Steyning
Sheep Down
HOVE PARISH
OVINGDEAN PARISH
NORTH LAINE
HILLY LAINE
WEST LAINE
TOWN
LITTLE LAINE
EAST LAINE
to Shoreham
to Rottingdean
English Channel

0 km 1
0 mile 1/2

Source: ESRO AMS 4106 and 4107, and Brighton Area Library SB9 B76 (acc 74318).

Between 1750 and 1780, tourism facilities such as private libraries, lodging houses, bathing machines, shops selling luxury goods, theatres and baths were built, mainly in East Street and around the Steine. After 1780, Brighton's growth was spectacular, and the old town was transformed into a modern Georgian town with town houses such as the building on the Steine that is now Marlborough House. A few villas were erected on the surrounding farmland.[8]

From 1780, urban development spilled out rapidly over the farmland. Much of that land was still owned and cultivated as if it was an open field system (map 2). The Old Steine became the focal point for the town because of the lack of a seafront promenade. By 1800 terraced houses were built over the narrow strips that belonged to the fossilised open field system to the north and east of the town. As the suburbs spread in both directions, so the old town became the business and resort centre.[9]

By the time that George, Prince of Wales, made his first visit to Brighton in 1783, it had already been established as the nation's premier seaside resort. Three of his uncles had already visited the town and it was the Duke of Cumberland who invited him to Brighton soon after he became of age. George liked the lively town and the wonderful opportunities that the rolling landscape of the surrounding South Downs gave for the enjoyment of horse-riding and racing.[10]

The Napoleonic Wars brought the threat of invasion to this very vulnerable stretch of coastline, and large numbers of troops were periodically garrisoned in and around Brighton.[11] The presence of large numbers of eligible young officers enhanced Brighton's reputation. In Jane Austen's *Pride and Prejudice*, Lydia Bennet exhorts her sisters to go to Brighton because the regiment that has been stationed near them is being moved there and they will lose the company of the officers.[12]

By 1821, Brighton was one of the fastest-growing towns in England, but by then the small bow-windowed terraced Georgian town houses were becoming old-fashioned. The new Regency style was grander, and suited the trend towards formal entertaining at home. Major projects, such as Kemp Town and Brunswick Town to the east and the

west of Brighton respectively, became the desirable locations for wealthy visitors who were now bringing their families, and for residents who had made fortunes from the success of tourism.[13]

During the 1830s, the town's growth rate again fell sharply. This was partly due to competition from other seaside resorts but also to economic depression. There were high levels of unemployment, poor returns on housing, and several areas of slums developed as a consequence.[14]

However, after many contentious debates, the railway line to London was opened in 1841 and this coincided with an economic revival that boosted the town's fortunes.

After 1841, Brighton became popular as a resort for short holidays from London. Day-trippers began to appear during the summer, whilst wealthy visitors came during the winter. More people began to commute to London, and middle-class families began to retire to modern houses in the new suburbs such as Cliftonville in Hove.[15] By 1851, when the Regency style that had dominated the look of the town since the 1820s was loosening its grip, 65,000 people were crowded into the town and royalty had deserted the Royal Pavilion.[16] But Brighton continued to flourish as a seaside resort.

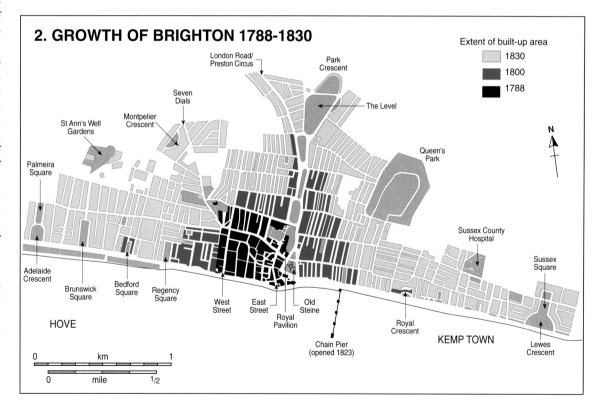

2. GROWTH OF BRIGHTON 1788-1830

Extent of built-up area
- 1830
- 1800
- 1788

London Road/Preston Circus
Park Crescent
Seven Dials
The Level
Montpelier Crescent
St Ann's Well Gardens
Queen's Park
Palmeira Square
Sussex County Hospital
Sussex Square
Adelaide Crescent
Brunswick Square
Bedford Square
Regency Square
West Street
East Street
Old Steine
Royal Pavilion
Royal Crescent
Lewes Crescent
Chain Pier (opened 1823)
HOVE
KEMP TOWN

0 km 1
0 mile 1/2

N

Although commercial and communication advances of the previous 100 years brought greater regional uniformity to England, Sussex agriculture by 1840 still demonstrated marked regional variation. Ten agrarian regions are set out on map 1.

At one extreme the Coastal Plain and the South Downs demonstrated prosperous farming, centred on arable production within various mixed farming operations. Wheat and barley, supplemented by the fattening of cattle and sheep on turnips and seeds, characterised these areas. Centuries of capital investment ensured that these were well-organised agrarian regions, yielding cereals from the folding of arable-fed downland sheep, imported seasonal harvest labour, fertilizer input, the erection of 'model farms' and proximity to growing coastal markets. Along the Coastal Plain [1] the productive brickearths ensured that grain production predominated

over livestock fattening. On the Downs [2], intensive cultivation was restricted to the lower slopes with large fields with boundaries which might be extended uphill when grain prices were favourable; there were sheepwalks on the flinty summits, and imported cattle were fattened in the brooklands where the Ouse, Arun and Adur cut through the chalk. High prices could, however, stultify farming as well as producing innovations: Caird noted with disapproval the downland four-field rotation and the heavy Sussex wooden plough 'which, for waste of opportunity, of power, and of time, could possibly not be matched in any other county in the United Kingdom'.[1]

In contrast, Southdown sheep had achieved international repute by 1840. They fitted the need for cheap meat in the growing industrial towns, the wool was used for blanket-making or knitting, and they still retained their folding qualities used in the nightly

improvement of arable fallows on the lower downland slopes. Much was owed to John Ellman of Glynde (1753-1832) who encompassed local, regional and national arenas as breeder of Southdowns, contributor to Arthur Young Sr.'s *Annals of Agriculture*, steward of the Trevor estate, expenditor of the Lewes and Laughton Levels, founder member of the Sussex Agricultural Society and of the Smithfield Society, and Deputy Lieutenant of Sussex 1814-20.[2] Men such as Ellman and the 'unincumbered capitalists' of the eastern Downs and Coastal Plain had therefore brought these regions to relative prosperity by 1840.[3]

Quite different were the High and Low Wealds of Sussex, where the headwater ghylls of the Ouse and Medway presented acidic slopes and uncertain drainage. At the very centre of the High Weald lay the grazings, heathlands and woodlands of Ashdown, Worth and St

1. Mid-19th-century farming regions

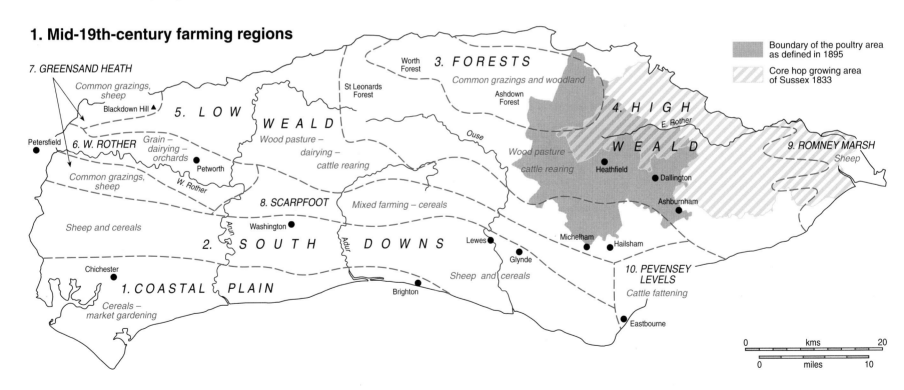

Leonards Forests [3], little given to commercial farming but where conflicts over common rights pitted manorial lords against commoners and squatters. Surrounding these areas was the High Weald itself [4], where animal husbandry was dominant within a mixed farming which was frequently sub-optimal commercially. There was less interest in mechanised farming: field size and morphology suited pastoral activities, the average field size at Dallington, for example, being 1.3ha in the 1840s; only with the addition of lime or marl could the deficient soils be made to yield cereals, mainly oats, and this only where pipe drainage had been implemented after 1840.[4] Caird was scornful of the small farms, with their yearly tenants 'unskilful and prejudiced in their methods of cultivation', and Leonce de Lavergne noted the farmers as 'men without capital, and as ignorant as they are poor'.[5] But one crop was grown very enthusiastically especially in the east: the hop acreage doubled in the High Weald between 1821 and 1874, with the 6,664ha of the latter date representing 25 per cent of the entire country's production. Although seen as an inferior hop-producing region to Mid-Kent, wealden poverty was often seen as only being mitigated by a successful hop season, with consequent excessive manure and time being spent in the minuscule hop fields of the region (map 2).

Animal husbandry fared somewhat better. In the 1830s Thomas Childs of Michelham began, with others, to exhibit the local Sussex breed of cattle at national shows, and enthusiasm grew for the breed such that a Sussex Herd Book was begun in 1878. And among the small, under-capitalised wealden farms at this time there also developed an interest in the 'cramming' (artificial fattening) of poultry, centred particularly on Heathfield by the 1860s, and with a network of rearers and crammers linked by specialist higglers who moved the birds around the countryside or to the railway stations.[6]

Wrapping around this area was the clay vale of the Low Weald [5], poorly-drained and heavily wooded in places from Hailsham to the Surrey border, with agricultural practices resembling the High Weald, but with dairying, pigs and more sheep. Although much of the area suffered from farmers who were, according to Siday Hawes, tied to their 'force of habit', later in the century dairy farming expanded, and with fruit

production brought further opportunities for wealden farmers, enabling them to resist the worst effects of the great depression after 1870 rather better than their counterparts elsewhere in Sussex.[7]

A quite different region was that of the Sandgate beds of the western Rother valley [6], from Petersfield to Washington, praised highly by Young, and providing a richer farming environment with more grain, dairy farming and orchards. This contrasted again with the neighbouring sterile Greensand heaths [7] which lay in an arc from Blackdown to the south of Petworth. And stretching eastwards from here to Eastbourne was a somewhat complex zone at the foot of the Downs escarpment [8] where chalk downwash mixed with Upper Greensand or Gault Clay amid gentle slopes and springs to provide an environment in which early settlement and well-organised capitalist agriculture centred around arable/livestock combinations. This 'scarpfoot zone', with a few remnant open field strips, partook of the characteristics of both Weald and Downland, with more barley and other cereals than the Weald but more woodland and fruit than on the chalklands above.

And finally, in the far east were the borders of Romney Marsh [9], with prestigious open breeding and fattening perennial ryegrass pastures given over to the statuesque Kentish sheep and to wool production, the flocks cared for by 'lookers' in the employ of large (but absentee) graziers. And in the Pevensey Levels [10], interests centred around the fattening of Scotch, Northern, Welsh and 'Country' (local) cattle on marshlands owned or rented by wealden or downland graziers. By 1830 the Ashburnham estate used 606ha in Pevensey as fattening land for its wealden farms. Neither area was well-drained and settlement was sparse. Sheep and cattle were moved between Downland, Weald and Marsh, maximising the environmental potential of each habitat.

The agricultural regions of Sussex can therefore be summarised at a macro-level as comprising an under-developed wealden wood-pasture environment on the one hand, and a more commercialised, grain-dominated mixed farming countryside to the south. But the intricately localised *pays*, places shaped by their particular combinations of soil and topography, habitation and agrarian history, permit an infinite subtlety of analysis.

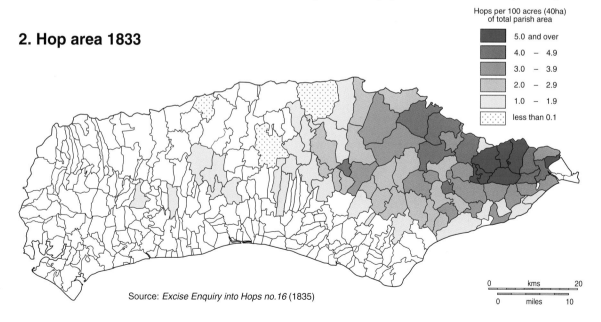

2. Hop area 1833

Hops per 100 acres (40ha)
of total parish area

■	5.0 and over
▨	4.0 — 4.9
▨	3.0 — 3.9
▨	2.0 — 2.9
□	1.0 — 1.9
⸭	less than 0.1

Source: *Excise Enquiry into Hops no.16* (1835)

Many generations of landowners in Sussex bought, sold and exchanged land according to their aspirations and needs. By the mid-Victorian period a picture emerged which bore the imprint of those multiple earlier transactions and which also set the scene for the general picture of landownership through at least to the 1920s.

A most useful snapshot of land ownership *c.*1870 is provided by J.M. Wilson's *The Imperial Gazetteer of England and Wales.*[1] Wilson derived information for a large majority of parishes, which he categorised as falling into one of five possible types. On the one hand there were those where the land was essentially held by larger landowners. Wilson referred to these as having 'most or all land in one estate' or 'not much divided' or 'divided among a few'. On the other hand there were parishes without significant large landowners, and these he classified as 'subdivided' or 'much subdivided'. To a large extent these two contrasting types can be correlated with the earlier Victorian concept of the 'open' and 'close' community, which terminology was employed quite largely by the 1840s.[2]

The 'open' community was typified by small occupiers rather than by large estates, a diverse rural economy, a society which was more independent, more likely to foster religious nonconformity, with a larger population, but with higher poor rates being paid by smaller farmers and businessmen who consequently had less capital to re-invest in their businesses. By contrast the 'close' community may have been dominated socially, economically and culturally by one or very few large landowners. Populations were kept low to keep the poor rates down, in-migration was discouraged except for the necessary seasonal harvesting migrations, the larger tenanted farms were commercialised, the minimum amount of housing was provided by the estate, and a conservative landowner might control jobs, housing and exert a hegemonic control through his presence on the parish vestry and possibly even owning the advowson of the parish church. At its most extreme, whole parishes were under the control of one family.

In practice, of course, there were very many parishes in Sussex which exhibited not only the extremes of fragmented and unified landownership, but which also fell somewhere along a spectrum between 'open' and

'close'. But the five categories employed by Wilson are nevertheless helpful here, and have been employed on the accompanying map and in the tables. Thus it can be seen that, of the 300 Sussex parishes analysed, 109 were 'in few hands', twice as many as were to be found in the more extreme 'close' parishes which were held in one estate (table 2). Where Wilson failed to classify a parish (the far western part of West Sussex is particularly deficient in *The Gazetteer*) surrogate information from the tithe apportionments *c.*1840 can be used to complete the map and the tables. One must, of course, be aware of the fact that the tithe information spans the years generally from 1837 to 1846, whereas Wilson's information was taken from the late 1850s and early 1860s. Nevertheless, a comprehensive picture of landownership patterns in mid-19th-century Sussex can now be seen for the first time.[3]

The overall pattern of landownership shows a contrast between wealden and non-wealden parishes. In the former there are many more 'open' parishes, with over 70% of High Weald parishes and nearly two-thirds of Low Weald parishes being essentially 'open'. The agrarian and settlement histories of these parishes is told elsewhere in this volume, but the later and dependent hamlet and individual settlements in these wood-pasture hills and valleys provided a base for small, owner-occupied family subsistence farms. The pattern is typified by the settlement history of such hamlets as Broad Oak, Punnetts Town, Cade Street, Three Cups, Cross-in-Hand, Burwash Common, Woods Corner or Maynards Green on the Forest Ridges of the central High Weald.[4] With a variety of tenures and the prevalence of poor soils and woodland and dual employments, this was not a promising area for investment through the collection of estate rentals. There were, it is true, some larger estates in the Weald, such as that of the Ashburnhams or Lord Sheffield's estate at Fletching, the Sackvilles at Buckhurst (Withyham) or the Pelhams, 18th-century magnates at East Hoathly. But these were the exceptions rather than the rule.

Instead, it is to the southern half of Sussex that one should turn to find the great landowners. The Downs, Scarpfoot, Coastal Plain and Marshland all had over two-thirds of their parishes 'close'. In the west were the greatest owners of all: the Duke of Richmond, and the powerful Duke of Norfolk at Arundel (table 1).[5] To the east,

landownership was on a more modest scale, but powerful local squires controlled the lives of whole communities such as Glynde, Alciston or West Firle. At the latter, Viscount Gage steadily acquired property throughout the late 18th and early 19th centuries until by 1840 the family owned 95% of the parish, and 5,550ha in Sussex by 1873. Similarly, virtually all of Falmer and Stanmer belonged to the Earl of Chichester at Stanmer House. The absentee Earl of Abergavenny owned 94% of Rodmell in the Ouse valley. On the Downs, 90% of the parishes were 'essentially close' (table 3). Here too were the great flockmasters and wealthy tenant farmers, holding large farms on long leases, epitomised perhaps by John Ellman of Glynde (see map 48).

The observed pattern is highly distinctive, and the traditions of deference and paternalism associated with landownership certainly lingered in rural Sussex, particularly in the south. But from the later Victorian period new families began to move in to challenge the old order, and the late 19th century depression forced many changes on the estates at the same time as rural out-migration and the advent of more democratic local authorities made older class distinctions less meaningful.

Table 1. The top Sussex landowners in 1873

Landowner	Centre	Area (ha)	Rental (£)
Lord Leconfield	Petworth	12,210	29,688
Duke of Norfolk	Arundel	7,956	29,760
Duke of Richmond	Goodwood	6,915	19,283
Earl of Chichester	Stanmer	6,558	13,650
Earl of Abergavenny	Eridge	6,208	12,753
Revd. J. Goring	Wiston	5,713	13,705
Earl of Ashburnham	Ashburnham	5,677	13,069
Earl of Egmont	Midhurst	5,665	11,022
Viscount Gage	West Firle	5,551	12,944
Earl de la Warr	Knole (Kent)	4,519	10,828

Source: *British Parl. Papers*, 'Return of Owners of Land (1872-3)' LXXII (1874)

Table 2. The pattern of Sussex landownership (by region and category)

	1	2	3	4	5	
	One estate 90%+	Not much divided 75–89%	In few hands 50–74%	Sub-divided 25–49%	Much sub-divided up to 25%	Total
Marshland	1	1	7	3	1	13
Low Weald	1	2	10	16	8	37
High Weald	3	2	10	19	19	53
Scarpfoot	11	10	40	7	6	74
Downs	21	8	25	5	1	60
Coastal Plain	17	8	17	14	7	63
Sussex total	54	31	109	64	42	300

1. The columns represent the categories assigned by J.M. Wilson in his *Imperial Gazetteer* (1870) or (in percentage figures) the amount of the total area of each parish owned by the three largest landowners in the tithe surveys of Sussex (taken from the 'Summary' at the rear of each tithe schedule).
2. The parish totals exclude those parishes which together constituted Chichester, Hastings and St Leonards, Lewes, and Newhaven, being primarily urban, and also Broomhill and West Thorney for which parishes no figures were available.

Table 3. The broad pattern of Sussex landownership

	Essentially 'Close'	%	Essentially 'Open'	%
Marshland	9	69.2	4	30.8
Low Weald	13	35.1	24	64.9
High Weald	15	28.3	38	71.7
Scarpfoot	61	82.4	13	17.6
Downs	54	90.0	6	10.0
Coastal Plain	42	66.7	21	33.3
Sussex total	194	64.7	106	35.3

1. 'Essentially Close' parishes are those in Columns 1–3 in Table 2; 'Essentially Open' are those in Columns 4 and 5.

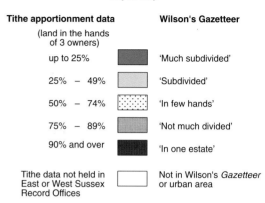

Key to map

Tithe apportionment data
(land in the hands of 3 owners)

	Wilson's Gazetteer
up to 25%	'Much subdivided'
25% – 49%	'Subdivided'
50% – 74%	'In few hands'
75% – 89%	'Not much divided'
90% and over	'In one estate'
Tithe data not held in East or West Sussex Record Offices	Not in Wilson's *Gazetteer* or urban area

Regions
1. Marshland
2. Low Weald
3. High Weald
4. Scarpfoot
5. Downs
6. Coastal Plain

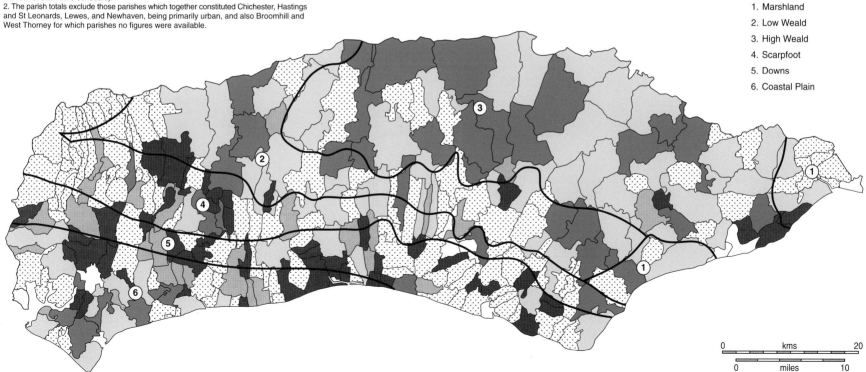

There has been a park attached to the manor house of the Honour and Manor of Petworth since at least the early 13th century. Small additions were gradually made to it, and in 1499 another 42ha were added.[1] While the Honour of Petworth was in the hands of the Crown, from 1537-1557, an area of common called Arbour Hill was enclosed into the Coney Park, and 'divers pleasant walks divided with quickset hedges' were laid out, and a banqueting house was built.

The survey of Petworth Manor made in 1557 describes the parks in some detail. The Conygre Park contained 32ha, and much fine timber. It was stocked with 60 deer and 200 couple of rabbits, and had a large fishpond. The Little Park was described as containing 121ha, 'well set with oaks and beech'. It was stocked with 200 deer and 300 couple of rabbits. There was also the Great Park, containing 161ha, which was detached from the other parks. This area of land was divided up and enclosed and let out to several tenants in 1635.[2]

By the time of the 1575 survey, the Conygre Park, with its additions, comprised 89ha, the Little Park 168ha. Shortly after this, the 81ha of the Outwood was enclosed into the park, the tenants of the manor being compensated for the loss of their rights over it.[3] The principal purpose of the park was clearly recognised by the tenants. John Wiltshire, in the court case between the 9th Earl of Northumberland and his tenants in 1596, deposed that 'the chiefest delight that [the 8th Earl] had in that park was in hunting … he …made little accompt otherwise of the pasture of the new park …'.[4]

On the map drawn by Ralph Treswell in 1610, the Home Park is shown as containing 76ha, and the New Park 332ha.[5] The park had still not reached its greatest extent, the northern boundary running from just south of Lodgefield Copse to White's Green. The house and its formal gardens and orchards comprised 2.4ha, and the Birch Walks, which were laid out and planted in 1589, comprised 3.4ha.[6] The view from the house towards the park was interrupted by the huge stable block built by the 9th Earl. An area of the park is shown as having been planted with acorns, which may have been the beginnings of Pheasant Copse.

When the Duke of Somerset was rebuilding the house with his wife's money in the late 17th century, he wanted a more fitting setting for his mansion. The garden was laid out by George London, with a formal approach to the house at the new west front.[7] The stable block which obstructed the view was demolished, and a new block built to the south of the house in 1716.[8] In 1702, the Duke bought up and demolished all the properties along the Tillington road, which ran immediately to the south of

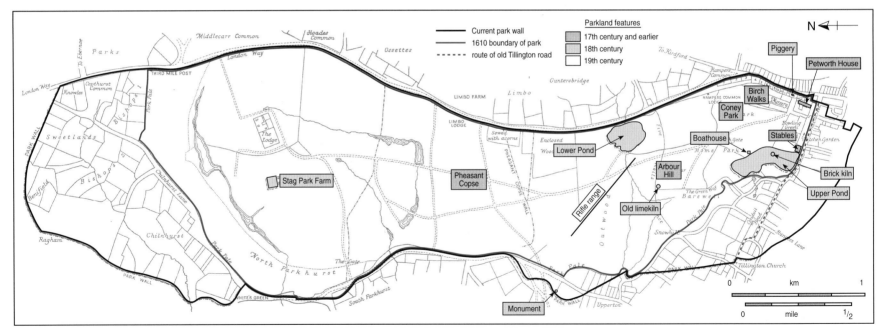

Petworth Park, based on the map by Ralph Treswell, 1610, with later additions of features mentioned in the text

the new house. While the Duke was building, a brick-kiln was set up in the park in 1703, so that Philp the brickmaker could produce the necessary bricks on site. In 1716 there were lime kilns in both Little Park and Home Park.

Surviving letters between the Duke and his stewards give details of the uses to which the Parks were put at this period. The parks were stocked with deer, indeed overstocked, according to the steward in 1702. Horses, cattle and oxen were grazed there, and Welsh runts and sheep were put into the parks to fatten. The parks also provided crops of hay, clover, tares and peas.[9]

Between 1752 and 1765, the southern end of the park was landscaped by 'Capability' Brown in the prevailing 'natural' style, which included the creation of a large lake in front of the house. Brown also moved the Tillington road further away from the house.[10] The long wall surrounding the park was built by the estate workmen from 1779.[11]

The last major change in the park was the enclosure of the northern end to form Stag Park Farm in 1782. This was the result of the 3rd Earl of Egremont's interest in agricultural improvement. In Stag Park he created a 'model farm', where he could try out his experiments in crop rotation and cultivation, and the breeding and feeding of animals. According to Revd Arthur Young, 'previously to its being improved, it was an entire forest scene, oversowed with bushes, furze, some timber and rubbish; of no kind of use, if we except a few miserable ragged stock which it annually reared...'. He went on to describe how, on the Earl's initiative, 'the timber [was] sold, the underwood grubbed, and burned into charcoal upon the spot; and every part of the park... drained in the most effectual manner: the whole of it enclosed and divided into proper fields'.[12]

Not only Stag Park was put to practical agricultural use. Thomas Phillips' painting of the park, dated 1798, shows deer, and also cattle and various breeds of sheep, including a long-haired sheep, grazing between the house and the lake. Turner's view of *The Lake, Petworth: Sunset, Fighting Bucks*, includes a group of pigs in the foreground,

which also grazed in the area of the park immediately in front of the House.[13] The Earl's piggery, built in the Pleasure grounds in 1798, was illustrated as a model of its kind in Revd Arthur Young's work on the agriculture of Sussex.[14]

Other activities went on in the park in the 3rd Earl's time. Horse races were run there before public races were established at Goodwood. Yeomanry exercises took place there. Later in the century, rifle butts were set up in the park, and one of the adjacent cottages was used for an armoury. Cricket was played in the park, and fêtes were also set up there.[15]

THE LANDSCAPE PARKS OF SUSSEX

Sue Berry

Many deer parks existed in Sussex and most of them are marked on some or all of the following cartographers' maps: Saxton (1575), Norden (1595), Speed (1610), Blaeu (1645). Some of these deer parks did not have houses used by their owners within their boundaries. Considerable numbers were disparked and converted to farmland before or during the 18th century. The remainder either had a house by 1575 or soon after. By 1700, some of these had also been disparked. Some new parks such as Stanmer were converted from farmland during the 18th century.

The map shows only parks that had been landscaped and had country houses within their boundaries at some point between c.1670 and 1820. The earliest landscaping was in the French style, remnants of which may survive at Stansted. The majority was developed in stages from the 1720s and most of the work appears to have been undertaken from about 1750. The key shows the sites where Brown and Repton worked, plus other possible sites. Most of the parks provided an income from timber and livestock but did not repay their costs. The majority of owners had income from trade and other activities in addition to agricultural rents. Many c.17th- to c.19th-century gardens still survive in Sussex.

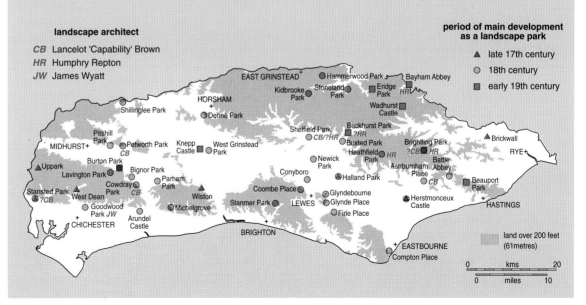

From the 16th to the 19th centuries, with the exception of the Civil War (map 29), fortifications were only constructed on the coast of Sussex. At the start of this period, coastal life was disrupted by piracy and French raids but fortification was confined to towns protecting themselves with some walls and a few cannon. Local look-outs were important and Cakeham Tower, for example, built near West Wittering in 1519, would have been a useful watch-tower. In 1539, faced with a threat of invasion from France and Spain, Henry VIII initiated a national policy of coastal defence by constructing artillery forts at important ports and anchorages. Most Sussex ports were then too small, or too silted, to accept the warships of the period and only one fort was built at this time in Sussex, embracing an earlier tower on a spit commanding the entrance to the Camber anchorage at Rye. This fort, Camber Castle, still stands, though the sea has long since receded.[1] In 1559 a small blockhouse was constructed at Brighton, which had suffered French raids.

In 1587, when England was threatened by Spain, a survey of the Sussex coast identified seven towns with artillery, as well as Camber Castle, and recommended the construction of 11 artillery batteries at other towns and anchorages.[2] These were to be earthworks, equipped with a few guns, and supplemented by trenches at places vulnerable to a landing. They were to be manned by local militia. Map 1 shows these batteries, though it is not certain that they were ever built. The same survey noted sites of fire-beacons along the coast. The map marks these and other traditional sites of fire-beacons, which, for many centuries, were set up to pass warning of seaborne landings via the inland hills of the High Weald and Lower Greensand of western Sussex to neighbouring counties and London, though not all sites may have been in use at any one time.[3] Although the Spanish Armada was defeated at sea in 1588, fears of invasion continued to disrupt the county until the end of the century.

Pirates and privateers posed a frequent threat along the Sussex coast in the 17th century but coastal defences were by this time suffering from neglect. Sussex ports were not of sufficient standing to warrant the considerable fortifications constructed at naval bases elsewhere during the Anglo-Dutch wars (1652-74). However, in the 18th-century wars with France, the vulnerability of the Sussex coast to an invading army in shallow-draught boats was of increasing concern. In 1759, orders were given for the construction of seven new batteries in Sussex: at Littlehampton (east of the harbour), Brighton, Newhaven, Blatchington, Seaford, Hastings and Rye (map 2). They were built of brick and equipped with guns which were mostly new. The battery at Brighton replaced the blockhouse, whose front had been destroyed in a storm. The new battery was itself to be washed away in 1786, and in 1793 two new batteries were built at the town on the east and west cliffs.[4]

During the French Revolutionary and Napoleonic Wars (1793-1815), the Royal Navy was the most important line of defence against invasion or raids. To help maintain contact with the navy's ships, and to provide manned look-out posts, the Admiralty established small signal stations on the coast. There were eventually 16 in Sussex, providing a chain of communication by visual signal, both out to sea and along the coast.[5] A mechanical shutter telegraph system was constructed between Portsmouth and London and this crossed the west end of the county, with a branch off to Plymouth. This was dismantled in 1814 but a semaphore telegraph system on a slightly different line operated from 1824, until replaced by the electric telegraph in 1847.[6]

Numerous earthwork batteries were constructed along the coast during the early Napoleonic era, and infantry trenches were associated with some of them. At many of the defences, and at major Sussex towns, barracks were built, or existing buildings were converted, to replace tented camps.[7] Defensive preparations ceased when a peace treaty was agreed in 1802 but when war broke out again the following year the threat of invasion was greater than ever. Napoleon had assembled large flotillas of flat-bottomed boats, suitable for landing an army on a shallow shore. The Sussex defences were manned again and new

earthworks and barracks were constructed. In 1804, work started on the construction of a vast dyke, the Royal Military Canal, around the north and west of Romney Marsh, which was intended to check the advance of an invading force. In Sussex it connects with the Rother at Rye and continues from near Winchelsea to Cliff End.[8]

Between 1805 and 1808, a chain of defensive towers was built on the low-lying coasts of east Sussex and south Kent, and later on the east coast. These Martello Towers (although the concept was older, the name was derived from a tower that hindered a British landing in Corsica in 1794) were circular and solidly built in brick, with one main gun mounted on the roof. Under the direction of the Board of Ordnance and the Royal Engineers, 46 towers were constructed between Eastbourne and Rye Harbour, sited where landings seemed possible.[9] A larger circular fort, or Redoubt, formed part of the scheme at Eastbourne.[10] A further Martello Tower was later built at Seaford. Ironically, the threat of invasion had gone before the Martello Towers were completed, and they were soon rendered obsolete by the introduction of rifled guns and iron-clad ships. Some Martellos were demolished and many were washed away by the sea; only ten and the Eastbourne Redoubt now remain in Sussex.

By the middle of the 19th century, the main external threat to England was considered to be one of attack on ports. The principal defences on the South Coast at this time were built in the 1860s around the naval base at Portsmouth, but at both Littlehampton (west of the harbour) in 1854, and Shoreham in 1857, a substantial new artillery fort was constructed, illustrating the rising significance of those ports.[11] By 1864, Newhaven was also considered to be of sufficient importance to merit the construction of a new artillery fort, and one that included the first use of massed concrete in a British fortification.[12]

As the century progressed, however, the Royal Navy was given the dominant role in defending the county from invasion and the coastal fortifications declined.

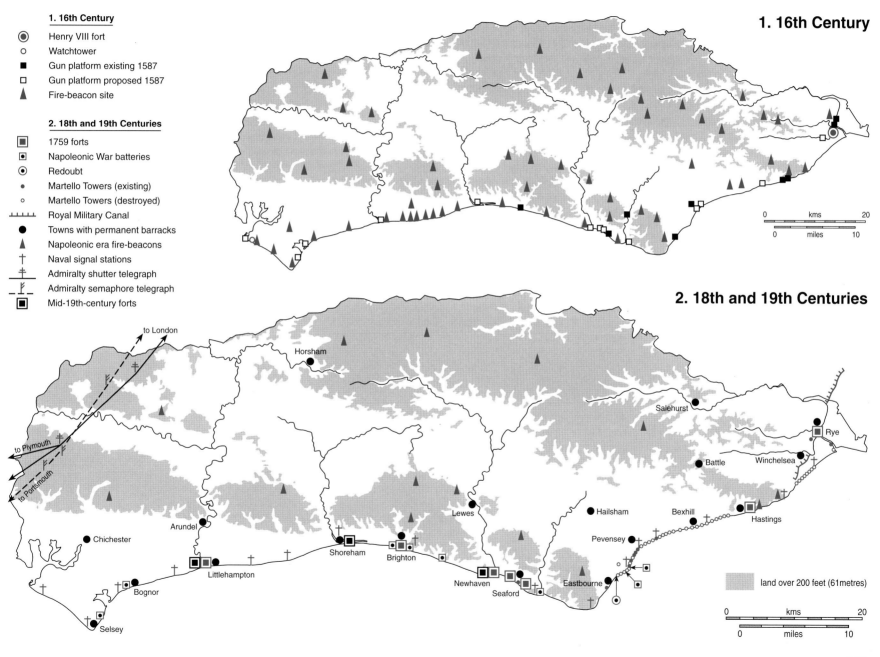

1. 16th Century

1. 16th Century

- ◉ Henry VIII fort
- ○ Watchtower
- ■ Gun platform existing 1587
- □ Gun platform proposed 1587
- ▲ Fire-beacon site

2. 18th and 19th Centuries

- ▣ 1759 forts
- ▣ Napoleonic War batteries
- ◉ Redoubt
- • Martello Towers (existing)
- ○ Martello Towers (destroyed)
- ┼┼┼ Royal Military Canal
- ● Towns with permanent barracks
- ▲ Napoleonic era fire-beacons
- † Naval signal stations
- ╪ Admiralty shutter telegraph
- ⌐ Admiralty semaphore telegraph
- ▣ Mid-19th-century forts

2. 18th and 19th Centuries

to London

to Plymouth

to Portsmouth

Horsham

Salehurst

Rye

Battle

Winchelsea

Hailsham

Bexhill

Hastings

Lewes

Pevensey

Chichester

Arundel

Shoreham

Brighton

Newhaven

Seaford

Eastbourne

Littlehampton

Bognor

Selsey

land over 200 feet (61 metres)

| 0 | kms | 20 |
| 0 | miles | 10 |

103

The 18th and 19th centuries were to bring great industrial change to parts of the British Isles. In the initial phases of the Industrial Revolution it was the textile and iron and steel industries that changed most. In Sussex, textile production had largely ceased by 1700, though isolated enterprises producing woollen and cotton cloth, linen, silk and sacking are recorded for later dates.[1] The iron industry proved more resilient, but as early as 1700 was not price-competitive with imported Swedish iron. The main product that sustained the industry until the end of the Seven Years War (1756-63) was ordnance. Coke-smelted pig iron and competition for ordnance orders from companies such as the Carron ironworks further reduced the ability of the Sussex industry to compete. Ten wealden furnaces and 13 forges were listed in 1717 but only three furnaces were in production 70 years later. The last furnace, Ashburnham, closed in 1813, the associated forge lingering on until 1826.[2]

The author of the introduction to *Pigot's Directory* could declare in 1839 that the manufactures of Sussex were 'neither various or extensive', but this statement tends to hide the considerable range that then existed. Even after the county had been opened up by improved roads, canals and river navigations and then railways, many markets were best served by local production. Industries such as brick, tile and pottery manufacture; lime, cement and plaster production; brewing and malting and the milling of grain were undertaken extensively and are dealt with in the sections that follow (see maps 53-56).[3] However, these were far from being the only industries.

Basic iron production may have ceased but foundries casting both iron and brass were to be found in most Sussex towns. Coastal locations were initially favoured, but inland towns also produced castings; Horsham had two foundries in 1882. Perhaps the best-known Sussex foundry was the Regent Foundry in Gloucester Lane, Brighton, which cast the chains for the Chain Pier (see p.92), iron spans for the New England Road railway bridge (1852-3) and also the bridge crossing Trafalgar Street allowing access to Brighton station. Three more foundries existed at Brighton and four more at Lewes in 1839. These met the growing demand for stoves and ovens, coal hole covers, iron railings and balconies and the ever growing list of goods that the public demanded to be made of iron or brass.[4]

Charcoal was in decline for the the iron industry but production continued. Often itinerant workmen, moving from one woodland area to the next, were the producers, but at Northchapel a substantial manufactory operated during the Napoleonic Wars, ceasing in 1831. This had a capacity of 27,500 tons per annum and the product went to the gunpowder works at Faversham (Kent) and Waltham (Essex). Gunpowder was also produced within the county, the main centre of production being Battle, where five mills operated at various dates between 1676 and 1874. Other works in the same area were at Sedlescombe, active in the 1760s, and Brede c.1770-1825. Further to the west was Maresfield, active until the 1850s.[5]

The forested nature of Sussex provided a resource for a number of trades. Wealden oak was actively sought by ship construction yards along the Thames estuary, but the Sussex coast also had active construction and repair yards. The fishing fleets of Rye, Hastings, Seaford, Brighton, Worthing, Bognor and Selsey provided trade for boat builders. Brighton had around 100 boats in 1813, declining to 53 in 1903, but in that year Hastings still had 103 and Worthing 56.[6] Sussex yards in the 18th and 19th centuries were, however, capable of producing larger ships for the North American and Australian trades. Shoreham in the mid-Victorian period could build vessels of 800-tons burthen and Littlehampton 450-tons. Rye had three shipyards and could produce 350-ton ships and even Hastings, launching from the beach, 200-ton vessels. Inland river and canal ports such as Lewes, Arundel and Chichester built ships. The last substantial vessel to be launched at Shoreham was in 1878 and by then Sussex yards had ceased to be viable for ocean-going vessels. Iron and steel shipbuilding, located in the north of Britain, was taking much of the trade and those seeking wooden vessels found it cheaper to use North American yards. Associated with shipbuilding were sail makers and rope works, though one of the largest rope making manufactories in the county was inland at Hailsham.[7]

Other industries reliant on woodland resources included furniture making, ranging from fashionable middle-class urban demand requiring imported veneer and carcass woods, to simple turnery and chair construction at village level. A branch of the Tunbridge Ware industry, producing decorative boxes and wooden souvenirs, flourished at Brighton c.1810-50 and at Lindfield a piano manufactory operated until 1886 when it was moved to Rugby. Trug baskets were the speciality of Herstmonceux, cricket bats of Robertsbridge and, at Selsey, Pullinger's works produced ingenious mouse traps and other goods aimed at a wider than local market. Coach building and repair was a trade found in most towns, some builders enjoying a more than local reputation. Paper manufacture was carried out on a limited scale in the county with works at West Ashling (Funtington), Iping, Isfield, Lewes and Hooe.[8]

Other Sussex industries relying on locally produced commodities included leather tanning, though by the end of the 19th century it was increasingly centred on Bermondsey in south-east London. Leather shoes, gloves, harness and saddles were widely produced within the towns and villages in Sussex. Another product of the agricultural sector was tallow. From this, candles and soap were manufactured. Potash, another ingredient required in soap manufacture, was produced in the Petworth area. Both candle and soap manufacture were town-based and in the 19th century factories were located at Brighton, Chichester, Hastings, Lewes, Petworth and Rye.[9]

The relative prosperity of farming in the mid-Victorian period, coupled with the development of improved agricultural implements and machinery and the advent of steam for ploughing and threshing, led to the development of a number of substantial manufacturers of agricultural equipment with the ability to install, hire and maintain steam plant. Typical of the larger firms were Penfolds of Arundel which commenced in 1833 and moved from the town to Tortington in 1871, and Carter Brothers of Billingshurst from the 1880s. Horsham had two farm implement manufacturers in the mid-19th century, edge tools were made at Chichester and elsewhere, and wooden tools such as rakes were widely produced, the Rich family of East Hoathly claiming to have the largest wooden goods manufactory in the county.[10] Steam engineering was also represented by the Brighton works of the London, Brighton & South Coast Railway. The works started producing locomotives in 1852, though the buildings were not completed until 1854. The works was expanded in 1870-73 and was in the late 19th century employing 2,000 workers. Lack of space on the site led to the removal of the marine engineering to Newhaven by 1901 and in the next year land was purchased at Lancing for a new carriage and wagon works. Signalling equipment was briefly manufactured by Saxby

& Farmer in the Haywards Heath area from 1862 but by the next decade production had been transferred to Kilburn.[11] Electrical equipment manufacture had made an appearance in the county by the last decade of the century.[12]

Printing was a craft widely practised in Sussex towns, in many of which newspapers or books such as local guides or histories for visitors were produced by the 19th century. *The Sussex Weekly Advertiser or Lewes Journal*, which commenced production in 1745, was the only paper in the town before the arrival of the enterprising George Baxter. He launched a rival, *The Sussex Agricultural Express*,

published Horsfield's two-volume history of Lewes (1824/1827) and his county history (1835) and devised a new method of inking plates using a roller. His talented son was to devise a multicolour printing system which achieved national fame.[13]

The pattern of industry was even more diversified than this short account can suggest, as numerous other trades are recorded in Sussex directories. These were small in scale, often one-person enterprises, but nevertheless significant in the totality of persons employed.

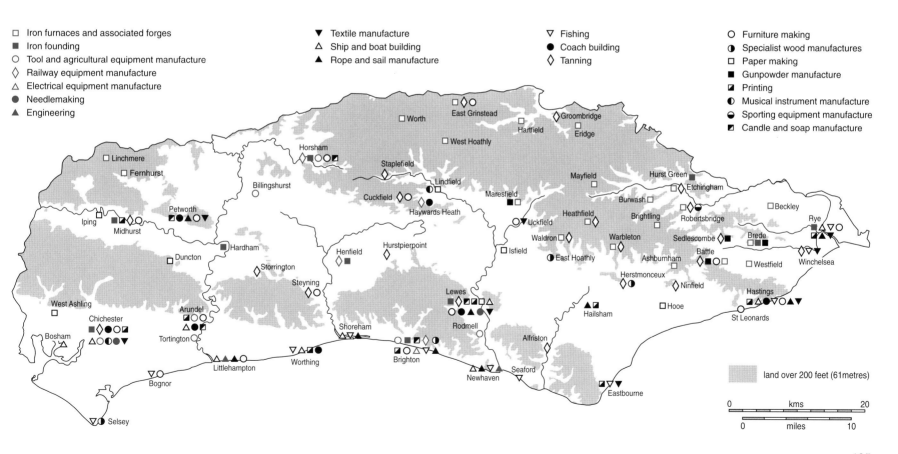

105

Bricks and tiles were first manufactured in Sussex during the period of the Roman occupation but, with the coming of the Saxons, who favoured timber as a building material, the skills were lost and not re-introduced from the Continent until the 13th century, when a tilery was established at Battle Abbey and most of the other monastic houses in the county followed suit. Bricks were being imported in small quantities from the early 14th century onwards but do not appear to have been made in Sussex until *c*.1440, when large quantities were produced, probably under Flemish supervision, for the building of Herstmonceux Castle.[1] Even then both bricks and tiles were slow to regain ground, as timber was plentiful and relatively cheap. However, from the mid-16th century onwards, increasing quantities were being made for use in the wealden iron industry, for the building of country houses and also for fireplaces and chimneys in timber-framed houses. The temporary kilns used by the itinerant brickmakers of the 15th and 16th centuries gradually gave way to permanent kilns, many of which were sited on the extensive commons in the Weald.

By the 18th century, brick had become established as the principal building material and tiles were replacing thatch on both houses and barns. They were also used, in the form of tile-hanging, to refurbish and insulate existing timber-framed buildings. The growth of the coastal resorts in the latter part of the century led to an increase in demand. This was met by the proliferation of small brickyards, using wood-burning kilns, particularly around Hastings, and of brickfields, where large quantities of bricks were burnt in open clamps, along the Coastal Plain to the west of Brighton. Brick was fashionable in the Georgian period and this led to older houses being re-faced in brick in towns such as Chichester and Horsham. In Lewes and elsewhere in East Sussex, mathematical tiles were used to clad timber-framed houses to resemble brick.[2]

The brick tax, imposed in 1787 and not finally repealed until 1850, did not greatly impede the spread of brickmaking, as the population of the county was rising steadily over this period and required housing. During the Napoleonic Wars the demand was further increased both by the presence in Sussex of large numbers of soldiers and camp followers, and by the decision to build the Martello Towers, each requiring around half a million bricks, along the flatter parts of the coast between Rye Bay and Seaford (see map 51).

By the mid-19th century there was at least one brickyard in practically every parish, with the exception of those situated on the chalk Downs and, even there, pockets of clay-with-flints and deposits of loess were occasionally exploited (see map 1). There were also brickyards on many of the large country estates, some of which, such as Ashburnham in the east and Goodwood in the west, not merely fulfilled their own requirements but supplied other customers in their locality.[3] Agricultural improvement, which encouraged the use of land drains, created additional work for the country brickyards where agricultural drainpipes were frequently produced in addition to bricks and tiles.

From *c*.1840 onwards the number of brickyards increased rapidly, mainly as a result of the coming of the railways and the consequent enlargement of the coastal towns (see maps 40 and 46). Whereas bricks had always been made adjacent to the building site whenever feasible to avoid the high costs of carriage, railway transport now made it possible to supplement the clamp-burnt bricks made along the Coastal Plain, with better-quality kiln-burnt bricks and quantities of tiles produced in the Weald. The new town of Burgess Hill grew up around the brickyards and potteries established specifically for this trade, clay deposits around Plumpton and Partridge Green were similarly exploited and bricks from Southwater, south of Horsham, were sent by rail to Worthing.[4]

Domestic pottery had been made in small quantities in Sussex from earliest times. There was a flourishing medieval pottery industry in Ringmer in East Sussex and around Graffham in West Sussex and kilns have been found in a number of other localities. By the late 18th century 'brownware', a red earthenware covered with a glossy lead glaze, was being made in commercial quantities in potteries in the Rye and Hastings area, on the Dicker near Hailsham, in Chailey and Ditchling and several other places. The clays used for these products were also eminently suitable for making terracotta and, when this became popular as a building material in the late-Victorian period, the 'potteries' of mid-Sussex in particular went into large-scale production. Crested ridge tiles, ornamental finials and chimney pots, as well as flower pots for the market gardens along the coast of West Sussex which were expanding to supply the London market, were manufactured.[5]

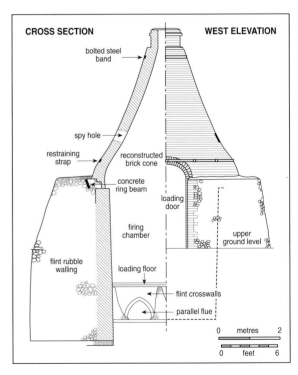

Restored 19th-century tile kiln at Piddinghoe

A peak in the number of brickyards in operation was reached in the 1890s, but already significant improvements in brick-making technology were beginning to make the smaller country brickyards redundant. The old methods of moulding bricks and tiles by hand, drying them in the open air and firing them in a simple wood-fired, open-topped kiln were being superseded by wire-cutting and moulding machines, heated drying sheds and larger, more sophisticated, coal-fired kilns. These changes also made continuous production possible, whereas work in the traditional brickyards had only been seasonal. Therefore, although the volume of brick production went on increasing into the 20th century, the number of brickyards rapidly dwindled, being replaced by large-scale brickworks such as the one which grew up at Warnham station, north of Horsham, which was able to dispatch its wares by rail across the county and also to London.

In spite of these developments, the old tradition of brick-burning in open clamps persisted, especially in the coastal area, up to the outbreak of the Second World War, largely because of the existence of a pool of cheap labour. Furthermore, a method of clamp-burning under open-sided sheds was developed on a few inland sites, where yards are still in operation at the present time.

The map shows the distribution of brickyards and potteries in the 18th and 19th centuries and does not take account either of earlier operations or of 20th-century developments. In consequence a number of parishes in the Arun valley and in the Bognor/Chichester area, in which the industry flourished briefly in the early years of this century, remain unshaded. In general, the greater concentrations of brickyards were to be found on the Weald Clay and the Hastings Beds in the centre and east of Sussex, reflecting not only the suitability of the materials available, including wood for fuel, but also the relatively higher population density of these areas (see maps 44 and 45). By contrast, the Downland is almost devoid of such sites.

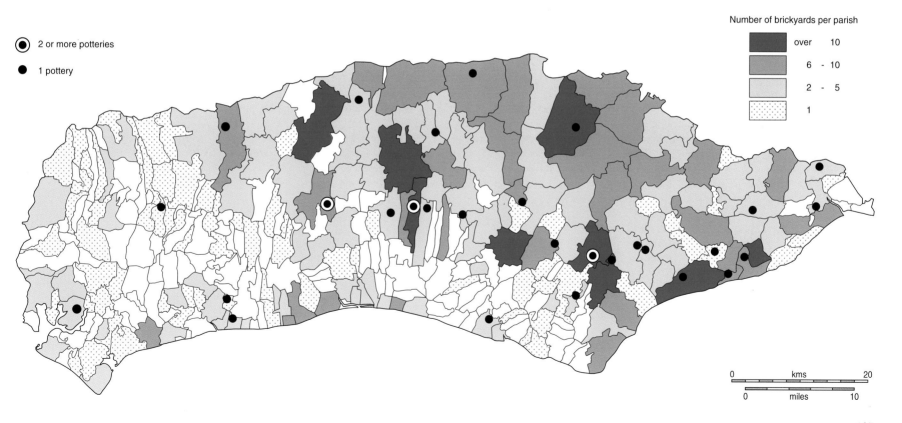

2 or more potteries

1 pottery

Number of brickyards per parish

over 10

6 - 10

2 - 5

1

0   kms   20

0   miles   10

The topography of Sussex has influenced the distribution of mills, which show a relatively uniform spread compared with many other counties. The conjunction of north-south flowing rivers and the higher land of the Downs and High Weald offer countryside that can provide both wind and water power. This is in contrast to neighbouring Hampshire, where most of the mills were water-powered.

Water Power

First recorded in the Greek part of the Roman Empire in the first century BC, a waterwheel on a horizontal shaft was geared to a vertical spindle rotating an upper stone over a stationary under stone. The watermill was in active use in Saxon England and Domesday Book records approximately 160 mills in the county. Actual sites are difficult to determine, both from Domesday Book and from other medieval sources. The full list from the Sussex Domesday folios notes the holding of 164 mills, five half-mills and one one-third of a mill, part of the 6,000 or so recorded there for the whole of England.[1] Although since the 11th century there have been many improvements to the machinery, dependence on water supply remained fundamental, and such supply could suffer from periods of drought as well as disputes from other users requiring to use the water for other mills or for irrigation.

The iron industry in Sussex utilised many of the sites and the ideas of corn mills, such as that at Boringwheel Mill on the edge of Ashdown Forest. The industry also developed new sites to operate the bellows and hammers required for those processes. But with the demise of the iron industry in Sussex in the 18th century, many sites were converted, or reverted, into corn milling. Ifield water mill and the one at Bewbush (Ifield) are examples of the change of use from iron manufacture to corn milling. At the former, the iron forge had been burnt by Waller's forces in 1643 and appears not to have been rebuilt for iron production, but rather to mill corn. At the latter, less than 1km away, the iron furnace was ruined by 1664. At Sheffield furnace site (Fletching), a corn mill had been built on the furnace site just below the bay and hammer pond by 1598, and continued in production until 1928.[2] This change of use accounts for the many mill streams

that even now contain slag from iron processing (see map 31).

There are individual records of at least 230 watermill sites in Sussex. Most mills were used for grinding corn for human or animal consumption. However, some had other uses, such as the fulling of cloth at Hempstead Mill (Uckfield), for providing power for sawing wood as at Brightling Park Mill, the pumping of water as at Coultershaw Mill (Petworth) and for driving farm machinery as at Durford Abbey Farm (Rogate). Today, examples of working mills can be seen at Michelham Priory Mill (restored using a Heritage Lottery Fund Grant from 1996) and the water pumping mill at Coultershaw.

Tidal Power

An alternative coastal development available in Sussex involved harnessing the power of the tide by trapping water at high tide and releasing this, as the tide receded, to drive a mill. Unlike the mill pond and stream, the tidal flow guaranteed the miller two periods in each day when the mill could operate, albeit that some of the times were unsocial. There was power in the tide, as can be seen by the fact that a tidemill at Bishopstone near Newhaven, built by 1768 and enlarged in the early 19th century, had 16 pairs of stones to grind corn.[3] Other smaller examples were at Birdham and Sidlesham amongst the tidal creeks of western Sussex. There are no working examples left in Sussex, the Bishopstone Mill having closed in the late 1880s.

Wind Power

The earliest Sussex windmills dated from at least the 1180s, when, out of 56 documented for England, three were in the county, at Amberley, Boxgrove and Ecclesdon (Ferring).[4] Earlier windmills, constructed before the mid-19th century, were of the wooden post-mill type. These were of simple design and the miller had to stop the mill every time there was a change in wind direction or speed. These changes required adjustments to the sails for an alteration in wind strength or the direction the mill was facing when the wind changed direction. Nutley open-trestle windmill was built in the early 19th century and is

a good example of the basic simplicity of the early post-mill. Other earlier examples of this type can still be seen at High Salvington (Worthing), Oldlands (Ditchling) and 'Jill' above Clayton.

During the 18th and 19th centuries increased technical knowledge provided the skills and the materials for many improvements to the workings of mills, enabling them to become a ubiquitous landscape feature. Thus we see the larger wooden smock-mill requiring only the cap to rotate to keep the mill facing into the wind. An example of this type is Punnetts Town Mill (Heathfield). This was then superseded by the more substantial brick tower mill, as at Halnaker (Boxgrove) or Patcham. The later versions of these, such as that at Stone Cross (Westham) and at Polegate, both to the north of Eastbourne, had all the refinements to enable the miller to operate the mill continuously on his own and without having to stop the mill working in order to make adjustments.

Most mills, both wind- and water-powered, originally built to operate by natural power and which survived into the 20th century, had some other source of power installed. This was achieved by adding a belt-driven pulley system in the mill that was connected to either a steam, oil or gas engine, placed externally, usually in an outbuilding. A good example of this is the weather-boarded Shipley Mill, preserved as a working mill, and now dedicated to the memory of a former owner, Hilaire Belloc.

Steam Power

This category of mill was purpose-built, originally constructed to be powered by a steam engine. Many were converted to operate by electrical power, and by the early-20th century there were mills being designed to operate by electricity from the outset. However, these are still normally referred to as steam mills. In addition to the change of the source of power, the milling process was different. Instead of two stones, one stationary and the other rotating, roller-milling now used two metal rollers mounted horizontally. A greater control of the end product could now be achieved, with higher productivity using less labour, and being run at times to suit the miller, who could now be assured of a constant power supply.

Without the requirement to be sited at the source of power these new mills were built in more central locations and close to the new railway network. A good example is the steam mill that was built in the 1890s at Three Bridges, close to the railway station. But with improved transport and the economies to be gained from operating port-based, larger mills, Sussex lost all the steam mills as such, although several of their buildings survive by being used for other purposes. One is that at Glynde, again adjacent to the railway station, and now used as a factory.

Distribution of Sussex Mills

The map demonstrates the fundamental distinction between the distribution of water-powered mills compared to windmills, the latter being in the majority on the Downs. In the High Weald the two were more equal, although the ubiquity of water power allowed for many sites in the river valleys and especially on the faster-flowing upper tributaries. A similar equality prevailed in the Low Weald and the Coastal Plain. The relative absence of windmills in the north-west and north-central areas of Sussex is very striking and not easily explicable. The smaller number of steam mills is associated with urban concentrations such as Brighton, Chichester and Crowborough. The map shows the distribution of mills according to their latest known position, but one problem in identifying sites for mills is that they were movable. Many Sussex mills, mainly post-mills but also some

smock-mills, have records of having been on other sites. The smock-mill at Chailey (Heritage Mill) for instance had two sites prior to being moved to Chailey; first at Highbrook in Kent, then near Newhaven, before finishing up at the present site. The demise of the wind- and water-powered mill started in the late-19th century, the Nutley post-mill closing in 1908, and gradually most mills succumbed to the inevitable with the last windmill to work commercially being that at Cross-in-Hand in 1971 and one of the last watermills being Cobb's Mill at Sayers Common that closed in 1966. At present there is a revival of interest in the working of mills. Nutley mill was restored from the late-1960s and there have been many appeals for restoration funds throughout Sussex. There are at present some 20 mills open to view by the public.

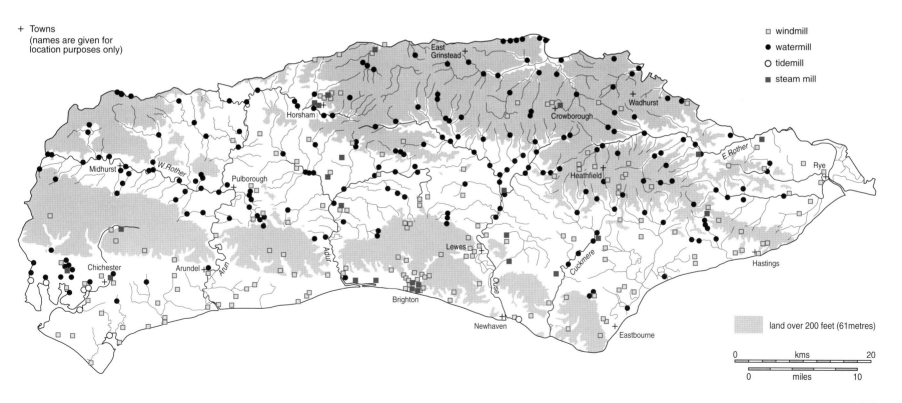

+ Towns
(names are given for location purposes only)

□ windmill
● watermill
○ tidemill
■ steam mill

land over 200 feet (61metres)

109

Limekilns

Historically, lime is one of the most widely used manufactured materials of all time other than from food related products. It is produced by the 'burning' of calcium carbonate in a kiln at a temperature of 900°C and this drives off carbon dioxide, leaving calcium oxide ($CaCO_3 = CaO + CO_2$). The resultant quick lime, when mixed with water in a violent reaction called slaking, produces hydrated lime. The most common source of calcium carbonate is limestone, which in Sussex is found in the form of chalk from the South Downs, although Sussex marble, commonly called winklestone, has been exploited by the Earl of Ashburnham and others.[1] Of all the uses of lime, the most common in Sussex were in building and in agriculture. Lime has been used since Roman times in building for binding together masonry blocks, right up to the introduction of Portland cement. The lime, once slaked, is left in troughs to mature and then mixed with sand or aggregates to make mortar or concrete, or it is used neat in the form of lime putty or plaster. When lime is diluted with water it is applied to walls as whitewash. Before the 16th century it was the normal practice to build a lime pit on site in order to produce lime for an individual building and several examples have been excavated, notably at Bramber Castle and Old Erringham Farm in Shoreham.[2] The increasing use of masonry in building in the 16th and 17th centuries, and the boom in building from the late 18th century onwards, required a considerably increased production of lime and encouraged the building of the many lime works situated along the line of the escarpment of the South Downs.

The pattern of the use of lime for agricultural purposes is different. Although arable agriculture was largely carried out on the lighter soils near the Downs and the Coastal Plain, by the 17th century the increasing population of the Weald made the production of arable crops necessary on a larger scale. The difficulty of working the heavy clay soils required the application of manures and, although various substances were also used to make the soils more easily worked, the most popular of these was lime.[3]

The data for limekilns on the map is based on information from the 1st Edition 25-inch Ordnance Survey maps, and kilns have also been included where they are described as 'Old Limekiln'. Inspection of tithe maps *c.*1840 has also been carried out but, although there was a recommendation to include topographical features on the maps, the symbol for limekilns has been rarely used. In fact there are only 15 parishes of the 306 in Sussex in which they are shown. The only indication of the presence of limekilns is when fields are named 'Limekiln Field' or similar in the tithe map schedules. However, this does not give any indication of kilns existing in fields which have other names. The map indicates the number of kilns found in each parish but, in addition, lime works where there was more than one kiln on a site have been individually shown.

The pattern of limekilns shows the greatest concentration in the areas of Weald Clay where each farm often had its own kiln, the chalk being fetched from the South Downs. An extant and restored example of such a farm kiln is at Ebernoe (Kirdford). The kilns of the South Downs were normally located at the foot of the scarp face and were often associated with a means of transport. Canals and river navigations were used during the late 18th and early 19th centuries and after the 1840s the railways were also available.

Cement and Plaster

Portland cement was invented by Joseph Aspdin in 1824, being manufactured by heating a mixture of limestone and clay at a temperature of 1400°C. The resulting clinker is finely ground and the resulting powder was bagged

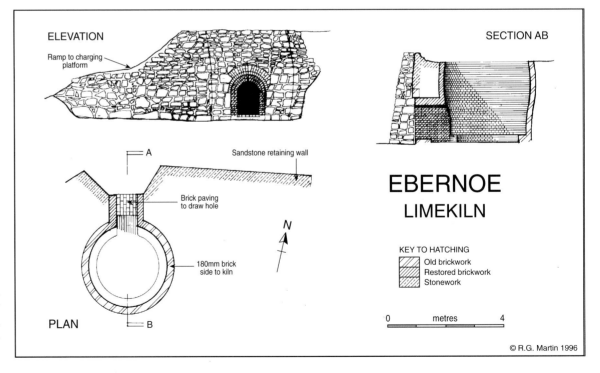

ELEVATION

Ramp to charging platform

SECTION AB

A

Sandstone retaining wall

Brick paving to draw hole

N

180mm brick side to kiln

PLAN

B

EBERNOE
LIMEKILN

KEY TO HATCHING
Old brickwork
Restored brickwork
Stonework

0   metres   4

© R.G. Martin 1996

and used to make mortar and concrete, increasingly throughout the latter part of the 19th and during the 20th centuries displacing lime in this respect. Cement was initially burnt in kilns similar to limekilns but by the beginning of the 20th century rotary kilns had been invented which resulted in considerably increased production. All the cement kilns in Sussex were located in the South Downs but only the one at Upper Beeding is still extant, although no longer in production.

Plaster is derived from gypsum which is mined at Mountfield and Brightling. Gypsum is hydrated calcium sulphate which, when heated, is converted into a hemi-hydrated plaster. These mines are still in production.

Extractive Industries

Sussex has been the source of a whole variety of minerals extracted for use mainly in the building industry. Flint, gravel, marl and chalk pits have not been noted on the map, as being too numerous to record, but in addition large chalk pits, as at Amberley, are always associated with both lime and cement works. Sand is excavated in large pits in the Washington area and there were sand mines in Pulborough for the excavation of moulding sand. Clay and brickearth were dug wherever brick- and pottery-making took place. Material from the beach deposits has been obtained from the Crumbles near Eastbourne, Rye Harbour and Chichester. Flints were

also either picked off the fields or derived from beach deposits in the form of cobbles or pebbles. Stone slabs used for roofing have been obtained in the Horsham area and copperas from the cliffs in Portslade. The sources noted on the maps are mainly quarries where squared stone has been derived – Lower Greensand from the Pulborough area and the Tunbridge Wells Sandstone, as well as Purbeck Limestone for lime and decorative work.

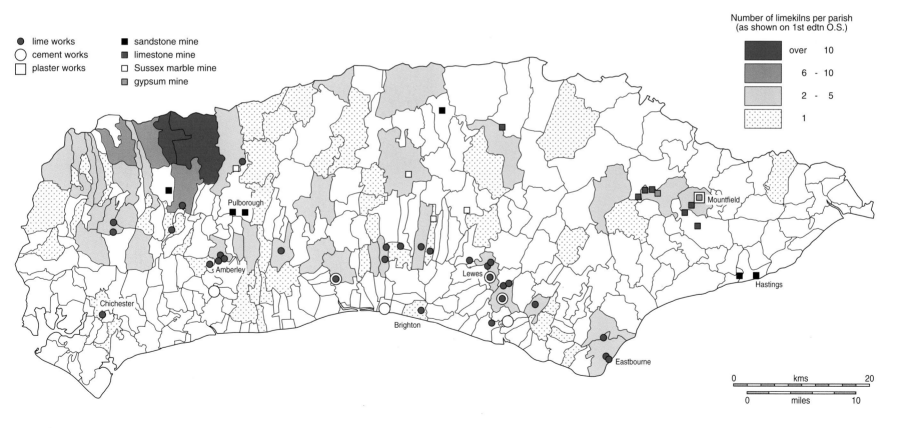

Malting

Malt, the brewer's main raw material, is produced from barley, the cultivation of which requires a soil giving a high nitrate content in spring and less later on for a high yield of low nitrogen content.[1] Such a soil is found on the South Downs where a light loam overlies the chalk and at several locations in the western interior of Sussex. In the malthouse the barley is first steeped in a cistern of water for up to 48 hours.[2] After the water has been drawn off it is spread on the floor and allowed to germinate for between 8 to 15 days. The sugars in the barley undergo a chemical change making them suitable for brewing. The resulting malt is finally dried in a kiln at various temperatures, depending on the kind of beer to be produced. Malting by brewers was usually carried out close to their brewery, although some malthouses were situated near to the barley fields where land and labour were cheaper, providing welcome work for farm labourers during the winter months, the usual malting season.

In the 18th and early 19th centuries there was a considerable export trade in malt, Chichester being the largest production area, reputed once to have had 32 malthouses, although not all these have been identified.[3] Not all maltsters were the users of the malt and a few, termed 'maltsters for sale', sold to local customers, mainly small publicans and private brewers who required small amounts and had neither the time nor the space to carry out their own malting. Production was often in the hands of the farmers who grew the barley, many of whom malted the barley of neighbours as well as their own. Sometimes the business was carried out in combination with milling, baking and corn-dealing, although some traders who were listed as maltsters in trade directories were probably only dealers.

No malting is now carried out in Sussex but several malthouses have survived, easily recognised by their rows of small ventilation windows on one or more low floors, and the drying kiln with its steep roof topped by a cowl. Surviving examples now put to an extraordinary variety of different uses include: a terrace of cottages to the east of the *Blacksmith Arms* at Adversane (Billingshurst); The Duke of York's Cinema in Brighton; the flats 'Drayman's Mews' at St Pancras, Chichester; village halls at Chidham and Cooksbridge; residences at Foundry Lane and Southover Manor, Lewes; East Grinstead British Legion Club; the Sussex Yacht Club at Southwick; and the East Sussex Record Office at The Maltings, Lewes.

The accompanying map for the period 1750 to 1900 shows 127 maltsters, three-quarters of whom were 'maltsters for sale'. Additionally, 38 common brewers had maltings adjacent to their breweries and 42 retail brewers were also maltsters.

Brewing

Beer is produced by the brewer adding hot water to ground malt in a malt-tun; boiling the resultant wort in a copper with hops and (only recently) with sugars; cooling; fermenting the wort by the action of yeast for about five days and finally either racking the beer into casks or bottling.[4] The process requires large quantities of water, for use in the actual brewing, to cool the worts and for cleaning purposes.

Brewing was one of the first industries in the 18th century to use steam power.[5] Furnaces used in the brewing could supply steam for an engine from which power could be taken by belts and pulleys to all parts of the brewery. Before steam, horse power via a horse wheel or gin operated the pumps, ground the malt and lifted the sacks. The same horses were often used to pull the delivery drays. Many small brewers stayed with horse power to the end of their existence, often into the 20th century. The coming of motor transport made deliveries over a large area much easier and beer was often transported from the country into the large towns, even to London. Most of the small firms suffered from the competition of larger concerns such as Tamplins, Henty and Constable and The Kemp Town Brewery, and either closed or were taken over.[6] The independent publican found it easier and cheaper to buy-in his beer rather than spend time brewing it himself.

There are two types of commercial brewer: the common brewer, brewing for wholesale or sale in his own tied public houses, and the retail or publican brewer, brewing for direct sale to the public for consumption either over the bar or at home. Many common brewers (such as the Stag Brewery at Petworth and the Frant Brewery) started as publican brewers and enlarged their plant so that they could supply other outlets. The terms

The Malthouse, Cooksbridge (Hamsey), now the village hall

'brewer' and 'publican' were often synonymous and it was not always certain whether a public house actually brewed its own beer.

Only two common brewers have survived: King and Barnes at Horsham and Harveys at Lewes.[7] Happily they have been joined recently by several small modern breweries. Many former brewing premises, however, have survived, their strong construction making them ideal for other uses. They can usually be recognised by their chimney and louvered roof on a building often resembling a tower. Examples are: the Eagle Brewery at Brewery Hill, Arundel; Battle Brewery and malthouse at the rear of 15 the High Street, Battle; the re-built Black Lion Brewery in Brighton; the Golden Hop Brewery at Seaside, Eastbourne; the Lion Brewery behind modern shop-fronts at Pevensey Road, Eastbourne; the Frant Brewery at Bells Yew Green; the Hailsham Brewery on the Battle Road, Hailsham; the Hurstpierpoint Brewery, Cuckfield Road, Hurstpierpoint; Beard's Brewery in Lewes; the Portslade Brewery in Old Portslade Village; Michell's Brewery in Steyning; Meryon's Brewery on the Strand at Rye; Ellis's Brewery and malthouse at Walberton; the Vine Brewery behind the 'Vine' pub at West Tarring; and the Tower Brewery at Warwick Road, Worthing.

The accompanying map shows that in Sussex, between 1750 and 1900, there were 83 common brewers and 231 retail brewers. The information for the map has been obtained from Trade Directories, Rate Books, Ordnance Survey and Tithe Maps found in both County Record Offices and, where available, preserved company records such as those of Messrs Tamplin, Whitbread and Allied Breweries.[8]

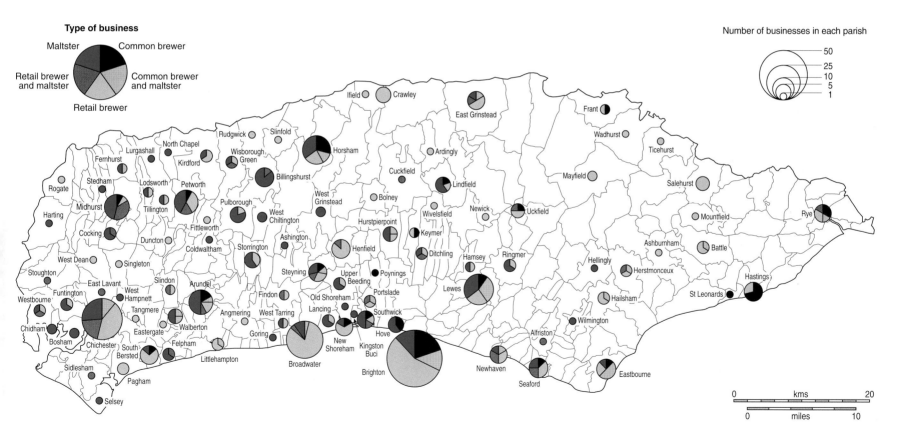

113

Between 1911 and 1951 the population of Sussex increased by 41%, from 663,378 to 937,339 people. Growth was faster in West Sussex than East Sussex, stronger after 1931 than before, and dominated by inward migration (the birth rate was relatively low and the death rate relatively high). The 43% increase for West Sussex in the two decades to 1951 was greater than for any other county in England and Wales, except Hertfordshire.

In 1931, 68% of the Sussex population lived in urban areas covering just 9% of the acreage, and over the four decades the county's population became ever more urban and suburban.[1] Away from the towns, a number of processes pushed people from the land, most obviously in the remoter and more isolated rural parishes of the Weald, and on parts of the Downs, where depopulation, or only a slight population increase, was normal. The situation provided rich pickings for Stella Gibbons in her classic rural parody: 'Sussex ... I don't much like the sound of that. Do they live on a decaying farm?'[2] Processes included the sale and fragmentation of many country estates which, especially in the Weald, were often the products of an earlier phase of immigration to Sussex during the 19th century, and unstable agricultural conditions – 'the "falling-down" of arable to poor pasture and the gradual disappearance of the sheep, so long the pride and mainstay of South Down farming'.[3]

The vacuum in the countryside attracted an immigrant literary and artistic metropolitan élite searching for a pastoral ideal, the likes of Kipling and Woolf, who moved to rural Sussex and in turn wove romanticised rural images of the county. Speculative developers also took advantage of cheap rural land, building houses in ribbon developments along main roads or in small greenfield estates. In parts of Sussex strong population growth took place: for example, Lindfield increased by 120%, Storrington by 100% and East Grinstead by 40%. The resulting 'discontinuous suburbs', with dormitory, retirement and service functions for London, had easy access to the stations on the main railway lines – many of which were electrified between the wars – and the developing arterial road system.

Resort towns remained the dominant population concentrations. Sussex seaside towns figured high in the national league table of resorts by population size. In 1911, Brighton, with a population of 131,237, was by far the largest resort in England and Wales, while Hastings ranked 4th (after Bournemouth and Southend). Eastbourne was 7th, Hove 11th, Worthing 16th, Bexhill 24th, and Littlehampton and Bognor 50th and 51st respectively.[4]

'Sussex by the Sea' was deluged by an annual seasonal influx of holidaymakers and resort workers. Municipal guide books encouraged holidaymakers to become residents, extolling the virtues of living by the sea. Many newcomers did, indeed, move to the coast, although they often avoided the lure of the great resorts, instead heading for new settlements. Between 1911 and 1951 population growth slowed in the older and larger resorts. Brighton, 'Old Ocean's Bauble', increased by 16%, Hastings by just 6%, and even Eastbourne, the great Victorian 'Empress of Resorts', by only 11%. Bexhill, an essentially Edwardian creation and the last traditional Sussex resort to be developed, bucked the East Sussex trend with its population increasing by 68%.[5]

Decades of untrammelled growth had left the older resorts with stark contrasts in the housing and living conditions of rich and poor. Tressell's famous political novel set in Edwardian Hastings described 'perpetual poverty which in many cases bordered on destitution', while three decades later the working-class areas of inner Brighton were presented by Graham Greene as 'the shabby secret behind the bright corsage'.[6] Municipal reactions to such conditions help provide a context for sometimes notable population change *within* some resorts and particularly in the second half of the period. With council renting emerging as a significant housing tenure, local authorities developed policies to re-house people from overcrowded private rented accommodation and began to clear the 'slums'.[7] People plucked from older inner urban areas by municipal authorities were likely to be deposited in new council estates on the edge of towns. Owner occupation also developed as an important housing tenure and private estates, too, were constructed on undeveloped land, becoming the new outer suburbs for resorts.[8] The older seaside resorts covered ever larger areas and there were boundary extensions to Brighton in

1923 and 1928, Hove in 1928, Hastings in 1925 and 1938, Eastbourne in 1912, 1927 and 1938 and Worthing in 1929.

Brighton between 1931 and 1951 well illustrates this doughnut pattern of urban population change. The population decline in many older central wards was considerable: Regency Ward declined by 48%, Pier by 37%, Pavilion by 39% and St John's by 36%. There were concomitant falls in population densities: in the extreme example of St John's, the number of persons per acre (0.4ha) declined from 157.6 in 1921 to 87.6 in 1951. On the outskirts of Brighton, however, the population of some wards soared: Rottingdean increased by 245% in the 20-year period to 1951, and Patcham by 528%.

Considerable technological change in public and private road transportation aided the growth of new suburbs by allowing people to live at ever greater distances from urban centres. It also helped produce another extraordinary development – the emergence of a remarkable linear urban form, stretching largely unbroken along the coast from the Selsey Peninsula in the west to Seaford in the east. This embryonic suburban city was broken by a few green fingers touching the coast and had larger nodes centred on the older seaside resorts.

The transformation of the coastal landscape was startlingly rapid. With the exception of the older urban parishes of Shoreham-by-Sea and Littlehampton, the population of all the coastal parishes and urban areas of West Sussex increased by at least 100% in the 40 years to 1951; between 400% and 800% was relatively common and at the extreme, Middleton-on-Sea rose by 2,600%. To the east of Brighton, Telscombe grew by 1,243% and Peacehaven by an extraordinary 3,926%.

There was no grand design to so-called 'Channel Street'; instead a string of new residential suburbs by the sea speedily developed and coalesced as the result of the separate decisions of a myriad of land owners, speculative house builders and thousands of individual households.[9] Apart from the extremes of the infamous Peacehaven – 'a disgusting blot on the landscape' – and arcardian 'plotlands' such as Pagham Beach and Shoreham Beach, more typical but less well documented were speculative low density estates of bungalows and 'Tudorbethan' semis and detached houses.[10]

In the 1920s and '30s some local authorities tried to control this new suburban beast, but it was the Second World War that halted unplanned sprawl.[11] Post-war, the greater acceptability of state intervention produced more rigorous land-use planning aimed at preserving the countryside and limiting untrammelled urban growth. Planned state new towns were also begun as communities designed to be self-contained and balanced for work and living. In Sussex, Crawley New Town, designated in 1947, was planned around a series of older settlements that had experienced considerable inter-war house building and inward migration.[12] The early post-war government, while despising the private enterprise suburban arcadias so prevalent in Sussex between the wars, was eager to devise its own version of the new Jerusalem.

The new towns and the control of urban sprawl – both with implications for Sussex population change, especially after 1950 – were, in part, an indirect outcome of the Second World War. Both world wars in the first half of the century had other consequences for population change. For example, the 1939-45 war resulted in extreme and abrupt population movements, particularly through evacuation (first to, and then from, Sussex) and the effects of military call-up and demobilisation. The civilian population in the string of coastal towns stretching from Newhaven eastwards to Rye declined by 45% in two years from 1939, although by 1947 the population total had reverted to the 1939 figure.[13] A quarter of a century earlier, the 1921 Census treated the thousands of war deaths that occurred abroad during the 1914-18 war as 'losses by migration'.[14] War memorials throughout Sussex tell another story, although the long term impact of war deaths on Sussex population change is unknown.

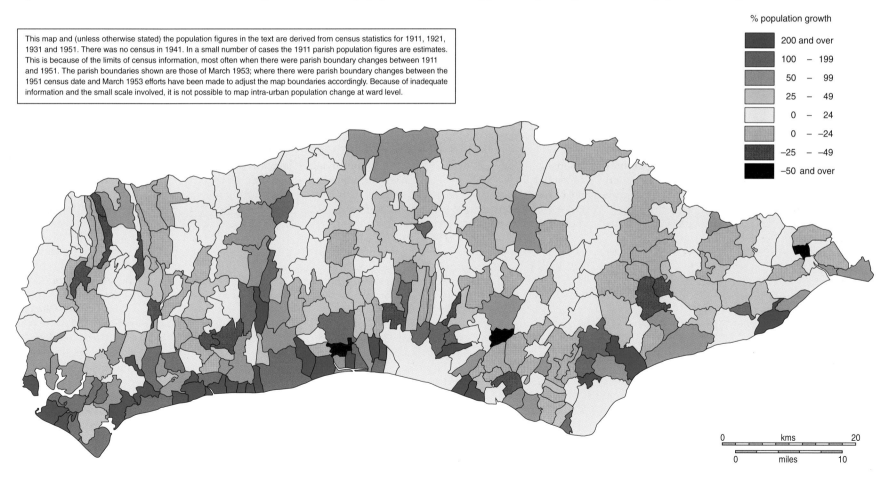

% population growth

▓	200 and over
▓	100 – 199
▓	50 – 99
▓	25 – 49
░	0 – 24
░	0 – –24
▓	–25 – –49
■	–50 and over

This map and (unless otherwise stated) the population figures in the text are derived from census statistics for 1911, 1921, 1931 and 1951. There was no census in 1941. In a small number of cases the 1911 parish population figures are estimates. This is because of the limits of census information, most often when there were parish boundary changes between 1911 and 1951. The parish boundaries shown are those of March 1953; where there were parish boundary changes between the 1951 census date and March 1953 efforts have been made to adjust the map boundaries accordingly. Because of inadequate information and the small scale involved, it is not possible to map intra-urban population change at ward level.

With the outbreak of war on 4 August 1914 the government depended on the patriotic endeavour of landed élites to mobilise manpower and material resources in each county on the age-old assumption that they would respond to the demands of a European war. At Arundel Castle the 17th Duke of Norfolk, Lord Lieutenant of Sussex, prepared the county's Emergency Scheme in the event of invasion and instigated recruiting plans as President of the Sussex Territorial Force Association. Deputy Lieutenants such as the Earl of Chichester, Baron Monk Bretton and G.W. Loder exerted their territorial influence in the expectation that recruits obtained for new 'service' battalions at Chichester, and for additional territorial battalions at Horsham and Hastings,would supplement sufficiently the two regular battalions of the Royal Sussex Regiment. The squadrons of Sussex Yeomanry mobilised at Chichester, Horsham, Brighton, Lewes and Rye, with horses requisitioned from hunts, would contribute to the mobile arm and the war would be over by Christmas.[1]

By the autumn months of 1914 the short-war illusion was shattered. The rhetoric of gentlemanly influence and authorised recruiters was overtaken by preparations for large-scale continental warfare. The War Office chose Shoreham and Seaford as divisional camps for Lord Kitchener's Third New Army.[2] Initially, atrocious conditions in the hutments led to the billeting of troops in coastal towns from Worthing to Eastbourne. Expressions of county identity were remarkably persistent in a war which became associated with anonymous and attritional forms of warfare. Beyond the control of the Lord Lieutenant, three 'Southdown' battalions were formed at Bexhill under the beneficent pseudo-patronage of Colonel Claude Lowther, owner of Herstmonceux Castle since 1911.[3]

Towns initially described as unresponsive to traditional recruiting pressures, such as Brighton and Eastbourne, became the focal points for enlistment by October 1914. From the shops as well as the sheep-fold, recruits participated in enthusiastic scenes of formalised departures from south coast railway stations for the Southdowners' new training camp at Cooden Beach. Edmund Blunden later remarked that these Southdown

battalions were a remarkable united expression of wartime Sussex.[4] The columns on 'Sussex and the War' in local newspapers highlighted the frequency with which men joined, served and died alongside each other. War memorials across Sussex bear testimony to complex, if still localised, patterns of recruitment. In Rusper men joined the Mayor of Kensington's battalion, which was training nearby. From Haywards Heath groups of 'pals' took the train to London to join the Queen's Westminster Rifles. Letters from the front contributed to the profound sense of local pride, which was a powerful element of wartime patriotism. [5] In Hassocks, and throughout mid-Sussex, the 'Fine Fourths' were celebrated for their Gallipoli record, Colonel Campion declaring that 'Sussex men are the right stuff after all'.[6] His wife turned their home, Danny at Hurstpierpoint, into a depot for comfort goods to send to the men. Increasingly the localised idiom of wartime service and sacrifice was expressed in another collective experience, church services to commemorate the war dead, which often took place at six-monthly intervals.

If the years 1914-16 were dominated in Sussex by the construction of large hutted camps, the billeting of troops for coastal defence and the exertion of landed influence, constant connections were forged between Sussex and the Great War in unforeseen and, often, poignant ways in the years 1917-18. Wounded soldiers were subject to charitable attention everywhere. From Southampton and Dover convoys of cot and sitting war-wounded arrived at the great Red Cross towns within 24 hours of departing from base hospitals in France.[7] The 2nd Eastern General Hospital was the focal point of many wards and annexes in Brighton and Hove which occupied buildings vacated by the boys' grammar school, elementary schools and the workhouse.[8] Innumerable private residences in Kemp Town accepted long-term medical cases. A further 24 auxiliary hospitals in Sussex formed part of a vast network of provision for the wounded Tommy whose arrival was too frequent and dismaying for cheering crowds to gather at railway stations after 1915. In Eastbourne six hospitals and provision for 1,000 wounded soldiers at Summerdown Convalescent Camp entitled the wartime capital of Sussex to the status of a Red Cross town.[9] The

sunshine records and recuperative qualities of the South Coast were mobilised in conditions of attritional war.

In the years 1917-18 the intensity and consequences of total war became apparent in Sussex in wide-ranging ways. Canadian and Australian forces occupied many training camps in the county and heavy artillery units were well represented as the war took the form of a 'wearing down' contest. The transport infrastructure of rail and port facilities assumed crucial strategic significance as the volume of war stores incessantly increased in preparation for the artillery battles in France after April 1917. In that year dock workers at Newhaven, including female labour, loaded stores onto transports for Italy as well as France. At sea, German U-boats managed to pass through the Dover Straits and merchant ships were sunk within sight of Beachy Head. German airships flew along the Sussex coast and naval air defence was reorganised and reinforced at Newhaven, Lancing and on the Portsmouth approaches. Plans for the defence of Britain against German invasion continued to require home defence units to maintain vigilance.[10]

On the political front the many visits of the Prime Minister, David Lloyd George, to the county assumed international significance when the War Cabinet discussed President Wilson's peace proposals in meetings at Danny Park and on walks over Wolstonbury Hill one month before the war ended.[11] For a county so ill-acquainted with industrial mass production, such a key feature of war in the modern age, Sussex experienced a diversity of roles which brought its encounter with the Great War uncomfortably close. In Fletching, Robert Saunders, the village headmaster, wrote of hearing the battles across the Channel: 'The great blot on everything is the Thud + Throb of the guns night and day in France'.[12]

As the war remorselessly continued, the contribution of Sussex shifted from the gentry and their estates in ways that acknowledged the demographic importance of that *other*, coastal and metropolitan, Sussex. As a consequence, the unexpected development of large integrated training and convalescent camps, and the military control of the enlarged port of Newhaven, formed the prime images of Sussex at war by 1918.

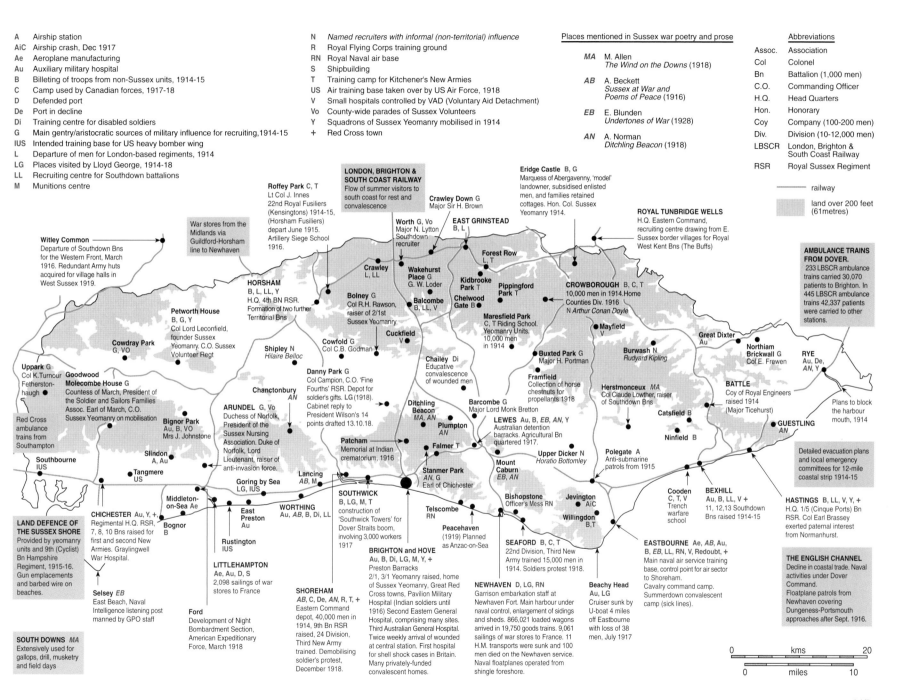

A   Airship station
AiC Airship crash, Dec 1917
Ae   Aeroplane manufacturing
Au   Auxiliary military hospital
B   Billeting of troops from non-Sussex units, 1914-15
C   Camp used by Canadian forces, 1917-18
D   Defended port
De   Port in decline
Di   Training centre for disabled soldiers
G   Main gentry/aristocratic sources of military influence for recruiting,1914-15
IUS Intended training base for US heavy bomber wing
L   Departure of men for London-based regiments, 1914
LG   Places visited by Lloyd George, 1914-18
LL   Recruiting centre for Southdown battalions
M   Munitions centre

N   *Named recruiters with informal (non-territorial) influence*
R   Royal Flying Corps training ground
RN   Royal Naval air base
S   Shipbuilding
T   Training camp for Kitchener's New Armies
US   Air training base taken over by US Air Force, 1918
V   Small hospitals controlled by VAD (Voluntary Aid Detachment)
Vo   County-wide parades of Sussex Volunteers
Y   Squadrons of Sussex Yeomanry mobilised in 1914
+   Red Cross town

Places mentioned in Sussex war poetry and prose

MA   M. Allen
     The Wind on the Downs (1918)

AB   A. Beckett
     *Sussex at War and
     Poems of Peace* (1916)

EB   E. Blunden
     Undertones of War (1928)

AN   A. Norman
     Ditchling Beacon (1918)

Abbreviations

Assoc.   Association
Col   Colonel
Bn   Battalion (1,000 men)
C.O.   Commanding Officer
H.Q.   Head Quarters
Hon.   Honorary
Coy   Company (100-200 men)
Div.   Division (10-12,000 men)
LBSCR   London, Brighton &
         South Coast Railway
RSR   Royal Sussex Regiment

———— railway

land over 200 feet
(61metres)

Witley Common
Departure of Southdown Bns for the Western Front, March 1916. Redundant Army huts acquired for village halls in West Sussex 1919.

War stores from the Midlands via Guildford-Horsham line to Newhaven

LONDON, BRIGHTON & SOUTH COAST RAILWAY
Flow of summer visitors to south coast for rest and convalescence

Roffey Park C, T
Lt Col J. Innes
22nd Royal Fusiliers
(Kensingtons) 1914-15,
(Horsham Fusiliers)
depart June 1915.
Artillery Siege School
1916.

Crawley Down G
Major Sir H. Brown

Worth G, Vo
Major N. Lytton
Southdown
recruiter

EAST GRINSTEAD
B, L

Eridge Castle B, G
Marquess of Abergavenny, 'model' landowner, subsidised enlisted men, and families retained cottages. Hon. Col. Sussex Yeomanry 1914.

ROYAL TUNBRIDGE WELLS
H.Q. Eastern Command, recruiting centre drawing from E. Sussex border villages for Royal West Kent Bns (The Buffs)

AMBULANCE TRAINS FROM DOVER.
233 LBSCR ambulance trains carried 30,070 patients to Brighton. In 445 LBSCR ambulance trains 42,337 patients were carried to other stations.

Forest Row
L, T

Crawley
L, LL

Wakehurst Place G
G. W. Loder

Kidbrooke Park T

Pippingford Park T

CROWBOROUGH B, C, T
10,000 men in 1914.Home Counties Div. 1916
N *Arthur Conan Doyle*

HORSHAM
B, L, LL, Y
H.Q. 4th BN RSR.
Formation of two further Territorial Bns

Petworth House
B, G, Y
Col Lord Leconfield, founder Sussex Yeomanry. C.O. Sussex Volunteer Regt

Bolney G
Col R.H. Rawson, raiser of 2/1st Sussex Yeomanry

Balcombe
B, LL, V

Chelwood Gate
B, LL, V

Maresfield Park
C, T Riding School. Yeomanry Units. 10,000 men in 1914

Mayfield V

Great Dixter
Au

**Northiam
Brickwall** G
Col E. Frewen

RYE
Au, De,
AN, Y

Cowdray Park
G, VO

Shipley N
Hilaire Belloc

Cowfold G
Col C.B. Godman

Cuckfield
V

Buxted Park G
Major H. Portman

Burwash N
Rudyard Kipling

Plans to block the harbour mouth, 1914

Uppark G
Col K.Turnour
Fetherston-
haugh

**Goodwood
Molecombe House** G
Countess of March, President of the Soldier and Sailors Families Assoc. Earl of March, C.O. Sussex Yeomanry on mobilisation

Chanctonbury
AN

Danny Park G
Col Campion, C.O. 'Fine Fourths' RSR. Depot for soldier's gifts. LG (1918). Cabinet reply to President Wilson's 14 points drafted 13.10.18.

Chailey Di
Educative convalescence of wounded men

Framfield
Collection of horse chestnuts for propellants 1918

Herstmonceux MA
Col Claude Lowther, raiser of Southdown Bns

BATTLE
Coy of Royal Engineers raised 1914
(Major Ticehurst)

Catsfield B

GUESTLING
AN

Red Cross ambulance trains from Southampton

ARUNDEL G, Vo
Duchess of Norfolk, President of the Sussex Nursing Association. Duke of Norfolk, Lord Lieutenant, raiser of anti-invasion force.

Bignor Park
Au, B, VO
Mrs J. Johnstone

Ditchling Beacon
MA, AN

Barcombe G
Major Lord Monk Bretton

Ninfield B

Slindon
A, Au

Southbourne
IUS

Tangmere
US

Goring by Sea
LG, IUS

Chichester Au, Y, +
Regimental H.Q. RSR. 7, 8, 10 Bns raised for first and second New Armies. Graylingwell War Hospital.

**Middleton-
on-Sea** Ae

Bognor

**East
Preston**
Au

WORTHING
Au, *AB*, B, Di, LL

Lancing
AB, M

SOUTHWICK
B, LG, M, T
construction of 'Southwick Towers' for Dover Straits boom, involving 3,000 workers 1917

Telscombe
RN

Peacehaven
(1919) Planned as Anzac-on-Sea

Falmer T

Stanmer Park
AN, G
Earl of Chichester

LEWES Au, B, *EB*, AN, Y
Australian detention barracks. Agricultural Bn quartered 1917.

Plumpton
AN

Upper Dicker N
Horatio Bottomley

**Mount
Caburn**
EB, AN

Polegate A
Anti-submarine patrols from 1915

Cooden
C, T, V
Trench warfare school

BEXHILL
Au, B, LL, V +
11, 12,13 Southdown Bns raised 1914-15

HASTINGS B, LL, V, Y, +
H.Q. 1/5 (Cinque Ports) Bn RSR. Col Earl Brassey exerted paternal interest from Normanhurst.

LAND DEFENCE OF THE SUSSEX SHORE
Provided by yeomanry units and 9th (Cyclist) Bn Hampshire Regiment, 1915-16. Gun emplacements and barbed wire on beaches.

Selsey *EB*
East Beach, Naval Intelligence listening post manned by GPO staff

Rustington
IUS

Ford
Development of Night Bombardment Section, American Expeditionary Force, March 1918.

LITTLEHAMPTON
Ae, Au, D, S
2,098 sailings of war stores to France

SHOREHAM
AB, C, De, *AN*, R, T, +
Eastern Command depot, 40,000 men in 1914, 9th Bn RSR raised, 24 Division, Third New Army trained. Demobilising soldier's protest, December 1918.

BRIGHTON and HOVE
Au, B, Di, LG, M, Y, +
Preston Barracks
2/1, 3/1 Yeomanry raised, home of Sussex Yeomanry, Great Red Cross towns, Pavilion Military Hospital (Indian soldiers until 1916) Second Eastern General Hospital, comprising many sites. Third Australian General Hospital. Twice weekly arrival of wounded at central station. First hospital for shell shock cases in Britain. Many privately-funded convalescent homes.

NEWHAVEN D, LG, RN
Garrison embarkation staff at Newhaven Fort. Main harbour under naval control, enlargement of sidings and sheds. 866,021 loaded wagons arrived in 19,750 goods trains. 9,061 sailings of war stores to France. 11 H.M. transports were sunk and 100 men died on the Newhaven service. Naval floatplanes operated from shingle foreshore.

Bishopstone
Officer's Mess RN

Jevington
AiC

Willingdon
B,T

SEAFORD B, C, T
22nd Division, Third New Army trained 15,000 men in 1914. Soldiers protest 1918.

Beachy Head
Au, LG
Cruiser sunk by U-boat 4 miles off Eastbourne with loss of 38 men, July 1917

EASTBOURNE Ae, *AB*, Au, B, *EB*, LL, RN, V, Redoubt, +
Main naval air service training base, control point for air sector to Shoreham. Cavalry command camp. Summerdown convalescent camp (sick lines).

Detailed evacuation plans and local emergency committees for 12-mile coastal strip 1914-15

THE ENGLISH CHANNEL
Decline in coastal trade. Naval activities under Dover Command. Floatplane patrols from Newhaven covering Dungeness-Portsmouth approaches after Sept. 1916.

SOUTH DOWNS MA
Extensively used for gallops, drill, musketry and field days

0   kms   20

0   miles   10

117

With the declaration of war on 3 September 1939, Sussex, along with many other parts of the United Kingdom, became part of the country's frontline defences. Its airfields played a key role in the Battle of Britain. Its towns were some of the most frequently attacked. Its fields and ports were an integral part of the build-up to the invasion of Europe, and its beaches some of the most heavily defended in the country.

The first line of defence was the 'coastal crust'. The overall plan was simple: defensive works guarded the Sussex coastline – pillboxes, machine-gun posts, trenches, rifle posts and anti-tank obstacles, reinforced by scaffolding, mines and barbed wire.[1] In locations such as Cuckmere Haven, where intelligence suggested a German invasion might occur, this 'coastal crust' was particularly thick. Less conventional warfare was also anticipated, such as installing equipment for setting the sea alight by petroleum at Church Norton, Rye and Camber Sands.

The coastal batteries were perhaps the most formidable part of these defences. In 1939 only one battery was in use – four 6-inch and two 12-pounder guns located at Newhaven, the only battery between Portsmouth and Dover.[2] By the end of the war nine major batteries existed on the Sussex coast, from Bognor Regis to Worthing and on to Hastings and Pett Level. Each location was different in design, often consisting of ex-Royal Navy 6-inch guns mounted in concrete structures. Excellent examples of surviving batteries can be seen at Pett Level and on the cliffs at Newhaven.

Inland, defences were no less weak. Generally these were arranged in six stop lines which, almost without exception, were based on Sussex rivers. Systems of mutually supporting pillboxes, trenches and other defences were used to defend the riverbanks, main roads, junctions and river crossings. These were: 1. part of the national General Headquarters Defence Line protecting Portsmouth which looped into Sussex through Midhurst and down to Chichester;[3] 2. the Arun Divisional Line following the Arun, from Bucks Green to Littlehampton and from Bucks Green to the Ouse via Horsham; 3. the Adur Divisional Line following the Adur from West Grinstead to Shoreham; 4. the Ouse Divisional Line stretching from Slaugham to Newhaven forming part of 5. the national General Headquarters Line which

extended northwards from Uckfield to Eridge and on to London;[4] 6. a Southeast Command Corps Defence Line running from Uckfield to Rye.[5]

To complement these defence lines 'nodal' defence points were set up at strategic locations. Often a nodal town, for example East Grinstead, was located on a defence line with its own defence system. In East Grinstead a Home Guard unit, 'B' Company 17th Battalion Royal Sussex Regiment, manned the defences, built in 1941 by Canadian Engineers.[6] Other nodal points were smaller, often at road junctions protected by a sandbagged rifle post, such as The Square in Findon. Shoreham Urban District had one of the largest number of nodal points at five; Southwick Urban District had four.[7]

Thankfully, these defences were never put to the use for which they were intended, unlike the airfields across Sussex which served long and hard throughout the war. The most famous were the RAF fighter stations at Tangmere, Westhampnett and Ford, the latter having served as a Royal Naval Air Station until September 1940. Tangmere was the sector airfield for A Sector of 11 Group, an area stretching from Brighton to Portsmouth. Westhampnett and Merston were satellite airfields for Tangmere. Others were located at Friston, Thorney Island and Shoreham.[8] Reminders of wartime activity can still be seen: at Merston a battle control centre, at Tangmere the runways, at Westhampnett the control tower, and at Ford a number of blister hangars.

Advanced Landing Grounds were constructed in the D-Day build up. The large number of aircraft preparing for the D-day operations used these basic airfields. In Sussex seven such airfields were established: Apuldram, Bognor Regis, Chailey, Coolham, Deanland (Ripe), Funtington and Selsey. As these were temporary sites almost nothing remains today. The Army established two airfields in Sussex for army observation aircraft at Hammerwood, near East Grinstead, and Parham. Shoreham was home to No. 277 Squadron, an Air-Sea Rescue unit which worked alongside the rescue launches of the air-sea rescue service, based at Shoreham, Littlehampton and Newhaven. Further D-Day preparation saw landing craft being built at Littlehampton, Itchenor and Bosham. Marshalling of the floating

Mulberry harbours took place off Pagham and Selsey. There were landing exercises in Bracklesham Bay and at Climping. The ports at Shoreham and Newhaven were major embarkation points.

As well as conventional defences, other devices were also employed, one of the most secretive being the deception sites. These consisted of equipment designed to draw the bombers from their intended target. At Gumber Farm (Slindon) the RAF established a decoy site of false runway lights to be switched on during an air raid, whilst the lights at nearby Tangmere would be extinguished. Another variation was at Cuckmere Haven, where a system of lights was arranged to convince the Luftwaffe that they were attacking Newhaven.[9]

At the outbreak of war, Britain possessed the technical advantage of radar for air defence. Development had begun in the early 1930s, and in 1935 authorisation was given for a national radar chain. By 1945 radar stations were at Poling, Durrington, Truleigh Hill, Beachy Head, Pevensey, Fairlight and Rye. The site at Pevensey remains remarkably complete for such a site some 50 years after the war. The transmitter and receiver blocks, air raid shelters, RAF housing and other miscellaneous buildings remain.[10]

Throughout 1939-45 every part of Sussex was affected by the war. Army camps, tented or more permanent, sprang up in fields and estates county-wide.[11] Large houses became home to military institutions: Bignor Manor was home to the French Resistance.[12] Army exercises destroyed farms and small hamlets, such as Tidemills, near Newhaven.[13] The community at Shoreham Beach was cleared. New tank roads were laid on the Downs.[14] Air raids were a daily hazard – on 9 July 1943 East Grinstead suffered the worst air raid in Sussex when bombs hit a cinema and the town centre, killing 108 people.[15] With the arrival of the V-1 rockets in 1944, East Sussex, with Kent, became known as 'Doodlebug Alley'. The second V-1 to hit the UK crashed at Cuckfield.[16] Industry turned to the war effort, and harbours became dominated by Naval and Merchant shipping.

Such was the impact of the war on Sussex that many reminders of the events of those years survive today in all corners of the county.

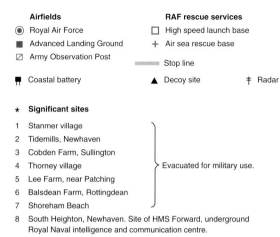

Airfields
- ◉ Royal Air Force
- ■ Advanced Landing Ground
- ☑ Army Observation Post
- 🔫 Coastal battery

RAF rescue services
- ☐ High speed launch base
- + Air sea rescue base
- ▥▥▥ Stop line
- ▲ Decoy site
- ☩ Radar

★ **Significant sites**

1 Stanmer village ⎫
2 Tidemills, Newhaven ⎪
3 Cobden Farm, Sullington ⎪
4 Thorney village ⎬ Evacuated for military use.
5 Lee Farm, near Patching ⎪
6 Balsdean Farm, Rottingdean ⎪
7 Shoreham Beach ⎭

8 South Heighton, Newhaven. Site of HMS Forward, underground Royal Naval intelligence and communication centre.

9 East Grinstead. Queen Victoria Hospital - pioneering burns unit.

10 Cowdray Park, Midhurst. Aircraft storage site.

11 Off Pagham Harbour and Selsey. Mulberry harbour marshalling site.

12 Linchmere. Mulberry harbour experimental site.

13 Horsham. Headquarters of No.2 Group Royal Observer Corps.

14 Shoreham. Experimental mine clearance centre.

15 Hailsham. Manufacture of dummy tanks and aircraft for decoy sites.

16 Broadbridge Heath. Headquarters of UK bomb disposal units.

17 Windlesham, near Washington. School of petroleum warfare.

18 Tottington Manor, near Small Dole. Regional Headquarters of the Sussex Home Guard Auxiliary units (special underground resistance units).

19 Chichester ⎫
20 Glynde ⎬ Railway gun depots.

21 Faygate, near Horsham. 49 Maintenance Unit RAF, a salvage centre for crashed German aircraft.

22 Thorney Island. Only major barrage balloon centre in Sussex, intended to protect Portsmouth.

23 Bracklesham Bay ⎫
24 Climping ⎬ D-Day landing exercises.

25 Bignor. Staging post for French Resistance and underground personnel en route to Europe.

26 Shoreham ⎫
27 Newhaven ⎬ D-Day embarkation ports.

28 Langhurst, near Rudgwick. Military equipment testing centre.

29 Rye ⎫
30 Church Norton, near Selsey ⎬ Petroleum warfare sites.
31 Camber Sands ⎭

32 Bosham ⎫
33 Littlehampton ⎬ D-Day landing craft construction sites.
34 Itchenor ⎭

35 Kings Standing, Ashdown Forest. Radio station for broadcasting propaganda to Germany.

36 Anti-tank ditch linking the Arun Divisional Defence Line and the Ouse Divisional Line.

37 Balcombe Place, national headquarters of the Women's Land Army.

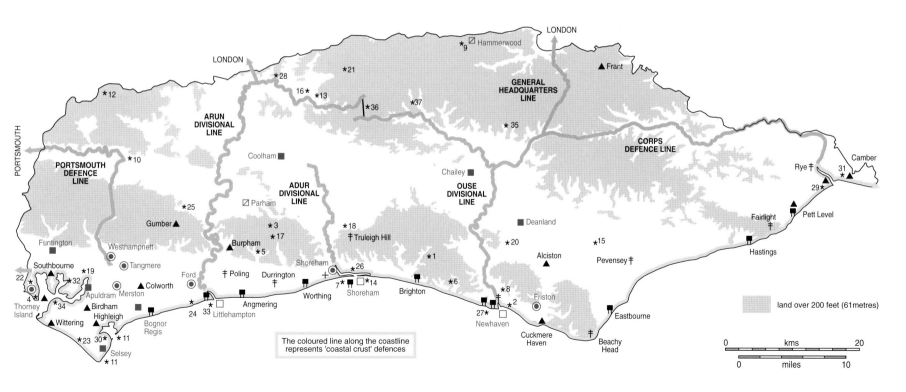

The coloured line along the coastline represents 'coastal crust' defences

land over 200 feet (61 metres)

119

The Map

The map shows the rate of population change over the half century to 2001 in each parish and urban borough.[1] Some parish boundaries have changed over the period, so where necessary the data has been adjusted to the boundaries as they were in 1991. Inset diagrams show the proportion of the population within the main age groups in 1951 and 1991, for Sussex and for two contrasting towns, Crawley and Bexhill.

Numerical Change

By 2001 the population of Sussex is expected to be 1,498,000, and will have grown by 60% – more than half a million – since 1951. The rate of increase was fastest in the 1960s and '70s, the decades that saw Crawley's main development and the greatest migration into the county generally from Greater London. Two-thirds of the growth took place in West Sussex, which saw its population almost double: the population of East Sussex grew by just over a third.

The number of households grew nearly twice as fast as the population, as the number of people per household – and hence the number living in each house – has reduced, in line with the national trend. Thus parishes where there has been little or no increase in living space have tended to lose population. This applies in rural parishes where development opportunities have been limited by planning controls – notably within the Sussex Downs Area of Outstanding Natural Beauty (AONB) – or ownership (villages on the major landed estates). It is true also in a few dense urban areas, especially Brighton, where expansion during the period has been curbed by its particularly constrained position between the Downs and the sea.

Most of the growth has been towards the edges of Sussex. Where coastal towns have been able to expand they have been among the fastest growing areas. The populations of Seaford and Littlehampton/Rustington have more than doubled. Those of Eastbourne, Bexhill and Shoreham-by-Sea have grown by around 60%, that of Bognor Regis by 45% and those of Hastings and Worthing by nearly 40%. Some of the parishes adjacent to established towns have grown fastest of all, sometimes coalescing, as with Pagham, Aldwick, Felpham and Middleton, adjoining Bognor; Rustington, adjoining Littlehampton; and Polegate, Willingdon and Westham,

adjoining Eastbourne. The coastal conurbation now extends from Pagham to Seaford, interrupted only by a few stoutly-defended gaps. Separated to the west by only five miles, a discernible 'ridge' of relatively rapid growth along the A27 and the railway between Emsworth and Chichester forms an extension of the South Hampshire conurbation.

Inland, the fastest growth has been at Crawley, where the building of the new town has led to an almost ninefold population increase (from under 11,000 to nearly 97,000). Other towns have grown rapidly, influenced by employment pressures and by planning policies focusing development on centres with relatively good transport links: the largest are on the London-Brighton axis close to Crawley and Gatwick. The population of Burgess Hill (nearly 29,000 by 2001) has more than tripled, and those of Horsham (44,000) and East Grinstead (26,000) have more than doubled. The smaller East Sussex towns of Crowborough, Hailsham and Uckfield have also grown fast, the last more than tripling its population.

Several detached groups of villages and small towns with easy access to employment centres and not subject to the severest planning controls have seen rapid population increase. Examples include Steyning, Bramber and Henfield; Pulborough, Billingshurst and Storrington; Ringmer, Wivelsfield and Newick. All these lie in the Low Weald just north of the Downs near the centre of the county. In contrast, the lack of population growth in the more remote AONB parishes north of Chichester and in northern East Sussex is striking.

The Causes of Population Change: the Importance of Migration

By 1951 the Sussex coast had become a favoured destination for retirement moves to the seaside, and inward migration was already the main cause of population growth in the principal coastal towns. The following decades brought an influx of working-age migrants to Crawley New Town and the other fast-growing towns in the centre of the county. However, retirement migration continued apace, and large numbers in the post-retirement age groups meant that throughout the period deaths exceeded births in Sussex as a whole.

Sussex is one of only a few counties where this is true. It means that the population would fall unless topped up by newcomers. In the early 1990s, every week saw, on

average, 310 births and 390 deaths in East and West Sussex – a net loss of 80 people. This was outweighed by a weekly net in-migration of 210 people, giving an average increase of about 130 people a week.

Migration flows are volatile and depend on national as well as local circumstances. With large gross flows into and out of Sussex (in 1996 there were 56,000 in-migrants and 42,000 out-migrants) small changes in either or both can substantially affect the net figure. In addition, the age profile of in- and out-flows can vary considerably, influencing the age composition of the total population. Contrary to national trends, in East Sussex the proportion of the population over retirement age is reducing, resulting in part from a younger net in-migrant age profile.

Changes in Age Structure

One result of high rates of inward migration during the three decades after the Second World War was to create, by 1981, two areas within Sussex with different demographic characteristics. In the north and centre the age structure was fairly youthful, and there were more births than deaths (a natural increase). Along the coast and in most rural areas there was more of a bias towards the elderly, and more deaths than births (a natural decrease). As in-migration has reduced since, these differences have become less marked.

The insets show, for 1991, a greater proportion of the county population aged 75 and over, compared with 1951, as the inflow of elderly migrants has continued and as people have survived longer. Among the working-age population the share of under-35s has grown and that of 35-50s has reduced, so that, on balance, the workforce was younger in 1991 than in 1951.

The diagrams for Crawley and Bexhill show the extremes concealed by the county averages. They illustrate the interaction of widely differing age structures of population and migrants. In Crawley, in 1991 the proportion of the younger working population was much higher than in 1951 and that of young children and older working population less: the proportion in the retirement age groups was little changed. In Bexhill, the growth in the population of retirement age over the 40 years was such as to reduce significantly the share in the two lowest age groups.

Changes in age structure 1951-91

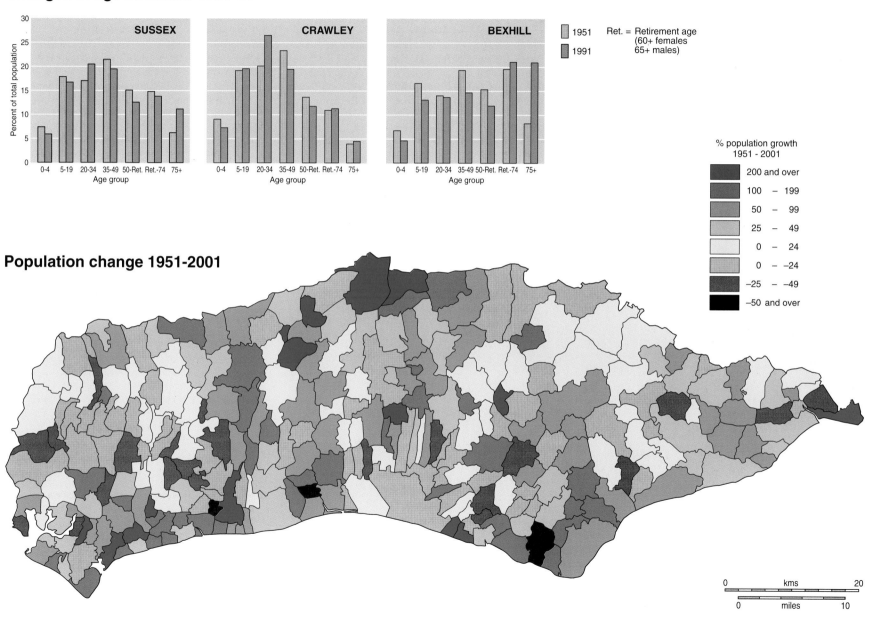

Population change 1951-2001

SUSSEX

CRAWLEY

BEXHILL

1951
1991

Ret. = Retirement age
(60+ females
65+ males)

Percent of total population

Age group

0-4   5-19   20-34   35-49   50-Ret.   Ret.-74   75+

% population growth
1951 - 2001

200 and over
100 – 199
50 – 99
25 – 49
0 – 24
0 – −24
−25 – −49
−50 and over

0   kms   20
0   miles   10

CRAWLEY NEW TOWN 1947–2000

Charles Kay

Crawley New Town was designated on 9 January 1947, the second town designated under the powers of the New Towns Act 1946.[1] In choosing Crawley, the Ministry of Housing and Local Government was meeting two objectives, the first being the requirement of the Greater London Plan 1944 for at least one new town south of London, and the second the resolution of a local planning problem which emerged in the 1930s, the subject of a 1944 agreement between the Ministry and the local planning authorities whereby Crawley and Three Bridges would be planned as a single unit with a possible eventual population of 25,000.[2] Crawley lay just outside the area covered by the Greater London Plan, but a twin-centred town of 30,000 to 40,000 based on Crawley and Three Bridges was proposed in the Ministry's initial response to the Plan.[3] In May 1946 the Minister, Lewis Silkin, obtained the agreement of the Lord President's Committee for a New Town of 50,000, and the decision to proceed with Crawley was announced on 10 July 1946.[4] A planning consultant, Thomas Sharp, was appointed in August 1946 and, following a public enquiry in December 1946, the boundaries were fixed and the Designation Order made.[5]

Map 1 shows the 1947 designated area, of which over half was then in East Sussex, though most of the population was in West Sussex. The population at the time was roughly 9,500. The main built-up areas are shown, together with the Anglican churches (Lowfield Heath and Worth were just outside the area). The small town of Crawley had a good range of shops, public houses and a cinema but its schools were inadequate. Three Bridges had several shops and three public houses, but the school was some distance away at Worth. Ifield was a very scattered community. There was a little recent industrial development in the area, some connected with war-work.

An Advisory Committee was appointed in September 1946 and this formed the basis for the Development Corporation whose membership was confirmed in February 1947 under the chairmanship of Sir Thomas Bennett.[6] Work was initially slow, pending the outcome of a legal challenge to the Development Order (dismissed in December 1947) and was further hampered by the resignation of Thomas Sharp. His replacement, Anthony

Minoprio, produced an outline Master Plan which was published in December 1947, the final version being completed in 1949.[7] This envisaged a town of 50,000 (later 55,000), to be completed in 15 years. Nine residential neighbourhoods each with a population of about 5,000 were arranged around the existing town of Crawley, where a new town centre, including shops and public buildings, would be built immediately to the east of the existing High Street (map 2). Each neighbourhood had a centre with shops for local needs, a public house, a primary school and an Anglican church (those at Ifield and West Green served those areas, but a new St Richard's was built in Three Bridges). Other denominations built new churches as required. Secondary schools were concentrated on three campuses. The industrial area was to the north-east of the town (and thus remote from some of the housing), with a small service industry area at Three Bridges. An area for heavy industry to the east of the railway was never built. Radial roads for through traffic separated the residential areas. Considerable areas of green belt were allocated, but a tenth neighbourhood, Furnace Green, was built in the 1960s on land reserved for future growth. Housing in the original nine neighbourhoods was almost exclusively managed by the Corporation for rent, but Furnace Green introduced private development on a large scale.

Despite early setbacks, the Development Corporation did achieve its target and the population of the town on 31 March 1962 was 55,800.[8] In 1956 the Development Corpor-

ation had started planning for the continued growth of the town and sanctioned the Furnace Green neighbourhood.[9] However, the government decided to wind up the Development Corporation, and its assets were transferred to the Commission for the New Towns on 1 April 1962. Strategic planning was left to West Sussex County Council, whose Town Map of 1961 proposed expansion to 70,000, mainly through a new and much larger neighbourhood at Broadfield (population 12,000).[10] A further large neighbourhood followed at Bewbush, though part lay physically separated by the railway and is now known as Ifield West. Considerable extensions were also made to Pound Hill, which now is regarded as

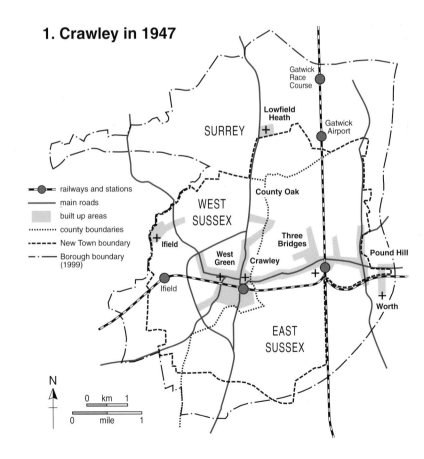

1. Crawley in 1947

two neighbourhoods. Most of Pound Hill was of more expensive private housing. A 13th neighbourhood, Maidenbower, was started in 1986 and now has a population of about 5,000. The 1996 estimate for the town was 92,710 and growth to well over 100,000 is now inevitable, with a 14th neighbourhood proposed for the North East Sector – as yet unnamed – between Tinsley Green and the M23. However, progress here is now subject to the outcome of a study into airport policy in the South East, announced by the Government in March 1999.[11]

The development of Gatwick Airport, sanctioned in 1954, was bitterly opposed by the Development Corporation but it is perhaps no coincidence that many of the industries in Crawley in the 1950s were of military importance.[12] Warehousing and airport-related industries have replaced many of the original manufacturing firms on the industrial estate, and considerable office developments have taken place recently. Other developments since 1980 include a large indoor shopping centre, County Mall, opened in 1992, and the Crawley Leisure Park, opening in phases from January 1999, which includes a 15-screen cinema, a fitness centre and restaurants. A long-awaited theatre and arts centre opened at The Hawth in 1988. It will be seen from map 3 that recent and proposed developments have taken almost

all of the original green belt to the east and south-west of the town, and the M23 motorway (opened in 1974) now forms the eastern borough boundary.

The housing assets and neighbourhood shopping centres owned by the Commission for the New Towns were transferred to Crawley Borough Council in 1977.[13] Other property was to be realised commercially, a task largely achieved by 1999. Although the development of the town has not been without problems, it is perhaps a tribute to the original planners and developers of Crawley New Town that the town has weathered economic changes and will enter the 21st century with a population almost twice that foreseen in 1947.

2. Crawley 1948-62

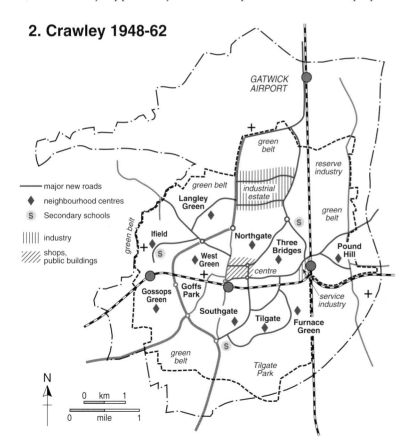

3. Crawley since 1962

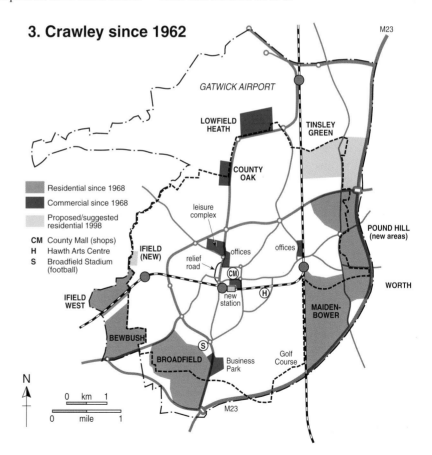

The Map

The map shows the main features of planning for land use, development and conservation over the period. The inset shows Sussex in the context of the South East region.[1]

Only the most significant changes in the pattern of road and rail links have been included. The three Areas of Outstanding Natural Beauty also contain other designated areas within them, notably Ashdown Forest. There are many other areas protected for their wildlife or other scientific interest (see map 70).

Planning and Communications 1947-2000

The 1947 Town and Country Planning Act introduced the first comprehensive system of land use planning. Plans were drawn up to allocate land for new housing and industry, to improve communications, to protect the best agricultural land and countryside, and to guide the future development of towns and villages. Piecemeal development, often on good quality land, had been one of the reasons for the introduction of planning controls. The inter-war development of Peacehaven had been one of the prime examples of this type of uncontrolled planning.

Although the planning system has been adapted over the last 50 years, its framework of regional, county and local plans, implemented through the promotion of policies and the control of development, has remained essentially the same. Public concern and involvement in both national and local planning issues have increased steadily. The main themes in planning policies in the period are described below.

The extent to which Sussex should provide housing, firstly for people moving out of London, and later for the growth in the region's population and the demand for housing generally, has been a major concern. The creation of a green belt around London has undoubtedly increased pressure for development in Sussex. In the 1960s and '70s Crawley/Gatwick was a designated area for major growth and Eastbourne/Hastings a growth area. Crawley was one of several New Towns planned around the outskirts of London. Hastings had the last overspill scheme with the Greater London Council.

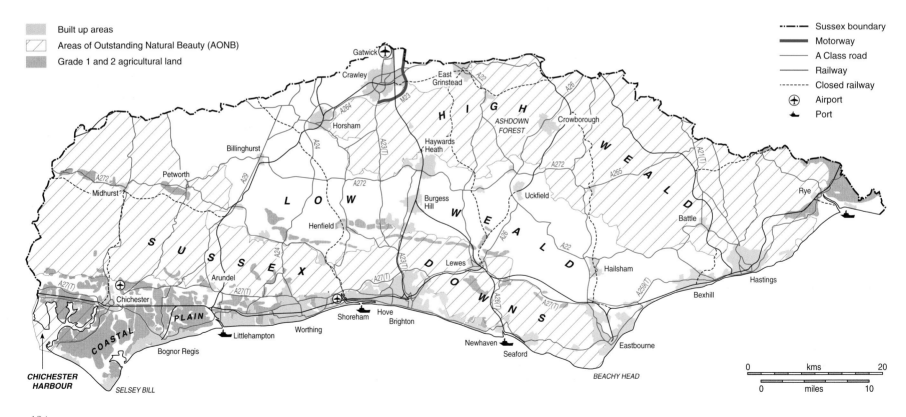

Elsewhere provision for more housing has been concentrated on the coastal towns, with a modest expansion of some inland towns and larger villages. Little additional development has been allowed in the majority of villages and many have been very severely restricted, as has development in the countryside more generally.

Much of this planned pattern of development has taken place. Crawley continues to expand, together with Gatwick Airport, and has been the centre of an area of strong economic growth and low unemployment in central Sussex. Planning policies here and in western Sussex have tried to manage and divert growth in jobs both to match infrastructure and prevent excessive housing development. Development in the Eastbourne/Hastings area has not been on the same scale, although some smaller towns have expanded more quickly than envisaged. Some housing areas on the edge of towns have experienced social problems, and development has narrowed the rural gaps between towns. These strategic gaps have been a key feature in maintaining the modern settlement pattern.

From the later 1970s there has been a steady decline in new council housing and housing for rent and a corresponding increase in owner-occupation. Generally, Sussex has had a relatively low proportion of its stock in social housing, with the exception of a few towns, notably Crawley. In recent years, housing associations have taken over the provision of social housing. Relatively low incomes in many parts of Sussex, and continuing demand for houses, have made it difficult for many local people to buy houses here.

The strong economy and low unemployment of the Crawley/Gatwick area and many of the western coastal towns have not been matched in eastern Sussex. Brighton and Hastings in particular have experienced problems of replacing and regenerating employment, sites and buildings. Increased car ownership and changing work and shopping patterns have led to concerns about the decline of rural life, resulting in policies to allow some small-scale and local housing and the conversion of redundant farm buildings for business use in rural areas.

There has been considerable investment in improving the main road network. The A23 and much of the A27 in West Sussex have been dramatically increased in capacity, and now link to the M25 and the motorway system. Most of the other main roads linking the coastal towns have been upgraded. Nevertheless Sussex has only 12km of motorway and relatively little dual carriageway. The road network in the west is significantly better than in the east. By contrast some of the strategic as well as local rail links have closed. The principal investment in rail has been on the London-Gatwick-Brighton line. The four small Sussex ports have seen changing, but gradually decreasing, trade. New leisure-based marinas have been created at Brighton and Eastbourne to add to existing harbours as at Chichester.

The Sussex Downs were included in the original 1947 proposals for National Parks but were not designated. This area was made an Area of Outstanding Natural Beauty in 1966, as was Chichester Harbour in 1964, and the High Weald in 1983. Public concern about changes in the natural environment has led to protection of other areas, such as the natural wetlands.

By contrast the combination of the pattern of investment in the road and rail network, the expansion of Crawley/Gatwick and many coastal towns, and the protection of sensitive environmental areas, has left the Low Weald as the current main area for planning major new developments for housing, business or tourism.

Increasing concern at the loss of the architectural and historic heritage of Sussex towns has led to the designation of Conservation Areas and schemes to conserve their buildings and character. In the later part of the period, policies for the comprehensive regeneration of towns were introduced to address problems of traffic congestion, redundant buildings, decline of the tourist trade, loss of population and jobs, and security. Many of these proposals were associated with proposed or completed by-passes of most of the main towns.

The relationship of Sussex to the Channel Tunnel and planning in northern Europe, possible new settlements, continuing concern about the loss of natural environment and the maintenance of buildings and townscape, the effect of a rise in sea levels, and the pursuit of sustainability, will all feature strongly in planning into the new Millennium.

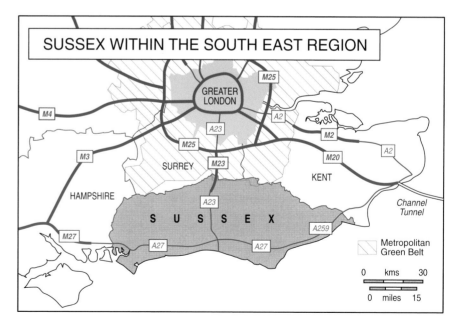

SUSSEX WITHIN THE SOUTH EAST REGION

'The English Shires are the most ancient units of local administration to have survived anywhere in the western world.'[1] In Sussex, local administration was based from the early Middle Ages on the three eastern and three western Rapes, the long-standing division between east and west being noted in 1585 when the Justices of the Peace for Sussex recorded that they held meetings of Quarter Sessions at Chichester for the west part of the shire and at Lewes for the east part 'as it hathe bene used tyme owte of mynde'.[2]

By the County of Sussex Act 1865, the arrangement which had developed over the preceding 800 years was put on a formal basis. The two divisions were to be regarded as separate counties for most administrative business (such as police, prisons, asylums, roads and bridges), leaving the militia and a few minor functions to be dealt with on the basis of Sussex as a whole.

The administration of local affairs by the county's justices had served Sussex well for hundreds of years, and the fact that the county gentry came together quarterly to transact business and dispense justice bolstered the strong sense of county community which was fundamental to the English system of local administration.[3] However, as the 19th century advanced, as towns grew and ideas about representative democracy gained support, the system of local administration by non-elected country gentlemen was increasingly seen as being at odds with the spirit of the times.

As a result, the Local Government Act 1888 established elected county councils for East and West Sussex, to whom the administrative functions of Quarter Sessions were transferred. It also provided that every town with more than 50,000 inhabitants (and some still smaller ones) could become county boroughs and operate independently of the county councils in whose areas they were located. Thus, Brighton and Hastings became county boroughs in 1889, and Eastbourne followed in 1911.

A number of towns (such as Arundel, Chichester, Hastings and Rye) enjoyed borough or similar status from an earlier period. Powers were provided by local or national legislation from the 18th century, enabling them to cope with such pressures as population growth and public health needs, and also to achieve more efficient and democratic forms of government. Improvement Commissioners were an early solution to improving town government (for example, Brighton 1773) and subsequent general legislation gave additional powers.

The poor law unions of 1834 formed the basis for developing district authorities in both rural and some urban areas, resulting in rural and urban sanitary authorities under the Public Health Act 1872. These (with the councils and local boards of health of other boroughs and towns) would be rationalised under the Local Government Act 1894 into a coherent system of boroughs and urban and rural districts. Parish meetings and councils were established for the most local units. By 1911 the local government of Sussex was thus in the hands of two county councils, three county borough councils, 21 borough and urban district councils and 20 rural district councils (map 1).

Under the Local Government Act 1929, county councils were encouraged to review the number and boundaries of district councils in their areas. In Sussex this led to the amalgamation of a number of urban and rural districts, a process completed by 1934 (map 2). In addition, the continuing growth of towns on the coast and in mid-Sussex was leading to a number of boundary changes as urban areas extended into what had previously been rural parishes. Substantial extensions were made to the boundaries of Brighton and Hove in 1928 and to those of Hastings in 1938. The structure of local government was then to remain substantially unchanged locally until 1974.

The post-war period saw an increasing interest in the reform of local government, allied to the inevitable tensions between the interests of rural communities and their expanding urban neighbours. There was also a belief that larger organisations were inherently more efficient than smaller ones. The Royal Commission on Local Government in England 1966-1969, chaired by Lord Redcliffe-Maud, recommended the replacement of all the local authorities in Sussex with three new, all-purpose authorities for West Sussex, East Sussex and Mid-Sussex, but this was not to be.[4]

Alternative proposals were, however, implemented by the Local Government Act 1972, and in 1974 the boundary between West and East Sussex was moved eastwards, taking the mid-Sussex area into West Sussex (map 3). The three county boroughs (Brighton, Eastbourne and Hastings) were abolished and taken into East Sussex as districts, and the number of district councils was further reduced (to seven in each county), producing some large geographical units with little community identity. Gatwick Airport, previously in Surrey, was transferred to West Sussex and the new borough of Crawley.

A further review of local government in Sussex took place in 1994, when the Local Government Commission investigated whether a pattern of so-called unitary authorities would suit the circumstances of Sussex. Outside the principal conurbation, the public displayed little enthusiasm for further costly disruption, however, and the only change made was to establish a unitary authority to serve Brighton and Hove, independent of East Sussex County Council. It came into operation on 1 April 1997, though some functions such as police, fire and strategic planning continued to be provided on a county-wide basis (map 4).

For hundreds of years, the parish dominated the daily lives of the 300 ancient communities which made up the county of Sussex, and elected town and parish councils continue to fulfil an important role in the modern local government system at grass-roots level.

Sussex was anciently a kingdom. Its boundaries (with its two historic divisions), largely coterminous with those of the diocese of Chichester, have survived centuries of development and reorganisation remarkably intact at the Millennium. New threats and opportunities lie ahead, not least those arising from the possible development of regional government, but it is to be hoped that the institutions which have served Sussex well throughout its long history will continue to be 'in touch with their local people and to get the best out of them', as they have in the past.[5]

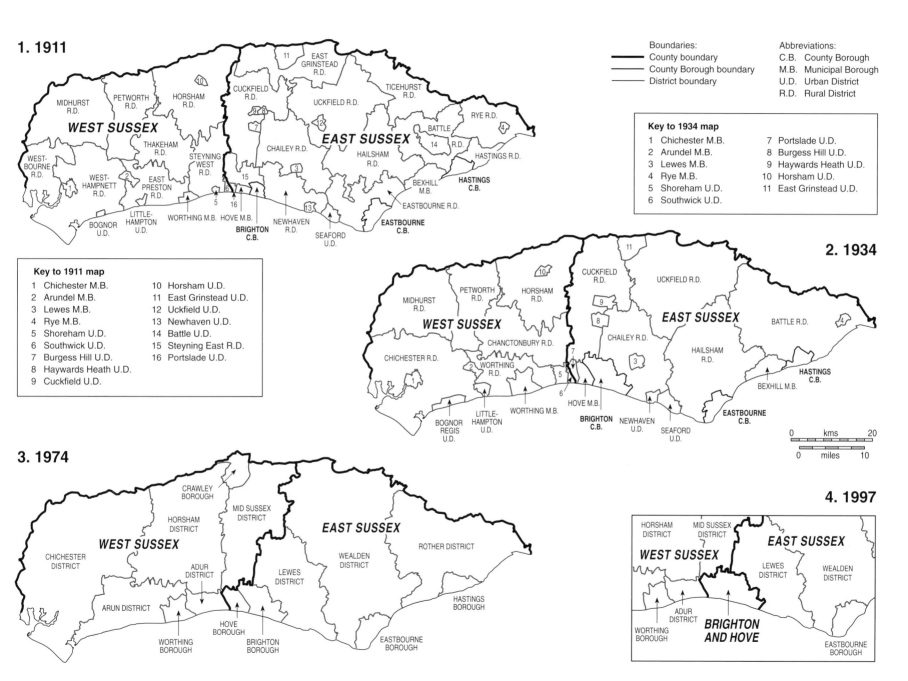

1. 1911

WEST SUSSEX

EAST SUSSEX

MIDHURST R.D.

PETWORTH R.D.

HORSHAM R.D.

10

CUCKFIELD R.D.

11 EAST GRINSTEAD R.D.

UCKFIELD R.D.

TICEHURST R.D.

9 8

7

BATTLE R.D.

RYE R.D.

4

WEST-BOURNE R.D.

WEST-HAMPNETT R.D.

2

THAKEHAM R.D.

EAST PRESTON R.D.

STEYNING WEST R.D.

CHAILEY R.D.

HAILSHAM R.D.

HASTINGS R.D.

1

15

3

12

BOGNOR U.D.

LITTLE-HAMPTON U.D.

WORTHING M.B.

5

6

16

HOVE M.B.

NEWHAVEN R.D.

13

BEXHILL M.B.

HASTINGS C.B.

BRIGHTON C.B.

SEAFORD U.D.

EASTBOURNE R.D.

EASTBOURNE C.B.

Boundaries:
━━━ County boundary
── County Borough boundary
── District boundary

Abbreviations:
C.B. County Borough
M.B. Municipal Borough
U.D. Urban District
R.D. Rural District

Key to 1934 map
1	Chichester M.B.	7	Portslade U.D.
2	Arundel M.B.	8	Burgess Hill U.D.
3	Lewes M.B.	9	Haywards Heath U.D.
4	Rye M.B.	10	Horsham U.D.
5	Shoreham U.D.	11	East Grinstead U.D.
6	Southwick U.D.		

2. 1934

WEST SUSSEX

EAST SUSSEX

MIDHURST R.D.

PETWORTH R.D.

HORSHAM R.D.

10

CUCKFIELD R.D.

11

UCKFIELD R.D.

CHICHESTER R.D.

CHANCTONBURY R.D.

9

8

CHAILEY R.D.

HAILSHAM R.D.

BATTLE R.D.

4

2

WORTHING R.D.

3

HASTINGS C.B.

BOGNOR REGIS U.D.

LITTLE-HAMPTON U.D.

WORTHING M.B.

1

5

7

6

HOVE M.B.

BRIGHTON C.B.

NEWHAVEN U.D.

SEAFORD U.D.

BEXHILL M.B.

EASTBOURNE C.B.

Key to 1911 map
1	Chichester M.B.	10	Horsham U.D.
2	Arundel M.B.	11	East Grinstead U.D.
3	Lewes M.B.	12	Uckfield U.D.
4	Rye M.B.	13	Newhaven U.D.
5	Shoreham U.D.	14	Battle U.D.
6	Southwick U.D.	15	Steyning East R.D.
7	Burgess Hill U.D.	16	Portslade U.D.
8	Haywards Heath U.D.		
9	Cuckfield U.D.		

0 ‖‖‖‖ kms ‖‖‖‖ 20

0 ‖‖‖‖ miles ‖‖‖‖ 10

3. 1974

WEST SUSSEX

EAST SUSSEX

CRAWLEY BOROUGH

MID SUSSEX DISTRICT

HORSHAM DISTRICT

ROTHER DISTRICT

CHICHESTER DISTRICT

ADUR DISTRICT

LEWES DISTRICT

WEALDEN DISTRICT

ARUN DISTRICT

HOVE BOROUGH

BRIGHTON BOROUGH

HASTINGS BOROUGH

WORTHING BOROUGH

EASTBOURNE BOROUGH

4. 1997

HORSHAM DISTRICT

MID SUSSEX DISTRICT

EAST SUSSEX

WEST SUSSEX

LEWES DISTRICT

WEALDEN DISTRICT

WORTHING BOROUGH

ADUR DISTRICT

BRIGHTON AND HOVE

EASTBOURNE BOROUGH

The Map

The most comprehensive information available about travel to work movements in England comes from the decennial Census of Population, which records, for each resident with a job, the addresses of both the home and the workplace. From that information it is possible to map the work trips between every pair of enumeration districts in England and Wales. Aggregating these, map 1 shows the gross flows between the Sussex local authority districts in 1991.[1] Flows of fewer than 1,000 are not shown.

Flows from Sussex districts to destinations outside the county are not shown on map 1, but the 1991 movements of 1,000 or more between Sussex as a whole and other counties are shown on map 3. In practice, flows of this size took place only between Sussex and Greater London, Hampshire, Surrey and Kent. Map 2 shows the same information for 1951.[2]

Travel to Work in 1991

Lengthy journeys to work have become the acceptable norm for an increasing proportion of the working population as the century has progressed: by 1991 the average distance travelled in East Sussex was 10.5km. The situation which existed after the Second World War, in which most people lived within walking distance, or that of a short bus ride, of their work, has changed out of all recognition. The maps understate this general mobility, since they show only those journeys which cross district or county boundaries; many journeys within the large districts which were created in 1974 are also quite long.

There are more workers resident in Sussex than there are jobs, so there is a substantial net outflow of travellers to work, especially from East Sussex. Large numbers of people travel out, offset by smaller numbers travelling in. This has long been the case. Nevertheless, most working residents both live and work within Sussex. West Sussex, in particular, has become more in balance as employment has grown strongly around Crawley and Gatwick Airport. This has provided jobs both for Sussex people who might otherwise have had to look elsewhere

for employment, and for workers resident elsewhere who travel into the county.

The main gross flows of Sussex residents to jobs outside are to Greater London (33,000), Surrey (16,000), Kent (11,000) and Hampshire (7,000). London has been getting relatively less important. There are smaller flows inward, except that the inflows from, and outflows to, Hampshire roughly balance. The main flows to London are from the central districts of Mid Sussex (7,000), Brighton and Hove (5,000), Horsham (4,000) and Crawley (3,000), and also from Wealden (4,000). Clearly closeness to the capital and the long-standing superiority of both rail and road transport in the centre of Sussex have been influential. Crawley actually has a 3,000 flow *from* London, much of it made up of workers at Gatwick.

Flows to and from the adjoining counties originate or end mainly in the Sussex districts that are closest to them. Crawley sends 4,000 workers to Surrey, and receives 7,000 in return (again many of them bound for Gatwick); Wealden sends 6,000 to Kent; and Chichester both sends and receives 5,000 to or from Hampshire.

There is a complex web of travel movements *within* East and West Sussex. Two broad features are evident. First, there is the attraction of workers resident in the more rural districts to the concentrations of jobs in the main urban centres. There are significant flows from Arun into Chichester (6,000); from both Arun and Adur into Worthing (both 4,000); from Adur (6,000) and Lewes (7,000) into Brighton and Hove; from Horsham (4,000) and Mid Sussex (6,000) into Crawley; from Wealden into Eastbourne (6,000); and from Rother into Hastings (4,000).

The second broad feature is a net movement from most of the coastal districts into the central districts of Crawley, Horsham and Mid Sussex - across the watershed formed by the lightly-populated areas of the Downs and the remote parts of the Weald in Chichester and Lewes districts. This is less clearly seen from the map than the magnetism of the main urban centres, but has been increasing in importance with the growing dominance of the Crawley/Gatwick area.

Labour Shortfalls and Surpluses

Map 1 gives an indication of the relationship between the size of the resident workforce and the number of jobs in each district. Crawley is a substantial net importer of labour, having a 28% shortfall of working residents compared with its jobs; no other district is in anything like this position, of which Gatwick is obviously a principal cause. The districts of Chichester, Worthing, Brighton and Hove, Eastbourne and Hastings have an approximate balance between jobs and working residents; Chichester is the odd one out in this list, as a large and very rural district, and its inclusion clearly shows the exceptional importance as an employment centre of its only significant town, the city of Chichester itself.

Arun, Horsham, Mid Sussex and Rother have substantial surpluses of working residents, and this is even more the case in Adur, Lewes and, particularly, Wealden (where the surplus is 42%).

Means of Transport to Work

In 1951 most Sussex residents with jobs travelled to work either on foot, by bicycle or by public transport. In 1991 over 65% of working residents travelled by car, 13% still walked and 3%, bravely, cycled. The share of rail and bus had fallen to 6% and 5% respectively.

Public transport was used less in the mainly rural districts and in Worthing, and more in Brighton and Hove – the only district where more than 20% of working residents used it. To some extent the use made of public transport correlates with the availability of a dense network of services: Eastbourne, Crawley and, particularly, Brighton and Hove have higher than average proportions travelling to work by bus. However, possibly the most accessible place in Sussex by public transport is Gatwick Airport, where almost 85% of workers arrive by car.

Finally it should be noted that, by 1991, 36,000 working people were avoiding the work journey altogether, by working from home: they amounted to 6% of the county's working residents, with higher percentages in the more rural districts.

1. Internal flows 1991

number of journeys (flows under 1000 not shown)

5000   3000

4000   2000

           1000

General relationship between jobs and resident workforce

substantial (11% or greater) shortfall of resident workers compared with jobs

reasonable balance (10% shortfall to 10% surplus of workers)

substantial (11% – 30%) surplus of workers

surplus of workers 31% or greater

● centres with 10,000 or more jobs in 1991

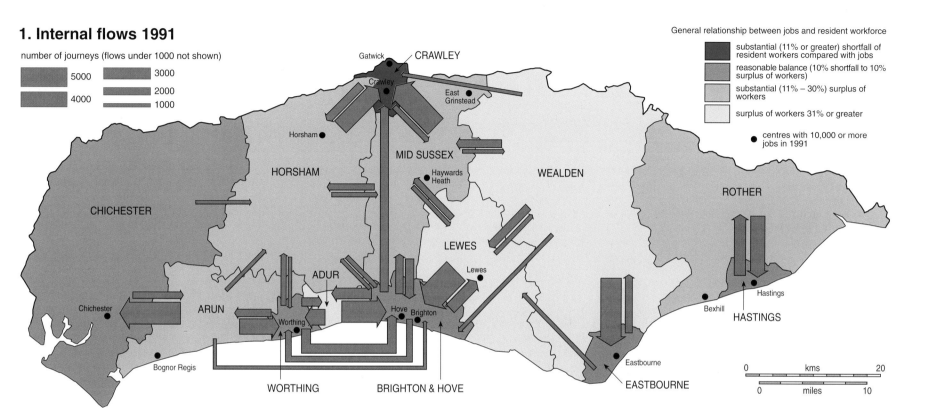

Gatwick   CRAWLEY

Crawley

East Grinstead

Horsham ●

MID SUSSEX

HORSHAM

Haywards Heath ●

WEALDEN

ROTHER

CHICHESTER

LEWES

Lewes ●

Chichester ●

ARUN

ADUR

Worthing

Hove   Brighton

Bexhill ●

Hastings ●

HASTINGS

Bognor Regis ●

WORTHING

BRIGHTON & HOVE

Eastbourne ●

EASTBOURNE

0   kms   20

0   miles   10

2. External flows 1951

3. External flows 1991

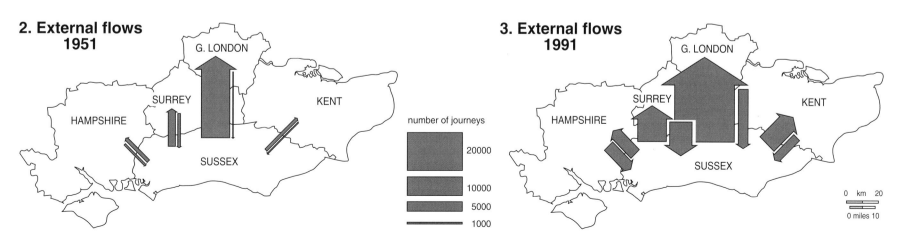

HAMPSHIRE   SURREY   G. LONDON   KENT

SUSSEX

number of journeys

20000

10000

5000

1000

HAMPSHIRE   SURREY   G. LONDON   KENT

SUSSEX

0   km   20

0 miles 10

129

Sussex is frequently portrayed as one huge leisure zone. This disguises much of its agricultural life as well as its considerable urbanisation, although the latter owes much both to attracting visitors and to the retirement patterns of those with fond memories of holidays. The accompanying map cannot show many of the minor attractions, such as teashops, let alone the zoning of the county by foxhunts. What it does show is the distribution and broad types of attraction, and clusters of facilities. Although much of the advertising is aimed at outside visitors, the local leisure industry depends on relatively local markets and plays a major role in attracting settlers both to older centres and new estates.

For many people the main lure is the coast, with its mixture of Georgian and Victorian resorts, reinforced by inter-war holiday camps and the marinas which have boosted yachting since Brighton Marina was begun in the late 1970s.[1] The resorts still retain many of the subtle class variations which fostered their development, but their clientele tends increasingly to be self-catering or short-stay, whilst organisations such as Saga Holidays offer bargain tours for pensioners, and the towns, particularly Brighton and Eastbourne, compete for conference business. The long ribbons of bungalows which developed during the 1920s and '30s, to be reinforced after the Second World War, produced a considerable backlash and movements to preserve threatened coastal beauty spots, such as Beachy Head and the Selsey Peninsula.[2] The creation of the Seven Sisters Country Park in the 1970s was prompted by this, and Chichester Harbour represents a careful balancing of potentially competing interests: dormitory and retirement homes, sailing, birdwatching, fishing, wildfowling and walking and cycling. Almost the whole coast sees regular use by shorefishers, whose sport has been boosted by extended harbour and marina defences. Another form of coastal heritage has appeared with increasing efforts to preserve fortifications and piers, of which the long campaign for Brighton's derelict West Pier has been the outstanding example.

The leisure use of inland Sussex owes much to several intertwining influences, including a sense of a 'vanishing' rural England, a loose nature mysticism, and changing transport systems. Many of the most influential magnets

may be grouped loosely as 'heritage' locations, with all the complications and controversies attached to that term. Apart from churches, the most prominent of these are the country houses and gardens, created originally for the private delight of the aristocracy and landed gentry. These were often open to the 'respectable' public as part of a sense of aristocratic duty in the later 19th century, but their availability now owes far more to economic necessity as part of estate management or to charitable organisations such as the National Trust or Charleston Trust, with the latter's dedication to keeping the myths of 'Bloomsbury on Sea' alive. Access is open, but to the fee-paying rather more than to the deferential. Locations are dependent on the landowning and leisure patterns of their former owners, and their uneven distribution in the Weald is particularly noticeable. One particular variation of this, famous far outside Sussex, has been at Glyndebourne, whose annual opera season was founded by the owner, John Christie, in 1934, as a commercial revival of a much older pattern of country house entertainment. The building of a new opera house there in the 1990s has sealed the enterprise's role as a major world venue, yet it remains far more accessible to locals at lower cost than is often imagined.[3]

Access to these sites grew in the later 19th century with the increasing numbers of excursion trains made possible by the completion of the railway system in the 1880s and '90s. Paradoxically, it was the closure of some of these minor lines in the 1960s that opened up a new heritage industry, the tourist railway, of which the best-known of the three Sussex examples is the Bluebell Line. The railways in their heyday made it possible for cyclists, after the 1890s bicycle boom, and walkers between the wars, to spread outwards into the countryside. Because they were largely 'respectable', they experienced little of the difficulties of access that their northern compatriots faced, but the walkers brought a pressure to land-use on the South Downs which eventually led to regulation and containment.[4] The South Downs Way and its companion routes represent a major adaptation to leisure use of existing economic routes, prehistoric pathways and farm tracks, and, in the case of the Downs Link and Cuckoo Trail, an imaginative adaptation of cleared railway lines. Walkers have long shared such paths with horse riders,

but the 1980s saw new, and as yet unresolved pressures, cross-country cycling and four-wheel drive vehicles bringing not always welcome travellers.

Some of these leisure features link with others, particularly wildlife parks and heritage sites, to bring an intense usage of some areas. Leisure use of the Sussex countryside has increased dramatically since the car-ownership boom of the 1960s cheapened and extended access. Containing the less adventurous to such viewpoints as Beachy Head and Ditchling Beacon has at least reduced environmental disruption, but has raised major problems for narrow access roads and exhaust pollution. Similar issues have emerged with new multiple-use sites such as the reservoirs constructed throughout the Weald for urban water supplies, which now offer sailing, fishing, birdwatching and picnicking, all of which have to be zoned to reduce user conflict. Ardingly, in the middle of Sussex, is perhaps the best example of this.

Perhaps the most intrusive and private use of semi-rural space has been the construction of golf clubs, averaging 40ha. The main ones were opened before 1914, with a steady inter-war extension, but it was the 1990s that saw the most rapid and sometimes controversial expansion, as agricultural land was set aside under EEC regulations for other uses. The investment promises of this boom were rarely realised.[5]

Two developments remain to be noted. The first is the adaptation of industrial and scientific facilities to other uses, including the Royal Greenwich Observatory at Herstmonceux, sharing with the railways a celebration of past technology. Secondly has been the use of literature and imagination. The childhood fantasies that produced *Winnie-the-Pooh* and *Puck of Pooks Hill*, and the adult fictions of Henry James and E.F. Benson, draw thousands to their imagined landscapes.

The complex influences that have dotted Sussex with such magnets continue to develop and to be refined by local authorities seeing their revenue potential. What was once a piecemeal agglomeration of individual sites is often packaged as a total experience, such as 'The Pooh Country' and '1066 Country'. Sussex does sometimes have to fight hard against becoming a total theme park.

1 Uppark (house) and (L): H.G. Wells
2 Hollycombe Steam Collection
3 Aldworth* (L): Alfred Lord Tennyson
4 Stedham Polo
5 Midhurst (L): H.G. Wells
6 Cowdray Ruins and Polo
7 Petworth House
8 Bignor Roman Villa
9 Bury* (L): John Galsworthy
10 Amberley Industrial Museum
11 Parham Airfield (gliding)
12 Parham House
13 Amberley Wildbrooks/Pulborough Brooks
14 Fishers Farm Park
15 Field Place* (L): Percy Bysshe Shelley
16 Shipley* (L): Hilaire Belloc
17 Southwater Country Park
18 Buchan Country Park
19 High Beeches (garden)
20 Nymans (garden)

21 Leonardslee (garden)
22 Woods Mill, Sussex Wildlife Trust
23 Hickstead, All England Jumping Course
24 Washbrooks Farm Centre
25 Ditchling Common Country Park
26 Plumpton Racecourse
27 Borde Hill (garden)
28 Sheffield Park (garden)
29 South of England Showground, Ardingly
30 Wakehurst Place, Royal Botanic Gardens
31 Priest House, West Hoathly
32 Saint Hill Manor
33 Standen (house)
34 Ashdown Llama Farm, Wych Cross
35 Hartfield* (L): A. A. Milne
36 Crowborough* (L): Sir Arthur Conan Doyle
37 Ringmer Airfield (gliding)
38 Bentley Wildfowl/Motor Museum
39 Bayham Abbey
40 Batemans (house) and (L): Rudyard Kipling

41 Bodiam Castle
42 Great Dixter (garden)
43 Brickwall (garden)
44 Doucegrove* (L): Sheila Kaye-Smith
45 Lamb House, Rye (L): Henry James
46 Battle Abbey
47 Ashburnham Place
48 Hastings Castle
49 Herstmonceux Science Centre
50 Pevensey Castle
51 Michelham Priory
52 Arlington Speedway
53 Long Man of Wilmington
54 Seven Sisters Sheep Centre
55 Drusillas Park (zoo)
56 Clergy House, Alfriston
57 Charleston (L): Bloomsbury Set
58 Firle Place
59 Glynde Place
60 Glyndebourne Opera House

61 Paradise Park, Newhaven
62 Newhaven Fort
63 Monks House, Rodmell (L): Virginia Woolf
64 Lewes Castle
65 Stanmer Park
66 Rottingdean* (L): Rudyard Kipling
67 Brighton Racecourse
68 Royal Pavilion, Brighton
69 Withdean Sports Stadium
70 British Engineerium, Hove
71 Museum of D-Day Aviation, Shoreham
72 Shoreham Airport
73 Church Farm, Coombes
74 St Mary's House, Bramber
75 Bramber Castle
76 Worthing (L): Oscar Wilde
77 Goring* (L): Richard Jefferies
78 Highdown (garden)
79 Rustington* (L): J. M. Barrie
80 Burpham* (L): Edward Lear/Mervyn Peake

81 Arundel Wildfowl and Wetlands Trust
82 Arundel Castle
83 Slindon* (L): Hilaire Belloc
84 Denmans (garden)
85 Fontwell Racecourse
86 Felpham* (L): William Blake
87 Butlins Family Entertainment Resort, Bognor Regis
88 Tangmere Military Aviation Museum
89 Goodwood Airfield/ Motor Racing Circuit
90 Goodwood House
91 Goodwood Sculpture Park
92 Goodwood Racecourse
93 Weald and Downland Open Air Museum, Singleton
94 West Dean Gardens
95 Earnley Gardens
96 Chichester Gravel Pits - watersports
97 Rymans, Apuldram (garden)
98 Fishbourne Roman Palace
99 Kingley Vale Nature Reserve
100 Telegraph House* (L): Bertrand Russell

Resort areas

Water sites; sailing, fishing and birdwatching

Yacht harbours

Principal wildlife reserves and country parks

☐ Literary sites (L) in key, (* house not open to public)

✿ Gardens

The map shows a representative selection of visitor/tourist attractions

- - - - - Steam railways

- - - - - Major footpath and cycle routes

▶ Golf courses

♦ Piers

Built up areas

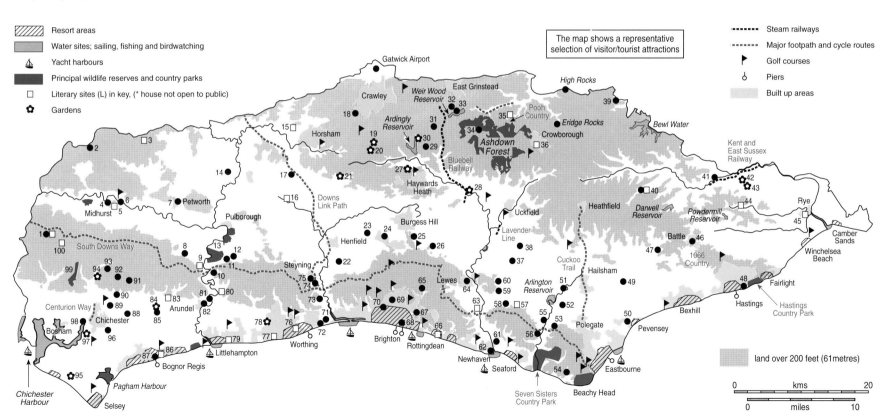

land over 200 feet (61 metres)

0 kms 20

0 miles 10

131

The Map

The map shows the total number of jobs within each of the 13 current Sussex administrative districts for 1991, the most recent date for which the Census of Population provides comprehensive information.[1] The total includes the self-employed, and is sub-divided into the four basic sectors of primary (agriculture, forestry, and fishing), manufacturing, construction and service employment.

Also shown, to the same scale, is the same information from the 1951 Census of Population, aggregated for the same areas.[2] For 1951, the primary sector also includes jobs in quarrying.

Changes in Employment in Sussex since 1951

The 40 years covered by the map saw a 60%, or 205,000, increase in total employment in Sussex. For much of the period labour demand from employers was strong, and shortage of particular skills was endemic. Sussex suffered severely in the national recession of the early 1990s, but growth has now resumed, continuing the trends of the previous 40 years and leading to a recurrence of skill shortages.

Six of the districts of post-1974 West Sussex accounted for three-quarters of the employment growth. The fastest increase was at Crawley, where the new town, Gatwick Airport and the associated improved road network led to 54,000 new jobs (more than a quarter of the total Sussex increase). The adjoining two districts of Horsham and Mid Sussex, heavily affected by the spin-off from Crawley, saw almost another quarter. Thus, half the growth in jobs was associated with the central part of the London-Brighton corridor, much the most prosperous part of Sussex already and benefiting further from Government decisions to invest at Crawley and Gatwick.

A further quarter of the growth took place in the three westernmost districts of Chichester, Arun and Worthing, with increases of 17,000 jobs in both Arun and Worthing (more than 70% growth in each). The final quarter was shared between the remaining seven districts in the Brighton conurbation and the current East Sussex – all of which had rates of increase below the Sussex average (despite growth of 13,000 jobs in Wealden). Brighton and Hove had the lowest rate of growth (4%, 4,000 jobs), and Rother the lowest amount (2,000 jobs).

Looking at the fortunes of the main industrial sectors, there was a marked decline in primary employment, which had employed almost 10% of the total in 1951 (over 20% in Horsham, Rother and Wealden), and lost 19,000 jobs during the 40 years.

Overall, manufacturing fell slightly as a proportion of total jobs but increased in amount. In Brighton and Hove there was an actual decline of 15,000 jobs, a loss of 65% of the 1951 figure, when 40% of the manufacturing jobs in Sussex had been in the borough. There were gains everywhere else, totalling 38,000 jobs, a figure that had been higher before 1991, but had fallen in line with the national trend. This was true especially in Crawley, where the manufacturing firms which had led the new town for its first three decades proved vulnerable to the recession of the early 1990s, and where service jobs, many associated with Gatwick, increased to replace the jobs lost.

In Sussex as a whole, service jobs increased by nearly 187,000: as a proportion the sector grew by 10%. The biggest increases were in Crawley (42,000), Horsham, Mid Sussex and Brighton and Hove. Most important were business services, public administration, education and health, and, in Crawley, transport.

Reflecting this growing dominance of services, women's jobs increased rapidly, growing from 34% to 46% of the county total. In 1991 women outnumbered men in the large group classified as other services and, in most places, in distribution and business services. A substantial increase in part-time employment also took place, much of it as a reflection of the growth in women's jobs.

Employment in Sussex in 1991

These changes have led to a Sussex economy with many growing industries and companies, the Crawley/Gatwick stimulant, and a pleasant living and working environment. There are, however, weaknesses: the county has a narrow economic base; a high dependence on vulnerable activities such as tourism, branch factories, the public sector and back-office functions of types called into question by the worldwide shake-up in financial services; and a poor record of attracting inward investment.

There are marked differences between West and East Sussex. West Sussex, with a much better strategic road network and fewer old urban concentrations, is much stronger and faster growing, with generally low unemployment; this applies especially to the central districts of Crawley, Horsham and Mid Sussex. Brighton and Hove apart, East Sussex is much less easily accessible, and Brighton and Hove and Hastings show many characteristics associated with inner cities, including high unemployment. Quite why Crawley and Gatwick fail to provide more of an economic stimulus to the Brighton conurbation, which is close by and connected by good communications, is an unanswered conundrum.

548,000 people worked in Sussex in 1991. The main concentration was in Brighton and Hove (97,000), the second most substantial in Crawley (59,000). The five largest predominantly rural districts of Mid Sussex, Horsham, Chichester, Wealden and Arun each had about 40,000 jobs.

Under 14,000 people worked in the primary sector, only 2.5% of the total and under one-third of the number working in construction. Unsurprisingly, the proportion was higher in the rural districts, particularly Wealden and Rother.

There were almost 80,000 manufacturing jobs, less than 15% of the total, compared with almost 18% in England and Wales as a whole. More than half the manufacturing jobs in the county were in engineering. Manufacturing was concentrated particularly at Crawley, and to a lesser extent in the districts of Arun (which had the highest amount, 23%), Brighton and Hove, and Horsham.

Nearly 75% of Sussex jobs were in the service sector. Almost 30% of these were in other services, which includes public administration, education, health and personal services; 22% were in distribution, including catering and hotels and vehicle repair; 14% were in business services. Brighton and Hove had the largest concentration of distribution jobs, and also of jobs in business services. Horsham, Mid Sussex and Worthing were also important for business services.

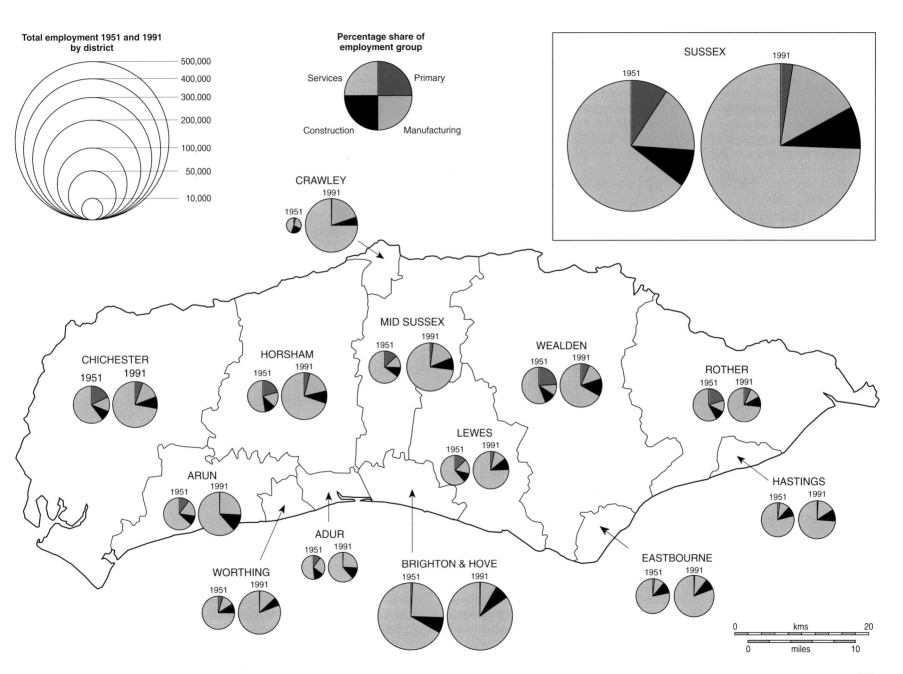

Total employment 1951 and 1991 by district

500,000
400,000
300,000
200,000
100,000
50,000
10,000

Percentage share of employment group

Services
Primary
Construction
Manufacturing

SUSSEX

1951
1991

CRAWLEY
1951
1991

CHICHESTER
1951
1991

HORSHAM
1951
1991

MID SUSSEX
1951
1991

WEALDEN
1951
1991

ROTHER
1951
1991

LEWES
1951
1991

ARUN
1951
1991

ADUR
1951
1991

WORTHING
1951
1991

BRIGHTON & HOVE
1951
1991

EASTBOURNE
1951
1991

HASTINGS
1951
1991

0   kms   20
0   miles   10

133

During the 20th century medical practice and hospitals in Britain have undergone major changes, transforming the piecemeal provision of the Victorian period into a comprehensive modern health-care system. The extent to which the introduction of the National Health Service in 1948 has been responsible for these changes, whether it was a truly radical initiative or whether it merely built upon existing structures and ideas, has been the subject of much debate. The NHS, having reached its 50th anniversary, has come under increasing scrutiny, both as to its past achievements and its future role. In this context a study of the origins of hospital provision in Sussex and its structure under the NHS can only serve to stimulate and inform this debate.

The map is based on *The Hospitals Year Book 1966* and shows the NHS hospitals in existence at that date. By 1966 the NHS had been in operation for almost 20 years, with sufficient time to establish and build upon the original proposals of the 1946 Act and far enough removed from the immediate post-war economic uncertainties and social upheavals. Alongside each hospital is shown its date of origin and pre-NHS status. Specialist hospitals are also shown.

For the first half of the 20th century, prior to 1948, patient care outside the private sector relied largely upon two types of institution: the voluntary hospitals, which were funded by charitable endowments and patients' fees, and the public hospitals, financed from the local rates and central government grants. Many of the hospitals in this second category originated as workhouse infirmaries. They were under the control of public assistance committees, appointed by the local authorities after the abolition of the poor law guardians in 1929. By that date local authorities had also acquired other public health roles and responsibilities; these included the establishment of clinics and hospitals for the treatment of infectious diseases such as tuberculosis and venereal disease, and for maternity care. In addition mental hospitals and asylums for the treatment of the mentally deficient were supervised at a national level by the Board of Control, which had been set up in 1913 to replace the Commissioners in Lunacy. All of these types of institution existed in Sussex prior to the advent of the NHS and are represented on the map.

The plethora of health-care provision and its geographical variability had become a growing cause for concern by the 1930s. The 1938 Hospital Survey carried out in preparation for the wartime Emergency Medical Service highlighted the inadequacy of the system. Resources were soon concentrated on improving the hospital services, unified for the first time under a regional administrative structure responsible to the Ministry of Health. New standards were set in health care and new services introduced, such as the National Blood Transfusion Service, the Ambulance Service, free food supplements, free school meals and a mass vaccination programme initiated to prevent the outbreak of epidemics during the blitz.[1]

It was this structure which paved the way for the introduction of the National Health Service immediately after the war. The Beveridge Report of 1942 had recommended the establishment of a comprehensive National Health Service and subsequent papers and reports continued to examine the options in the face of growing opposition from the British Medical Association on behalf of general practitioners, the voluntary sector and the Board of Control. The 1945 General Election brought the Labour Party to power and Aneurin Bevan to the Ministry of Health. Proposals for a National Health Service were drawn up later the same year and the National Health Service Act 1946 came into force in July 1948. Under the new service, existing hospitals were nationalised and grouped into 377 local Hospital Management Committees, which were themselves controlled by a national network of 14 Regional Hospital Boards.[2]

In Sussex the hospitals were administered from 1948 by ten different Hospital Management Committees divided between the South East and South West Metropolitan Regional Hospital Boards. In 1974 a further reorganisation resulted in the replacement of the HMCs by Health Districts, covering distinct geographical areas and possessing wider powers. Six Health Districts were created in Sussex, as shown on the map, together with the East Sussex and West Sussex Area Health Authorities. These were controlled in turn by the South East Thames and South West Thames Regional Health Authorities. In 1982 the Area Health Authorities were dissolved and their

powers divided between District Health Authorities, which replaced the Health Districts, and the existing Regional Health Authorities. The six new District Health Authorities in Sussex were based on the 1974 Health Districts, with the Mid Downs District Health Authority replacing the Cuckfield and Crawley Health District.

Although the NHS brought many administrative changes to the system of health care in Britain it did not radically alter the existing hospital network. One of the most interesting features of the hospital map of Sussex is the lack of new hospital building in the first 20 years of the NHS. By 1966 few new institutions had been erected and most of the service was still based on Victorian sites and earlier foundations. From the outset the NHS faced serious financial difficulties. Expenditure levels were much higher than anticipated and the consequences of inflation and other post-war factors resulted in severe economic restraints upon the development of the service. It was not until Enoch Powell's Hospital Plan of 1962 that a long-term programme of capital investment in hospitals was agreed as part of a wider scheme to control the future growth of expenditure and manage the hospital budget more effectively.

Under the 1962 Plan the NHS was to be based on a network of district general hospitals, each serving a catchment area of 100,000-150,000 people, with all the main medical services concentrated on these sites. This inevitably involved the closure of smaller, more isolated rural hospitals, continuing the process of concentrating resources on larger hospitals in the main centres of population. By 1966 a number of cottage hospitals and isolation units had ceased to exist, such as Newick Cottage Hospital, the Hastings Borough Small Pox Hospital at Brede and the Victoria Hospital for Infectious Diseases at Hailsham. However the availability of major hospital services just outside the county boundary, as at Tunbridge Wells, Guildford and Portsmouth, should be borne in mind when looking at the apparent lack of health care provision in the north and west of the county. The development and use of specialist hospitals in London would also have been an important factor.

By 1966, despite the good intentions of the 1962 Hospital Plan, little progress had been made. J F Milne, the editor of *The Hospitals Year Book 1966*, commented that 'much less hospital building will be accomplished in the next decade than was envisaged three years ago .... there must be an expensive continuance of the use of old buildings and plant, and a prolongation of the endeavour to practice twentieth century medicine in nineteenth century hospitals'.[3] The map shows the extent to which Milne's comments were justified. Whilst many hospitals, particularly in the urban areas, continued to expand with additional buildings and services, most owed their existence to Victorian benefactors, poor-law institutions or early 20th-century foundations.

The National Health Service did not rewrite the hospital map of Sussex, serving instead to provide a unified and comprehensive administration, which allowed the service to be available to all free of charge at the point of delivery. The national structure created in 1948 and adapted in 1974 and 1982 remained in place until the creation of the NHS Trusts, which began in 1991 and opened up yet a further new chapter in the history of 20th-century health care in Britain.[4] This latest period has also seen the opening of several new hospitals in Sussex, including the Princess Royal Hospital in Haywards Heath in 1991, built in the grounds of St Francis Hospital but replacing Cuckfield Hospital as a new district

general hospital for the area; the Conquest Hospital in Hastings, which opened in July 1992 replacing The Royal East Sussex and Buchanan Hospitals; and Mill View Hospital in Nevill Avenue, Hove, which started taking patients in June 1998, and took over the functions of the New Sussex Hospital in Brighton, together with the Hove out-patient services previously based at Aldrington House. The official opening of Mill View on 2 October 1998 makes this the most recent addition to the hospital network in Sussex.

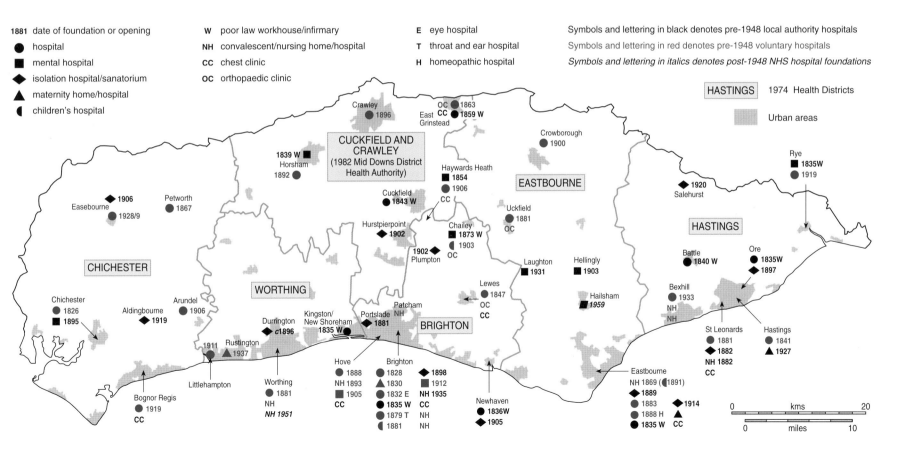

135

Theatres (Robert Elleray)

During the later 18th century the circuit system of travelling companies operated, each usually based on a particular town and directed by an actor manager, performances often being given in makeshift accommodation. These visits occasionally led to the building of a permanent theatre as at Arundel by Henry Thornton in 1792, and Worthing, where Thomas Trotter erected the Ann Street Theatre by invitation in 1807.[1] At this period national circumstances benefited Sussex: sea bathing became fashionable and the war with France curtailed travel abroad, encouraging visitors to the new resorts. Here entertainment became an essential requirement. Brighton, with the advantage of royal patronage and Doctor Russell's salt water cure, soon became the centre of social activity. Other Sussex resorts developed, leading to the coastal concentration of entertainment facilities which subsequently characterised the county.

Social changes in the later 19th century – paid and bank holidays, improved transport and the proximity of London – all conspired to transform the Sussex resorts into areas rich in theatre opportunity, the years 1880-1910 seeing the building of theatres mainly financed by local entrepreneurs. Fine auditoria by Frank Matcham survive at the Devonshire Park Theatre at Eastbourne (1884) and the former Brighton Hippodrome (1901).[2] These developments, prior to 1914, were so successful that outside promotion and investment in theatres became frequent, especially from London, encouraging an influx of 'flying matinées', repertory and concert parties. Although the intensive provision of resort entertainment had visitors as its prime target, the Sussex hinterland, hitherto dependent on local amateur initiatives and occasional touring shows, now began to benefit, the percentage of country people attending coastal theatres increasing steadily. As the century advanced, however, the theatres faced serious competition, first from the cinema and later television, resulting in numerous closures and conversions, and more recently the compromise of dual-use auditoria. Yet successful theatre continued – at the Theatre Royal, Brighton, with its popular pre-London performances, the Devonshire Park Theatre, Eastbourne, and the excellent repertory at the Worthing Connaught (1932) later backed by the Rank Organisation.[3]

Since the founding of the Arts Council in 1946 and the subsequent work of South-East Arts, many new theatre developments have taken place in Sussex, with an impressive increase in diversity and availability of drama and a growing financial participation by local authorities. The Chichester Festival Theatre, with its epoch-making design, opened in 1962, to be followed by the Brighton Festival in 1967.[4] A number of Arts and Community Centres, often linked to colleges and schools, have provided undreamed of facilities for the enjoyment of theatre at both professional and amateur level. Significantly, these new venues, by their occasional inland locations such as The Hawth at Crawley (1988) and the Christ's Hospital Arts Centre (1974), have begun to counter the resort monopoly of entertainment to the advantage of people inland. Other initiatives such as the Stables Theatre, Hastings (1959) and the successful New Venture Theatre in Brighton (1947) have enriched the scope of theatre in Sussex and point to an encouraging future.[5]

A   Major theatres

B   Pier theatres

C   Music halls, hippodromes, variety

D   Smaller theatres

E   College, school theatres

F   Arts, community, leisure centres with theatres

G   Concert and assembly halls with some theatre use

H   Theatres converted to cinema or dual use

I   Open air and beach venues

J   Pleasure grounds, amusement parks with theatres

The map ignores village and school halls occasionally used for plays. More than one theatre in a category is indicated by a number e.g. B2.

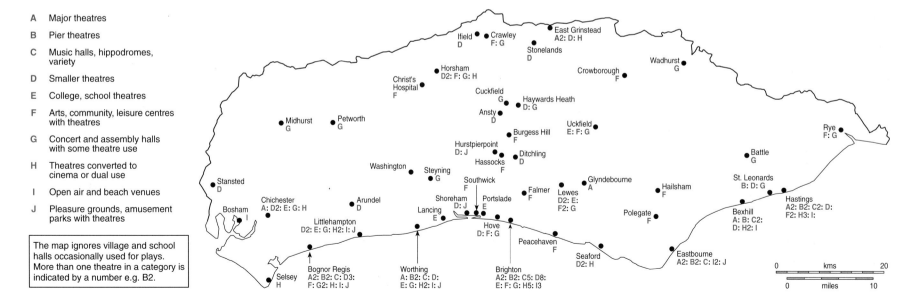

Cinemas (Allen Eyles)

After the first public screening of films in London on 20 February 1896, the new entertainment of moving pictures spread rapidly. The first venue outside London was the Pandora Gallery in King's Road, Brighton. In the early years films were shown in converted shops and halls, fairgrounds and music halls.

When it became clear that films were no passing novelty, the first purpose-built cinemas emerged. The Duke of York's cinema in Brighton, opened in 1910, is probably the oldest, largely unaltered, purpose-built cinema still operating in the UK.

The First World War brought cinema building to a close. A few larger cinemas began to appear after the war. None of these was more spectacular than the Regent, Brighton, opened in 1921 with 2,200 seats, and with a dance hall and restaurant.[6]

From the late 1920s there was frantic expansion in the film trade. One of the first cinemas opened by the ABC circuit was the Savoy in Brighton in 1930 – the largest ever built in Sussex, with 2,567 seats. ABC later acquired other existing cinemas at Bexhill, Eastbourne,

Hastings, Haywards Heath, Horsham, Hove, St Leonards-on-Sea and Worthing as part of its spread to become a major national circuit.[7]

A second circuit, Gaumont-British, ensured more than adequate representation in the key entertainment centre of Brighton, when it acquired the Regent, along with the older Academy, although it added only one further outlet in Sussex, the purpose-built Gaumont in Chichester.[8]

Oscar Deutsch, founder of what became the third national chain, Odeon, built his first notable Odeon, with tower and streamlined façade, at Worthing. Odeons at Bognor Regis, Kemp Town, Lancing, Lewes and Littlehampton were comparatively undistinguished, but his 1936 Odeon at Horsham showed the circuit style at its distinctive best. In Brighton, Deutsch's new Odeon joined the Savoy and Regent as the pre-eminent cinemas not only here but in Sussex as a whole. All the Sussex Odeons have been demolished except for Lancing and an earlier cinema taken over at Chichester, neither building now being used for entertainment.[9]

Independent entrepreneurs filled some of the gaps in the distribution of cinemas until the Second World War

prevented further developments. The last to open in Sussex was the Luxor at Lancing in January 1940.

Although there were few additions to the cinema scene in the immediate post-war period, this was a time when cinemas had some of their highest attendances. But they were soon to start closing in a gradual stream during the 1950s and later, under the impact of television and rival attractions. Many were converted to bingo halls or demolished for flats, supermarkets and offices.

Cinema attendances reached their lowest level in 1984. Then the first UK 'multiplex' – an idea from America – opened in 1985 and thereafter admissions began a dramatic recovery as cinema-going became fashionable once more. Multiplexes have opened in Sussex at Brighton and Eastbourne. The multiplex has been enlarged into the 'megaplex', the 15-screen Virgin at Crawley, opened in January 1999, being the first in Sussex.

These new complexes, and the survival of some small town cinemas, seem certain to place the long-established tradition of 'going to the pictures' among the top leisure attractions in Sussex for the foreseeable future.

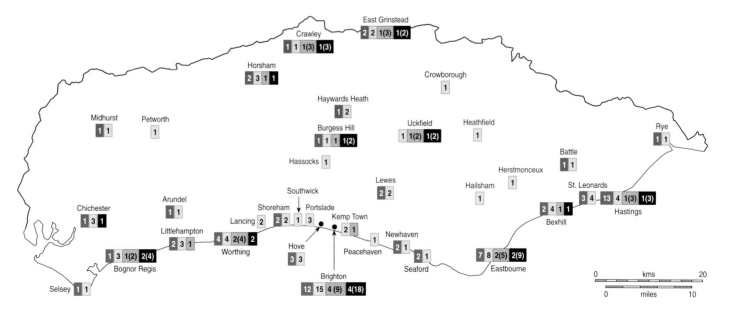

Cinemas are regarded as buildings used exclusively or very predominantly for showing films. They were not necessarily purpose-built, often being a conversion of existing buildings.

The map shows the number of cinemas in each town at the end of 1914, 1940, 1984 and 1998. This is not indicative of the number of cinemas ever built in a town as many cinemas were replaced between the dates shown. Numbers in brackets are the number of screens within the cinemas when there was more than one per cinema.

137

Anthony Freeman

Overview 1

Balfour's Education Act (1902) abolished the Victorian School Boards. Their schools, the funding of voluntary schools, and power to provide secondary and further education were handed to local government – to county councils, county boroughs and (for elementary education only) the larger urban districts and municipal borough councils. Sussex, therefore, had ten Local Education Authorities (LEAs) in 1902. This has declined overall to 5 from 1944, 2 from 1974 and 3 from 1997. The LEAs' core task has always been to provide for the compulsory years of schooling – to 12 until 1918, to 14 until 1947, to 15 until 1972 and thereafter to 16. Until the 1950s they did this mainly through elementary schools – 'all-age' schools from 5 to 14. Until the 1980s the LEAs' roles grew constantly, encompassing further education and a vast range of services, from teacher training to school meals and educational cruises, careers and youth services.

The LEAs have always had to accept partnership. Particularly in elementary schools, teachers themselves decided what to teach. In 1905 the Board of Education declared that 'each teacher shall think for himself and work out methods of teaching best suited to the school'. The LEA role was also limited by the churches. Until the 1950s almost two-thirds of West Sussex elementary or primary schools were denominational and, although the churches' influence has declined, half the East Sussex LEA primary schools, over a third in West Sussex and a quarter in Brighton, were church schools in 1998.

The LEAs did not educate all children of school age resident in their areas. In 1998, 4% of East Sussex children of secondary age attended maintained schools outside the county and some 20% of Brighton and Hove children and 27% of those from Wealden District were educated privately or elsewhere. Throughout the 20th century, Sussex has maintained a strong tradition of independent schooling. Despite the Depression there were 360 small private educational establishments in Sussex in the mid-1930s. Half were in East Sussex seaside towns. Every decade saw new independent schools opening, although most of the major independent schools date from the second half of the 19th century. Figures from the Independent Schools Information Service show over 17,000 pupils in these schools in Sussex in 1998; over a third were boarders, twice the national average.

1902-1944

It was, nevertheless, local government which took centre stage after 1902. West Sussex seized the initiative immediately, in 1904 opening three pupil-teacher schools for girls aged 14-18 in Chichester, Horsham and Worthing. Otherwise it was not until the 1930s that the LEAs really started to take advantage of the opportunities to develop new schools for pupils above the age of 11. Certainly Horsham and Midhurst, as well as the coastal belt, gained 'senior' schools, but otherwise rural West Sussex depended upon the 5-14 'all standard' school until well after the Second World War. The picture in East Sussex is very similar, with work on secondary schools in Heathfield, Uckfield and Wadhurst being a priority after the war. In Brighton, 84% of 11-14 year olds were still in 'all-age' schools in 1944, despite the opening of 'senior' and grammar schools. Tuition was not necessarily free at grammar schools. Horsham High School for Girls charged £5 5s per term in the mid-1920s and, in 1939, 61% of West Sussex 'secondary' (i.e. grammar) pupils paid fees, whereas in Brighton all such education was by then free. The Sussex LEAs recognised their deficiencies but, as elsewhere, had to wait until after the Second World War before replacing elementary education by 5-11 and 11-14+ schools. The war itself caused considerable, but survivable, dislocation, Sussex initially receiving large numbers of evacuee children before evacuating its own, mainly to the North and the Midlands.

1944-1999

The Butler Education Act (1944) had a profound effect on Sussex, bringing secondary education to all areas: secondary modern schools for the rural areas and a mix of grammar and secondary modern schools in towns. In addition, West Sussex, developing pre-war practice, created three secondary technical schools, though this policy was abandoned in 1957. Its Development Plan gives an idea of the enormity of the task. It gave priority to the rural secondary moderns, 'to train boys and girls to grow up good countrymen and women'.[1] In total there would be 32 new secondary moderns, four new grammar schools and the three technical schools. Boarding accommodation for girls was added at Midhurst and new hostels were opened at Steyning. But 46 elementary schools were to close, including all one-teacher schools, and 87 were to be substantially rebuilt or transferred to new sites and 45 new primary schools would be built – without making any allowance for the needs of Crawley New Town.

The Development Plans were to be implemented over 15-16 years – and in 1963 East Sussex LEA still had 'all-age' schools – but in one respect the 1944 Act was out of date before it was fully implemented. Selecting pupils for different types of secondary education came under immediate criticism.[2] Brighton Education Committee disliked selection and in West Sussex the first 'grammar-modern' (i.e. comprehensive), the Thomas Bennett School in Crawley, was opened in 1958, long before the Labour government's 1965 directive requiring LEAs to submit proposals for the introduction of comprehensive schools.[3] East Sussex was at first very cautious, but willing to introduce the changes during the next 15 years wherever population increased, and so selective education in Sussex ceased.[4] In parts of Brighton, and adjacent areas of West Sussex, Middle Schools were developed.

In the 1980s LEAs began to lose power. Schools were allowed to manage their own budgets and control over Further Education was surrendered in 1993. However, when offered the opportunity, only one Sussex school – the Greenway Junior School, Horsham – chose to leave LEA control altogether and attempts to create a City Technology college, independent of the LEA, failed in Brighton.

Except for the University of Sussex (opened in 1961), Further and Higher Education in Sussex developed piecemeal through mergers and municipal Technical and Art Colleges. The 1944 Act was an opportunity to bring coherence, but the plans at that time for a University, 17 County Colleges, a Regional College of Art and a College of Music and Dance all foundered. Nevertheless, Further Education saw massive growth from the 1960s as well as increasing diversity. In 1998 Sussex had six Colleges of Technology, seven Sixth-Form Colleges, two Agricultural Colleges and one Tertiary College. All became autonomous in 1993. The Universities of Sussex and Brighton and the Chichester Institute of Higher Education educated over 17,000 students in 1997. In 1999 the Chichester Institute was granted degree-awarding power and renamed University College Chichester.

Adult Education flourished in a variety of guises. From its Evening Institute classes in 1928 with 776 students,

West Sussex had 37,000 Adult Education students in 1997. The Workers' Education Association took over the work of the University Extension Scheme in 1918 and in 1998 had over 3,000 enrolled on its courses. A similar number were studying for Open University degrees at this date in Sussex.

Overview 2

Sir Arthur Conan Doyle described Board Schools as 'Beacons ... out of which will spring the wiser, better England of the future'.[5] The future arrived and during the 1990s a number of measures became available to permit at least a tentative view of how well Sussex is being educated. Except in Brighton and Hove, reading and mathematics levels for 7-year-olds in 1997 matched performance elsewhere in England. At 11 and 14 West Sussex moved slightly ahead, especially in mathematics, in which Brighton and Hove also made faster than average progress.[6] At 16, however, GCSE results reflected a widening range of performance, as the map for 1998 demonstrates. In the same year the Basic Skills Agency described 20,511 of Brighton and Hove's working-age population as having 'low or very low' literacy. More encouragingly, the Labour Force Survey of the same date had a quarter of the employed workforce in Sussex qualified to degree level – exactly in line with U.K. averages.

Source for map data:
Department for Education and Employment, *Secondary School Performance Tables 1998: 845-East Sussex; 846-Brighton and Hove; 938- West Sussex* (1998).

Percentage of pupils gaining 5 or more GCSE Grades A–C in 1998

Independent	Comprehensive				
■	●	95 and over	◩ ⊘	35	44
⊠	⊗	85 – 94	◩ ⊘	25	34
⊠	⊗	75 – 84	◩ ⊘	15	24
◩	⊘	65 – 74	■ ●	below	15
◩	⊘	55 – 64			
◩	⊘	45 – 54		England average 46.3%	

139

During this century Sussex has been in the forefront of pioneering new ways to protect and enhance its diversely beautiful landscape in the face of some of the strongest development pressure in England.

Countryside conservation became a matter of extreme urgency in the 1920s and '30s when a rash of indiscriminate development, mainly in coastal locations, began to destroy some of the least unspoiled landscape in the country. Notwithstanding the very limited planning powers of county councils and other local authorities before 1947, the tangible achievements in conservation were very substantial, notably in defence of the South Downs, then in danger of being routed and forced into full retreat by the bungalow merchant. Meanwhile (Sir) Herbert Carden's Brighton came to be regarded as a model municipality, buying up her open hinterland of Downs for preservation amid a chorus of praise, though Brighton's policies for mass leisure in the Downs later came under severe criticism.[1]

Immediately after the Second World War there was substantial support for National Park status as a fitting conclusion to the Downs' survival from the holocaust. A National Park for the central area of the South Downs between the Arun and Adur had been proposed by Vaughan Cornish in 1929, and John Dower's 1945 White Paper on *National Parks in England and Wales* and Sir Arthur Hobhouse's 1947 *Report of the National Parks Committee* both identified the South Downs amongst areas which met requirements for designation as a National Park.[2] The character of the Downs had greatly changed, however, with the ploughing-up of much of the traditional sheep pasture during the war, and by 1957, when the National Parks Commission considered the status of the Downs, the arable transformation was proceeding on a scale unimaginable a generation earlier. In the changed circumstances the Commission concluded that the recreational value of the Downs had been so severely reduced by cultivation that designation as a National Park was no longer appropriate.

Frantic attempts to rescue fragments of heritage were much frustrated. The scheduling of ancient monuments and areas of scientific importance had begun before the war, but progress was slow owing to the lack of national funds and qualified staff. In the extensive ploughing-up of the early post-war years less than one-half of both historic and scientifically significant sites then recognised had been scheduled, and these not necessarily the most important.[3]

The most decisive step in the 1950s was the designation of the Kingley Vale yew forest, considered to be the finest in Europe, in the first tranche of National Nature Reserves (NNRs) in 1952. This fulfilled a 40-year old ambition of Sir Arthur Tansley, then Chairman of the Nature Conservancy, whose familiarity with the area had begun with his ecological research at the beginning of the century. Three more NNRs have been subsequently designated on the Downs.[4]

Another notable event was the designation of the South Downs Way in 1963, the ridgeway track along the crest covering some 113km, the first long-distance trail to be created in Britain. This was extended to Winchester in 1981.

The most significant steps forward in rural conservation at this time were the creation of Areas of Outstanding Natural Beauty (AONBs). Chichester Harbour was so designated in 1964, followed in 1966 by the Sussex Downs which included not only the chalklands but also the clays and sands on the north-west.[5] The High Weald of Sussex was included in the High Weald AONB in 1983. More than half of East and West Sussex was included in these AONBs and, ever since, the protection and enhancement of the quality of their landscape and habitats have been a key issue.

In 1973 added protection was given to the magnificent chalk cliffs from Splash Point near Rottingdean to the edge of Eastbourne by means of one of the first of three Heritage Coast designations in England which aimed to conserve the zone between low water mark and one mile inland.

Meanwhile the notification of Sites of Special Scientific Interest proceeded steadily and has continued apace in recent years. Approximately 4% of land in West Sussex is now in this category; in East Sussex the figure is 6.5%. A strong drive has been given to the protection of the best surviving lowland heathland and, increasingly, the most significant geological exposures are now being scheduled. The remaining wetlands have also come to be regarded as very special places and the extensive shingle beaches, sand dunes and grazing marshes between Dungeness (Kent) and Pett Level make this area a candidate in the Natura 2000 scheme identifying sites of European importance.[6]

However, despite AONB status, the continued vulnerability of the Downs to urban encroachment on the fringes of coastal towns, especially around Brighton, together with adverse changes resulting from their intensified cultivation, gave rise to increased public concern in the 1980s. These urgent problems led to two new ways of protection. One was the Ministry of Agriculture's Environmentally Sensitive Area Scheme, newly introduced in 1987 and immediately applied to the eastern South Downs and extended westwards to cover the West Sussex and Hampshire Downs in the following year. The second step stemmed from the public debate on the future of the organisation administering the South Downs. The result was the setting up of the Sussex Downs Conservation Board in 1992 as a unique experiment in the management of a threatened landscape. At the end of its six-year experimental period its functions were extended into the next century; in September 1999 the Deputy Prime Minister announced that he had asked the Countryside Agency to consider designating a National Park in the South Downs.[7]

It will be apparent that in this century countryside conservation has been marshalled on behalf of places *special* in terms of outstanding scenery or importance for wildlife. Oh that future generations will continue this but that they will also value, maintain and enhance normal, *ordinary*, Sussex landscape as in the Low Weald, now so precariously threatened by rapidly advancing suburbia, spreading like so much spilt treacle.

Sites of Special Scientific Interest

1 Forest Mere
2 Chapel Common
3 Rake Hanger
4 Fyning Moor
5 Woolbeding and Pound Commons
6 Northpark Copse to Snapelands Copse
7 Perry Copse Outcrops
8 Shillinglee Lake
9 Chiddingfold Forest
10 Ebernoe Common
11 The Mens
12 Upper Arun
13 Bognor Common Quarry
14 Kingley Vale
15 Pads Wood
16 West Harting Down
17 Harting Downs
18 Rook Cliff
19 Iping Common
20 Treyford to Bepton Down
21 West Dean Woods
22 Singleton and Cocking Tunnels

23 Heyshott Down
24 Ambersham Common
25 Lavington Common
26 Burton Park
27 Coates Castle
28 Duncton to Bignor Escarpment
29 Fairmile Bottom
30 Arundel Park
31 Levin Down
32 East Dean Park Wood
33 Halnaker Chalk Pit
34 Eartham Pit, Boxgrove
35 Chichester Harbour
36 Bracklesham Bay
37 Selsey, East Beach
38 Pagham Harbour
39 Bognor Reef
40 Felpham
41 Climping Beach
42 Arun Banks
43 Amberley Mount to Sullington Hill
44 Cissbury Ring
45 Chanctonbury Hill
46 Chantry Mill

47 Sullington Warren
48 Parham Park
49 Amberley Wild Brooks
50 Waltham Brooks
51 Pulborough Brooks
52 Hurston Warren
53 Marehill Quarry
54 Park Farm Cutting
55 Coneyhurst Cutting
56 Coppedhall Hanger
57 Slinfold Stream and Quarry
58 Warnham
59 House Copse
60 Buchan Hill Ponds
61 St Leonards Park Ponds
62 St Leonards Forest
63 Cow Wood and Harry's Wood
64 Worth Forest
65 Wakehurst and Chiddingly Woods
66 Philpots and Hook Quarries
67 West Hoathly
68 Stonehill Rocks
69 Mills Rocks
70 Wolstonbury Hill

71 Horton Clay Pit
72 Beeding Hill to Newtimber Hill
73 Adur Estuary
74 Brighton to Newhaven Cliffs
75 Castle Hill
76 Kingston Escarpment and Iford Hill
77 Lewes Brooks
78 Offham Marshes
79 Clayton to Offham Escarpment
80 Ditchling Common
81 Chailey Common
82 Rock Wood
83 Ashdown Forest
84 Weir Wood Reservoir
85 Penn's Rocks
86 Eridge Green
87 High Rocks
88 Eridge Park
89 Bream Wood
90 Hastingford Cutting
91 Stackland Farm Meadows
92 Paines Cross Meadow
93 Willingford Meadow
94 Dallington Forest

95 Bingletts Wood
96 St Dunstan's Farm Meadows
97 Heathfield Park
98 Sapperton Meadows
99 Waldron Cutting
100 Buxted Park
101 Plashett Park Wood
102 Park Corner Heath
103 Burgh Hill Farm Meadow
104 Lower Dicker
105 Lewes Downs
106 Southerham Grey Pit
107 Southerham Machine Bottom
108 Southerham Works Pit
109 Asham Quarry
110 Firle Escarpment
111 Arlington Reservoir
112 Milton Gate Marsh
113 Wilmington Downs
114 Lullington Heath
115 Seaford to Beachy Head
116 Willingdon Downs
117 Folkington Reservoir
118 Pevensey Levels

119 Herstmonceux Park
120 Ashburnham Park
121 Darwell Wood
122 River Line
123 High Woods
124 Combe Haven
125 Fore Wood
126 Marline Valley Woods
127 Blackhorse Quarry
128 Hemmingford Meadow
129 Maplehurst Wood
130 Brede Pit and Cutting
131 Northiam
132 Hastings Cliffs to Pett Beach
133 Pett Levels
134 Rye Harbour
135 Winchelsea Cutting
136 Leasam Heronry Wood
137 Houghton Green Cliff
138 Walland Marsh
139 Camber Sands and Rye Saltings
140 Dungeness

Source for map data:
English Nature, *Sites of Special Scientific Interest and other statutory sites in East and West Sussex* (1993) with later additions.

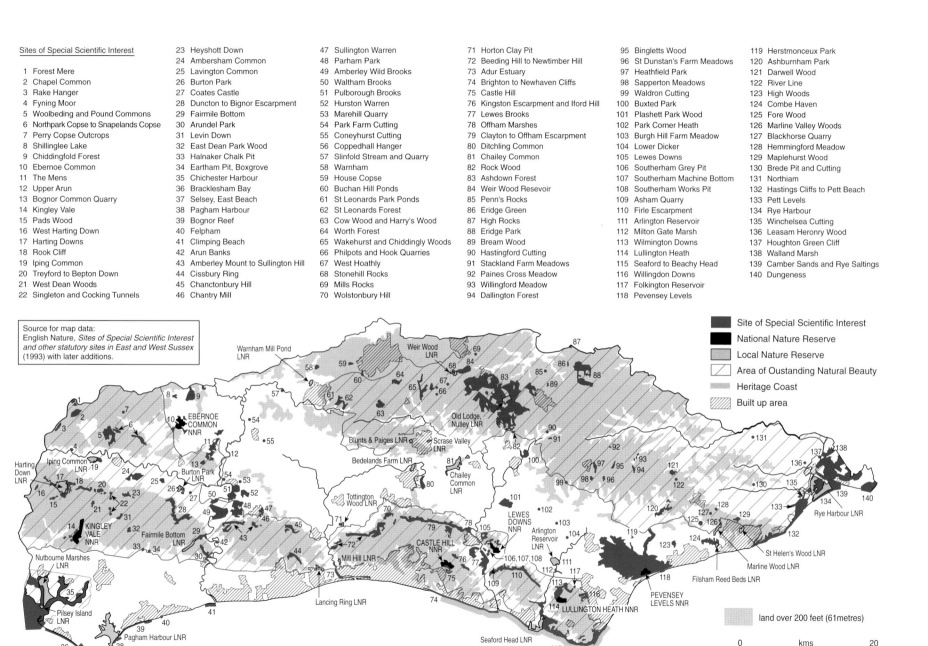

Site of Special Scientific Interest
National Nature Reserve
Local Nature Reserve
Area of Oustanding Natural Beauty
Heritage Coast
Built up area

land over 200 feet (61metres)

141

NOTES AND FURTHER READING

Place of publication is London, unless otherwise specified.

The following abbreviations are used throughout:

Arch in Sx: P.L.Drewett (ed), *Archaeology in Sussex to AD 1500* CBA Research Report **29** (1978)
CBA: Council for British Archaeology
ESRO: East Sussex Record Office, Lewes
PRO: Public Record Office
PPS: *Proceedings of the Prehistoric Society*
SAC: *Sussex Archaeological Collections*
SE to AD 1000: P.Drewett, D.Rudling and M.Gardiner, *The South East to AD 1000* (1988)
SE from AD 1000: P.Brandon and B.Short, *The South East from AD 1000* (1990)
SIH: *Sussex Industrial History*
SNQ: *Sussex Notes and Queries*
SRS: *Sussex Record Society*
Sx ELS: Geography Editorial Committee (eds), *Sussex: Environment, Landscape and Society* (Gloucester 1983)
VCH Sx: *Victoria County History of Sussex*
WSRO: West Sussex Record Office, Chichester

INTRODUCTION

1. Apart from *The Historical Atlas of Cheshire*, a pioneering work published in 1958, it has been only in more recent years that this county-based approach has gained favour, perhaps even prompted by the deliberations of the Local Government Commission for England which brought home to many residents the full meaning of county affiliation. We now therefore have county atlases for Suffolk (1988), Durham (1992), Norfolk (1993), Lincolnshire (1993), East Yorkshire (1996) and Berkshire (1998). A slightly different approach is adopted in the *Historical Atlas of South-West England* (1999) which encompasses both Cornwall and Devon.
2. J. Black, *Maps and History: Constructing Images of the Past* (1997), 224-5. The development of the English county atlas does not, however, feature in this otherwise fascinating book.
3. W.G. Hoskins, *English Local History: the Past and the Future* (Leicester 1966), 5.
4. J.B. Harley, 'Historical Geography and the Cartographic Illusion', *Journal of Historical Geography* **15** (1989), 87.
5. *VCH Hampshire and the Isle of Wight* **III** (1908), 77-8; *VCH Sx* **IV** (1953), 2, 54, 80; the latter is incorrect in the dating of the transfer of the Ambershams to surrounding parishes. We thank Peter Wilkinson (WSRO) for correcting these dates.

1. GEOLOGY

1. W. Gibbons, *The Weald - a Geological Field Guide* (1981); R.N. Mortimore, *The Chalk of Sussex and Kent. Geologists' Association Guide* **57** (1997); R.W. Gallois, *The Wealden District* (British Geological Survey, 1965). See also the individual sheet memoirs of the British Geological Survey, e.g. R.D. Lake, B.Young, C.J. Wood and R.N. Mortimore, *Geology of the Country around Lewes* (1987); B.Young and R.D. Lake, *Geology of the Country around Brighton and Worthing* (1988); R.D. Lake and E.R. Shephard-Thorn, *Geology of the Country around Hastings and Dungeness* (1987) and R.W. Gallois and B.C. Worssam, *Geology of the Country around Horsham* (1993).
2. A. Ruffell, A. Ross and K.Taylor, *Early Cretaceous Environments of the Weald. Geologists' Association Guide* **55** (1996).
3. R.N. Mortimore, 'The Geology of Sussex', in *Sx ELS*, 15-32.
4. D.K.C. Jones, *Southeast and Southern England* (1981).

2. SOILS

1. The classification and terminology of soil types follows B.W. Avery, 'Soil classification in the Soil Survey of England and Wales', *Journal of Soil Science* **24** (1973), 324-38; and M.G. Jarvis, R.H. Allen, S.J. Fordham, J. Hazelden, A.J. Moffat and R.G. Sturdy, *Soils and their use in South East England,* Soil Survey of England and Wales, Bulletin **15** (1984).
2. S.G. McRae and C.P. Burnham, 'The soils of the Weald' *Proceedings Geologists Association* **86** (1975), 593-610.
3. J.M. Hodgson, *Soils of the West Sussex Coastal Plain,* Soil Survey of England and Wales, Bulletin **3** (1967).
4. Ministry of Agriculture, Fisheries and Food, *Agricultural Land Classification Map of England and Wales* (1968).
5. J. Loveday, 'Plateau deposits of the southern Chiltern Hills', *Proceedings Geologists Association* **73** (1962), 83-102.
6. J.P. Hodgson, J.A. Catt and P.H. Weir, 'The origin and development of clay-with-flints and associated soil horizons on the South Downs', *Journal of Soil Science* **18** (1967), 85-102.
7. McRae and Burnham, 'The Soils of the Weald'.
8. Macrae and Burnham, 'The Soils of the Weald'; Jarvis *et al.*, *Soils and their use.*
9. R.M.S. Perrin, 'The nature of "Chalk Heath" soils', *Nature* **178** (1956), 31-2.
10. D.A. Robinson and R.B.G. Williams, 'The soils and vegetation history of Sussex' in *Sx ELS*, 109-26.

3. NATURAL REGIONS

1. See, for example, R.B.G. Williams and D.A. Robinson, 'The landforms of Sussex', in *Sx ELS*, 33-49. Other authors recognise as few as three major regions (e.g. the Weald, Downs and Coastal Plain) or as many as eight or ten. For planning purposes very large numbers of more minor units are sometimes recognised.
2. Countryside Commission, *The High Weald: Exploring the Landscape of the Area of Outstanding Natural Beauty* (Cheltenham 1994); English Nature, *High Weald Natural Area profile* (Wye, Kent 1998).
3. D.A. Robinson and R.B.G. Williams, *Classic Landforms of the Weald.* Geographical Association Landform Guide **4** (Sheffield 1984).
4. English Nature, *Romney Marsh Natural Area Profile* (Wye, Kent 1998).
5. English Nature, *Low Weald and Pevensey Natural Area Profile* (Wye, Kent 1998).
6. English Nature, *Wealden Greensand Natural Area Profile* (Wye, Kent 1998).
7. English Nature, *South Downs Natural Area Profile* (Wye, Kent 1998); Countryside Commission and Sussex Downs Conservation Board, *The Sussex Downs AONB Landscape Assessment* (Landscape Design Associates, Peterborough 1994).
8. D. Streeter, 'Biogeography, ecology and conservation in Sussex', in *Sx ELS*, 127-47; Sussex Wildlife Trust, *Vision for the Wildlife of Sussex* (Henfield 1996); F. Rose, *The Habitats and Vegetation of Sussex* (Brighton 1995).
9. F. Rose and J.H. Patmore, *Weald Gill Woodlands* (English Nature, 1997); A. Jackson and M. Flanagan, *Conservation of cryptogams in the Weald* (Royal Botanic Gardens, Kew 1997).
10. R. Williamson, *The Great Yew Forest: the Natural History of Kingley Vale* (1978).
11. English Nature, *Folkestone to Selsey Bill Natural Area Profile* (Wye, Kent 1998).

4. THE COAST AND COASTAL CHANGES

1. G.F. Mitchell, 'Raised beaches and sea-levels' in F.W. Shotten, (ed), *British Quaternary Studies* (1977), 169-86.
2. Mitchell, 'Raised beaches'; R.J.N. Devoy, 'Flandrian sea-level changes in the Thames Estuary and the implications for land subsidence in England and Wales', *Nature* 270 (1977), 712-15; R.J. Devoy, 'Analysis of the geological evidence for Holocene sea-level movements in South East England', *Proceedings Geologists Association* 93 (1982), 65-90; D.A. Robinson and R.B.G. Williams, 'The Sussex coast past and present', in *Sx ELS*, 50-66.
3. D.K.C. Jones, *Southeast and Southern England* (1981); P. Burrin, 'The coastal deposits of the southern Weald', *Quaternary Newsletter* 38 (1982), 16-24; P.J. Burrin, D.K.C. Jones, S. Jennings and C. Smyth, 'A preliminary interpretation of coastal deposits from East Sussex', *Quaternary Newsletter* 37 (1982), 12-19.
4. Jones, *Southeast and Southern England*.
5. J. Eddison, 'Flandrian barrier beaches off the coast of Sussex and south-east Kent', *Quaternary Newsletter* 39 (1983), 25-9; S. Jennings and C. Smyth, 'Coastal sedimentation in East Sussex during the Holocene', *Progress in Oceanography* 18 (1987), 205-41; S. Jennings and C. Smyth, 'Holocene evolution of the gravel coastline of East Sussex', *Proceedings Geologists Association* 101 (1990), 213-24.
6. For details see H.C. Brookfield, 'A critical period in the history of Shoreham Harbour, 1760-1816', *SAC* 88 (1949), 42-50; H.C. Brookfield, 'The estuary of the Adur', *SAC* 90 (1952), 153-63; P.F. Brandon, 'The origin of Newhaven and the drainage of the Lewes and Laughton Levels', *SAC* 109 (1971), 94-106; J.H. Farrant, 'The evolution of Newhaven Harbour and the lower Ouse before 1800', *SAC* 110 (1972), 44-60; R. Castleden, *Classic Landforms of the Sussex Coast* (The Geographical Association, 2nd edtn, Sheffield 1996); *VCH Sx* V (pt 1) (1997).
7. Castleden, *Classic Landforms*.
8. P. Brandon, *The Sussex Landscape* (1974), 116-17.
9. J. Cleeve and R.B.G. Williams, *Cliff erosion in East Sussex*, Sussex Studies 5 (Geographical Educational Material for Schools, University of Sussex 1987); Castleden, *Classic Landforms*.
10. R.W.G. Carter, 'Rising Sea Level', *Geology Today* 5 (1989), 637; L. Shennon, 'Holocene crustal movements and sea level changes in Great Britain', *Journal Quaternary Science* 4 (1989), 77-89; South Downs Coastal Group, *South Downs Shoreline Management Plan, Selsey Bill to Beachy Head* (1996).
11. J.B. Redman, 'On the alluvial formations and local changes of the south coast of England', *Proceedings Institute of Civil Engineers* 11 (1851-2),162-226; M.F. Tyhurst, 'Eastbourne's sea defences', *Journal Society Civil Engineering Technicians* 2 (1972), 3-8; Jennings and Smyth, 'Holocene evolution'. The dates BP are obtained from radio-carbon dates by means of the tree-ring calibration of radiocarbon ages. BP indicates calendar years before present, calculated from AD 1950.
12. South Downs Coastal Group, *South Downs Shoreline* (1996).
13. H. Lovegrove, 'Old shorelines near Camber Castle', *Geographical Journal* 119 (1953), 200-7; R. Millward and A. Robinson, *South-East England - The Channel Coastlands* (1973), 63-4; J. Eddison, 'The evolution of barrier beaches between Fairlight and Hythe', *Geographical Journal* 149 (1983), 39-53.
14. T.M.L. Wigley and S.C.B. Raper, 'Implications for climate and sea level rise of revised IPCC emissions scenarios', *Nature* 357 (1992), 293-300; J. Houghton, *Global Warming: The complete briefing* (2nd edtn 1997).

5. EARLIEST INHABITANTS

1. A. Parfitt, forthcoming in D. Rudling (ed), *The Archaeology of Sussex to AD 2000*; Wessex Archaeology, *The Southern Rivers Palaeolithic Project Report 3 1993-1994; The Sussex Raised Beaches and the Bristol Avon* (1994), 40-83; A.G. Woodcock, 'The Palaeolithic in Sussex', in *Arch in Sx*, 8-14; A.G. Woodcock, *The Lower and Middle Palaeolithic Periods in Sussex*, British Archaeological Reports 94 (1981), 1-418; A.G. Woodcock, 'The Lower and Middle Palaeolithic Periods in Sussex', in S.N. Colcutt (ed), *The Palaeolithic of Britain and its nearest neighbours - Recent trends* (University of Sheffield 1986), 31-5.
2. A number of papers which discuss the latest evidence for dating these deposits can be found in J.M. Murton, C.A. Whiteman, M.R. Bates, D.R. Bridgland, A.J. Long, M.B. Roberts and M.P. Waller (eds), *The Quaternary of Kent and Sussex: Field Guide* (Quaternary Research Association 1998), 121-213.
3. Evidence from near Dover (Kent) suggests that Palaeolithic material may have survived on the chalk Downs close to where it was originally deposited; see G. Halliwell and K. Parfitt, 'Non-river gravel Lower and Middle Palaeolithic discoveries in East Kent', *Kent Archaeological Review* 114 (1993), 80-3.

6. BOXGROVE

1. M.B. Roberts, S.A. Parfitt, M.I. Pope and F.F. Wenban Smith, 'Boxgrove, West Sussex: Rescue excavations of a Lower Palaeolithic Landsurface (Boxgrove Project B 1989-1991)', *PPS* 63 (1997), 303-58.
2. M.B. Roberts and S.A. Parfitt, *A Middle Pleistocene hominid site at Eartham Quarry, Boxgrove, West Sussex* (English Heritage Archaeological Report 17 1999).
3. M.R. Bates, S.A. Parfitt and M.B. Roberts, 'The chronology, palaeoecology and archaeological significance of the marine Quaternary record of the West Sussex Coastal Plain, Southern England, UK', *Quaternary Science Reviews* 10 (1997), 127-52.
4. R.C. Preece, J.D. Scourse, S.D. Houghton, K.L. Knudsen, and D.N. Penney, 'The Pleistocene sea-level and neotectonic history of the eastern Solent, southern England', *Philosophical Transactions of the Royal Society of London* (1990), B 328, 425-77.
5. C.S. Gamble, *Timewalkers: The Prehistory of Global Colonisation* (Bath 1993).

7. LATER HUNTERS AND GATHERERS

1. R.M. Jacobi, 'The Mesolithic in Sussex' in *Arch in Sx*, 15-22.
2. P.A.M. Keef, J.J. Wymer, and G.W. Dimbleby, 'A Mesolithic site on Iping Common, Sussex, England', *PPS* 31 (1965), 85-92.
3. D. Garton, 'An Early Mesolithic site at Rackham, West Sussex', *SAC* 118 (1980), 145-52.
4. J.G.D. Clark, 'The Affinities of the Farnham Industry: the Horsham Culture' in J.G.D. Clark and W.F. Rankine, 'Excavations at Farnham, Surrey (1937-38): The Horsham Culture and the Question of Mesolithic Dwellings', *PPS* 5 (1939), 91-8.
5. R.M. Jacobi and C.F. Tebbutt, 'The excavation of a Mesolithic rock-shelter site at High Hurstwood, Sussex', *SAC* 119 (1981), 1-36.
6. J.H. Money, 'Excavations at High Rocks, Tunbridge Wells, 1954-1956', *SAC* 98 (1960), 173-221.
7. P. Drewett, 'The excavation of four round barrows of the second millennium B.C. at West Heath, Harting, 1973-75', *SAC* 114 (1976), 126-50.
8. G.W. Dimbleby, 'Pollen Analysis' in P.L. Drewett, 'The Excavation of a turf barrow at Minsted, West Sussex, 1973', *SAC* 113 (1975), 54-65.
9. P. Drewett, *The Archaeology of Bullock Down, Eastbourne, East Sussex: The Development of a Landscape* (Sussex Archaeological Society Monograph 1, 1982), 42-4.
10. M.W. Pitts, 'A Gazetteer of Mesolithic finds on the West Sussex Coastal Plain', *SAC* 118 (1980), 153-62.
11. Jacobi, 'The Mesolithic in Sussex'.

8. FIRST FARMING COMMUNITIES AND COMMUNAL MONUMENTS

1. *SE to AD 1000*, 35.
2. M. Bell, 'Excavations at Bishopstone, Sussex', *SAC* 115 (1977), 1-241.
3. J. Sheldon, 'The Environmental Background' in *Arch in Sx*, 3-7.
4. R.G. Scaife and P.J. Burrin, 'Floodplain development in the vegetational history of the Sussex High Weald and some archaeological implications', *SAC* 121 (1983), 1-10.
5. K.D. Thomas, 'The Land Mollusca from the Enclosure on Offham Hill' in 'The Excavation of a Neolithic Causewayed Enclosure on Offham Hill, East Sussex, 1976', *PPS* 43 (1977), 234-9.
6. O. Bedwin, 'Excavations at the Neolithic Enclosure on Bury

Hill, Houghton, West Sussex 1979', *PPS* **47** (1981), 69-86; O. Bedwin, 'The excavation of a small hilltop enclosure on Court Hill, Singleton, West Sussex 1982', *SAC* **122** (1984), 13-22; O. Bedwin, 'Prehistoric Earthworks on Halnaker Hill, West Sussex: Excavations 1981-1983', *SAC* **130** (1992), 1-12.

7. P. Drewett, 'Dr V. Seton Williams' excavations at Combe Hill, 1962, and the role of Neolithic causewayed enclosures in Sussex', *SAC* **132** (1994), 7-24.

8. P. Drewett, 'The excavation of a Neolithic Causewayed Enclosure on Offham Hill, East Sussex 1976', *PPS* **43** (1977), 201-41.

9. *SE to AD 1000*, 52-60.

10. R. Holgate, *Prehistoric Flint Mines* (Princes Risborough 1991).

11. N.H. Field, C.L. Matthews and I.F. Smith, 'New Neolithic sites in Dorset and Bedfordshire with a note on the distribution of Neolithic storage pits in Britain', *PPS* **30** (1964), 352-81.

12. J. Thomas, *Rethinking the Neolithic* (Cambridge 1991).

13. *SE to AD 1000*, 46-7.

9. EMERGING HIERARCHIES AND THE RISE OF THE INDIVIDUAL

1. R. Bradley, 'The excavation of a beaker settlement at Belle Tout, East Sussex, England', *PPS* **36** (1970), 312-79.

2. M. Bell in P. Drewett, *The Archaeology of Bullock Down, Eastbourne, East Sussex: the development of a landscape* (Sussex Archaeological Society Monograph **1**, 1982); R. Holgate, 'Further investigations at the later Neolithic domestic site and Napoleonic "camp" at Bullock Down, near Eastbourne, East Sussex', *SAC* **126** (1988), 21-30.

3. E.C. Curwen, 'Excavations at Whitehawk Neolithic Camp, Brighton 1932-3', *Antiquaries Journal* **14** (1934), 99-133; G.P. Burstow and G.A. Holleyman, 'Late Bronze Age settlement on Itford Hill, Sussex', *PPS* **23** (1957), 167-212; O. Bedwin and M.W. Pitts, 'The excavation of an Iron Age settlement at North Bersted, Bognor Regis, West Sussex 1975-76', *SAC* **116** (1978), 293-346.

4. O. Bedwin, 'Bronze Age Pottery from Cross Lane, Findon, West Sussex', *SAC* **117** (1979), 254-5.

5. C. Butler, 'A fieldwalking project at Breechlands Farm, near Hurstpierpoint, West Sussex', *SAC* **128** (1990), 21-32; C. Butler and J. Funnell, 'Further fieldwalking at Novington Manor, Plumpton, East Sussex', *SAC* **130** (1992), 13-21; M.J. Allen, 'The prehistoric land-use and human ecology of the Malling-Caburn Downs: two late Neolithic/early Bronze Age sites beneath colluvial sequences', *SAC* **133** (1995),19-43.

6. P. Drewett in O. Bedwin, 'Excavations at Chanctonbury Ring, Wiston, West Sussex, 1977', *Britannia* **11** (1980), 173-222; R. Holgate and A. Woodcock, 'A later Mesolithic site at Pannel Bridge, near Pett Level, East Sussex', *SAC* **127** (1989) 1-10; E.W. Holden and R.J. Bradley, 'A Late Neolithic site at Rackham', *SAC* **113** (1975), 85-103.

7. C. Greatorex, 'The excavation of an Early Bronze Age Barrow at Crowlink, near Eastbourne, East Sussex',

(forthcoming).

8. *SE to AD 1000*, 84.

9. E.C. Curwen, *The Archaeology of Sussex* (1954), 152-7; L.V. Grinsell, 'Sussex Barrows', *SAC* **75** (1934), 220; H.B.A. Ratcliffe-Densham, 'A Woman of Wessex Culture', *SAC* **106** (1968), 40-8; C. Butler, 'The excavation of a Beaker Bowl Barrow at Pyecombe, West Sussex', *SAC* **129** (1991), 1-28.

10. *SE to AD 1000*, 86.

11. R. Bradley, *The Social Foundations of Prehistoric Britain* (1984), 74.

12. *SE to AD 1000*, 86.

13. C. Greatorex, 'The Excavation of a later Bronze Age settlement site at Patcham Fawcett School, Carden Avenue, Brighton, East Sussex' (forthcoming).

14. R. Bradley, 'Working the land: imagining the landscape', *Archaeological Dialogues* **4** (1997), 40.

15. D. Rudling and J. Funnell, 'Excavations at Downsview' in D. Rudling (ed) 'Downland Settlement and Landuse: The Archaeology of the Brighton By-pass' (forthcoming); I. Greig, 'Excavation of a Bronze Age settlement at Varley Halls, Coldean Lane, Brighton, East Sussex', *SAC* **135** (1997), 7-58.

16. E. Curwen, 'Prehistoric remains from Kingston Buci', *SAC* **72** (1931), 185-217.

17. S. Stevens, 'Excavations at Potlands Farm, Patching, West Sussex', *SAC* **135** (1997), 59-70.

18. Drawn by Jane Russell (Archaeology South-East, University College London).

10. REGIONAL TRADITIONS c.1000-100BC

1. O. Bedwin, 'Iron Age Sussex: the Downs and the Coastal Plain', in *Arch in Sx* , 41-51; S. Hamilton and J. Manley, 'Points of view: prominent enclosures in 1st millennium BC Sussex', *SAC* **135** (1997), 93-112.

2. O. Bedwin, 'The excavation of a cross-dyke at Old Erringham Farm, Upper Beeding, West Sussex 1976', *SAC* **117** (1979), 11-19.

3. E. Curwen and E.C. Curwen, 'Excavations in the Caburn, near Lewes', *SAC* **68** (1927), 1-56.

4. P. Drewett, *The Archaeology of Bullock Down, Eastbourne, East Sussex: the development of a landscape* (Sussex Archaeological Society Monograph **1**, 1982).

5. M. Bell, 'Excavations at Bishopstone' *SAC* **115** (1977).

6. O. Bedwin and R. Holgate, 'Excavations at Copse Farm, Oving, West Sussex', *PPS* **51** (1985), 215-45.

11. THE END OF PREHISTORY c.100BC-AD43

1. S. Hamilton and J. Manley, 'Points of view: prominent enclosures in 1st millennium BC Sussex', *SAC* **135** (1997), 93-112; J. Money, 'Aspects of the Iron Age in the Weald', in *Arch in Sx,* 38-40.

2. O. Bedwin and R. Holgate, 'Excavations at Copse Farm, Oving, West Sussex', *PPS* **51** (1985), 215-45.

3. S. Hamilton, 'The Iron Age pottery', in M. Bell, ' Excavations at Bishopstone' *SAC* **115** (1977), 83-117.

4. S. Hamilton, 'The Iron Age pottery', in O. Bedwin and R. Holgate, 'Excavations at Copse Farm, Oving, West Sussex', *PPS* **51** (1985), 220-8.

5. H. Cleere and D. Crossley, *The Iron Industry of the Weald* (2nd edtn, ed. J. Hodgkinson, Cardiff 1995).

6. A.P. Fitzpatrick, 'Archaeological Excavations on the route of the A27 Westhampnett Bypass, West Sussex, 1992. Vol 2: the Cemeteries', *Wessex Archaeology Report* **12** (1997).

7. O. Bedwin, 'Excavations at Lancing Down, West Sussex 1980', *SAC* **119** (1981), 37-56.

8. O. Bedwin and C. Place, 'Late Iron Age and Romano-British occupation at Ounces Barn, Boxgrove, West Sussex; excavations 1982-83', *SAC* **133** (1995), 45-101.

9. Coin distribution map kindly supplied by Philip de Jersey.

10. Dyke map kindly supplied by John Magilton.

12. ROMAN SUSSEX

1. J.G.F. Hind, 'The Invasion of Britain in AD43: An Alternative Strategy for Aulus Plautius', *Britannia* **20** (1989), 1-21.

2. See map 13.

3. Until recently this individual, who was probably a kinsman of Verica, was known as Cogidubnus. The reasons for the change in spelling have been put forward by R.S.O. Tomlin, 'Reading a 1st century Roman gold signet ring from Fishbourne', *SAC* **135** (1997), 127-30.

4. See map 13; B. Cunliffe, *The Regni* (1973), ch. 4; D. Rudling, 'The development of Roman villas in Sussex', *SAC* **136** (1998), 41-65.

5. Cunliffe, *The Regni*, 79.

6. Suggestion from Ernest Black, *pers. com.*

7. B.W. Cunliffe, *Excavations at Fishbourne 1961-1969, vol.1: The Site*. Reports of the Research Committee of the Society of Antiquaries of London, **XXVI** (Leeds 1971), 75 and 153.

8. Cunliffe, *The Regni*.

9. The whole subject of Roman roads in Britain, and especially those in the South-East, formed the basis of a lifetime of research by the late Ivan Margary, who was a prominent member of the Sussex Archaeological Society. Although the reader is referred to the published results of Margary's work, it should be noted that not all of Margary's roads and routes have been confirmed by excavation. See I.D. Margary, *Roman Ways in the Weald* (1965) and *Roman Roads in Britain* (1967).

10. J. Magilton, 'Roman Roads in the Manhood Peninsula', *The Archaeology of Chichester and District 1995* (Chichester 1996), 31-4.

11. For a review of the fragmentary evidence concerning the *Classis Britannica,* see H. Cleere, 'The Classis Britannica', in D.E. Johnston (ed), *The Saxon Shore* (CBA Research Report **18**, 1977), 16-19.

12. A.L.F. Rivet and C. Smith, *The Place-Names of Roman Britain* (1979), 45.

13. See map 13.

14. The posting stations (*mansiones*) were part of the imperial

communications system and provided accommodation for official travellers, and perhaps also some 'local policing' and administrative functions. At Alfoldean, Hardham and Iping the posting stations consisted of rectangular earthworks. At Alfoldean rescue investigations outside the earthwork enclosure revealed traces of settlement extending up to 600m to the south of the posting station. See J. English and J.L. Gower, 'Alfoldean Roman Posting-Station (TQ 118330), Interim Report', *Sussex Archaeological Society Newsletter* **47** (1985), 456-7; at Hassocks various finds, including settlement evidence and a large cemetery, have been discovered in the vicinity of the intersection of two major Roman roads. See M.A.B. Lyne, 'The Hassocks cemetery', *SAC* **132** (1994), 53-85.

15. K.J. Evans, 'Excavations on a Romano-British site, Wiggonholt, 1964', *SAC* **112** (1974), 97-151.
16. Cunliffe, *The Regni*, 74.
17. D. Rudling, '"Round House" to Villa: The Beddingham and Watergate Villas', in R.M. and D.E. Friendship-Taylor, *From Round House to Villa,* The Upper Nene Archaeological Society (1997), Fascicule 3, 1-8; Rudling, 'The development of Roman villas', 52-8.
18. F.W. Black, 'The Roman villa at Bignor in the fourth century', *Oxford Journal of Archaeology* **2**, 93-107; F. Aldsworth and D. Rudling, 'Excavations at Bignor Roman Villa, West Sussex 1985-1990', *SAC* **133** (1995), 103-88; Rudling, 'The development of Roman villas', 58-63.
19. M. Bell, 'Excavations at Bishopstone', *SAC* **115** (1977), 1-299.
20. O. Bedwin, 'Excavations at Chanctonbury Ring, Wiston, West Sussex, 1977', *Britannia* **11** (1980), 173-222; O.R. Bedwin, 'Excavations at Lancing Down, West Sussex 1980', *SAC* **119** (1981), 37-56; there are various references to, and illustrations of, the Hayling Island temple in A. Woodward, *Shrines and Sacrifice* (1992), *passim.*
21. Some prehistoric round-barrows were used in Roman times as sites for votive deposits of coinage, and are often known as 'money mounds'. An example, which was enclosed in the Roman period by a square fence, was excavated on Slonk Hill. See R. Hartridge, 'Excavations at the Prehistoric and Romano-British site on Slonk Hill, Shoreham, Sussex', *SAC* **116** (1978), 69-141.
22. The Roman iron industry of the Weald has been reviewed by Henry Cleere. See H. Cleere and D. Crossley, *The Iron Industry of the Weald* (2nd edtn, ed. J.Hodgkinson, Cardiff 1995), 57-86.
23. D.R. Rudling, 'The excavation of a Roman Tilery on Great Cansiron Farm, Hartfield, East Sussex', *Britannia* **17** (1986), 191-230; A.P. Middleton, M.R. Cowell and E.W. Black, 'Romano-British relief-patterned flue tiles: a study of provenance using petrography and neutron activation analysis', in S. Mery (ed), *Earth sciences and archaeological ceramics, experimentation, applications,* Documents et Travaux, IGAL Cergy **16** (1992), 49-59.
24. For reviews of the Saxon Shore Forts see V.A. Maxfield

(ed), *The Saxon Shore. A Handbook* (Exeter 1989). For details of the significant re-dating of the Pevensey fort see M. Fulford and I. Tyres, 'The date of Pevensey and the defences of an Imperial Britanniarium', *Antiquity* **69** (1995), 1009-14; and see map 13.
25. See map 14.

Further Reading

F.W. Black, *The Roman Villas of South-East England,* British Archaeological Research Reports, British Series **171** (1987).
B. Cunliffe, *Fishbourne Roman Palace* (Stroud 1998).
A. Down, *Roman Chichester* (Chichester 1988).
P. Drewett, D. Rudling and M. Gardiner, *The South-East to AD 1000* (1988), ch.6, 'A Colony of Rome, AD 43-410'.

13. ROMAN CHICHESTER AND FISHBOURNE

1. See A.L.F. Rivet and C. Smith, *The place-names of Roman Britain* (1979), 427. The full name was *Noviomagus Reg(i)norum,* the second element being a Celtic tribal name meaning 'proud ones, stiff ones' (see K. Jackson in A.L.F. Rivet, 'The British Section of the Antonine Itinerary', *Britannia* **1** (1970), 34-82). It used to be read as Latin *Reginorum* or *Regnensium,* meaning 'the people of the kingdom' and this is still found in some publications (eg B. Cunliffe, *Fishbourne Roman Palace* (1998), 22). The first element 'Newmarket' implies that the Roman city replaced a late Iron Age centre. The range of early imported fine wares from Chichester/Fishbourne now equals those from Camulodunum and Braughing/Puckeridge, two other late Iron Age proto-towns, although the volume of material is less. See V. Rigby, 'Early imported, traded and locally produced fine and specialist wares' in B. Cunliffe, A. Down and D. Rudkin, *Excavations at Fishbourne 1969-1988,* Chichester Excavations **9** (1996), 117-36.
2. For discussions of the road network see J. Magilton, 'Roman Roads in the Manhood Peninsula', *The Archaeology of Chichester and District 1995* (1996), 31-4; and D. Turner, 'The course of the Roman road north of Chichester', *The Archaeology of Chichester 1996* (1997), 42-7.
3. This is the individual known by Tacitus as 'Cogidumnus'. For a discussion of the name see R.S.O. Tomlin, 'Reading a 1st-century Roman gold signet ring from Fishbourne', *SAC* **135** (1997), 127-30. The invasion has traditionally, although with little foundation, been held to have taken place in Kent. It has, however, been argued that the main landing was in the Solent area, assumed to have been friendly territory. See J.G.F. Hind, 'The Invasion of Britain in AD43 – An Alternative Strategy for Aulus Plautius', *Britannia* **20** (1989), 1-21.
4. Discussed at length by J.E. Bogaers, 'King Cogidubnus in Chichester. Another reading of *RIB 91*', *Britannia* **10** (1979), 243-54; for *RIB 92* see R.G. Collingwood and R.P. Wright, *The Roman Inscriptions of Britain* **I** (1965), 26-7.
5. For a general discussion of the buildings of Roman Chichester, A. Down, *Roman Chichester* (Chichester 1988),

ch. 3, is a good summary, although there is some doubt about whether the earliest timber buildings, attributed to a military phase of occupation beneath the Roman town, have any distinctive military characteristics.
6. The walls were traditionally dated to the later 2nd century, a time when many Romano-British towns received their first defences, but investigations in 1987-8 of the western defences of Chichester have suggested this later date. A. Down and J. Magilton, *Chichester Excavations* **8** (Chichester 1993), 99-130.
7. See Down, *Roman Chichester,* ch. 4, for a general discussion of the cemeteries, and Down and Magilton, *Chichester Excavations* **8**, ch. 4, for detail of the West Gate cemetery.
8. The amphitheatre was investigated on a small scale in the 1930s but has not been examined since. See G.M. White, 'The Chichester Amphitheatre: Preliminary Excavations', *The Antiquaries Journal* **XVI** (1936), 149-59. For a general discussion of the eastern suburbs, see J. Magilton, 'Roman Chichester beyond the East Gate – putting it all together', *The Archaeology of Chichester and District 1996* (Chichester 1997), 31-6.
9. Down, *Roman Chichester,* ch. 6, gives a fuller account of the archaeological evidence.
10. B.W. Cunliffe, *Excavations at Fishbourne 1961-1969, Vol.1: The Site.* Reports of the Research Committee of the Society of Antiquaries of London **XXVI** (Leeds 1971).
11. Bogaers, 'King Cogidubnus'.
12. Fishbourne Roman Palace is owned and administered by the Sussex Archaeological Society and is open to the public daily between mid-February and mid-December.
13. This event was roughly contemporary with the erection of Chichester's first defences and both may have had a common cause.
14. A.G. Down, 'Rescue excavations on the line of the A27 road in 1983 and 1985-6' in B.W. Cunliffe, A.G. Down and D.J. Rudkin, *Excavations,* 9-62; J. Kenny, 'Fishbourne: Westward House', *The Archaeology of Chichester and District 1992* (Chichester 1993), 32-7; S. Woodward (ed), *The Archaeology of Chichester and District 1995* (Chichester 1996), 11-16, *1996* (1997), 11-19 and *1997* (1998)16-18.
15. Tomlin, 'Reading a 1st-century Roman gold signet ring'.
16. The results to date are summarised in *Britannia* **27** (1996), 437-8; **28** (1997), 448-50, and future work will appear in subsequent volumes.

14. EARLY SAXON SUSSEX *c.*410-*c.*650

1. M.G. Welch, *Early Anglo-Saxon Sussex,* British Archaeological Research Reports, British Series, **112** (Oxford 1983), 215.
2. S. White, 'The Patching Hoard', *Medieval Archaeology* **XLII** (1998), 88-93.
3. Welch, *Early Anglo-Saxon Sussex,* 211-28; 461-84.
4. A. Down and M. Welch, *Apple Down and the Mardens,* Chichester Excavations **7** (Chichester 1990); A.B. Powell and A.P. Fitzpatrick, 'The Anglo-Saxon Cemetery and un-dated Features', in A.P. Fitzpatrick (ed), *Archaeological Excavations*

on the Route of the A27 Westhampnett Bypass, West Sussex, 1992 (Salisbury 1997), 287-95.

5. M. Bell, 'Saxon Settlements and Buildings in Sussex', in P. Brandon (ed), *The South Saxons* (Chichester 1978), 36-53; D. Rudling, 'The development of Roman villas in Sussex', *SAC* **136** (1998), 41-65; M. Gardiner, ' An Anglo-Saxon and Medieval Settlement at Botolphs, Bramber, West Sussex', *Archaeological Journal* **147** (1990), 216-75.

15. LATE SAXON SUSSEX *c.*650-1066

1. D. Austin, 'Central place theory and the Middle Ages', in E. Grant (ed), *Central Places, Archaeology and History* (Sheffield 1986), 95-103.
2. E. Miller, 'La société rurale en Angleterre (Xe-XIIIe siècles)', *Settimane di Studio del Centro Italiano di Studi sull' Alto Medioevo* **13** (1966), 111-34.
3. The identifications given by S. Keynes and M. Lapidge, *Alfred the Great. Asser's Life of King Alfred and other Contemporary Sources* (1983), 173-8, have been followed here.
4. F.M. Stenton, *Anglo-Saxon England* (3rd edtn, Oxford 1971), 298-9; R.H. Britnell, 'English markets and royal administration before 1200', *Economic History Review* 2nd ser. **31** (1978), 183-96.
5. W. Page, 'Some Remarks on the Churches of the Domesday Survey', *Archaeologia* **66** (1914-15), 79-81.
6. M. Gardiner and R. Coates, 'Ellingsdean, A Viking Battlefield Identified', *SAC* **125** (1987), 251-2.
7. D.H. Hill (ed), *The Defence of Wessex: The Burghal Hidage and the Anglo-Saxon Fortification* (Manchester 1996). I have accepted the identification of *Eorpeburnan* in N.P. Brooks, 'The unidentified forts of the Burghal Hidage', *Medieval Archaeology* **8** (1964), 81-5, and not that of F. Kitchen, 'The *Burghal Hidage:* towards the identification of *Eorpeburnan*', *Medieval Archaeology* **28** (1984), 175-7.
8. P.H. Sawyer, *Anglo-Saxon Charters: An Annotated List and Bibliography* (1968), no. 708.
9. M.F. Gardiner, 'Trade, Rural Industry and the Origins of Villages: Some Evidence from South-East England' in G. de Boe and F. Verhaeghe (eds), *Rural Settlements in Medieval Europe - Papers of the 'Medieval Europe Brugge 1997' Conference* **6** (1997), 63-73.

16. PLACE-NAMES BEFORE 1066

1. J.McN. Dodgson, 'The significance of the distribution of English place-names in -*ingas*, -*inga* in South-East England', *Medieval Archaeology* **10** (1966), 1-29.
2. M. Gelling, 'English place-names derived from the compound *wicham*', *Medieval Archaeology* **11** (1967), 87-104; M. Gelling, *Signposts to the Past* (3rd edtn, Chichester 1997), ch.3.
3. H. Hamerow, 'Settlement mobility and the "Middle Saxon Shift": rural settlements and settlement patterns in Anglo-Saxon England', *Anglo-Saxon England* **20** (1991), 1-17.
4. A. Mawer and F.M. Stenton, *The Place-Names of Sussex* (Cambridge 1929-30).
5. TRE – *Tempus Rex Edwardii* – In the time of Edward the Confessor, a standard term and abbreviation used in Domesday Book.
6. D. Sanders, 'The Saxon *tun*', *Locus Focus, Forum of the Sussex Place-Names Net* **2** (1) 1998, 33-4 (preliminary report).
7. R. Coates, 'New light from old wicks: the progeny of Latin *vicus*', *Nomina* **22** (forthcoming, 1999).

17. DOMESDAY SETTLEMENT

The authors wish to acknowledge the help of Leslie Lloyd, Annabelle Hughes, Diana Chatwin, and Derek and Hylda Rawlings.

1. The principal studies of Domesday Sussex are: J.H. Round, 'Domesday Survey', *VCH Sx* **I** (1905), 351-451; S.H. King, 'Sussex', in H.C. Darby and E.M.J. Campbell (eds), *The Domesday Geography of South-East England* (Cambridge 1962), 407-82; J. Morris (ed), *Domesday Book 2: Sussex* (Chichester 1976). The *Domesday Geography* analysis fails, however, to allow fully for exploitation of wealden Sussex. To aid more refined analyses in the future, data collected on Sussex Domesday manors as background for this contribution is being deposited in the library of the Sussex Archaeological Society, Lewes.
2. P.F. Brandon, *The South Downs* (Chichester 1998). For parish case histories in Bramber Rape, see *VCH Sx* **VI** (pts 1-3) (1980-87).
3. H. Warne, 'Stanmer: a restructured settlement', *SAC* **127** (1989), 192-4.
4. ESRO ADA 1; PRO LRRO 1/1138.
5. H. Warne (ed), *Wivelsfield: The History of a Wealden Parish* (Hurstpierpoint 1994), ch.1. The area of the Stanmer settlement in Wivelsfield is kindly supplied by Margaret Goodare, Wivelsfield History Study Group.
6. Previous analyses of Domesday Sussex have, wrongly, attributed this area to a tiny ½-hide manor of that name in Surrey held of Richard FitzGilbert, also referred to as Richard of Tonbridge, in order to justify the existence of the church. Worth was always firmly in Sussex, its church sited on demesne land of the Saxon royal manor of Ditchling held by Earl Warenne after 1066.
7. For the nation-wide context and the re-emergence of 'Englishness', see A. Williams, *The English and the Norman Conquest* (Woodbridge 1995).

Further Reading

M. Chibnall, *Anglo-Norman England* (Oxford 1986).
R. Lennard, *Rural England 1086-1135: A study of Social and Agrarian Conditions* (Oxford 1997).
R. Welldon Finn, *Domesday Book: A Guide* (Chichester 1986).

18. THE PAROCHIALISATION OF SUSSEX 1000-1086-1291

The author wishes to acknowledge the help of Brian Golding, John Blair, Mark Gardiner, David Hinton, Christopher Currie, and Gwen Jones.

1. See also N. Rushton, 'Parochialisation and Patterns of Patronage in 11th-Century Sussex', *SAC* **137** (forthcoming, 1999). All references to Domesday Book (DB) are from *Libri Censualis Vocati Domesday Book*, in 4 volumes, Record Commission (1816).
2. W. Page, 'Some Remarks on the Churches of the Domesday Survey', *Archaeologia* **16** (1915), 61-102; D. Gifford, 'The Parish in Domesday Book' (unpub. University of London Ph.D. thesis, 1952), esp. 91-153; R.V. Lennard, *Rural England 1086-1135* (Oxford 1959), 288-338; J. Blair, 'Local Churches in Domesday and Before', in J.C. Holt (ed), *Domesday Studies* (Woodbridge 1987), 265-78; and D.C. Douglas (ed), *The Domesday Monachorum of Christ Church Canterbury* (1944).
3. Rushton, 'Parochialisation', discusses the available evidence which can be used to assess whether a church can be said to have been standing by 1100.
4. There is much debate as to the dating, on architectural grounds, of 11th-century churches. The main national survey is H.M. Taylor and J. Taylor, *Anglo-Saxon Architecture,* 3 volumes (Cambridge 1965-78), which periodises Anglo-Saxon architecture in nine periods from 600-1100, periods C2 and C3 being *Saxo-Norman*. R. Gem, 'The English Parish Church in the 11th and Early 12th Centuries: a great rebuilding?', in J. Blair (ed), *Minsters and Parish Churches: the local church in transition 950-1200* (Oxford 1988), 21-30, provides a critique. See also L.A.S. Butler and R.K. Morris (eds), *The Anglo-Saxon Church*, CBA Research Report **60** (1986). Specifically for Sussex, H. Poole, 'The Domesday Book Churches of Sussex', *SAC* **87** (1948), 29-76; F.A. Fisher, *The Saxon Churches of Sussex* (Newton Abbot 1970). The archaeological excavations which have demonstrated the existence of otherwise unknown 11th-century churches are from Angmering, Greatham, Walberton and West Blatchington (Rushton, 'Parochialisation', appendix 1).
5. For Sussex pre-Conquest charters see E.E. Barker, 'Sussex Anglo-Saxon Charters', *SAC* **86** (1947), 42-101; **87** (1948), 112-63; **88** (1949), 51-113; and S.F. Kelly (ed), *Charters of Selsey,* Anglo-Saxon Charters **VI** (Oxford 1998). For the post-Conquest cartularies see L.F. Salzman (ed), *The Chartulary of the Priory of St Pancras of Lewes,* 2 vols, *SRS* **38** and **40** (1932 and 1934); W.D. Peckham (ed), *The Chartulary of the High Church of Chichester, SRS* **46** (1943); L.F. Salzman (ed), *The Chartulary of Sele* (Cambridge 1923). The existence of Westfield church in Hastings Rape, pre-1100, is recorded in a charter (British Library Add. Ch. 20161). Mayfield church, in Pevensey Rape, was standing in St Dunstan's time; W. Stubbs, *Memorials of St Dunstan*, Rolls Series **63** (1874), 204.
6. R. Morris, *Churches in the Landscape* (1989), 140-67, esp. fig. 37, 166, argues for large-scale parochialisation by 1100, with many parish churches made of wood. But allowances need to be made for localised conditions – in Sussex the wealden population is a vital element. For the chronology of settlement see P. Brandon, 'The South Saxon *Andredesweald*' in P. Brandon (ed), *The South Saxons* (Chichester 1978), 138-59; P. Brandon, *The Sussex Landscape* (1974), 66-104; D.

Haselgrove, 'The Domesday Record of Sussex' in Brandon *The South Saxons*, 204-5; *SE from AD 1000*, 49-56. Brandon, Haselgrove and Short all argue for minimal settlement by 1000. Conversely, P.H. Sawyer, 'Medieval English Settlements: New Interpretations', in P.H. Sawyer (ed), *English Medieval Settlement* (1979), 3; M. Gardiner, 'Medieval Settlement and Society in the Eastern Sussex Weald before 1420' (unpub. University of London Ph.D. thesis, 1995) argue that wealden settlement was more extensive by 1086. The extent to which DB silently includes wealden outliers within their head-manor entry does leave the issue ambiguous.

7. J. Blair and R. Sharpe (eds), *Pastoral Care before the Parish* (Leicester 1992), 137 *passim*; J. Blair, 'Secular Minster Churches in Domesday Book', in P. Sawyer (ed), *Domesday Book: a reassessment* (1985), 104-42; Blair, 'Local Churches'. These works reach a broad agreement as to the development of the minster system, but E. Cambridge and D. Rollason, 'The Pastoral Organization of the Anglo-Saxon Church: a review of the "Minster Hypothesis"', *Early Medieval Europe* 4 (1995), 87-104, have questioned the legitimacy of the established model, and the extent of pastoral care carried out by mother-churches, basing their argument largely on the definition of the word *monasterium* and that its use in Anglo-Saxon England had much the same meaning as it did in the 12th century. John Blair's comprehensive reply is 'Ecclesiastical Organization and Pastoral Care in Anglo-Saxon England', *Early Medieval Europe* 4 (1995), 193-212.

8. Page, 'Churches of the Domesday Survey', 66; Kelly, *Charters of Selsey*, 105. *Monasterium* is taken as meaning a 'minster' church, see S. Foot, 'Anglo-Saxon Minsters: a review of terminology', in Blair and Sharpe, *Pastoral Care*, 212-25.

9. Kelly, *Charters of Selsey*, 103-6; M.G. Welch, *Early Anglo-Saxon Sussex, British Archaeological Research Series* 112 (1983), 271-4.

10. DB I 16a, 16b,17a; Blair, 'Secular Minster Churches', 106.

11. H. Mayr-Harting (ed), *The Acta of the Bishops of Chichester 1075-1207*, Canterbury and York Society (1964), 17; *Chartulary of Lewes*, 2 , 77. See Rushton, 'Parochialisation' for a full discussion of the evidence for the formation and erosion of Petworth's *parochia*.

12. J. Caley (ed), *Taxatio Ecclesiastica Angliae et Walliae Auctoritate Papae Nicolai IV*, Record Commission (1802), 3. For the background to the *Taxatio*, see R. Graham, 'The Taxation of Pope Nicholas IV', *English Historical Review* 23 (1908), 434-54.

19. THE MEDIEVAL RURAL ECONOMY AND LANDSCAPE

1. P.F. Brandon, 'Demesne arable farming in coastal Sussex during the later Middle Ages', *Agricultural History Review* 19 (1971), 127; Arundel Castle Muniments A420.

2. H.L. Gray, *English Field Systems* (1915), frontispiece.

3. A.R.H. Baker, 'Field systems of southeast England', in A.R.H. Baker and R.A. Butlin (eds), *Studies of Field Systems in the British Isles* (Cambridge 1973), 425-9.

4. The data for the boundary of the open-field area is drawn very largely from P.F. Brandon, 'The Common Lands and Wastes of Sussex' (unpub. University of London Ph.D. thesis, 1963); see also P.F. Brandon, *The Sussex Landscape* (1974), 145-8; M.F. Gardiner, 'The geography and peasant rural economy of the eastern Sussex High Weald, 1300-1420', *SAC* 134 (1996), 126-7.

5. J.H. Round (ed), *Calendar of Documents Preserved in France* 1 (1899), 37; DB i, *25a*.

6. D. Martin, 'Three moated sites in north-east Sussex. Part 2: Hawksden and Bodiam', *SAC* 128 (1990), 89-116.

7. L.F. Salzman (ed), *Ministers' Accounts of the Manor of Petworth, 1347-1353, SRS* 55 (1955).

8. M. Clough (ed), *Two Estate Surveys of the Fitzalan Earls of Arundel, SRS* 67 (1969), 93.

20. MEDIEVAL ADMINISTRATION

1. Revd W. Hudson, 'The Ancient Deaneries of the Diocese of Chichester and their relation to the Rapes of the County of Sussex', *SAC* 55 (1912), 108-22.

2. Hudson, 'Deaneries', map facing 116.

3. W. Hudson (ed), *The three earliest subsidies for the County of Sussex in the years 1296, 1327, 1332, SRS* 10 (1909), 47.

4. *VCH Sx* I (1905), 538.

5. Hudson, 'Deaneries', 113-14.

6. L.F. Salzman, 'The Hundred Roll for Sussex, part 1', *SAC* 82 (1942), 20-34; 'part 2', *SAC* 83 (1943), 35-54; 'part 3', *SAC* 84 (1945), 60-81.

7. This map is based on Hudson, 'Deaneries', map facing 116; that in A. Mawer and F.M. Stenton, *The Place-Names of Sussex*, English Place-Name Society 6 (Cambridge 1929), Pt 1; and also on that in P.M. Wilkinson, *Genealogist's Guide to the West Sussex Record Office* (3rd edtn, Chichester 1994).

Further Reading

H. Cam, *The Hundred and the Hundred Rolls* (1930).
J. Hudson, *The Formation of English Common Law* (1976).
T.P. Hudson, 'The origins of Steyning and Bramber, Sussex', *Southern History* 2 (1980), 11.
J.F.A. Mason, 'The Rapes of Sussex and the Norman Conquest', *SAC* 102 (1964), 68-93.
L.F. Salzman, 'The Rapes of Sussex', *SAC* 72 (1931), 20-29.
VCH Sx: Introductions to the rapes in the relevant volumes: Hastings IX (1937), 1; Lewes VII (1940), 1; Bramber VI, pt 1(1980), 1; Arundel V, pt 1 (1997),1 and Chichester IV (1953), l.

Medieval Chichester (inset)

1. WSRO Chichester City Archives A1; Calendar of the Patent Rolls preserved in the Public Record Office (1891-2) (1300-1326), 314, (1377-81), 297; WSRO Episcopal Archives Ep VI/1/6 f.cxv, *v*.

2. *Annales Monastici* (rolls series) ii, 29; *Gesta Pontifici*, William of Malmesbury (rolls series) 68; J.Caley et al. (eds), 'W. Dugdale, *Monasticon Anglicanum*', **vi**, 1168; Gibson

Miscellanies, 1; *Rotuli Chartae* (Record Commission) 129; WSRO Ep VI/1/6 f.cxxxix *v.* and f.lxiv *v.*; Ep VI/1/6 f.cxvii; Ep VI/1/3 f.cxxxiv.

3. *Patent Rolls of the Reign of Henry III preserved in the Public Record Office* (1901-3), 37 Henry III; Pat Roll 53 Henry III m.3; WSRO Ep VI/1/6 f.lxix *v*, Ep III/4/7 ff.96-8.

4. WSRO Ep VI/1/4 f.165; Pat Roll 17 Edward I m.11; Cal. Pat. Rolls, 13 Henry III m.7; WSRO Ep I/I/6 f.62r.

21. MEDIEVAL MARKETS AND PORTS

The authors wish to thank Bob Edwards, Senior Conservation Officer (Hampshire County Council) for his help in identifying relevant medieval markets in Hampshire.

1. Relevant references to all locations identified on the map will be made available for study at the library of the Sussex Archaeological Society, Barbican House, Lewes. Major sources for the study of medieval markets include: R.H. Britnell, *The commercialisation of English society 1000-1500* (Cambridge 1993); R.H. Britnell, 'The Proliferation of Markets in England, 1200-1349', *Economic History Review*, 2nd ser., 34 (1981), 209-21; D.L. Farmer, 'Marketing the Produce of the Countryside, 1200-1500', in E. Miller (ed), *The Agrarian History of England and* Wales *III: 1348-1500* (Cambridge 1991), 324-430; J. Masschaele, *Peasants, Merchants and Markets: Inland Trade in Medieval England, 1150-1350* (1996); M. Mate, 'The Rise and Fall of Markets in Southeast England', *Canadian Journal of History* XXXI (1996), 59-86. Roads and fairs do not appear on the map. Very little research has been done on medieval roads in Sussex, but the network of 'major' roads recorded by Budgen on his map of Sussex 1723-4 was probably not dissimilar to that existing 300 years earlier (see map 39 in this volume). For a discussion and listing of Sussex medieval fairs see Mate, 'Markets'.

2. The county boundary was no barrier to travel or trade, and a number of other places within 5 miles (8km) of the boundary were named in market grants. They include Havant, Emsworth, Selborne, Chiddingfold, Cranleigh, Ockley, Burstow, Edenbridge, Groombridge, Cranbrook, Hawkhurst, Newenden and Appledore (Mate, 'Markets'; B.A. McLean, 'Factors in market establishment in Medieval England: the evidence from Kent 1086-1350', *Archaeologia Cantiana* CXVII (1997), 83-103.

3. For an estimate of the number of markets surviving from the Middle Ages to the early-modern period in Sussex see J. Chartres, *Agricultural markets and trade 1500-1750* (chapters from the *Agrarian History of England and Wales, vols. IV and V*, ed J. Thirsk, 1967, 1984-5), 3-4, 24.

22. WINCHELSEA – A MEDIEVAL NEW TOWN

1. W.M. Homan, 'The Founding of New Winchelsea', *SAC* 88 (1949), 22-41. In Winchelsea each individual block of land divided by the streets is traditionally called a 'Quarter' and each is numbered, there being 39 in all. In his reconstruction of the town Homan misplaced quarters 36-38 by one block.

2. W.M. Homan, 'The Black Friars at Winchelsea', *SNQ* **5** (1935), 225-9.
3. W.M. Homan, 'Winchelsea, the founding of a 13th Century Town' (Unpublished, 1940 – ESRO AMS 2497), 58-81.
4. *VCH Sx* **IX** (1937), 66. See also W.M. Homan, 'The History of Winchelsea' (Unpublished, December 1942 – ESRO AMS 2497).
5. *VCH Sx* **IX**, 70; Homan, 'Winchelsea' (1940), 39-71.
6. *VCH Sx* **IX**, 66; Regarding the likely attack in 1326 see Homan, *Winchelsea* (1942), 77.
7. Inquiry into intended town wall of Winchelsea, Dec. 1414 (ESRO RYE 146); Homan, 'Winchelsea' (1940), 80. At the time he wrote this article Homan did not have access to the 1414 inquiry.
8. C.E. Brent, 'Urban Employment and Population in Sussex between 1550 and 1660', *SAC* **113** (1975), 36; Homan, 'Winchelsea' (1942), 238; F. Aldsworth and D. Freke, *Historic Towns in Sussex; an Archaeological Survey* (1976), 65. For the decay of the urban centre see ESRO RYE 146.
9. W.D. Cooper, *History of Winchelsea* (1850), 107.

23. RELIGIOUS FOUNDATIONS
1. M. Hobbs (ed), *Chichester Cathedral: An Historical Survey* (Chichester 1994), 2 and 25; J. Munby, 'Saxon Chichester and its predecessors' in J. Haslam (ed), *Anglo Saxon Towns in Southern England* (1984), 315-30; F. Aldsworth, '"The mound" at Church Norton, Selsey, and the site of St. Wilfrid's Church', *SAC* **117** (1979), 104.
2. J. Blair, 'Secular Minster Churches in Domesday Book' in P. Sawyer (ed), *Domesday Book: a Reassessment* (1985), 115.
3. H. Clarke, *The Archaeology of Medieval England* (1984), 89-92.
4. D. Knowles and R.N. Hadcock, *Medieval Religious Houses in England and Wales* (1907); *VCH Sx* **II** (1907), 45-124.
5. R. Allen Brown, *The Normans and the Norman Conquest* (1969), 260.
6. Hobbs, *Chichester Cathedral*, 25.
7. The following were dependencies or 'alien' granges, that is the property of another monastery (shown in bold type): Atherington (Bailiffscourt, Climping) founded before 1102 – a grange of **Séez**; Boxgrove Priory, founded after 1105, an alien priory of **Lessay**; Hooe, founded 1106 – a grange of **Bec-Hellouin**; Lyminster nunnery, founded *c.*1082, was an alien priory of **Almenesches**; Rotherfield, founded pre-Conquest possibly as early as 790, was an alien priory of **St. Denis**; Runcton, founded before 1086 – **Troarn**; Sele, founded before 1126 – an alien priory of **St. Florent-de-Saumur**; Steyning church and manor were granted to **Fécamp** by Edward the Confessor, seized from them by Harold Godwinson, and returned by William I; Warminghurst, founded *c.*1085 – a grange of **Fécamp**; Wilmington, founded before 1086, an alien grange of **Grestein**; and Withyham a cell of **Mortain** (see Knowles and Hadcock, *Medieval Religious Houses* and *VCH Sx* **II** (1907), 45-124).
8. E. Searle (ed), *The Chronicle of Battle Abbey* (Oxford 1980).

9. For details of the Religious Houses of the various Orders, including Friars, Military Orders, hospitals and collegiate churches, see Knowles and Hadcock, *Medieval Religious Houses,* and *VCH Sx* **II** (1907).
10. R.W. Southern, *Western Society and the Church in the Middle Ages* (1975), 224-30.

Further Reading
L. Butler and C. Given-Wilson, *Medieval Monasteries of Great Britain* (1979).
A.W. Clapham, *English Romanesque Architecture after the Norman Conquest* (1964).
F.M. Stenton, *Anglo-Saxon England* (1971).

24. DESERTED SETTLEMENTS 1066-1500
We are grateful to the following for information: Mark Gardiner, John Mills, Christopher Whittick and Andrew Woodcock, none of whom necessarily agrees with each other!
1. G.R. Burleigh, 'An Introduction to Deserted Medieval Villages in East Sussex', *SAC* **111** (1973), 45-83; G.R. Burleigh, 'Medieval Earthworks at Arlington, Sussex', *SAC* **112** (1974), 80-5; G.R. Burleigh, 'Further Notes on Deserted and Shrunken Medieval Villages in Sussex', *SAC* **114** (1976), 61-8; M. Gardiner, 'Trade, rural Industry and the origins of Villages: Some Evidence from South-East England' in G. de Boe and F. Verhaeghe (eds), *Rural Settlements in Medieval Europe - Papers of the 'Medieval Europe Brugge 1997' Conference* **6** (1997), 63-73; E.W. Holden, 'Deserted Medieval Villages', *SNQ* **15** (1962), 312-17; E.W. Holden, 'Slate Roofing in Medieval Sussex', *SAC* **103** (1965), 67-78; E.W. Holden, 'Excavations at the Deserted Medieval Village of Hangleton, Part I', *SAC* **101** (1963), 54-181; E.W. Holden, 'Excavations at Old Erringham, Shoreham, West Sussex, Part II; the "Chapel" and Ringwork', *SAC* **118** (1980), 257-97; E.W. Holden, 'Slate Roofing in Medieval Sussex – A Reappraisal', *SAC* **127** (1989), 73-88; J.G. and D.G. Hurst, 'Excavations at the Deserted Medieval Village of Hangleton, Part II', *SAC* **102** (1964), 94-142; C.F. Tebbutt, 'Two Newly-Discovered Medieval Sites', *SAC* **110** (1972), 31-6.
2. M. Beresford, *The Lost Villages of England* (1954), 21.
3. C. Taylor, *Village and Farmstead. A History of Rural Settlement in England* (1984 edtn), 174.
4. E.W. Holden, 'Excavations, Part I', 67-8. The late Eric Holden (1911-89) was the authors' father and his archaeological journals and working papers have been deposited by them with the Sussex Archaeological Society's Library at Lewes. The authors' working papers for this map have also been deposited at the same location.
5. Burleigh, 'An Introduction', 47-8, 53, 57.
6. *SE from AD 1000*, 105; Burleigh, 'An Introduction', 49; Taylor, *Village*, 171.
7. Burleigh, 'An Introduction', 66.

25. CASTLES AND OTHER DEFENSIVE SITES
1. D. Hill and A. Rumble, *The Defence of Wessex: the Burghal*

Hidage and Anglo-Saxon fortifications (Manchester 1996).
2. The hierarchical relationship between Knepp and Bramber can be seen clearly in an order from the king to Reuland Bloet dated 18 May 1214 which stated that 'we command you, without delay, to transfer all the stores which you have at Knapp or elsewhere, and which you are able to gather, to Bremble; and that you fortify that house in the best possible manner you can...; that you destroy altogether the houses at Knapp'. This appears not to have been undertaken since a further order dated 13 June 1216 commanded that the castle of Knepp should be burnt and destroyed (C.M. Burrell, 'Documents relating to Knepp Castle', *SAC* **3** (1850), 1-12).
3. In 1447 the bishop received a block licence to crenellate Amberley together with 11 other of his manors in Sussex (*Calendar of the Charter Rolls preserved in the Public Record Office*, **VI** (HMSO, 1903-27), 94-5).
4. C. Coulson, 'Bodiam Castle: Truth and Tradition', *Fortress* **10** (1991), 3-15.
5. P. Brandon, *The Sussex Landscape* (1974), 134-43.

26. THE STRUGGLE FOR A PROTESTANT REFORMATION 1553-1564
1. M.J. Kitch, 'The Reformation in Sussex' in M.J. Kitch (ed), *Studies in Sussex Church History* (University of Sussex 1981), 94.
2. Kitch, *Studies*, 96.
3. Kitch, *Studies*, 96; J. Goring, 'Reformation and reaction in Sussex, 1534-1559', *SAC* **134** (1996), 149.
4. Information on Marian deprivations has been compiled from original sources by Peter and Jane Wilkinson. In addition to the Chichester Episcopal Archives in WSRO, the most valuable sources are the Calendars of Chichester Diocesan Institution, compiled by W.D. Peckham (WSRO MP 1095-6 and 1099) and the Dunkin MSS in the British Library (BL Add MSS 39326-39546).
5. J.M. Horn (comp.), *John Le Neve, Fasti Ecclesiae Anglicanae, 1547-1857*, **II**, *Chichester Diocese* (1971).
6. For information on the impact of the Elizabethan Settlement on Sussex I am heavily indebted to T.J. McCann, and his 'The Clergy and the Elizabethan Settlement in the Diocese of Chichester', in Kitch, *Studies*, 99-124.
7. McCann, 'The Clergy', 99-123.
8. McCann, 'The Clergy', 99-123.

27. TUDOR AND STUART GREAT HOUSES
1. The pattern described here follows that suggested by the comparison of three counties (Hertfordshire, Northamptonshire and Northumberland) made by L. Stone and J.C. Fawtier Stone, *An Open Elite? England 1540-1880* (Oxford 1984), ch. XI 'Building and Builders'.
2. On both Bodiam and Herstmonceux, see M.W. Thompson, *The Decline of the Castle* (Cambridge 1987). See also C. Coulson, 'Some Analysis of the Castle at Bodiam', *Medieval Knighthood* **IV** (Woodbridge 1992), 51-108.
3. On houses and health, see M. Howard, 'The ideal house

and the healthy life: the origins of architectural theory in England', in J. Guillaume (ed), *Les Traités d'Architecture de la Renaissance* (Paris 1988), 425-34.

4. P. Hembry, 'Episcopal Palaces 1535-1660', in E.W. Ives, J.J. Scarisbrich and R.J. Knecht (eds), *Wealth and Power in Tudor England* (1978), 146-66.

5. C. Breight, 'Caressing the Great: Viscount Montague's Entertainment of Elizabeth at Cowdray, 1591', *SAC* **127** (1989), 147-66.

6. W.H. Godfrey, 'An Elizabethan Builder's Contract', *SAC* **65** (1924), 211-23.

7. Michelgrove is key to M. Girouard's discussion of the later Elizabethan prodigy house of Wollaton, Nottinghamshire, in *Robert Smythson and the Elizabethan Country House* (1983), 100.

Further Reading

J.R. Armstrong, *A History of Sussex* (3rd edtn Chichester 1974).

W. Berry, *County genealogies: pedigrees of the families in the county of Sussex* (1830).

P.F. Brandon and B.M. Short, *The South East from AD 1000* (1990).

D.G.C. Elwes and C.J. Robinson, *A History of the Castles, Mansions and Manors of Western Sussex* (1876).

M. Holmes, *The Country House Described. An Index to the Country Houses of Great Britain and Ireland* (1986).

M.A. Lower, *A Compendious History of Sussex, topographical, archaeological and anecdotical* 2 vols. (Lewes 1870).

I. Nairn and N. Pevsner, *The Buildings of England: Sussex* (1965).

28. RELIGIOUS OBSERVANCE IN THE 17TH CENTURY

1. William Salt Library, Stafford; WSRO MP 185 is a photocopy. See also J.H. Cooper, 'A Religious Census of Sussex in 1676', *SAC* **45** (1902), 142-8. And see also map 33 in this Atlas.

2. BL Harleian MS. 280, f.158.

3. WSRO Ep.II/24/1, printed in W.C. Renshaw, 'Ecclesiastical Returns for 81 Parishes in East Sussex made in 1603', *SRS* **4** (1905), 3-17; WSRO Ep1/15/1, 1624, 1626 and 1628.

4. WSRO QR/W14.

5. R. Garraway Rice, *West Sussex Protestation Returns 1641-2, SRS* **5** (1906); and see T.J. McCann, 'Midhurst Catholics and the Protestation Returns of 1642', *Recusant History* **16** (1983), 319-23.

6. WSRO Ep1/17/28, ff.30, 31. See C.E. Welch, 'Roman Catholics in Midhurst in 1641', *SNQ* **14** (1956), 166-9.

7. ESRO Q/RE51. See Cynthia Herrup, 'Recusants 1641', *Sussex Family Historian* **3** (1978), 142-4.

8. A. Fletcher, *A County Community in Peace and War. Sussex 1600-1660* (1975), 97.

9. Archives of the Archdiocese of Westminster, **XXIV**, f.639.

10. A. Foster, 'Chichester Diocese in the early 17th Century', *SAC* **123** (University of Sussex 1981), 187-95.

11. A.J. Fletcher, 'Puritanism in seventeenth century Sussex', in M.J. Kitch (ed), *Studies in Sussex Church History* (University of

Sussex 1981), 141-56.

12. A.G. Matthews, *Calamy revised: being a revision of Edmund Calamy's Account of the Ministers and others ejected and silenced, 1660-2* (1934).

13. G. Lyon Turner, *Original Records of Early Nonconformity under Persecution and Indulgence* 3 (3 vols. 1911-14); N. Caplan, 'The Numerical Strength of Nonconformity, 1669-76: Sussex', *Transactions of the Unitarian Historical Society* **13** (1963), 13-18.

14. N. Caplan, 'Presbyterian Ministers in Sussex: Checking the Accuracy of the Common Fund Surveys, 1690-91', *Journal of the Presbyterian Historical Society of England* **XII** (1966), 106-8.

29. CIVIL WAR

The Author wishes to acknowledge the assistance given by Dr Andrew Foster and Dr John Gurney.

1. J.R. Armstrong, *A History of Sussex* (3rd edtn Chichester 1974), 105.

2. *SE from AD 1000*, 147.

3. *SE from AD 1000*, 148.

4. Armstrong, *History*, 105-6.

5. See the narratives of the war in C. Thomas-Stanford, *Sussex in the Great Civil War and Interregnum 1642-1660* (1910), *passim*; and L.F. Salzman's account of the political history of the county in *VCH Sx* I (1905), 521-8.

6. The national picture of destruction is discussed by S. Porter, *Destruction in the English Civil Wars* (Stroud 1994), *passim*.

7. Porter, *Destruction*, 63.

8. Porter, *Destruction*, 75.

9. *SE from AD 1000*, 151-2.

10. The 1669 survey is documented in J. Lowerson, *A Short History of Sussex* (Folkestone 1980), 105-6.

11. Armstrong, *History*, 108-9.

30. TIMBER-FRAMED BUILDINGS

1. R.T. Mason, *Framed Buildings of the Weald* (2nd edtn, Horsham 1969); J. Warren (ed), *Wealden Buildings: studies in the timber-framed tradition of building in Kent, Sussex and Surrey in tribute to R.T. Mason* (Horsham 1990).

2. H.M. and U.E. Lacey, *The Timber-Framed Buildings of Steyning* (Worthing 1974); A. Hughes, *Horsham Houses: A Study of Early Buildings in a Market Town* (Chichester 1986); D. Chatwin, *The Development of Timber-Framed Buildings in the Sussex Weald: The Architectural Heritage of the Parish of Rudgwick* (Rudgwick 1996).

3. K. Leslie, *Weald & Downland Open Air Museum: The Founding Years 1965-1970* (Singleton 1990); the work of David and Barbara Martin for the Rape of Hastings Architectural Survey, published in a series of volumes and research papers, is now in the East Sussex Record Office (ESRO HBR).

4. It should be noted that space prohibits discussion of farm buildings in Sussex. But see, for example, D. and B. Martin, *Old Farm Buildings in Eastern Sussex 1450-1750* (Historic Buildings in Eastern Sussex 3, Robertsbridge 1982); L. Caffyn, 'A study of farm buildings in selected parishes of

East Sussex', *SAC* **121** (1983), 149-71; G. Jones and J. Bell, *Oasthouses in Sussex and Kent* (Chichester 1992).

31. IRON AND GLASS INDUSTRIES

1. M. Zell, *Industry in the Countryside: Wealden Society in the Sixteenth Century* (Cambridge 1994), 200-1.

2. R.H. Tawney and E. Power, *Tudor Economic Documents* **1** (1924), 231-8.

3. H. Cleere and D. Crossley, *The Iron Industry of the Weald* (2nd edtn, ed J. Hodgkinson, Cardiff 1995), 133-6.

4. G.H. Kenyon, *The Glass Industry of the Weald* (Leicester 1967); E.S. Godfrey, *The Development of English Glass-making 1560-1640* (Oxford 1975).

5. D. Crossley and R. Saville, *The Fuller Letters 1728-1755: Guns, Slaves and Finance, SRS* **76** (1991), xxi-xxiv.

6. N. Bjorkenstam, 'The blast furnace in Europe during medieval times', in O. Magnusson (ed), *The Importance of Ironmaking: Technological Innovation and Social Change* **1** (Stockholm 1995), 143-53; A. Jockenhövel, 'The beginning of blast furnace technology in central Europe', *Historical Metallurgy Society News* **37** (1997), 4-5.

7. B.G. Awty, 'The continental origins of Wealden iron-workers', *Economic History Review* 2nd ser. **34** (1981), 524-39.

8. O. Bedwin, 'The excavation of a late 16th-century blast furnace at Batsford, Herstmonceux, East Sussex, 1978', *Post-Medieval Archaeology* **14** (1980), 89-112; D.W. Crossley, *The Bewl Valley Ironworks* (1975); *The Archaeology of Chichester and District 1989* (1990), 30-5; *1990* (1991), 41-4; O. Bedwin, 'The excavation of a late sixteenth/early seventeenth-century gun-casting furnace at Maynard's Gate, Crowborough, East Sussex 1975-76', *SAC* **116** (1978), 163-78; D.W. Crossley, 'A 16th-century Wealden blast furnace: excavations at Panningridge, Sussex, 1964-70', *Post-Medieval Archaeology* **6** (1972), 42-68; D.W. Crossley, 'Cannon manufacture at Pippingford, Sussex: the excavation of two iron furnaces of *c.*1717', *Post-Medieval Archaeology* **9** (1975), 1-37; D.W. Crossley, 'A guncasting furnace at Scarlets, Cowden, Kent', *Post-Medieval Archaeology* **13** (1979), 235-49.

9. O. Bedwin, 'The excavation of Ardingly fulling mill and forge, 1975-6', *Post-Medieval Archaeology* **10** (1976), 34-64; C. Place and O. Bedwin, 'The sixteenth-century forge at Blackwater Green, Worth, West Sussex: Excavations 1988', *SAC* **130** (1992), 147-63; Crossley, *Bewl Valley*.

32. ELIZABETHAN AND EARLY STUART LEWES

1. *VCH Sx* **VII** (1940), 7.

2. D. Hill and A. Rumble (eds), *The Defence of Wessex: the Burghal Hidage and Anglo-Saxon Fortifications* (Manchester 1996), 207-8.

3. J. Goring, 'The Fellowship of the Twelve in Elizabethan Lewes', *SAC* **119** (1981), 157-72; C. Brent, 'The Neutering of the Fellowship and the Emergence of a Tory Party in Lewes (1663-1688)', *SAC* **121** (1983), 95-107.

4. Maps: (a) 'A Description of the scite of ye Burrough Towne and Castle of Lewes ...' by George Randoll, 1620 (ESRO

ACC 3476 (previously SAS/ E5)). A copy was made by W.H. Godfrey in 1934 of that part of the map showing the town, and it is most recently published in J. Houghton, *Unknown Lewes: an historical geography* (Horam 1997), 32. (b) One of three companion maps showing the Ouse and Glynde Reach, from Newhaven to Barcombe Mills and Laughton 1620 – probably by John de Ward (ESRO ACC 2187; the other two maps are ESR0 SRA 6/13/1 and 2). Much detail of Lewes from this map appears in the cover design of C. Brent, *Historic Lewes and its buildings* (rev. edtn, Lewes 1995). 'Bounderstone' and 'bridge': W.H. Godfrey (ed), *The Book of John Rowe*, SRS **34** (1928), 121-2.

5. D.J. Freke, 'Further Excavations in Lewes, 1975', *SAC* **114** (1976), 176-93. For 15th-century references to a disused lane called Ladderes or Lodders Lane (perhaps derived from O.E. *loddere* – a beggar) in this part of the town, see L.F. Salzman, 'The Borough of Lewes in 1498', *SNQ* **5** (1934), 99 and fn 2.

6. Houghton, *Unknown Lewes,* 35, 175-80.

7. F. Kitchen, 'Sussex Towns in 1595', *Sussex History* **24** (1987), 15.

8. A. Fletcher, *A County Community in Peace and War. Sussex 1600-1660* (1975), 48.

9. C. Brent, *Georgian Lewes 1714-1830: The Heyday of a County Town* (Lewes 1993), 51.

10. 'Dodson': note on Dodson-owned property in Lewes in Anon., 'Sussex Deeds in Private Hands', *SAC* **66** (1925), 116; 'Vine Inn': Brent, *Historic Lewes,* 21-2; 'Market House': L.F. Salzman (ed), *The Town Book of Lewes 1542-1701*, SRS **48** (1945-6), 15; 'Sessions House' and 'House of Correction': Brent, *Historic Lewes,* 4. For the High Street in the late 16th and early 17th centuries, see also Fletcher, *County Community,* 9; W.H. Godfrey, 'The High Street of Lewes', *SAC* **93** (1955), 1-33. For a recent study of what has become known as 'the great rebuilding' *c.*1560 to 1630, see C. Platt, *The Great Rebuildings of Tudor and Stuart England: Revolutions in architectural taste* (1994).

11. 'Camden': G.J. Copley, *Camden's Britannia: Surrey and Sussex* (1977), 49; E.H.W. Dunkin, *Calendar of Sussex marriage Licences … Archdeaconry of Lewes, August, 1585, to March, 1642-3*, SRS **1** (1902).

12. Godfrey, *John Rowe,* 122. John Rowe (1560-1639) was a lawyer and lived in Lewes for many years. From 1597 to 1622 he was steward to Lord Bergavenny, one of the lords of Lewes.

13. The 'broken church' (called Little St Peter by Rowe, and St Nicholas by most later commentators) was one of a number of parish churches in Lewes which did not survive into the later l6th century. For a full account of these churches, see Houghton, *Unknown Lewes,* 83-105, 118-19.

14. The East Gate (if it existed) has not been identified with any certainty on (or under) the ground. For a discussion of a possible 'Burh-gate' in School Hill, see Houghton, *Unknown Lewes,* 24.

33. POPULATION IN 1676 AND 1724

1. E. Carpenter, *The Protestant Bishop: being the life of Henry Compton, 1632-1713 Bishop of London* (1956), 31.

2. Carpenter, *The Protestant Bishop,* reveals some of these problems (p.32); and see map 28.

3. The original manuscript collection is housed in the William Salt Library, Stafford as MS. 33. The returns are transcribed in A. Whiteman (ed), *The Compton Census of 1676: A Critical Edition* (Oxford 1986), 137-9; and the difficulties of interpretation are dealt with in A. Whiteman, 'The Compton Census of 1676' in K.Schurer and T.Arkell (eds), *Surveying the People* (Oxford 1992), 78-96; A. Whiteman and M. Clapinson, 'The use of the Compton Census for demographic purposes', *Local Population Studies* **50** (1993), 61-6; and A. Crockett and K.D.M. Snell, 'From the 1676 Compton Census to the 1851 Census of Religious Worship: Religious Continuity or Discontinuity', *Rural History* **8** (1997), 55-89. The Sussex data is also transcribed in J.H. Cooper, 'A religious census of Sussex in 1676', *SAC* **45** (1902), 142-8.

4. A multiplier of 31% is suggested in E.A. Wrigley and R.S. Schofield, *The Population History of England 1541-1870* (Cambridge 1981), 218.

5. Thomas Bowers, Archdeacon of Canterbury, was consecrated as Bishop of Chichester in October 1722 but died in August 1724 shortly after the survey was conducted.

6. For a transcription of the survey see W.K. Ford, *Chichester Diocesan Surveys 1686 and 1724*, SRS **78** (1994), 55-223.

7. The parishes for which Archbishop Wake's Visitation data is incorporated into the 1724 returns are Bersted, Buxted, Durrington, Edburton and Fulking, Framfield, Glynde, Heene, East Lavant, Lindfield, South Malling, Pagham, Patching, Ringmer, West Tarring and Uckfield.

8. D. Turner, 'A lost seventeenth century demographic crisis? The evidence of two counties', *Local Population Studies* **21** (1978), 11-18. On localised demographic crises in Sussex see also I. Nelson, 'Famine and Mortality crises in Mid-Sussex, 1606-1640', *Local Population Studies* **46** (1991), 39-47; Turner and Wightman make comparisons with the 1641-2 Protestation Returns as recorded in R. Garraway Rice, *West Sussex Protestation Returns 1641-42*, SRS **5** (1906).

9. C.E. Brent, 'Employment, land tenure and population in eastern Sussex, 1540-1640' (unpub. University of Sussex D.Phil. thesis, 1973); *SE from AD 1000,* 190-6. A long-term comparison of taxpayers in 1524-5 with 1665 or 1670 shows that in 13 out of 16 wealden localities population had risen by between 12% and 38%, compared with declines of 13% to 44% in the Downland. But of the 245 parishes for which information is available in 1676 and 1724, 51.5% remain in the same quartile for both years and a further 38.4% move by just one quartile. There are therefore few startling changes in adult or family densities per 100 acres (40ha) in the period considered here.

10. Much again depends on the choice of multiplier. Here 31% is used for Compton. Whiteman, *The Compton Census,* xcvii-

xcviii and 140-1, finds a higher population of between 89,500 and 109,000. The whole of Chichester Archdeaconry was excluded from Whiteman's calculations. For her total population estimate see Whiteman, *The Compton Census,* ciii and cx-cxi.

34. INNS AND ALEHOUSES IN 1686

1. PRO WO/30/48/7788. Returns & accommodation for men and horses 1686. Sussex, ff.437-43. Thanks to Richard Coates, Mark Gardiner, Tim Hudson, Michael Leppard, Max Wheeler and Christopher Whittick for place-name suggestions.

2. *The Journals of the House of Commons, from October the 10th 1667, in the Nineteenth Year of the Reign of King Charles the Second to April the 18th 1687 In the Third Year of the Reign of King James the Second. Reprinted by Order of the House of Commons* (1803), **9**.

3. *The Journals of the House of Commons, from December 16th 1688 – October 26th 1693* (1803), **10**.

4. *The Journals of the House of Commons* **10**, 5. However, William of Orange came ashore in Devon on 5 November 1688.

5. J. Hunter, 'Legislation, Royal Proclamations and other National Directives affecting Inns, Taverns, Alehouses, Brandy Shops and Punch Houses 1552-1757 (unpub. University of Reading Ph.D. thesis, 1994), 236-41, 266-8.

6. Sidlesham served the Pagham harbour area, and possibly provided a more local turn-around service, rather than landing travellers who then needed to ride away. Perhaps goods were landed rather than people, with carriers coming from Chichester to collect. Chichester's difficult harbour bar could then be avoided. Dell Quay and Fishbourne to the north only provided 3/3 and 4/4 beds and stablings respectively.

7. Revd E. Turner, 'High Roads in Sussex, at the end of the Seventeenth and at the Commencement of the Eighteenth Centuries', *SAC* **19** (1867), 153-69.

8. 'Extracts from the Journal and Account Book of the Rev. Giles Moore, Rector of Horstead Keynes, Sussex, from the year 1655 to 1679. With remarks by Robert Willis Blencowe Esq', *SAC* **1** (1848), 104, fn.

35. THE POOR LAW 1700-1900

1. Despite the development of Sussex as the most pauperised county in the land, and widespread workhouse provision, there is a surprising dearth of scholarly studies of either poverty or workhouses at both the county and local levels in the 18th and 19th centuries. Much of the following is therefore based on central and local poor law material, the former now located at the PRO, the latter at ESRO and WSRO. See, in particular PRO MH 1/series (minutes of the Poor Law Commission); MH 34 (expenditure on workhouses); MH 32/series (private letters from the assistant poor law commissioners to the Commission); and especially MH 12/series (correspondence between (and about) individual unions and the central authorities). A guide to

the Sussex Poor Law Union minutes and other material up to the date of its publication is J. Coleman (ed), *Sussex Poor Law Records: A Catalogue* (Chichester 1960), but the maps in this volume contain mistakes, especially over the Gilbert Union parishes. Although generally more reliable, there are similar problems in F.A. Youngs, *Guide to the Local Administrative Units of England I, Southern England* (1979). Material on the Gilbert Unions can be gleaned from WSRO, especially via the Petworth House Archives.

2. See P. Slack, *The English Poor Law, 1531-1782* (1990); J.D. Marshall, *The Old Poor Law 1795-1834* (1968); P. Dunkley, *The Crisis of the Old Poor Law in England 1795-1834* (1982).
3. J.S. Taylor, 'The unreformed workhouse, 1776-1834', in E.W. Martin (ed), *Comparative Development in Social Welfare* (1972). And see M.N. Pilbeam and I. Nelson, *Mid Sussex Poor Law Records 1600-1835, SRS* (forthcoming 1999).
4. S.G. and E.O.A. Checkland, *The Poor Law Report* (1974), which contains a reprint of the 1834 Report of the Royal Commission into the Poor Laws. The conditions in many individual Sussex parishes are detailed in *British Parliamentary Papers* (Irish University Press reprints), *Poor Law* **10**.
5. The standard text on New Poor Law workhouses is M.A. Crowther, *The Workhouse System 1834-1929* (1981), but see also F. Driver, *Power and Pauperism: the Workhouse System 1834-1884* (1993) and A. Digby, *Pauper Palaces* (1978) which focuses on Norfolk.
6. R. Wells, 'Social protest, class, conflict and consciousness in the English countryside 1700-1880', in M. Reed and R. Wells (eds), *Class Conflict and Protest in the English Countryside 1700-1880* (1990), 121-214; R. Wells, 'Resistance to the New Poor Law in the Rural South', in J. Rule and R. Wells (eds), *Crime, Protest and Popular Politics in Southern England 1740-1850* (1997), 91-125.
7. A good exemplar of a local Sussex study is I. Watson, *The Westbourne Union: Life in and out of the New Workhouse* (Westbourne 1991).

36. PARLIAMENTARY REPRESENTATION
1. E.J. Evans, *The Great Reform Act of 1832* (2nd edtn 1994), 6.
2. A. Olson, *The Radical Duke: The Career and Correspondence of Charles Lennox Third Duke of Richmond* (1961), 48-9.
3. R. Pearce and R. Stearn, *Government and Reform 1815-1918* (1994), 70.

Further Reading
T.W. Horsfield, *The History, Antiquities, and Topography of the County of Sussex*, **2** (Lewes 1835), Appendix III.

37. RIOTS AND UNREST
1. D. Jones, 'Rural crime and protest', in G. Mingay (ed), *The Victorian Countryside* **2** (1981), 569.
2. For a general account of food riots in Britain see R. Wells, *Wretched Faces: Famine in Wartime England 1793-1801* (1988); A. Charlesworth (ed), *An Atlas of Rural Protest in Britain 1548-1900* (1983), 63-118; A. Charlesworth, 'Labour protest 1780-

1850' in J. Langton and R. Morris (eds), *Atlas of Industrialising Britain 1780-1914* (1986), 185-9; R. Wells, 'The development of the English rural proletariat and social protest, 1700-1850', *Journal of Peasant Studies* **6** (1979), 115-39.
3. The classic account of the riots is E.J. Hobsbawm and G. Rudé, *Captain Swing* (1969). This includes a table of incidents although subsequent research has amplified the number considerably. See also R. Wells, 'Rural rebels in southern England in the 1830s', in C. Emsley and J. Walvin (eds), *Artisans, Peasants and Proletarians 1760-1860* (1985), 126-36.
4. For the spatial incidence of the riots see A. Charlesworth, *Social Protest in a Rural Society: the Spatial Diffusion of the Captain Swing Disturbances of 1830-1831* (Historical Geography Research Series **1,** 1979); *SE from AD 1000*, 232-7; a detailed account of the wealden disturbances is also to be found in M.Reed and R.Wells (eds), *Class, conflict and protest in the English countryside 1700-1880* (1990), especially the contributions of Wells, Reed, and Mills and Short. For the link between the rioters and the reform movement see A. Charlesworth, 'The spatial diffusion of riots: popular disturbances in England and Wales, 1750-1850', *Rural History* **5** (1994), 1-22.
5. J. Lowerson, 'Anti poor law movements and rural trade unionism in the South East 1835' in Charlesworth, *Atlas of Rural Protest*, 155-8.
6. For the spatial context of the KSLU and NALU see A. Charlesworth, D. Gilbert, A. Randall, H. Southall and C. Wrigley (eds), *An Atlas of Industrial Protest in Britain 1750-1990* (1996), 59-121.
7. R. Wells, 'Southern Chartism', *Rural History* **2** (1991), 37-59.

38. RELIGIOUS WORSHIP 1851
1. J.A. Vickers, *The Religious Census of Sussex 1851, SRS* **75** (1989).
2. B.I. Coleman, 'Southern England in the Census of Religious Worship, 1851', *Southern History* **5** (1983), 154-88.
3. Based on figures recorded at the best-attended service of the day and given in Table N of the Census *Report.*

Further Reading
Clive D. Field, 'The 1851 religious census of Great Britain: a bibliographical guide for local and regional historians', *The Local Historian*, **27** (1997), 194-217.
J.A. Vickers, *The 1851 Religious Census*, Historical Association, 'Short Guides to Records', **45** (1995).

39. GROWTH OF COMMUNICATIONS 1720-1840
1. I.D. Margary, 'Traffic Routes in Sussex, 1724 as shown by "Milestones" on Richard Budgen's Map', *SAC* **109** (1971), 20-3, with minor amendments.
2. On waterways, see C. Hadfield, *The Canals of South and South East England* (Newton Abbot 1969), chs. II and VI; P.A.L. Vine, *Kent and East Sussex Waterways* (Midhurst 1989) and P.A.L. Vine, *West Sussex Waterways* (Midhurst 1985). On harbours, see J.H. Farrant, *The Harbours of Sussex 1700-1914* (Brighton 1976), chs.1 and 2.

3. On turnpikes, see G.D. Johnston, 'Abstract of Turnpike Acts relating to Sussex' (transcript *c.*1948 in Sussex Archaeological Society Library); I.D. Margary, 'The development of turnpike roads in Sussex', *SNQ* **13** (1950), 49-53; G.J. Fuller, 'The development of roads in the Surrey-Sussex Weald and coastlands between 1700 and 1900', *Trans. Inst. British Geographers* **19** (1953), 37-49 (the figures in which are the basis for the turnpikes in the map); and B. Austen, 'John Loudon McAdam and the Lewes to Eastbourne turnpike', *Transport History* **7** (1974), 41-59. On bridges, see G.D. Johnston, 'The repair of Sussex bridges', *SAC* **91** (1953), 164-84.
4. J.H. Farrant, 'The seaborne trade of Sussex, 1720-1845', *SAC* **114** (1976), 100.

40. GROWTH OF COMMUNICATIONS 1840-1914
1. R.H. Clark, *A Southern Region Record* (Lingfield 1964) is the authoritative chronology. C.F.D. Marshall, *A History of the Southern Railway,* 2 vols (2nd edtn rev. R.W. Kidner, 1963), is the classic official history. I.T.H. Turner, *The London, Brighton & South Coast Railway*, **1**, *Origins and Formation* (1977), **2**, *Establishment and Growth* (1978) and **3**, *Completion and Maturity* (1979), is the most recent and, on the civil engineering works, exhaustive work on the dominant company in Sussex.
2. I.L. Griffiths, 'Road and Rail in Sussex' in *Sx ELS*, 237-41.
3. W.H. Parker, 'Settlement in Sussex 1840-1940', *Geography* **35** (1950), 9-20. Also S. Farrant, 'The Early Growth of the Seaside Resorts c.1750 to 1840', in *Sx ELS*, 208-20; and J.R. Lowerson, 'Resorts, Ports and "Sleepy Hollows": Sussex Towns 1840-1940', in *Sx ELS*, 221-34.
4. H.R.C. Inglis, quoted in *SRS* **66** (1968), 70; G.J. Fuller, 'The development of roads in the Surrey-Sussex Weald and coastlands between 1700 and 1900', *Trans. Inst. British Geographers* **19** (1953), 49.
5. C. Hadfield, *The Canals of South & South East England* (Newton Abbot 1969), Appendix I; P.A.L. Vine, *London's Lost Route to the Sea* (3rd edtn Newton Abbot 1973), ch. XVI.
6. J.H. Farrant, *The Harbours of Sussex 1700-1914* (Brighton 1976), chs. 3 and 4.

41. SCHOOLS IN THE 18TH CENTURY
1. W.B. Stephens and R.W. Unwin, *Materials for the Local and Regional Study of Schooling, 1700-1900*, British Records Association, Archives and the User **7** (1987); the documentary sources of all data featured in the map or mentioned in the text are given in J.M. Caffyn, *Sussex Schools in the 18th Century, SRS* **81** (1998).
2. M.G. Jones, *The Charity School Movement* (1938). B. Unwin, 'The Established Church and the Schooling of the Poor: the Role of the SPCK 1699-1720', *The Churches and Education*, History of Education Society (1984) (SPCK archives).
3. M. Dick, 'Religion and the origins of mass schooling: the English Sunday School *c.*1780-1840', *The Churches and Education*, History of Education Society (1984).

42. SCHOOLS IN THE 19TH CENTURY

1. General sources used in compiling school schedules include: *VCH Sx,* especially **II** (1907), 397-440 'Schools', and sections on individual parishes; *Reports of the Commissioners appointed … to inquire concerning Charities and Education,* 34, 'Sussex' (1839); Board of Education (List 32), *Tenure and Trusts of Voluntary Schools,* 923-51 'Sussex' (1907); 19th-century Sussex trade directories; parish and town histories; lists of school, etc, records deposited in ESRO and WSRO; WSRO EpI/47/la, 4, lists of National Schools in the archdeaconry of Chichester, 1838, 1855, and EpII/40/l, list of National Schools in the archdeaconry of Lewes, 1855.

2. G.S. Minchin, 'Table of Population' in *VCH Sx* **II**, 217-28.

3. The full titles of these societies were The National Society for Promoting the Education of the Poor in the Principles of the Established Church throughout England and Wales; and the British and Foreign School Society (originally founded in 1808 as the Royal Lancasterian Society).

4. For later Brighton schools see particularly ESRO PAR 277/7/2 series, several volumes of printed parochial, etc, reports, 1870-88; and ESRO RE2/1/6-30, minutes and reports of the Brighton (later Brighton and Preston) School Board, 1871-1903.

5. *Post Office Directory of Sussex 1867,* 2271-3.

Further Reading

W.B. Stephens and R.W. Unwin, *Materials for the Local and Regional Study of Schooling, 1700-1900,* British Records Association, Archives and the User **7** (1987).

C.R. Davey (ed), *Education in Hampshire and the Isle of Wight* (Winchester 1977).

43. FORESTS, COMMON LAND AND ENCLOSURE 1700-1900

1. See P. Brandon, 'The common lands and wastes of Sussex', (unpub. University of London Ph.D. thesis, 1963) appendix D; in which he also notes enclosures that were contentious. To his list add Binsted (area 5), see *VCH Sx* **V** (pt 1) (1997), 121. For Sussex case histories, see P. Jerrome, *Cloakbag and Common Purse: Enclosure & Copyhold in 16th Century Petworth* (Petworth 1979) on the contested enclosure of Petworth Park; H. Warne, 'Stanmer. A restructured settlement', *SAC* **127** (1989), 189-210; and H. Warne (ed), *Wivelsfield: the History of a Wealden Parish* (Hurstpierpoint 1994).

2. Figures based on W.E. Tate, 'Sussex Inclosure Acts and Awards', *SAC* **88** (1949), 114-56. Commons enclosed by private agreement after 1700 are not shown because comprehensive statistics are not available.

3. Information from Christopher Whittick (ESRO). See ESRO CHR/18/1-7 (rentals); CHR/18/8-19 (maps by Yeakell and Gardner, 1787); ASH/500-501; AMS/5735/53.

4. Lack of tidal commons in the far east of Sussex perhaps resulted from medieval monastic reclamation programmes, as at Broomhill (area 26), see *VCH Sx* **IX** (1987); and at Barnhorne near Bexhill (area 25), see P.F. Brandon, 'Agriculture and the effects of floods and weather at Barnhorne, Sussex, during the late middle ages', *SAC* **109** (1971), 69-93; in the far west of Sussex the manor of Bosham holds two commons, one of which, at 862ha, is the single largest common in West Sussex. The only remaining common brooks in Sussex today are at Coldwaltham (49 ha) in the Arun valley.

5. For bounds of the forest, etc see W.D. Peckham, *The Chartulary of the High Church of Chichester, SRS* **46** (1946), 164, 188-9; for a map *c.*1595 see Arundel Castle MS PM 193. For the Great Park, see *VCH Sx* **V** (pt 1), 52-3; for Downley see Joy Ede, *Drovers Estate, West Sussex: an archaeological and land-use history report* (Slindon 1997). There were settlements, and their commons, within the forest.

6. For instance, see S.M. Jack, 'Ecological destruction in the 16th century: the case of St Leonards Forest', *SAC* **135** (1997), 241-7. Agriculture had, however, advanced around the edges of the forest: P. Brandon, 'Common lands', appendix D (Eridge and Horsham); and *VCH Sx* **VI** (pt 3), (1987), 7-29 (Lower Beeding); WSRO MF673 (Worth); W. Marshall, *Review and Abstract of the County Reports to the Board of Agriculture … 5* (repr, Newton Abbot 1969), 459; and J.S. Hodgkinson, 'The decline of the ordnance trade in the Weald: the Seven Years' War and its aftermath', *SAC* **134** (1996) with map of furnaces producing iron, 1750-70 (p.59).

7. Common meadows not apparently associated with common arable systems had also existed in the Weald beside the larger streams. I have detected such at Wivelsfield, but more research and field work needs to be done. See Warne, *Wivelsfield,* ch.6.

8. The fact that virtually every parish in the relevant areas had such a system makes plotting them pointless. The area of arable enclosed can be obtained from the Awards themselves, from copies in ESRO or WSRO. Typically, the arable was around 25% or less, of the whole. For example, the 577ha at Houghton (area 5) enclosed in 1809 (having been bought up by the 11th Duke of Norfolk) were: 143ha common arable, 44ha common meadow, 5ha 'open waste' and 385ha common down (ref. Arundel Castle MSS D6023-4).

9. R.M. Tittensor, 'A History of the Mens: A Sussex Woodland Common', *SAC* **116** (1978), 347-74.

10. They were encouraged by the agricultural pundits of the day. See, for instance, Revd A.Young, *General View of the Agriculture of the County of Sussex* (1813, repr. Plymouth 1970); for Burgess Hill, comprising St John's Common, Keymer, enclosed 1828 and St John's Common, Clayton, enclosed 1855, see B. Short (ed), *'A very improving neighbourhood': Burgess Hill 1840-1914* (University of Sussex 1984). For the actual procedure of enclosure see P.F. Brandon, 'The Enclosure of the Keymer Commons', *SNQ* **15** (1960), l8l-6; J. Chapman, 'The unofficial enclosure proceedings: a study of the Horsham (Sussex) enclosure 1812-1813', *SAC* **120** (1982), 185-91; Arundel Castle MS MD657 (Littlehampton). Registering of village greens has restored at least one former coastal common, the 18ha enclosed at Bexhill (area 25) in 1895.

11. *Biological Survey of Common Land: 16,* East Sussex and **19**, *West Sussex* (English Nature 1994). This does not cover registered village greens, statistics of which have to be obtained from East and West Sussex Councils. For statistics of commons registered in Sussex in 1961, see also L.D. Stamp and W.G. Hoskins, *The Common Lands of England and Wales* (1963).

12. Account Book of the reeve of the Common, ESRO AMS/5782.

13. *VCH Sx* **II** (1907), 313-23; J.E. Small, 'A review of Ashdown Forest and the Common rights thereon', *SAC* **126** (1988), 155-65; L. Merricks, 'Without violence and by controlling the poorer sort: the enclosure of Ashdown Forest 1640-1693', *SAC* **132** (1994), 115-28; for transcripts of commoners' evidence see B. Short (ed), *The Ashdown Forest Dispute. 1876-1882: Environmental Politics and Custom, SRS* **80** (1998); 2616 ha were registered as common in 1961 in which 566 commoners' rights were claimed, covering all sorts of livestock, estovers including bracken, turbary, pannage and piscary; and, moving with the times, the right to 'erect a clothes line' and tether a goat.

44. POPULATION CHANGE 1801-1851

1. E.A. Wrigley and R.S. Schofield, *The Population History of England, 1541-1871: a Reconstruction* (1981), 528-9; D. Mills and K. Schurer (eds), *Local Communities in the Victorian Census Enumerators' Books* (*Local Population Studies* supplement 1996), 72.

2. Calculated from *Abstract of the Population Returns of Great Britain, 1831* (Enumeration Vols **I** and **II**, *British Parl. Papers* 1833, XXXVI-XXXVII); see also B.M. Short, 'The changing rural society and economy of Sussex 1750-1945' in *Sx ELS,* 148-66.

3. The Registrar-General's post was created in 1837 and the census was then administered through the geographical framework of the Poor Law Unions, established from 1834. The country was divided into 624 Registration Districts in 1841, 2,190 sub-districts, and over 30,000 Enumeration Districts.

4. Census of England and Wales 1851 Index, **1** Pt I.

5. W. Cameron, 'The Petworth Emigration Committee: Lord Egremont's Assisted Emigrations from Sussex to Upper Canada, 1832-1837', *Ontario History* **65** (1973), 231-46.

6. T.J. McCann, *Restricted Grandeur: Impressions of Chichester 1586-1948* (Chichester 1974), 32-3.

45. POPULATION CHANGE 1851-1911

1. J.K. Walton, *The English Seaside Resort: a social history 1750-1914* (Leicester 1983), ch. 4.

2. R. Lawton and C.G. Pooley, *Britain 1740-1950: an Historical Geography* (1992), 127-36.

Further Reading

Census of Great Britain 1851 Population Tables I (1852-53) Cmnd. 1631.

Census of England and Wales 1911 Summary Tables (1915) Cmnd. 7929.

P. Brandon, *The Sussex Landscape* (1974), 258-60.

P. Brandon and B. Short, *The South East from AD 1000* (1990), ch. 6.

R. Lawton, 'Population changes in England and Wales in the later nineteenth century: an analysis of trends by registration districts', *Trans. Institute of British Geographers* 44 (1968), 55-74.

R. Lawton, 'Population' in J. Langton and R. Morris (eds), *Atlas of Industrialising Britain 1780-1914* (1986), ch. 2.

R. Lawton, 'Population and society 1730-1914', in R.A. Dodgshon and R.A. Butlin (eds), *An Historical Geography of England and Wales* (2nd edtn 1990), ch.11.

R. Lawton and C.G. Pooley, *Britain 1740-1950: an Historical Geography* (1992).

J. Lowerson, 'Resorts, ports and "sleepy hollows": Sussex towns 1840-1940', in *Sx ELS*, 221-34.

G.S. Minchin, 'Table of Population' in *VCH Sx* II (1907), 215-28.

M. Ray, 'Domestic servants in a superior suburb: Brunswick Town, Hove', *SAC* 131 (1993), 172-84.

46. URBAN DEVELOPMENT 1750-1914

1. J.P. Huzell, 'Population change in an East Sussex town: Lewes 1660-1800', *SIH* 3 (1971-2), 11; For Chichester and Hastings see J.H. Cooper, 'A religious census of Sussex in 1676', *SAC* 45 (1902), 142-8, and Decennial Census for 1801; P. Brandon, *The Sussex Landscape* (1974); P. Corfield, *The impact of English towns 1700-1800* (Milton Keynes 1982), 67-8; C. Chalklin, *The Provincial Towns of Georgian England* (1974), 318; P. Hohenburg and L. Hollen Lees, 'Urban systems and economic growth: town populations in Metropolitan Hinterlands 1600-1850' and M. Reed, 'London and its hinterland 1600-1800: the view from the provinces' in P. Clark and B. Lepetit (eds), *Capital cities and their hinterlands in early modern Europe* (Aldershot 1996), 26-83; C. Brent, *Georgian Lewes* (Lewes 1993).
2. Brent, *Lewes*.
3. See S. Farrant, 'The role of landowners and tenants in changing agricultural practice in the Valley of the River Ouse South of Lewes (East Sussex), 1780-1930 and the consequences for the landscape' (unpub. University of London Ph.D. thesis, 1978).
4. J. Lowerson (ed), *Crawley: Victorian New Town* (University of Sussex 1980); F. Gray (ed), *Crawley: old town, new town* (University of Sussex 1983); W. Ford, *Metropolis of Mid Sussex* (Haywards Heath 1981) are amongst the studies of these towns.
5. J.H. Farrant, *The Harbours of Sussex 1700-1914* (Brighton 1976) covers key points.
6. Farrant, *Harbours*.
7. S. Farrant, 'The early growth of the seaside resorts c.1750 to 1840', in *Sx ELS*, 208-20; S. McIntyre, 'Bath: the rise of a resort town', in P. Clark (ed), *Country Towns in Pre-industrial England* (Leicester 1981), 198-249.

8. J. Whyman, *The early Kentish seaside* (Gloucester 1985), 20-2.
9. S. Farrant, *Georgian Brighton, 1740-1820* (Brighton 1981) covers these themes.
10. Farrant in *Sx ELS*, 208-20; C.L. Sayer, *Correspondence of Mr. John Collier (deceased) and his family* 2 (1907), 316 (27 July 1762, letter from Mrs. Green, p.492); L.F. Salzman, *Hastings* (1921), 74 notes *Universal Magazine* 1760; *Sussex Weekly Advertiser* 17 July and 9 July 1799; *The Times* 21 September 1820; W. Moss, *History of Hastings* (1824); *Powell's Hastings Guide* (1825); *Diplock's Hastings Guide* (7th edtn c.1830); J.M. Baines, *Burton's St. Leonards* (Hastings 1956); R. Phillips, *Guide to all the Watering Places* (1806), 249.
11. *The Times* 3 August 1782, August-September 1798, 6 October 1799; J. Dallaway and E. Cartwright, *A History of The Western Division of the County of Sussex, Bramber Rape* (1830); Worthing Section, Property to let, *Sussex Weekly Advertiser*, 30 August 1790, 10 August 1792, 22 June 1795; *VCH Sx*, 6 (pt l) (1980), 94-5; D. Cannadine, *Lords and Landlords: the Aristocracy and the Towns, 1774-1967* (Leicester 1980), ch.16.
12. M. Schoberl, *A Topographical and Historical Description of the County of Sussex* (1813), 155; *The Times* 20 September 1806; T.W. Horsfield, *The History, Antiquities and Topography of the County of Sussex* (1835); J. Mackcoull, *A Sketch of Worthing and its environs* (1813); D.R. Elleray, *Worthing Theatres 1780-1984* (Worthing 1985), 1-3; J. Evans, *Picture of Worthing* (2nd edtn, 1814); A. Hudson, 'Volunteer soldiers in Sussex during the Revolutionary and Napoleonic Wars, 1793-1815', *SAC* 122 (1984), 165-81; A. Hudson, 'Napoleonic Barracks in Sussex' *SAC* 124 (1986), 267-8; S. Berry, *Brighton: Georgian Seaside Resort 1740-1820* (forthcoming 1999).
13. S. Farrant, 'London by the Sea: resort development on the south coast of England', *Journal of Contemporary History* 22 (1987), 137-62.
14. S. Farrant (ed), *The Growth of Brighton and Hove, 1840-1939* (University of Sussex 1981) examines the Stanford Estate. Cannadine, *Lords*, is devoted to Eastbourne and the Devonshires.
15. Both Cannadine, *Lords*, and the town guide books pick up the point about use of the countryside by residents. J. Lowerson and J. Myerscough, *Time to Spare in Victorian England* (Hassocks 1977) describe some of the emerging leisure habits.

47. BRIGHTON IN THE EARLY 19TH CENTURY

1. S. Farrant [now Berry], 'The early growth of the seaside resorts c.1750 to 1840', in *Sx ELS*, 208-20; S. Farrant, 'London by the sea: resort development on the South Coast of England, 1880-1939', *Journal of Contemporary History* 22 (1987), 137-62.
2. E.W. Gilbert, *Brighton Old Ocean's Bauble* (1954), 209-36.
3. *VCH Sx* VII (1973), 245.
4. C. Brent, *Georgian Lewes* (Lewes, 1993); S. and J.H. Farrant, *Aspects of Brighton: 1650-1800* (University of Sussex 1978), 20-8.
5. S. and J.H. Farrant, *Brighton before Dr Russell* (University of

Sussex 1976), 1-4.
6. S. Farrant, *Georgian Brighton: 1740-1820* (University of Sussex 1981), 3-5,13-24.
7. S. Farrant, 'The development of coaching services from Brighton, 1750-1822', *Sussex Genealogist and Local Historian* 7 (1986), 85-91.
8. Farrant, *Georgian Brighton*, 25-42.
9. Farrant, *Georgian Brighton*, 43-8.
10. Farrant, *Georgian Brighton*, 23; S. Farrant, 'The physical development of the Royal Pavilion Estate and its influence on Brighton (E. Sussex) 1785-1823', *SAC* 120 (1982), 171-84.
11. R.C. Grant, 'The Brighton Garrison' (Brighton n.d. c.1994) covers some of this theme and see also S. Berry, *Brighton: Georgian Seaside Resort 1740-1820* (forthcoming 1999).
12. J. Austen, *Pride and Prejudice* (1813, Norton Critical Edtn 1966), 150-53.
13. A. Dale, *Fashionable Brighton 1820-1860* (Newcastle-on-Tyne 1967) is still the best study; see for some corrections, N. Bingham (ed), *C.A. Busby: The Regency Architect of Brighton and Hove* (1991).
14. S. Farrant, 'The drainage of Brighton: sewerage and outfall provision as an issue in a famous seaside resort c.1840-80', *SAC* 124 (1986), 213-26.
15. J. Lowerson (ed), *Cliftonville, Hove: Victorian Suburb* (University of Sussex 1977).
16. S. Farrant (ed), *The growth of Brighton and Hove 1840-1939* (University of Sussex 1981),13-35; S. Farrant (ed), *Changes in Brighton and Hove's suburbs 1841-1871* (Hove 1985); C. Musgrave, *Life in Brighton* (Rochester 1981) has interesting sections on the later 20th century.

48. AGRICULTURAL REGIONS, IMPROVEMENTS AND LAND USE c.1840

1. J. Caird, *English Agriculture in 1851-2* (1852), 128.
2. For the cordial relations between Ellman and Arthur Young (1741-1820) see J.H. Farrant, '"Spirited and Intelligent Farmers": the Arthur Youngs and the Board of Agriculture's Reports on Sussex, 1793 and 1808', *SAC* 130 (1992), 200-12. And see S. Farrant, 'John Ellman of Glynde in Sussex', *Agricultural History Review* 26 (1978), 77-88.
3. J. Farncombe, 'On the farming of Sussex', *J. Royal Agricultural Society England* 11 (1850), 84.
4. B. Short, 'The Turnover of tenants on the Ashburnham Estate, 1830-1850', *SAC* 113 (1975), 157-74.
5. L. de Lavergne, *The Rural Economy of England, Scotland and Ireland* (1865), 203.
6. B. Short, '"The art and craft of chicken cramming": poultry in the Weald of Sussex 1850-1950', *Agricultural History Review* 30 (1982), 19-30.
7. S. Hawes, 'Notes on the Wealden Clay of Sussex and on its Cultivation', *J. Royal Agricultural Society England* 19 (1858), 188.

Further Reading
P. Brandon, *The South Downs* (Chichester 1998), chs. 8 and 9.

E. Collins (ed), *The Agrarian History of England and Wales VII, 1850-1914* (Cambridge, forthcoming 2000).

G. Mingay (ed), *The Agrarian History of England and Wales VI, 1750-1850* (Cambridge 1989).

B. Short, 'The changing rural society and economy of Sussex 1750-1945', in *Sx ELS*, 148-66.

M. Overton, *Agricultural Revolution in England: the Transformation of the Agrarian Economy 1500-1850* (Cambridge 1996).

49. LANDOWNERSHIP IN VICTORIAN SUSSEX

1. J.M. Wilson, *The Imperial Gazetteer of England and Wales* (6 vols 1870, or 2-volume edition 1875).

2. Differing interpretations of 'open' and 'close' communities in Sussex can be gained from B. Short, 'The evolution of contrasting communities within rural England' in B. Short (ed), *The English Rural Community: Image and Analysis* (Cambridge 1992), 19-43; and in *SE from AD 1000*, 322-59.

3. Material from the tithe can be translated to approximate to one of Wilson's five categories using the following criteria: 'Most or all in one estate', over 90% of the parish area belonging to between one and three owners; 'not much divided', 75% to 89% belonging to between one and three owners; 'divided among a few', 50% to 74% belonging to between one and three owners; 'subdivided', 25% to 49% belonging to between one and three owners; and 'much subdivided', less than 25% owned by between one and three owners. The information was extracted readily from the summaries at the rear of each tithe apportionment schedule at ESRO and WSRO.

4. J.C. Kirk, 'Colonists of the Waste: the structure and evolution of 19th-century economy and society in the central Forest ridges of the Sussex Weald', (unpub. University of Sussex MA dissertation, 1986).

5. 'Return of Owners of Land, England and Wales (1872-3)', *British Parliamentary Papers LXXII*, 1874.

50. THE HISTORY OF PETWORTH PARK

1. M.T. Martin (ed), 'Percy Cartulary', *Surtees Society*, **117** (1911), 407, 409; WSRO Petworth House Archives (subsequently PHA) 1403.

2. PHA 1409; N21/4, Nos 14-20.

3. PHA 1413.

4. PHA 7362.

5. PHA 3574.

6. PHA 424.

7. PHA 230.

8. PHA 6375.

9. PHA 6323-5; 6375.

10. PHA 5177; 5178; 6623.

11. PHA 3606; the map of 1779 shows palings round the park. PHA 9333 contains documents concerning the extent and course of the wall.

12. PHA 1966; Revd A. Young, *General View of the Agriculture of the County of Sussex* (1808), 188-9; for more details of the 3rd Earl's agricultural experiments, see H.A. Wyndham, *A Family*

History 1688-1837 (Oxford 1950); M. Butlin, M. Luther and I. Warrell (eds), *Turner at Petworth* (London 1989), appendix 1: '"Lord of the Soil": a reappraisal of Turner's Petworth Patron'; PHA 90; PHA 91.

13. Collection, Lord Egremont; Collection, National Trust, Petworth.

14. PHA 2238; Young, *General View*, between pp.380-1.

15. PHA 2225, 2244, 2246; PHA 5531; F.H. Arnold, *Petworth: A Sketch of its History and Antiquities* (1864), 91-2; Ordnance Survey 25-inch map, 1875.

Further Reading

Lord Leconfield, *Petworth Manor in the Seventeenth Century* (1956).

P. Jerrome, *Cloakbag and Common Purse: Enclosure & Copyhold in 16th Century Petworth* (1979).

F. Aldsworth, 'Petworth House and the Formal Gardens', *SAC* **118** (1980), 373-7.

F.W. Steer and N.H. Osborne (eds), *The Petworth House Archives: A Catalogue* **I** (1968).

A. McCann (ed), *The Petworth House Archives: A Catalogue* **II** (1979).

A. McCann (ed), *The Petworth House Archives: A Catalogue* **III** (1997).

The Landscape Parks of Sussex (inset)
Further Reading

G. Copley, *Camden's Britannia* (1977).

East Sussex County Council, *Inventory of Parks and Gardens in East Sussex* (n.d. *c.*1997).

English Heritage, *Register of Parks and Gardens of historic interest in England: East and West Sussex* (revision forthcoming 1998-9).

S. Farrant, 'The development of landscape parks and gardens in eastern Sussex *c.*1700-1820: a guide and gazetteer', *Garden History* **17** (1989), 166-81.

T. Grose, *The Antiquities of England* (1784-7) Sussex section.

J. Harris, *The Artist and the Country House* (1995).

T. Horsfield, *The History, Antiquities and Topography of the County of Sussex* (Lewes 1835).

I. Nairn and N. Pevsner, *The Buildings of England: Sussex* (1965).

West Sussex County Council, *List of Parks and Gardens* (n.d. *c.*1997).

Maps of Sussex used in construction of the Landscape Parks map: C. Saxton, *Map of Kent Surrey Sussex and Middlesex* (1575); J. Norden *Sussex with inset plan of Chichester* (1595); J. Speed after Norden, *Sussex with inset plan of Chichester* (1610); J. Blaeu, *Sussex* (1645); R. Budgen, *Sussex* (1724); P. Overton and T. Bowles (after Budgen), *Sussex* (*c.*1740); T.Yeakell and W. Gardner, *Sussex* (1778); J. Cary, *Sussex* (1787); W. Gardner and T. Gream, *Sussex* (partly after Yeakell and Gardner) (1795); 1st-Edition Ordnance Survey, *Sussex* (1813); C. and J. Greenwood, *Sussex* (1825).

51. FORTIFICATIONS AND DEFENSIVE WORKS
1500-1900

The author wishes to acknowledge the help of John Goodwin, Anne Hudson and Frank Kitchen.

1. H.M. Colvin (ed), *The History of the King's Works IV, 1485-1660* (Pt II), (1982), 415-47.

2. M.A. Lower, *A Survey of the Coast of Sussex made in 1587* (Lewes 1870).

3. F. Kitchen, 'The Ghastly War-Flame: Fire Beacons in Sussex until the mid 17th Century', *SAC* **124** (1986), 179-91.

4. F. Kitchen, 'Brighton's Batteries', *Sussex History* **21** (1986), 2-13.

5. F. Kitchen, 'The Napoleonic War Coast Signal Stations in Sussex', *Sussex History* **27** (1989), 13-16.

6. G. Wilson, *The Old Telegraphs* (Chichester 1976).

7. A. Hudson, 'Gazetteer of Barracks in Sussex During the Revolutionary and Napoleonic Wars (1793-1815)' (1986 typescript in Sussex Archaeological Society Library).

8. P.A.L. Vine, *The Royal Military Canal* (Newton Abbot 1972).

9. The location of defensive works of the Napoleonic era is given on early editions of the Ordnance Survey maps but for the numbering and history of Martello Towers see S. Sutcliffe, *Martello Towers* (Newton Abbot 1972); and W.H. Clements, *Towers of Strength* (Barnsley 1999).

10. J.E. Goodwin, 'Circular Masonry Redoubts', *Fort* **2** (1976), 5-6, 16.

11. F. Aldsworth, 'A Description of the Mid Nineteenth Century Forts at Littlehampton and Shoreham, West Sussex', *SAC* **119** (1981), 181-94.

12. A. Powter, 'Concrete in nineteenth-century fortifications constructed by the Royal Engineers', *Fort* **9** (1981), 31-42.

Further Reading

J. Goodwin, *The Military Defence of West Sussex: 500 Years of fortifications of the coast between Brighton and Selsey* (Midhurst 1985).

J. Goring, *Sussex and the Spanish Armada* (Lewes 1988).

F. Kitchen, 'Aspects of the defence of the south coast of England: 1756-1805', *Fort* **19** (1991), 11-22.

N. Longmate, *Island Fortress* (1991).

A. Saunders, *Channel Defences* (1997).

52. INDUSTRIAL SUSSEX

1. *VCH Sx* **II** (1907), 257-8.

2. H. Cleere and D. Crossley, *The Iron Industry of the Weald* (2nd edtn, ed. J.Hodgkinson, Cardiff 1995), 191-209; Revd A. Young, *General View of the Agriculture of the County of Sussex* (1813), 431.

3. See maps 53-6.

4. *Pigot and Co's National and Commercial Directory of Kent, Surrey and Sussex* (1839); P. and J. Holtham, 'The North Laine of Brighton', *SIH* **15** (1986), 24; *Sussex Industrial Archaeology Society Newsletter* (hereafter *SIAS Newsletter*) **25** (1980), 10; **52** (1986), 5-6; **80** (1993) 10; *Sussex Archaeological Society Newsletter* **45** (1985), 415; *VCH Sx* **VI** (pt 2) (1986), 176.

5. Young, *General View*, 432-5; *VCH Sx* **II**, 237; B. Austen *et al.*, *Sussex Industrial Archaeology* (Chichester 1985), 21, 25; *Sussex Industrial Archaeology Study Group Newsletter* **3** (1969) 5; **4** (1969), 5-6; *SIAS Newsletter* **31** (1981), 3-4; *Sussex Weekly*

Advertiser 2 November 1761, 10 December 1764.

6. *A Guide to All the Watering and Sea-Bathing Places* (1813), 18; *Pigot*; *VCH Sx* **II**, 270.

7. M. Rome, 'Sussex Sailing Ships', *Sussex County Magazine* **10** (1936), 22-7, 116-18, 198-203, 240-42, 313-15, 385-6, 469-72, 540-43; J. Hornell, 'The Fishing Boats of Hastings', *Sussex County Magazine* **11** (1937), 700-5, 766-71; *VCH Sx* **II**, 235; **9** (1987), 56; *Pigot* (1839), 260, 266, 268; *The Stranger's Guide to Hastings and St Leonards* (Hastings n.d. *c.*1837), 35.

8. G. Beard and C. Gilbert (eds), *Dictionary of English Furniture Makers 1660-1840* (1986); B. Austen, 'Brighton's Tunbridge Ware Industry', *SIH* **27** (1997), 8-17; H. Hall, *Lindfield Past and Present* (2nd edtn, Haywards Heath 1963), 57; *VCH Sx* **II**, 236, 238; *SIAS Newsletter* **88** (1995), 2; D. Drummond, 'Colin Pullinger and his Perpetual Mouse Trap', *SIH* **24** (1994), 2-9; *Pigot*; *SIAS Newsletter* **92** (1996), 7; **93** (1997), 3-4.

9. G. Mead, 'The Sussex Leather Industry in the 19th Century', *SIH* **19** (1989), 2-10; *Pigot*; F. Aldsworth, 'A Prefabricated Cast Iron Tanyard Building at Brighton Road, Horsham, West Sussex', *SAC* **121** (1983), 173-9; S. Lewis, *A Topographical Dictionary of England* **4** (4th edtn 1840), 253.

10. *SIAS Newsletter* **30** (1981), 7-8, **40** (1983), 5; *VCH Sx* **VI** (pt 2) (1986), 176; **5** (pt 1) (1997), 71; G. Pennethorne, 'Country Factory', *Sussex County Magazine* **30** (1956), 90-2; *Pigot*.

11. P. and J. Holtham, 'North Laine', 24; *SIAS Newsletter* **65** (1990), 4-5; J.T. Howard Turner, *The London Brighton & South Coast Railway* **2** (1978), 233, 240, 285-6; C.F.D. Marshall and R.W. Kidner, *The Southern Railway* (1968), 240, 251.

12. Anon., 'Industrial Romance', *Sussex County Magazine* **27** (1953), 362-3.

13. *Pigot*; *SIAS Newsletter* **86** (1995), 5; *VCH Sx* **II**, 238; **5** (Pt 1), 70.

53. BRICK, TILE AND POTTERY MANUFACTURE

1. W.D. Simpson, 'Herstmonceux Castle', *Archaeological Journal* **99** (1942), 110-22; D. Calvert, *The History of Herstmonceux Castle* (1982), 8-13. Another early (16th-century) brick building is discussed in J. Farrant, M. Howard, D. Rudling, J. Warren and C. Whittick, 'Laughton Place: A manorial and architectural history, with an account of recent restoration and excavation', *SAC* **129** (1991), 99-164.

2. S. Farrant, 'The Sources of Building Materials for Brighton', *SIH* **10** (1980), 23-7.

3. K. Leslie, 'The Ashburnham Estate Brickworks 1840-1968', *SIH* **1** (1970-1), 2-22.

4. B. Short (ed), *Scarpfoot Parish: Plumpton 1830-1880* (University of Sussex 1981), 32-3; B. Short (ed), *'A very improving neighbourhood': Burgess Hill 1840-1914* (University of Sussex 1984), 38.

5. J.M. Baines, *Sussex Pottery* (1980).

Further Reading

M. Beswick, *Brickmaking in Sussex: A History and Gazetteer* (Midhurst 1993).

54. WIND, WATER, TIDE AND STEAM MILLS

1. J. Morris (ed), *Domesday Book: Sussex* (Chichester 1976) *passim*; for further information on medieval mills, see R. Holt, *The Mills of Medieval England* (1988).

2. H. Cleere and D. Crossley, *The Iron Industry of the Weald* (Leicester 1985), 338, 356.

3. S. Farrant, 'Bishopstone Tidemills', *SAC* **113** (1975), 199-202.

4. E.J. Kealey, *Harvesting the Air: Windmill Pioneers in Twelfth-Century England* (Berkeley 1987), 256-8.

Further Reading

M. Brunnarius, *The Windmills of Sussex* (Chichester 1979).
F. Gregory and R. Martin, *Sussex Watermills* (Seaford 1997).
D. Stidder and C. Smith, *Water Mills of Sussex: 1* East Sussex (Whittlebury, Towcester 1997).
D. Stidder and C. Smith, *Water Mills of Sussex: 2* West Sussex (Whittlebury, Towcester forthcoming 1999).

55. LIME, CEMENT, PLASTER AND THE EXTRACTIVE INDUSTRIES

1. Revd A. Young, *General View of the Agriculture of the County of Sussex* (1813), 205-12.

2. K.J. Barton and E.W. Holden, 'Excavations at Bramber Castle, second season's work, 12th-29th August, 1967', *SNQ* **16** (1967), 333-5; E.W. Holden, 'Excavations at Old Erringham, Shoreham', *SAC* **49** (1981), 272-4.

3. Young, *General View*, 199-203.

56. MALTING AND BREWING

1. H.M. Lancaster, *The Maltster's Materials and Method* (1936).

2. J. Brown, *Steeped in Tradition* (Reading 1983).

3. R. Morgan, *Chichester – A Documentary History* (Chichester 1994).

4. H.S. Corran, *A History of Brewing* (Newton Abbot 1975).

5. P. Mathias, *The Brewing Industry in England, 1700-1830* (Cambridge 1959).

6. N. Barber, *A Century of British Brewing* (New Ash Green 1994).

7. King & Barnes Ltd., *A Guide to King & Barnes Houses* (Heathfield n.d.); Harvey & Son Ltd., *Harvey & Son, Bridge Wharf Brewery, Lewes Bicentenary Year* (Tunbridge Wells 1990).

8. N.O. Faulkner, *Allied Breweries: A Long Life* (1988).

Further Reading

A. Barritt, 'Kingston Malthouse 1844-1971', *SIH* **3** (1971-2), 20-8.
P. Holtham, 'Seven Brighton Brewers', *SIH* **22** (1992), 9-13.
P. Holtham, 'The Portslade Brewery', *SIH* **25** (1995), 22-4.
H.A. Monckton, *The Story of the Publican Brewer* (Sheffield 1982).
K. Neale, *Victorian Horsham: The Diary of Henry Michell 1809-1874* (Chichester 1975).

57. POPULATION CHANGE 1911-1951

1. 'Urban areas' defined as the Boroughs, Municipal Boroughs and Urban Districts; *Census of England & Wales 1931, County of Sussex (Part I)* (1933), vii.

2. S. Gibbons, *Cold Comfort Farm* (1932, 1954 edtn), 16.

3. E.W.H. Briault, *Sussex (East and West), Parts 83-84* (1942), 508.

4. J.K. Walton, *The English Seaside Resort: A Social History 1750-1914* (Leicester 1983), 65.

5. F. Gray (ed), *Bexhill Voices* (Brighton 1994).

6. R. Tressell, *The Ragged Trousered Philanthropists* (St Albans 1914, 1965 edtn), 585; G. Greene, *Brighton Rock* (1938, 1970 edtn), 173.

7. P. Dickens and P. Gilbert, 'Inter-War Housing Policy: A Study of Brighton', *Southern History* **3** (1981), 201-31.

8. E.W. Gilbert, *Brighton Old Ocean's Bauble* (1954), 209-36.

9. J. Sheail, *Rural Conservation in Inter-War Britain* (Oxford 1981), 102.

10. P. Dickens, 'A disgusting blot on the landscape', *New Society* (17 July 1975), 127-9; D. Hardy and C. Ward, *Arcadia for All: The Legacy of a Makeshift Landscape* (1984).

11. Sheail, *Rural Conservation*, ch.7, provides an account of attempts at inter-war planning around Brighton and downland preservation in West Sussex. See also Sussex Rural Community Council, *To-Morrow in East Sussex* (Lewes 1946).

12. F. Gray (ed), *Crawley: Old Town, New Town* (Brighton 1983); and P. Dickens, S. Duncan, M. Goodwin and F. Gray, *Housing, States and Localities* (1985), 214-22.

13. *Census 1951 England and Wales County Report, Sussex* (1954), xiv.

14. *Census of England and Wales 1921, County of Sussex* (1923), x.

Further Reading

P.A. Barron, *The House Desirable: A handbook for those who wish to acquire homes that charm* (1929).
P.A. Barron (ed), *Sussex Homes: a pocket magazine for those who choose to live in England's fairest county* (Worthing 1936-7).
H. Belloc, *The County of Sussex* (1936).
H. Clun, *Famous South Coast Pleasure Resorts* (1929).
C. Williams-Ellis (ed), *Britain and the Beast* (1937).

58. SUSSEX IN THE FIRST WORLD WAR

1. H.I. Powell-Edwards, *The Sussex Yeomanry and 16th (Sussex Yeomanry) Battalion, Royal Sussex Regiment, 1914-1919* (1921), 18.

2. PRO W0163/44. Minutes of meetings of military members of the Army Council, 3, 10 September 1914.

3. *The Times*, 3 September 1914; WSRO MP 2426. General O'Brien to the Duke of Norfolk, 31 March 1915.

4. WSRO RSR 11/73. E. Blunden, 19 September 1954.

5. Many letters were published in the local press and parish magazines, as at Fernhurst. See K. Leslie, *The Great War illustrated by Documents from the West Sussex Record Office* (Chichester 1989), 24-5, 59-61.

6. *Sussex Daily News* (hereafter *SDN*), 14 September 1915, 4.

7. *SDN*, 3 January 1918, 4.

8. H.M. Walbrook, *Hove and the Great War* (Hove 1920), 14-23.

9. *SDN*, 2 January 1917, 5.

10. B. Millman, 'British home defence planning and civil dissent 1917-1918', *War in History* **5** (1998), 210-13.
11. Lord Ridell, *War Diary* (1933), 368-72.
12. Imperial War Museum, R. Saunders MS 79/15/1. Saunders to his son in Canada, 1 June 1918.

Further Reading

C. Ashworth, *Action Stations 9. Military airfields of the Central South and South-East* (Wellingborough 1985).

J. Goodwin, *The Military Defence of West Sussex: 500 Years of fortifications of the coast between Brighton and Selsey* (Midhurst 1985).

K. Grieves, '"Lowther's Lambs": rural paternalism and voluntary recruitment in the First World War', *Rural History* **4** (1993), 55-75.

P. Holden, *Brave Lads of Sunny Worthing: A Seaside Town during the Great War* (Worthing 1991).

E.A. James, *British Regiments 1914-18* (1978).

A.E. Readman (ed), *Records of the Royal Sussex Regiment: A Catalogue* (Chichester 1985).

O. Rutter (ed), *The History of the Seventh (Service) Battalion, The Royal Sussex Regiment, 1914-1919* (1934).

59. SUSSEX DEFENCES IN THE SECOND WORLD WAR

1. M. Mace, *Frontline Sussex: The Defence Lines of West Sussex 1939-1945* (Storrington 1996).
2. J. Goodwin, *The Military Defence of West Sussex: 500 years of fortifications of the coast between Brighton and Selsey* (Midhurst 1985), 84.
3. H. Wills, *Pillboxes: A Study of UK Defences 1940* (1985), 10,12.
4. I.D. Greeves, 'The Construction of the GHQ Stop-Line: Eridge to Newhaven, June-November 1940', *Fortress* **16** (February 1993), 52-61.
5. C. Alexander, *Ironside's Line* (forthcoming 1999).
6. WSRO BO/AR/24/3/5.
7. WSRO Add Ms 17,932.
8. C. Ashworth, *Action Stations 9. Military airfields of the Central South and South-East* (Wellingborough 1985); R.J. Brooks, *Sussex Airfields in the Second World War* (Newbury 1993).
9. H. Fairhead, *Colonel Turner's Department: Memoirs of the Men that operated the Secret Decoy Sites of Wartime Britain* [Norwich 1997], 1-3; P. Longstaff-Tyrrell, *Operation Cuckmere Haven: An investigation into military aspects of the Cuckmere Valley, East Sussex* (Polegate 1997), 1.
10. M.F. Mace, *Sussex Wartime Relics and Memorials: Wrecks, Relics and Memorials from Sussex at War 1939-1945* (Storrington 1997), 23-8.
11. For a list of D-Day camps in West Sussex see I. Greig, K.Leslie and A. Readman, *D-Day West Sussex: Springboard for the Normandy Landings 1944* (Chichester 1994), 85-8.
12. B. Bertram, *French Resistance in Sussex* (Pulborough 1995).
13. For a survey of the impact of the war on the countryside see A.W. Foot, 'The Impact of the Military on the Agricultural Landscape of Britain in the Second World War' (unpub. University of Sussex M.Phil. thesis, 1999).

14. P. Longstaff-Tyrrell, 'Tank Roads on the Downs', *SIH* **28** (1998), 27-32.
15. P. Burgess and A. Saunders, *Bombers over Sussex 1943-45* (Midhurst 1995), 52-5.
16. B. Ogley, *Doodlebugs and Rockets: The Battle of the Flying Bombs* (Westerham 1992), 31.

Further Reading

C. Adams *et al.*, *Local History Mini Guide No. 2: West Sussex at War 1939-1945* (Chichester 1995).

S. Angell, *The Secret Sussex Resistance 1940-1944* (Midhurst 1996).

P. Crook, *Sussex Home Guard* (Midhurst 1998).

G. Ellis, *The Secret Tunnels of South Heighton* (Seaford 1996). Underground intelligence centre.

G. Farebrother (ed), *Hailsham at War 1939-41* (Brighton 1986).

G. Humphrey, *Wartime Eastbourne: the story of the most raided town in the south-east* (Eastbourne 1989).

G. Huxley, *Lady Denman G.B.E.1884-1954* (1961). The Director of the Women's Land Army, its national HQ at her home at Balcombe.

Lewes University of the Third Age Oral History Group, *Lewes Remembers The Second World War (1939-1945)* (Lewes 1993).

Sussex Express and County Herald, *The War in East Sussex: A short account of the main war events in East Sussex, September 3, 1939-May 7, 1945, and the bombing of the county* (Lewes 1945).

60. POPULATION CHANGE 1951-2001

1. *Census 1961 England and Wales County Report, East Sussex* (1964); *Census 1961 England and Wales County Report, West Sussex* (1964). For population projections, see East Sussex County Council Transport and Environment Department statistics, departmental ref. 1996/SPDEP2; and West Sussex County Council, *Population in West Sussex* (Chichester 1996).

61. CRAWLEY NEW TOWN 1947-2000

1. For a full account of the development of Crawley see C.R.J. Currie, 'Crawley New Town' in *VCH Sx* **VI** (pt 3) (1987), 74-95 and the *Annual Reports* of the Crawley Development Corporation for 1948-62 and of the Commission for the New Towns from 1963 to date; *London Gazette*, 10 January 1947, 231.
2. P. Abercrombie, *Greater London Plan 1944* (1945); PRO HLG 91/153; *Sussex & Surrey Courier*, 24 June 1944, 3, and 22 July 1944, 1.
3. PRO HLG 91/153.
4. PRO CAB 124/878; CAB 124/879; LP(46); *Hansard*, 10 July 1946; *Sussex & Surrey Courier*, 12 July 1946, 1.
5. PRO HLG 91/153; HLG 91/159; HLG 91/165.
6. PRO HLG 91/159.
7. Preliminary Outline Plan, 6 December 1947; *The New Crawley: preliminary outline plan reprinted from the Kent and Sussex Courier, 12 December 1947* (1947); A. Minoprio, *A Master Plan for Crawley New Town June 1949* (1949).
8. *Crawley Development Corporation Fifteenth Annual Report 31 March 1962* (1962).

9. *Crawley Development Corporation Ninth Annual Report 31 March 1956* (1956).
10. *West Sussex County Development Plan, Crawley Town Map July 1961* (1961).
11. *Crawley Borough Local Plan Deposit Draft 1995* (1995); *Crawley Observer*, 14 April 1999, 1; Crawley Borough Council Policy and Resources Committee, 7 May 1999, minute 140; for up-to-date population estimates and projections see West Sussex County Council's Internet Website http//www.westsussex.gov.uk
12. *Report of an Inquiry into the proposed development of Gatwick Airport July 1954* (Cmnd 9215, 1954).
13. *New Towns (Amendment) Act 1976. Crawley Transfer Scheme* (1976).

Further Reading

R. Bastable, *Crawley: The Making of a New Town* (Chichester 1986).

P. Gwynne, *A History of Crawley* (Chichester 1990).

C. Kay and T.J. McCann, *Local History Mini Guide No 1: Crawley* (Chichester 1994).

62. PLANNING AND COMMUNICATIONS 1947-2000

1. East Sussex County Council, *East Sussex County Council County Structure Plan 1991* (Lewes 1992); West Sussex County Council, *West Sussex Structure Plan 1993: The Approved Structure Plan* (Chichester 1993) and associated reports.

63. LOCAL GOVERNMENT IN THE 19TH AND 20TH CENTURIES

1. J. Campbell, *The History of the English Shires* (Chichester 1992), 1.
2. *A Descriptive Report on the Quarter Sessions, Other Official, and Ecclesiastical Records in the custody of the County Councils of West and East Sussex* (Chichester and Lewes 1954), 199.
3. Campbell, *The History*, 4.
4. *Royal Commission on Local Government in England 1966-1969, Volume I: Report* (1969), 300-2.
5. Department of the Environment, Transport and the Regions, *Modern Local Government. In Touch with the People* (1998), 6.

Further Reading

D. Arscott, *Tales from the Parish Pump: A hundred years of parish councils in East Sussex* (Seaford 1994).

C.R.V. Bell, *A History of East Sussex County Council 1889 - 1974* (Chichester 1975).

J. Godfrey, K. Leslie and D. Zeuner, *A very Special County: West Sussex County Council: The First 100 Years* (Chichester 1988).

V. Porter, *The Village Parliaments: The Centenary of West Sussex Parish Councils, 1994* (Chichester 1994).

F.A. Youngs, *Guide to the Local Administrative Units of England I, Southern England* (1979).

64. JOURNEYS TO WORK 1951-1991

1. *1991 Census Workplace and Transport to Work, Great Britain, Part 1* (1994), **1**, tables 2, 3; **2**, table 4; **3**, table 6.

2. *Census 1951 England and Wales Report on Usual Residence and Workplace* (1956), table 5.

65. LEISURE MAGNETS IN THE LATER 20TH CENTURY
1. J. Lowerson, 'Resorts, ports and "sleepy hollows": Sussex towns 1840-1940', in *Sx ELS*, 221-34.
2. P. Brandon, *The South Downs* (Chichester 1998), 157-94.
3. P. Mandler, *The Fall and Rise of the Stately Home* (1977); W. Blunt, *John Christie of Glyndebourne* (1968).
4. J. Lowerson, 'Battles for the Countryside', in F. Gloversmith (ed), *Class, Culture and Social Change: a new view of the 1930s* (Brighton 1979).
5. J. Lowerson, 'Golf' in T. Mason (ed), *Sport in Britain: a social history* (Cambridge 1989), 187-214.

Further Reading
P. Brandon, *The Sussex Landscape* (1974).
F. Gray, *Walking on the Water: the West Pier Story* (Brighton 1998).
J. Lowerson and J. Myerscough, *Time to Spare in Victorian England* (Hassocks 1977).
J. Lowerson, *A Short History of Sussex* (Folkestone 1980).
J. Lowerson, *Sport and the English Middle Classes, 1870-1914* (Manchester 1993).
C. Wilson, *Hamlyn Leisure Atlas: Southern England* (1982).
T. Wright, *The Gardens of Britain, 4: Kent, East and West Sussex and Surrey* (1978).

66. EMPLOYMENT 1951-1991
1. *1991 Census Workplace and Transport to Work, Great Britain Part 1* (1994), **2**, table 4.
2. *Census 1951 England and Wales Industry Tables* (1957), tables 2, 3.

67. HEALTH PROVISION
1. A. Land, R. Lowe and N. Whiteside, *The Development of the Welfare State 1939-1951: A Guide to Documents in the Public Record Office* (1992), 92-105.
2. P. Brigden and R. Lowe, *Welfare Policy under the Conservatives 1951-1964: A Guide to Documents in the Public Record Office* (1998), 41-88.
3. *The Hospitals Year Book 1966* (1965), 7.
4. A. Pudell (ed), *The Pillar Directory, volume 1: Managers in UK Health Care* (1992); J. Spiers, *The Invisible Hospital and the Secret Garden: an insider's commentary on the NHS reforms* (1995).

Further Reading
C.H. Bailey, *St Richard's Hospital and the NHS: An Oral History* [Chichester] (Chichester 1998).
J. Gooch, *A History of Brighton General Hospital* (Chichester 1980).

S.E. Large, *King Edward VII Hospital Midhurst 1901-1986: The King's Sanatorium* (Chichester 1986).
J. Surtees, *The Princess Alice Memorial Hospital Eastbourne and other Eastbourne hospitals* (Eastbourne 1994).
P. Thane, *Foundations of the Welfare State* (2nd edtn 1996).

68. ENTERTAINMENT IN THE 19TH AND 20TH CENTURIES
1. P. Ranger, 'The Thornton Circuit 1784-1817', *Theatre Notebook* **32** (1978), 130-6; D.R. Elleray, *Worthing Theatres 1780-1984* (Worthing 1985), 1-10.
2. D. Adland, *Brighton's Music Halls* (Brighton 1994), 10-17.
3. A. Dale, *The Theatre Royal Brighton* (Stocksfield, Northumberland 1980).
4. L. Evershed-Martin, *The Impossible Theatre: The Chichester Festival Theatre Adventure* (Chichester 1971).
5. T. Sobey, *Dramatic Story of the Stables Theatre Hastings* (Hastings 1978).
6. J. House, 'Regent Brighton', *Picture House* **10** (1987), 10-14.
7. A. Eyles, *ABC The First Name in Entertainment* (Burgess Hill 1993).
8. A. Eyles, *Gaumont British Cinemas* (Burgess Hill 1996).
9. A. Eyles, 'Oscar and the Odeons', *Focus on Film* **22** (1975), 38-57.

Further Reading
D.R. Elleray, *A Refuge from Reality: The Cinemas of Brighton and Hove* (Hastings 1989).
L. Evershed-Martin, *The Miracle Theatre: The Chichester Festival Theatre's Coming of Age* (Newton Abbot 1987).
A. Eyles, F. Gray and A. Readman, *Cinema West Sussex: The First Hundred Years* (Chichester 1996).
P.R. Hodges, *Temples of Dreams: An affectionate celebration of the cinemas of Eastbourne* (Seaford 1994).
T. Hounsome, *Three Pennyworth of Dark* (East Grinstead 1995). Cinemas of East Grinstead.
R.A. Jerrams, *Weekly Repertory: A Theatrical Phenomenon* (Droitwich 1991). Includes Worthing.
A. Northcott, *Popular Entertainment in Horsham 1880-1930* (Horsham 1988).
C. Robinson and N. Roger, *The Theatre Royal Brighton* (Brighton 1993).
F.T.P. Windsor, *The Dream Palaces of Worthing* (Birmingham 1986).

69. EDUCATION
1. *West Sussex County Council Development Plan for the provision of primary and secondary education* (1947), 3.
2. A. Pinsent, *The Principles of Teaching-Method* (1949), 10.
3. Ten years after its opening the Thomas Bennett School claimed the distinction of being the largest school in the

UK, with 2,125 pupils: N. and R. McWhirter (ed), *The Guinness Book of Records* (1968), 227.
4. *East Sussex County Council Plan for the Reorganisation of Secondary Education* (Lewes 1966).
5. Sir A. Conan Doyle, *The Memoirs of Sherlock Holmes* (1893, 1974 edtn), 225.
6. For a general treatment of LEA performance see J. Marks, *An Anatomy of Failure: Standards in English Schools for 1997* (1998).

Further Reading
R. Dunn, *Moulsecoomb Days: Learning and Teaching on a Brighton Council Estate 1922-1947* (Brighton 1990).
E. Garrett, *Farlington School 1896-1996: A Centenary History* [Haywards Heath and Slinfold] (Horsham 1996).
P. Gordon, R. Aldrich and D. Dean, *Education and Policy in England in the Twentieth Century* (1991).
J. Hackworth, *Sir Henry Fermor C of E School 1744-1994: A History* [Crowborough] (Crowborough 1994).
M.D.W. Jones, *Brighton College 1845-1995* (Chichester 1995).
E.M. Marchant, *Horsham High School for Girls 1904-1954* (Horsham n.d.).
N. Sexton, *Journal of the First 25 Years of Broadfield North First & Middle School* [Crawley, 1971-96] (Horsham 1997).
B. Simon, *Education and the Social Order 1940-1990* (1991).

70. COUNTRYSIDE CONSERVATION
1. P. Brandon, *The South Downs* (Chichester 1998), 167-80.
2. V. Cornish, *National Parks* (1930), 38-44.
3. Brandon, *South Downs*, 187-9.
4. Brandon, *South Downs,* 12-13, 184, 207.
5. Brandon, *South Downs,* 191-2.
6. Brandon, *South Downs,* 207; Department of the Environment, *The Habitats Directive* (1997); English Nature, *European Birds Directive: Natura 2000* (Lewes 1999).
7. Brandon, *South Downs,* 218.

Further Reading
Countryside Commission, *The Chichester Harbour Landscape* (Cheltenham 1992).
Countryside Commission, *The High Weald: Exploring the Landscape of the Area of Outstanding Natural Beauty* (Cheltenham 1994).
Countryside Commission and Sussex Downs Conservation Board, *The Landscape of the Sussex Downs Area of Outstanding Natural Beauty* (Cheltenham and Storrington 1996).
Kernon Land Use Consultants, *The High Weald Land Management Initiative Outline Project Framework* (1999).
Sussex Wildlife Trust, *Vision For the Wildlife of Sussex* (Henfield 1996).

SUSSEX PARISH BOUNDARIES PRE-1894

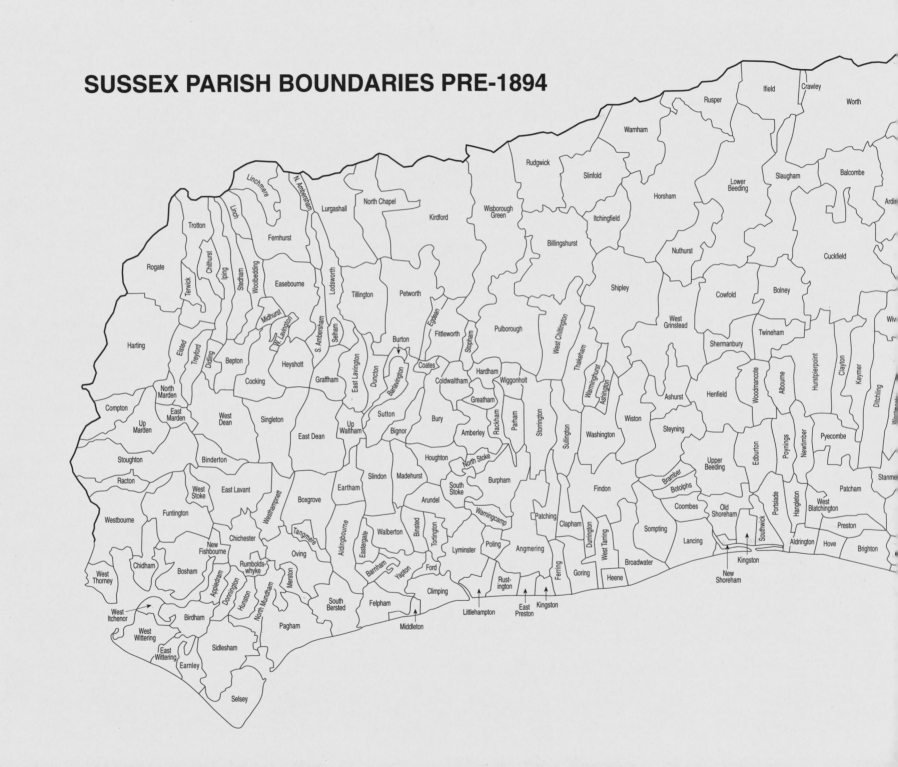